The Story of
Western Architecture

The Story of
Western Architecture

Bill Risebero

The Herbert Press

Contents

To Christine

Acknowledgements

Many people have helped me with their interest, ideas and encouragement, including Ian Boutell, Colin Davis, Peter Lennard, Scott Melville, Alan Seymour, David Stevenson, Dr Pamela Tudor-Craig and Rev. Keith Ward. My particular thanks go to Tim Sturgis for having read the manuscript and suggested many improvements, to David and Brenda Herbert for their continued enthusiasm and patience, and to my wife Christine, not only for her typing and helpful criticism but also for having looked after an almost fatherless family for two years.

The background to the story

Europe in the 5th century

As men journeyed in the east, they came upon a plain in the land of Shinar and settled there. They said to one another, 'Come, let us make bricks and bake them hard'; they used bricks for stone and bitumen for mortar.
– *Genesis* 11:2 (*New English Bible*)

Since earliest times, men and women like those of the kingdom of Nimrod described in Genesis have tried to adapt their surroundings to their needs, clearing forests, growing crops, making weapons and tools. Building a shelter against sun, wind or rain is one of the most fundamental of human needs, essential to our physical and social life. But it is also an act which in an important way goes beyond functional necessity: the response to climate and weather, the finding and shaping of building materials, are a creative partnership with the natural world through which man develops his intellect and skills. They become, in fact, an act of self-creation in which man, as Marx says, 'starts, regulates and controls the material reactions between himself and Nature . . . by thus acting on the external world and changing it, he at the same time changes his own nature. He develops his slumbering powers and compels them to act in obedience to his sway.'

In primitive societies, with a system of shared labour, there may be few specialist building designers; often designer, builder and user are the same person. When a whole community is involved in putting up its own buildings, what is lost in sophistication may be amply gained in both personal and social satisfaction. The story told by this book begins in a barbaric and cruel age, but an age in which self-creation through the art of building was common enough to be the rule rather than the exception. The society of the Gauls and the Germans of the early centuries AD was oppressive and unequal, with many people living in virtual slavery. At the same time there was little division of labour. Warfare was the prerogative of nobles and freemen, but the rest of society had the same way of life, tending the land, growing food, making clothes and building homes. The specialist skills of poets, craftsmen and musicians, many of whom occupied honoured places in society, were largely used to improve the lives of the ruling classes. Nevertheless, the difference between the house of a noble and that of a tribesman was of degree rather than of kind.

The story ends in an age of uncertainty, in which creative collaboration between man and the world around him has been all but extinguished, in which the division of labour has cut the link between those who provide buildings and those who use them. Architecture is a commodity, produced by an alienated designer for an anonymous public. Its technical excellence is undeniable, but its emotional and intellectual content is too often based on spurious theories which bear little relationship to what its users really need. The transition between these two states, from primitive creativity to sophistication and remoteness, some 1500 years apart, is the story of western architecture.

7

The setting of the story, for most of that time, has been Europe, an area of mountain, plain, marsh and forest stretching from Scandinavia in the north to the Mediterranean in the south, and from the Atlantic in the west to the Black Sea in the east. During the first century AD the whole area was controlled by one man, the Roman emperor Augustus. His efforts to weld this large and varied empire into a cohesive whole almost succeeded. Roman fleets dominated the Mediterranean and newly-built roads linked Rome with the frontiers, which were defended by twenty-five legions and armies of provincial auxiliaries. The city of Rome, political and legal focus of the empire, was splendid with marble buildings and great public works. To pay for all this, a smoothly-running administrative and legal system collected taxes from all citizens. The offering of citizenship to provincials was one of several ways in which Rome attempted to create an imperial identity among its diverse population. But although Jews, Celts, Germans and Greeks could become citizens, the Roman way of life merely overlaid existing local cultures. In response to the complex and varied physical and climatic conditions of Europe, local ways of life, languages, laws and customs – and local building methods – still persisted.

Because of Europe's varied geology and climate, each local area has different materials suitable for building. With transport difficult and expensive – historically even more so than today – materials, except for the most important buildings, are sought, locally, and an enormously varied architectural character is the result. Generally, and quite logically, the use of a particular material reaches its highest degree of perfection in areas where it is most abundant: the ancient Greeks' use of limestone and marble and the use of timber in medieval England are two examples. However, the existence of a material does not imply its use at all periods of history, nor that it is used particularly well. Architecture, like history itself, is a contingent process, in which many circumstances combine to produce certain results. If the circumstances are not propitious or appropriate, materials go unexploited. In Greece, almost the only suitable building materials in ancient times were stone and marble, but it took the particular cultural circumstances of the 5th century BC to raise the working of marble to unparalleled heights.

In the Islamic world, natural building materials, except in some isolated areas, were not freely available locally. In such a sophisticated and cultured society, however, a virtue was made out of necessity and synthetic products like brick, *pisé*, ceramics and glass were developed to perfection.

Spain, France and Belgium are rich in materials, particularly stone. Limestone is found in southern Spain, Catalonia and Normandy, granite in Belgium and northern Spain, volcanic stones in Spain and the Auvergne, sandstone in Belgium, Andalucia and the Pyrenees. These have been exploited spasmodically throughout history; their use in the early Middle Ages depended on the existence of Arabic and Byzantine craftsmen and they were not fully developed as an indigenous tradition till about the 11th century.

Holland, with virtually no stone or timber, relied on imported materials till increasing wealth in the Middle Ages allowed it to develop its own brick industry. Brickmaking also flourished in Germany, north and east of the Elbe, an area less rich in building-stone than the Rhine valley. Scandinavia's main material has always been softwood, from its dense forests of pine, spruce and birch, and here a tradition of very accomplished timber-building grew up in the early Middle Ages, dominating all the areas linked by the Vikings' Baltic trade routes. Britain is richer in building materials than most European countries, with indigenous hardwoods and a variety of building stone including limestone, sandstone, granite and flint. Brick was not widely used until the late Middle Ages when there was sufficient wealth to develop the industry and more permanent materials than timber were demanded in areas short of stone.

Imperial Rome, like Greece, had marble and limestone, but it also had earth for terracotta and brickmaking, volcanic tufa, lava and pumice, and the volcanic earth known as *pozzolana*, which became the basic material for Roman concrete. All these materials might have gone unexploited if the particular economic and political circumstances of Rome had not demanded buildings of a certain character.

Climatic variations from one part of Europe to another were fundamental to building design. The steep roofs of the north, designed to shed water and snow, were unnecessary in the south: the steeply-pitched outline of the northern long-house and the low-lying, horizontal silhouette of the Roman villa are therefore a contrast of function as well as of mood. Southern houses, with their *atria* and peristyles, were designed to allow the free circulation of cooling air; northern buildings to keep out the cold north and east winds.

Rome's wealth was based on what could be produced within the empire: raw materials such as iron-ore and furs, foodstuffs such as wheat, maize and meat, and manufactured goods. The basic economy was that of the Celtic peasant, the production of food by farming small-holdings. Over this was superimposed the system of the Roman *villae*, large holdings of rich landowners worked by slaves. Applied to the light-weight 'mountain' soils of the Mediterranean area, this system, with its intensive methods, produced high yields and generally there was little need to open up the inherently much more fertile lands of the north, which remained locally farmed for local use. In Augustus' time the south still dominated, economically and culturally. The city of Rome, living on the taxes of the empire and enormously wealthy, demanded luxuries of every kind, and its merchants ventured ever farther afield to supply them. Transport by sea was quicker and cheaper than by land and the Mediterranean became the main trade route in and out of Rome. To the west lay the unknown Atlantic, still full of terrors for the traveller, so traders turned to the eastern routes, through the Red Sea and the Persian Gulf, to India and China, bringing back silk, ivory, resins and spices. As a result, the staging-posts between the Mediterranean and the east grew in both size and wealth: Constantinople, Antioch and Alexandria soon surpassed the economic importance of Rome itself.

Economic growth does not in itself bring social progress, and although wealth can offer a society opportunities to apply its knowledge, distribute its resources and educate its people, imperial Rome was not one to do this. Its chief preoccupations were how to administer its vast provinces and how to keep its unwieldy economic system going, problems caused by the conspicuous consumption of the city itself and its ever-greater demand for goods and services. For centuries the Romans' view of their own society had included concepts of freedom and justice, but it is important to realise that concepts are usually those of the ruling class: they can be unreliable guides to the truth about a society.

The design of buildings bears this out. To all appearances, the great buildings of Rome were a celebration of the Roman ideal of freedom; luxurious temples, baths, amphitheatres and circuses, available to all. But in the context of imperial Rome's economic ills – increasing inflation, unemployment, a troublesome urban working-

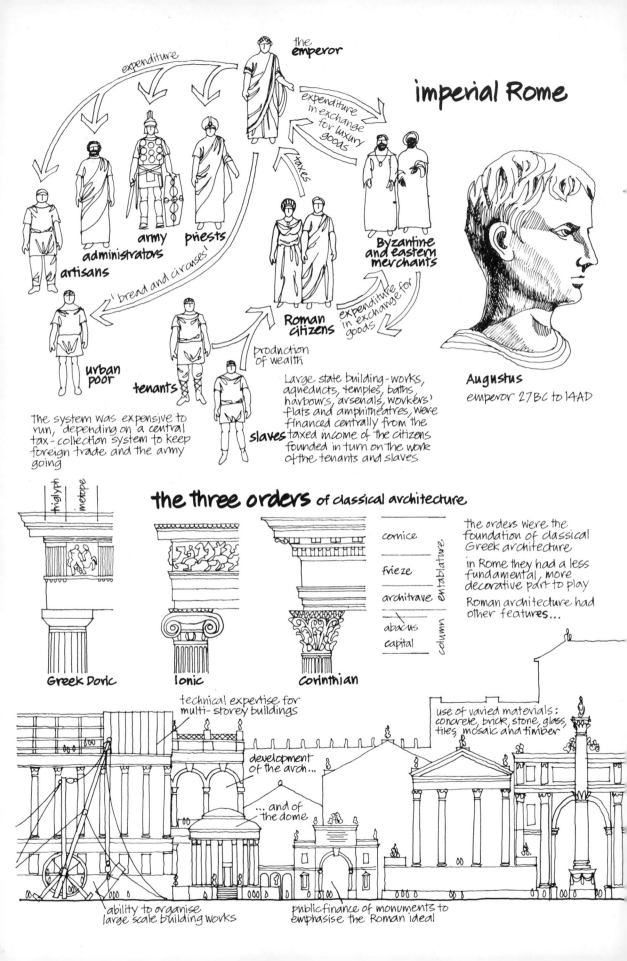

imperial Rome

expenditure

the **emperor**

expenditure in exchange for luxury goods

taxes

army

administrators

priests

artisans

Byzantine and eastern merchants

urban poor

'bread and circuses!'

tenants

Roman citizens

production of wealth

expenditure in exchange for goods

slaves

Augustus
emperor 27BC to 14AD

The system was expensive to run, depending on a central tax-collection system to keep foreign trade and the army going

Large state building-works, aqueducts, temples, baths, harbours, arsenals, workers' flats and amphitheatres, were financed centrally from the taxed income of the citizens founded in turn on the work of the tenants and slaves

the three orders of classical architecture

triglyph

metope

Greek Doric

Ionic

Corinthian

cornice

frieze

architrave

abacus

capital

entablature

column

the orders were the foundation of classical Greek architecture

in Rome they had a less fundamental, more decorative part to play

Roman architecture had other features...

technical expertise for multi-storey buildings

use of varied materials: concrete, brick, stone, glass, tiles, mosaic and timber

development of the arch...

... and of the dome

ability to organise large scale building works

public finance of monuments to emphasise the Roman ideal

class – they can be seen as an investment in the security of the city, an antidote to discontent.

The great Flavian amphitheatre in Rome, built in AD 70 and known also as the Colosseum, was archetypal. Amphitheatres were built all over the Roman world and used for extravagant and deadly displays of all kinds. Despite its political purpose and the use to which it was put, we can still see that by any definition the Colosseum was a great building. Some 200 metres long, an ellipse on plan, it was enclosed by a sheer external wall on which Doric, Ionic and Corinthian columns were superimposed in three tiers. Inside, continuous rows of seats raked down to the oval amphitheatre in which the displays took place. Beneath the seats, a complex of vaults on three levels contained accommodation for the gladiators, the beasts' cages and the cells of the victims. The audacity of the structure and the use of varied materials according to their constructional role – lava for strength in the foundations, tufa and brick for the walls, and pumice to reduce the weight of the vaulting – made the building both monumental and subtle.

The architectural achievement of the Greeks had been to bring exquisite refinement of detail and proportion to a simple, even banal, structural system. By contrast Roman architecture was aesthetically crude but structurally much more advanced. The semi-circular arch, the barrel-vault and its derivatives the cross-vault and the dome, the use of different materials for different constructional purposes, and above all the use of concrete, were brought to a high degree of development, and they were used in buildings of great size which relied on mass for stability (rather than on the counter-balancing of forces displayed by a Gothic cathedral), but which were nevertheless structurally audacious.

Roman structural advances, although among history's great architectural achievements, were slow and tentative, the result of gradually gathered experience rather than creative experiment. It was a pragmatic rather than an intellectual age, which placed many constraints on the freedom of the artist and craftsman, not least his servile place in society. Tramelled by ideas and circumstances inherited from the past, he could not develop original ideas except along rigidly determined lines.

Under these circumstances it was even more remarkable that the unknown builders of Rome succeeded as they did. Among their finest achievements was the temple known as the Pantheon, a building of great character, uniquely Roman and still the best preserved building of ancient Rome. Built in 120 by Hadrian on the site of an earlier temple by Agrippa, Augustus' son-in-law, it used some features of the original building but adapted them in a highly individual way. The rectangular foundations of the old temple formed the basis of a massive portico, built with salvaged material, and Agrippa's inscription remained on the re-used entablature. The new portico was reduced in width but the height of the pediment was retained, so that, with a fine disregard for Greek theories of proportion, it appears unusually steep. The main body of the temple is a domed rotunda, its width of 43 metres exactly corresponding with its internal height. Walls and roof are structural concrete, faced with a variety of materials including brick and marble. From inside, the supports are apparently eight huge piers, alternating with eight large *exedrae* or niches, but as the piers are hollowed out behind they form in effect a wall, serpentine on plan, the shape of which is self-buttressing. The drum of the rotunda is three tiers high on the outside but only two inside, since the dome springs from the top of the second tier. The structure between the second and third tiers is therefore thicker and helps contain

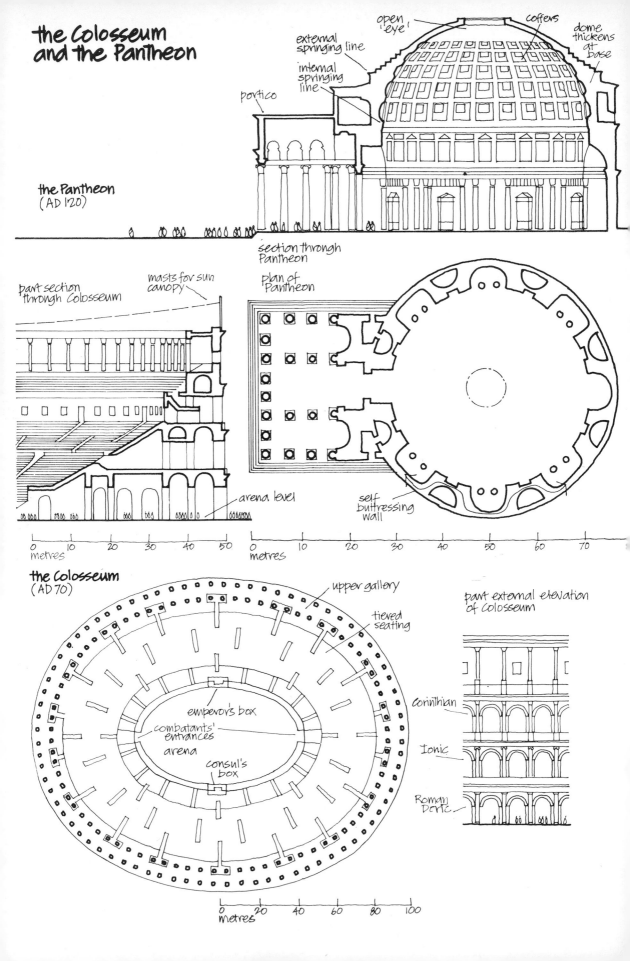

the Colosseum and the Pantheon

open 'eye'

coffers

dome thickens at base

external springing line

internal springing line

portico

the Pantheon (AD 120)

part section through Colosseum

masts for sun canopy

section through Pantheon

plan of Pantheon

arena level

self buttressing wall

```
0    10    20    30    40    50
metres
```

```
0    10    20    30    40    50    60    70
metres
```

the Colosseum (AD 70)

upper gallery

tiered seating

emperor's box

combatants' entrances

arena

consul's box

part external elevation of Colosseum

Corinthian

Ionic

Roman Doric

```
0    20    40    60    80    100
metres
```

the thrust of the dome, the surface of which is coffered to reduce weight. The circular opening or 'eye' in the roof was, and still is, the only means of lighting the interior, adding to the drama of one of the most impressive buildings in Rome.

Rome's great buildings, like its army, its administrators and its luxury goods from the east, were paid for by the taxes from its agricultural estates. The economy depended on safeguarding a large enough area of productive land to meet the demands placed on it; this was the main role of the legions whose elaborate system of camps defended the boundary formed by the Black Sea coast, the Danube and the Rhine. In time, the cost to the tax-payer of permanently defending 5000 kilometres of frontier began to tell, and during the 3rd century towns throughout the empire were hit by inflation, higher death-rates, decreasing fertility and the migration to the country of citizens trying to escape the punitive taxes. The massing of enemy armies on the borders reduced trade and hastened the decline.

The cities of the eastern Mediterranean, stronger economically, were capable of weathering the storm, but Rome was not. Constantine, with great foresight, moved his capital to Byzantium in the early 4th century, leaving Rome a political backwater as well as the economic backwater it had already become. The Roman system had outgrown its strength; decline was almost inevitable.

However, growing within it were the seeds of a new order founded on the local tribal society of the Gauls and Belgae which had survived the superimposed Roman system. The arrival of Germanic tribes from north of the Rhine acted as a catalyst. Since the 2nd century, infiltrations of Germans into the empire had been assimilated without conflict because the land was not intensively farmed. When in the 4th century the Huns from the far east pushed west to the Caspian Sea, the Germanic tribes themselves migrated south and west in a movement the demoralised legions could no longer resist. During the 5th century the Visigoths, Vandals, Alans and Suevi crossed the Rhine and established themselves throughout the north-west. Traditionally, these barbarians 'destroyed' the empire, but in effect it had collapsed already: all they did was to occupy and defend the land and develop its agriculture according to a simpler, older system of local production for local needs. Trade declined, and money went out of use.

The barbarians were generally tolerant of local customs and laws, and many of them not only tolerated but also professed the official religion of the dying empire. Christianity had gradually grown in influence till astute emperors saw its adoption as a means to political unity. In 325 Constantine recognised it as the empire's established religion, and its adherents were able to end their semi-clandestine existence.

The first Christians had met in secret, where they could, in houses or buildings adapted from other purposes. The eventual establishment of the religion called naturally for a period of church-building, in the Holy Land and in Rome itself. In 330 Constantine founded both the Church of the Nativity, Bethlehem, and the Church of the Holy Sepulchre, Jerusalem, and in Rome he built the original church of St Peter and the church of San Giovanni in Laterano.

Pagan temples were shrines to their gods, and worshippers had gathered outside. A church, however, had to house the congregation inside, so a new architectural form was needed. From the beginning the form adopted by western Christians was that of the basilica. In imperial Rome, this was a hall for public administration and business transactions. Typically, a long straight nave, spanned with a barrel vault or

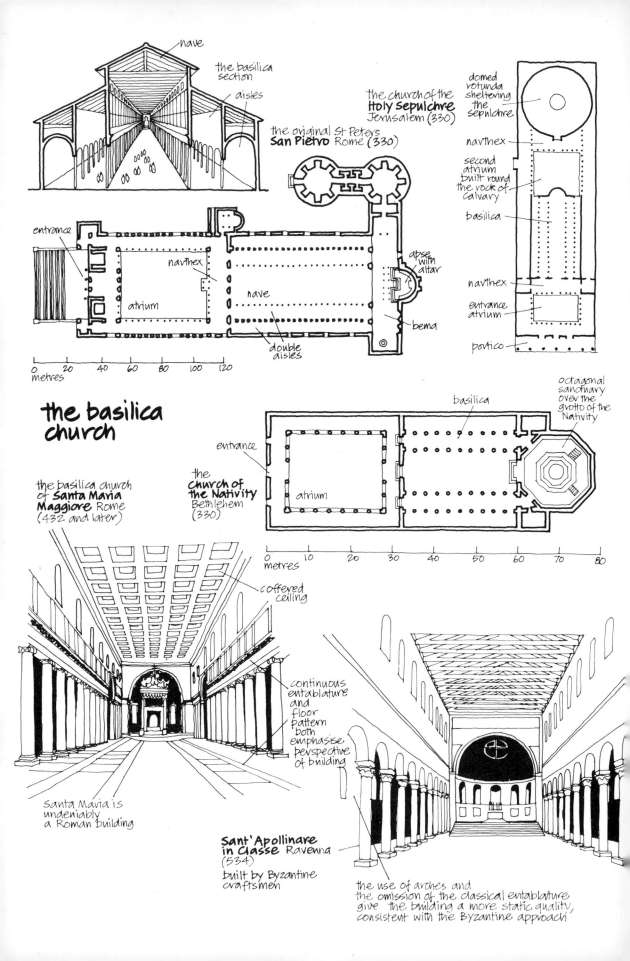

nave

the basilica section

aisles

the church of the **Holy Sepulchre** Jerusalem (330)

the original St Peters **San Pietro** Rome (330)

domed rotunda sheltering the sepulchre

narthex

second atrium built round the rock of Calvary

basilica

entrance

narthex

entrance atrium

portico

narthex

atrium

nave

apse with altar

bema

double aisles

0 20 40 60 80 100 120
metres

the basilica church

basilica

octagonal sanctuary over the grotto of the Nativity

entrance

the **Church of the Nativity** Bethlehem (330)

the basilica church of **Santa Maria Maggiore** Rome (432 and later)

atrium

0 10 20 30 40 50 60 70 80
metres

coffered ceiling

continuous entablature and floor pattern both emphasise perspective of building

Santa Maria is undeniably a Roman building

Sant'Apollinare in Classe Ravenna (534)
built by Byzantine craftsmen

the use of arches and the omission of the classical entablature give the building a more static quality, consistent with the Byzantine approach

groined vaults, or more often a trussed timber roof, was flanked by lower aisles above which clerestories let light into the centre part of the building. One or both ends terminated in an apse containing the votive altar (every important decision was accompanied by a sacrifice), the seats of the assessors and the throne of the *praetor*. The basilica was a relatively utilitarian building and its simple construction an economical way of roofing a large rectangular space. In the straitened economic circumstances in which the early church grew, the basilica form was ideal for worship, and the long straight nave, flanked by aisles and leading to an end altar, became a pattern for future church-planning in the west. The form was second nature to the Roman craftsmen who built the early examples, sometimes with columns salvaged from the ruins of pagan temples. Some of the best early basilica churches are in Rome and Ravenna. San Paulo fuori le Mura, Rome (380, rebuilt 1823 to the original design) is one of the largest and finest, and Santa Maria Maggiore, Rome (432), among the most beautiful. In both, the rows of columns lining the nave support a classical entablature. In the Ravenna church of Sant' Apollinare Nuovo (493) and its sister Sant' Apollinare in Classe (534), the columns support a row of semi-circular arches. Ravenna was the capital of the Ostrogoth Theodoric the Great during his short-lived but powerful kingship of Italy, and Sant' Apollinare Nuovo, elegant, spacious and rich with Byzantine mosaic, is a memorial to kingly ambition.

The Roman empire did not die: many of its institutions were finished, but others lived on in forms adapted to the new circumstances. Its legal system was incorporated into the various complex codes of the Germans. Its road system fell into disrepair – the barbarians' self-sufficient rural communities had less need for trade and travel – to be rediscovered, at least in part, several centuries later. Towns began to decay, some surviving as farmsteads, monasteries, bishops' palaces or castles, others disappearing completely.

Economically, Byzantium became the inheritor of the empire, providing a degree of continuity, preserving the use of money and keeping alive the Roman traditions of craftsmanship and building.

The church became Rome's cultural inheritor, the repository of what classical learning and literature still remained. Above all, the Celts and barbarians were there to develop a new economic system out of which feudalism, the basis of medieval society, was to emerge. These complex factors interacted with each other to produce a culture and an architecture, which is the theme of this book.

Barbarian Christianity

AD 500-1000

During the Roman empire, western Europe was essentially Celtic, an indigenous culture which had gradually been developing since prehistoric times, and particularly during the last few hundred years BC, with its Druidic religion and a complex code of civil and moral law. The Celtic people were not only warriors but also weavers, jewellers and smiths, sculptors and musicians.

Agriculture was the economic base of Celtic society and the extended family its main social unit: a society based on local production for local needs but with a surprisingly developed system of exchange, of both goods and ideas. Its buildings were therefore produced locally, but to common traditions of construction which existed all over Europe. Each local community had a two-tier social structure, with the local ruler, his warriors and priests, bards and advisers, dominating a class of peasants whose status was little above that of slaves. All over the Celtic world, but particularly in Britain, Ireland and western Gaul, these communities lived together as complete social units. Local farmsteads contained a small group of dwellings, byres and store-houses protected by ditch, stockade and gatehouse.

The most common building form in western Gaul was circular, for all types of building. A typical store-building or small dwelling would consist of a ring of wooden rafters, their ends embedded in the ground, meeting at the top to form a cone and carrying a covering of heather-thatch or turf. Headroom inside was very restricted, so often the floor would be lowered, the excavated earth being placed round the outside to help stabilise the feet of the rafters, thereby forming rudimentary walls. A single fireplace in the centre provided heating and cooking; the smoke escaped through a central hole in the roof. The size of any building was strictly limited by the length of timber available for rafters. When the owner's status required a larger building a composite structure would be employed, using two sets of rafters: a lower set spanning from the ground to a ring-beam supported on a circle of short timber posts, and an upper set spanning from the ring-beam to the apex. This produced a building capable of housing a local chieftain's family and retainers; typically, there would be a series of cubicles round the edge each housing a family group, the centre being reserved for meetings, entertainments and meals.

Europe's Celtic population had been declining over the last centuries of the Roman empire, leaving sparsely inhabited areas into which the migrating Germanic tribes were assimilated without difficulty. The Visigoths, Vandals, Suevi and Franks found themselves land in Gaul without much Celtic opposition. The Angles and Saxons had to fight rather harder for a foothold in Britain, and it took them almost 400 years from about the mid-5th century to the early 9th century to achieve dominance. Like the Celts, the Germans were by tradition subsistence farmers. Most of the migrants were young men, interested less in military conquest than in establishing new homelands for themselves and their families. The settlements of their northern homelands provided the pattern for the new ones they established farther south.

the tribal system:
the structure of Celtic society

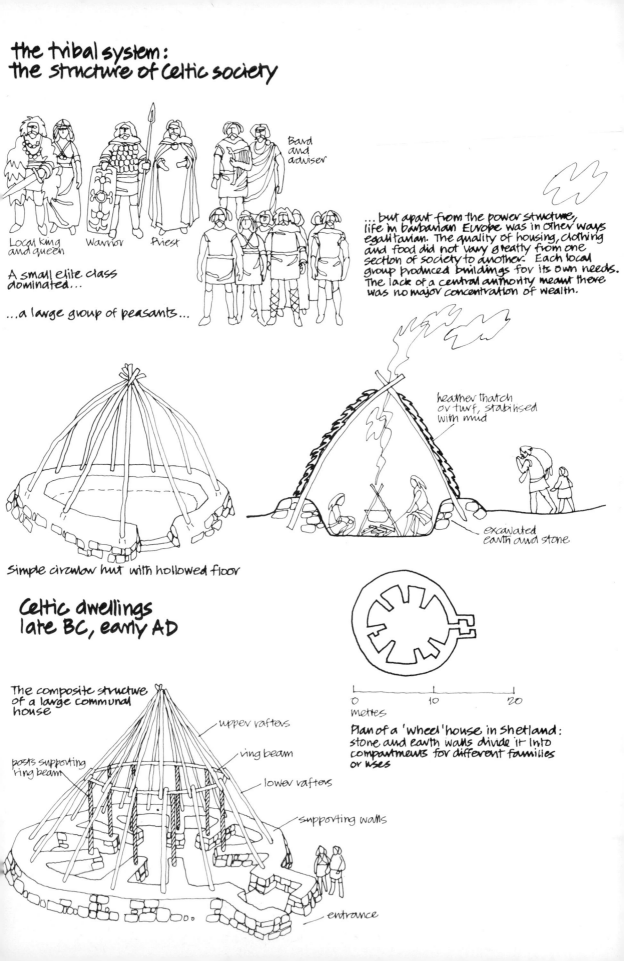

Local king and queen   Warrior   Priest

Bard and adviser

A small elite class dominated...

...a large group of peasants...

... but apart from the power structure, life in barbarian Europe was in other ways egalitarian. The quality of housing, clothing and food did not vary greatly from one section of society to another. Each local group produced buildings for its own needs. The lack of a central authority meant there was no major concentration of wealth.

heather thatch or turf, stabilised with mud

excavated earth and stone

Simple circular hut with hollowed floor

Celtic dwellings
late BC, early AD

Plan of a 'wheel' house in Shetland: stone and earth walls divide it into compartments for different families or uses

0   10   20
metres

The composite structure of a large communal house

posts supporting ring beam

upper rafters

ring beam

lower rafters

supporting walls

entrance

Julius Caesar in his Commentaries draws a sharp distinction between the culture and civilisation of the Germans and the Celts, greatly to the disadvantage of the former whom he calls *feri* or 'savages'. There is certainly little evidence that the Germans had the poetical and musical skills of the Celts, but in other respects there was in fact much cultural overlap. Continued contact between the races over the centuries had given the barbarians many of the Celtic skills in weaving, weapon-making and jewellery, and in one respect the barbarians were more skilful: their life on Europe's northern coasts had given them an affinity with the sea and a ship-building tradition. From this would develop, in later centuries, great masterpieces of Viking ship construction and Scandinavian and Anglo-Saxon timber building, but for the present it gave Germanic building construction an edge in quality over that of the Celts. Germanic society had a social pattern similar to the Celtic one: an agricultural base and a hierarchical structure in which local rulers, their warriors, priests and peasants played a part. However, both their settlement patterns and their building types were more varied. Isolated homesteads, rectangular villages surrounded by palisades, circular villages planned with buildings radiating from a central space, and fortified hill-top refuges were all built at various times and places during the first few centuries AD. Most striking were the *Terpen*, loosely-planned villages built in the low-lying coastal areas of northern Friesland on high artificial mounds to raise them above flood level. The best-known is Feddersen Wierde, dating from the 1st century AD.

Building types included a conical timber hut with a hollowed-out floor, similar to Celtic dwellings and known as the *Grubenhaus*; and, much more sophisticated, the 'aisled' or 'long' house which solved the problem of how to roof over large areas and thus produced rectangular buildings of great length. Extant foundations vary from 10 to 30 metres in length and up to 10 metres in width. Ingenious structures were needed to support the large thatched roofs on these buildings. Rafters spanned between a long ridge-pole and similar poles at eaves level. The latter were supported on stout columns embedded in the ground, from which hung the wattle hurdles that served as walls. A large span would require very long rafters so these might be laid in sections, carried at mid-span on purlins, themselves supported on posts from the ground. The whole provided a large building, capable by its modular construction of subdivision into different uses. A likely subdivision would be between people and animals, with a hearth and home at one end and rows of stalls at the other.

The northern invaders brought their Germanic languages to Europe, creating a linguistic diversity which still remains today. In other respects, barbarian and Romano-Celtic culture gradually merged. As Christianity spread, intermarriage became more common and the birthrate rose. The greater social responsibility taught by Christianity meant better care for the underprivileged, and the death-rate fell. Between 600 and 800 Europe's population began gradually to increase.

The Romans had grown most of their crops on the Mediterranean littoral where light soils demanded no more than a lightweight 'scratch' plough and production was kept up by intensive cultivation and plot rotation. These farming methods died out in Europe with the collapse of the Roman system, but the increase of population in western Europe as a whole demanded new methods, which came from the north. For the heavier, wetter soils a heavy, wheeled plough drawn by a large team of oxen was developed. Its appearance as early as the 7th century implies a degree of co-operation already existing in the north, since no single farmer would have owned

buildings of
the Germanic tribes

section through long-house
showing structure

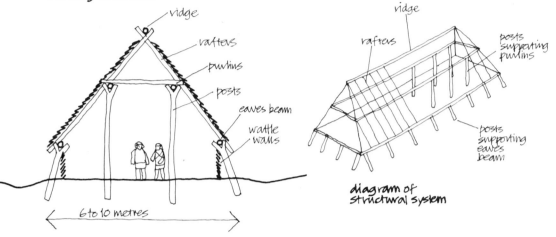

ridge

rafters

purlins

posts

eaves beam

wattle walls

6 to 10 metres

ridge

rafters

posts supporting purlins

posts supporting eaves beam

diagram of structural system

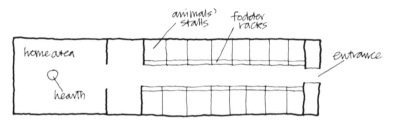

animals' stalls

fodder racks

home area

hearth

entrance

plan of aisled long-house at Feddersen Wierde, Friesland
1st century

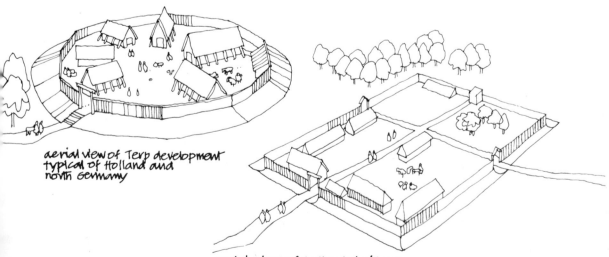

aerial view of Terp development
typical of Holland and
north Germany

aerial view of palisaded village

the number of oxen required. This is consistent with a general inventiveness among the northern population who in the next 300 years or so were to introduce into their agriculture the marling of top-soil, water-mills for grinding, the harrow and the flail, and a number of new cereal crops. Forests were cleared and strip-farming of large open fields, tended communally, became the pattern.

Political and economic uncertainty lay ahead, however. Central government was limited and farmers needed protection from local anarchism. The continued process, begun in the last years of the empire, of surrendering their freedom in return for the protection of local landlords, laid the foundations for the gradual replacement of the tribal system by that of the feudal manor.

Throughout the troubled times of the next four centuries the growing feudal system provided the unifying economic force of western Europe and Christianity provided the cultural continuity, the one common thread amid the political turmoil. This is not to say that the church spoke with one voice, nor that it was uninvolved in politics. The political history of the early Middle Ages is that of the church, and many of its early leaders, Constantine, Theodosius, Justinian, Gregory, were men of temporal as well as spiritual power. It was soon discovered, and repeatedly exploited, that religious unity helped to create national or imperial identity; the building of churches could also be used as a manifestation of both spiritual and political power.

Between the 5th and 9th centuries, with major building projects in western Europe almost at a standstill, architectural development was left to Byzantium which remained economically advanced and had, from its trade with the orient, a plentiful supply of commodities – silk, spice, jewellery, grain – which the west wanted. This economic stability encouraged building in general and constructional innovation in particular. Byzantine architecture developed into a remarkable synthesis between imperial Roman and middle-eastern architecture. From Rome came knowledge of brickwork and concrete construction; from the east the use of the dome. The Pantheon in Rome (120) had been roofed with a dome over a circular space, a shape which has a limited number of architectural applications. The Byzantine solution to the problem of how to put domes over square and rectangular spaces gave architects the freedom to devise varied and complex plan forms. The development of brickwork technique was one of the keys to this: the physical properties of brickwork, which can be shaped in innumerable ways, permitted builders to realise a variety of geometric forms of which the 'pendentive' was the most ingenious. Brickwork also encouraged the use of secondary materials for internal cladding of walls and ceilings, particularly mosaic. Constantinople itself produced the chief architectural glories of early Christendom, east or west. The church of St Sergius and St Bacchus (525) is an early example of a dome on eight piers over a square building. San Vitale, Ravenna (526), built by Byzantine craftsmen during the Ostrogothic domination of Italy, has a dome on eight piers within a basic octagon. A lightweight dome of clay pots allows the columns and walls to be reduced in weight and the result is a remarkably elegant building. The church of St Irene, Constantinople (564, altered 740), has two domes of different sizes over the nave of a basilica plan, the larger of which is the earliest example of a dome raised on a drum pierced with windows. The longitudinal plan-form departs from the symmetrical centralised forms of St Sergius and San Vitale.

The supreme example of a dome placed over a longitudinal plan form is at Haghia Sophia, the great church built for Justinian in Constantinople in 532. Architectural

20

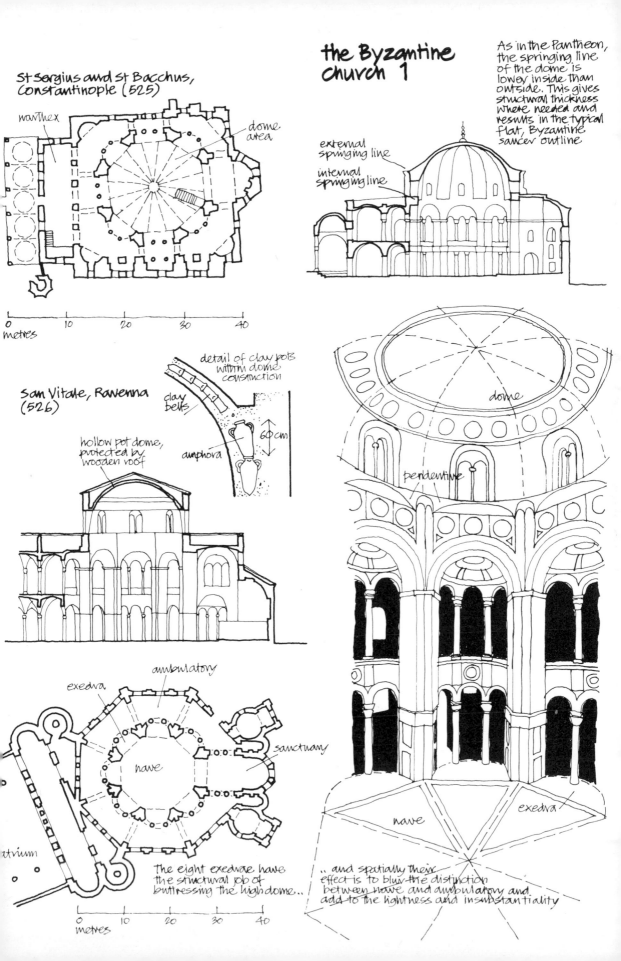

St Sergius and St Bacchus, Constantinople (525)

narthex

dome area

0 10 20 30 40
metres

the Byzantine church 1

As in the Pantheon, the springing line of the dome is lower inside than outside. This gives structural thickness where needed and results in the typical flat, Byzantine saucer outline

external springing line

internal springing line

detail of clay pots within dome construction

clay bells

amphora

60 cm

San Vitale, Ravenna (526)

hollow pot dome, protected by wooden roof

dome

pendentive

nave

exedra

exedra

ambulatory

sanctuary

nave

atrium

0 10 20 30 40
metres

The eight exedrae have the structural job of buttressing the high dome..

.. and spatially their effect is to blur the distinction between nave and ambulatory and add to the lightness and insubstantiality

ingenuity gives the building an effect of great simplicity. Four huge stone piers stand at the corners of a square some 30 metres across, and are linked by semi-circular arches which in turn support a huge hemispherical dome. This central space is extended to east and west by the addition of semi-domes supported on further piers. Together, dome and semi-domes form a vast oval-shaped nave some 70 metres long, beyond which lie the lower structures of the entrance narthex, aisles and apse. The semi-domes and their supports buttress the main dome to the east and west, and four massive buttresses over the aisles give support to the north and south sides. The interior is lit by windows in the dome and surrounding walls, and is alive with the colour of varied marbles and mosaics. The richness of decorative detail is in admirable contrast to the majestic simplicity of the overall design: characteristics of Byzantine architecture in its most developed form.

The Byzantine domed churches of the 6th century are to eastern Christendom what the basilica form is to the west: they crystallised the form which was to be the basis of eastern Christian architecture for the next 1000 years.

But not all Christendom expressed itself by building great churches: there were those who felt that the Christian life could only be one of poverty and hardship. As early as the 3rd century, Christians had gone into the Egyptian desert as hermits, and now, in disenchantment with the established church, a hermetic movement grew up, searching for spiritual fulfilment through poverty, abstinence and solitude.

The first European monastery is thought to have been at Lérins near Marseilles early in the 5th century, and the movement reached Ireland, with St Patrick, in 461. The first English monastery was probably Tintagel in 470, and St Columba established his in Iona in 563. The early monasteries were rough and primitive by comparison with the serenity of contemporary Byzantine churches, owing as much to religious conviction as to the backwardness of local building methods; but there is nothing unsophisticated about the magnificently appropriate siting of some of these simple buildings, such as Tintagel on its rocky coastal promontory or Sceilg Mhichil clinging to the side of the Great Skellig Rock.

Though originating as a search for truth through poverty and solitude, the movement attracted also the rich and self-indulgent who sought a quiet, romantic life or wished to acquire merit by excesses of abstinence. Observing this, St Benedict of Nursia (d. 543) established a 'Rule' at his monastery of Monte Cassino, prescribing poverty, celibacy, obedience to the abbot, a disciplined prayer-life and fellowship through communal manual labour. The Rule transformed monastic life throughout Europe and helped to develop it into a powerful spiritual force. Under the influence of Cassiodorus (575), learning and scholarship also became the monks' responsibilities and thereafter, for hundreds of years, the monastic movement was a major cultural influence in western Europe.

St Benedict's Rule did not require a church: at this early stage, communal worship had not fully developed, and small cells or oratories for individual monks to pray in were sufficient. The early communal hermitages on the rocky outposts of Europe were groups of beehive-like stone huts, some of them living-quarters and some oratories, enclosed within defensive stone walls.

Gradually, however, communal life became a monastic feature, and it was important to have a church for group worship. In a localised and fragmented society which practised its own local building methods, the early monks represented the nearest thing to a pan-European culture, and it is fascinating to see the traditions they

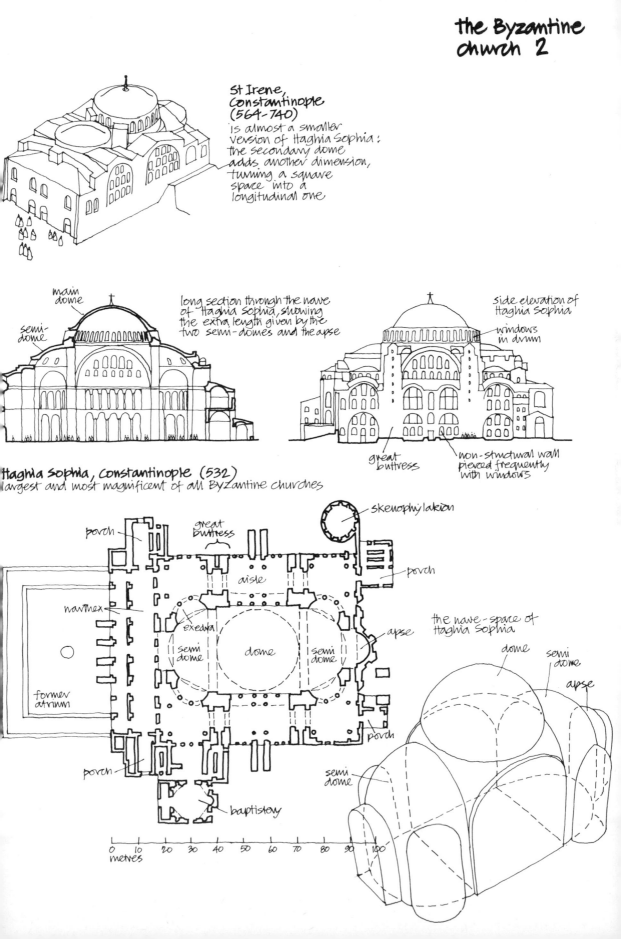

St Irene, Constantinople (564-740) is almost a smaller version of Haghia Sophia: the secondary dome adds another dimension, turning a square space into a longitudinal one

main dome

semi-dome

long section through the nave of Haghia Sophia, showing the extra length given by the two semi-domes and the apse

side elevation of Haghia Sophia

windows in drum

great buttress

non-structural wall pierced frequently with windows

Haghia Sophia, Constantinople (532)
largest and most magnificent of all Byzantine churches

porch

great buttress

skenophylakion

aisle

porch

narthex

exedra

apse

semi dome

dome

semi dome

the nave-space of Haghia Sophia

dome

semi dome

apse

former atrium

porch

semi dome

porch

baptistery

0 10 20 30 40 50 60 70 80 90 100
metres

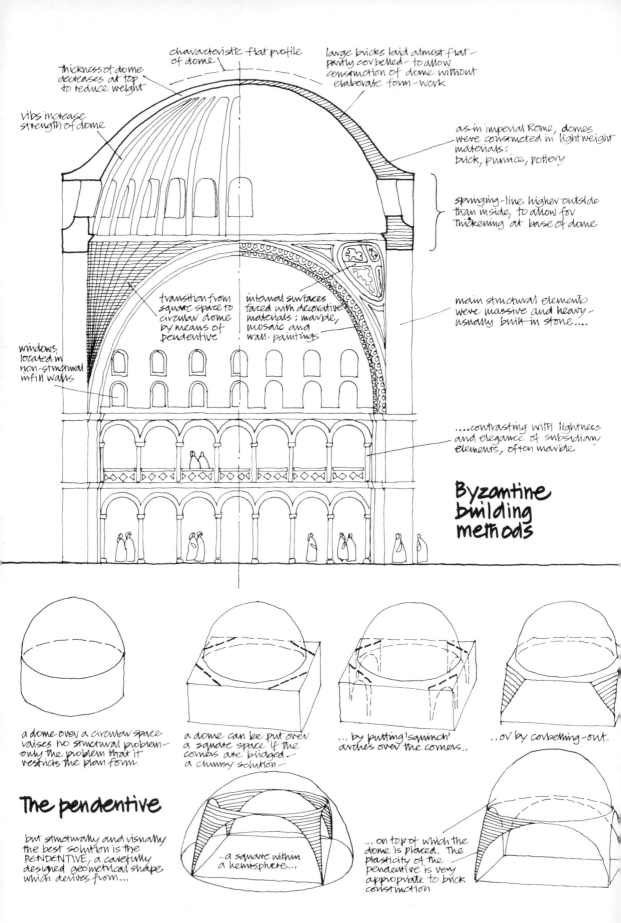

characteristic flat profile of dome

large bricks laid almost flat — partly corbelled — to allow construction of dome without elaborate form-work

thickness of dome decreases at top to reduce weight

ribs increase strength of dome

as in imperial Rome, domes were constructed in lightweight materials: brick, pumice, pottery

springing-line higher outside than inside, to allow for thickening at base of dome

transition from square space to circular dome by means of pendentive

internal surfaces faced with decorative materials: marble, mosaic and wall-paintings

main structural elements were massive and heavy — usually built in stone....

windows located in non-structural infill walls

....contrasting with lightness and elegance of subsidiary elements, often marble

Byzantine building methods

a dome over a circular space raises no structural problem — only the problem that it restricts the plan form.

a dome can be put over a square space if the corners are bridged — a clumsy solution —

... by putting 'squinch' arches over the corners..

..or by corbelling-out.

The pendentive

but structurally and visually the best solution is the PENDENTIVE, a carefully designed geometrical shape which derives from...

..a square within a hemisphere...

... on top of which the dome is placed. The plasticity of the pendentive is very appropriate to brick construction brought to these primitive outposts. Essentially they had two architectural models for a church: some form of longitudinal plan deriving more or less from the basilica of the Romano-Christian tradition, or a centralised plan deriving from the domed churches of Byzantium. These forms were adapted to local conditions and newly-emerging monastic needs.

The Celtic church of Ireland and Northumbria, deriving its traditions direct from Rome, built churches whose plan-forms have a distinct longitudinal emphasis. At the same time, a continental tradition was developing among the newly-Christianised barbarians of Europe for whom the cultural leader was still Byzantium, guardian of the only living tradition of masonry building on which the Germans and Anglo-Saxons could draw. The church of San Juan de Baños (661), built by the Visigoths in Spain, has a square, centralised plan and the early 8th-century Anglo-Saxon church of Bradford-on-Avon in Wiltshire, though basically Roman in form, has a cruciform plan of Byzantine origin. Most typically Byzantine of small European churches is Germigny-des-Prés near Orléans (806), a Carolingian design with a square plan and a central dome.

Almost all the survivals of the period are in stone; it is likely however that most church buildings of the time were timber and failed to survive the political turmoil of the 9th century. Timber was the most commonly available material and the most easily worked by the local craftsmen with their ship-building traditions. Though there are no direct survivals, contemporary descriptions of wooden Anglo-Saxon churches built on 'four great posts' suggest a Byzantine plan with a central tower. The later 'stave' churches of Norway, combining both Roman and Byzantine influences with mastery of timber techniques, show the heights to which north European timber craftsmanship may have aspired in these early centuries.

Out of the ruins of the old Roman empire a new indigenous culture was thus emerging. Far away in Asia Minor, in place of the old Persian empire, a religious, cultural and political movement was growing which would once more throw the world into turmoil. In 569 Muhammad was born in Mecca. His new religion, described in his great work the Qur'ān, was being spread by devoted followers among the Arabian tribes. Motivated by economic forces as well as religious zeal, Muhammadan armies embarked in the mid-7th century on a journey of conquest. The middle east, India and north Africa fell. Byzantium was barely able to hold out, Spain collapsed and western Europe was threatened.

Of the barbarian tribes, only the Franks were organised enough to show resistance. After the near-collapse of the Merovingian dynasty which had united the Franks under Clovis in 481, Pepin of Heristal assumed virtual control of the kingdom in 687, paving the way for his son Charles Martel (714–41) to defeat the Islamic forces at Tours and Poitiers and drive them back into Spain. Western Europe became more united and confident, but Islamic control of the Mediterranean drastically limited trade. Society became increasingly introspective. The art of building requires some wealth and some interchange and development of ideas if it is to expand, and these were not available. There were only certain isolated intellectual contributions, in particular those made by the monasteries. This was the age of Isidore of Seville (d. 636) and his scientific researches, of the Lindisfarne Gospels (late 7th century), and of Bede's (d. 735) *Ecclesiastical History of the English People.*

While western Europe looked inwards, the power of Islam expressed itself in marvellous architectural works. Islam was a complete way of life, religious, political

the early development of the church plan

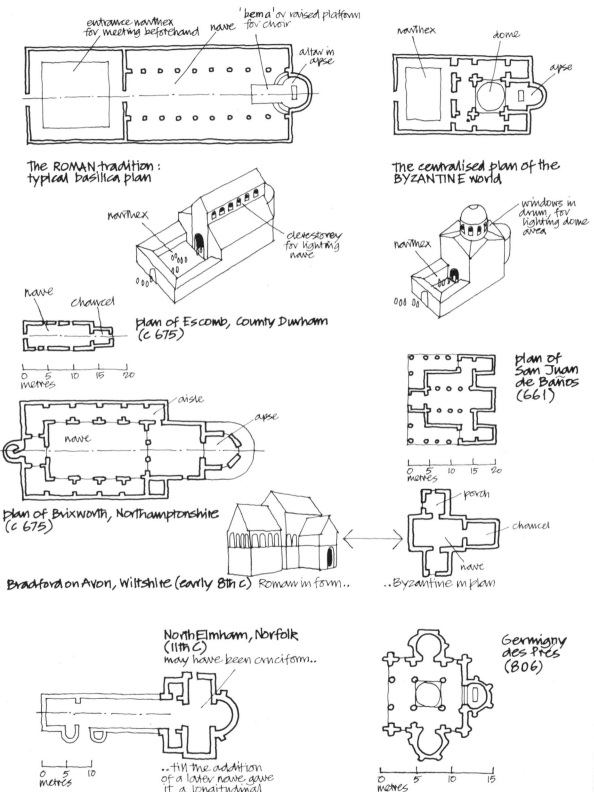

entrance narthex for meeting beforehand

nave

'bema' or raised platform for choir

altar in apse

The ROMAN tradition: typical basilica plan

narthex

dome

apse

The centralised plan of the BYZANTINE world

narthex

clerestorey for lighting nave

Plan of Escomb, County Durham (c 675)

nave

chancel

0 5 10 15 20
metres

windows in drum, for lighting dome area

narthex

plan of San Juan de Baños (661)

0 5 10 15 20
metres

aisle

apse

nave

plan of Brixworth, Northamptonshire (c 675)

Bradford on Avon, Wiltshire (early 8th c) Roman in form..

..Byzantine in plan

porch

chancel

nave

North Elmham, Norfolk (11th C)
may have been cruciform..

..till the addition of a later nave gave it a longitudinal plan

0 5 10
metres

Germigny des Prés (806)

0 5 10 15
metres

and social, carrying its search for religious truth into a striving for excellence in all aspects of life. The followers of Muhammad were tolerant of other religions, seeing themselves as the inheritors of the ancient Judaeo-Christian tradition. Nor did they despise the architectural traditions which they had inherited. They drew inspiration from Hellenistic, Syrian, Roman and Byzantine sources, and re-interpreted them in terms of the local craft techniques of the many regions of the world which their empire eventually covered. They developed brick and stone techniques into a fine art and with them perfected the use of the barrel-vault and the cross-vault, semi-circular and pointed arches, often in colonnades, and above all the dome, which first appears in Islamic architecture at the Kubbet es-Sakhra (the Dome of the Rock) in Jerusalem (688). This appears to have been designed as a direct counterpart to Constantine's domed Church of the Holy Sepulchre, and though its genealogy is obvious, it displays characteristically Islamic features which make it archetypal for centuries to come. In particular, it has a high dome of distinctly oriental rather than western profile, and the interior, clad in marble and glass mosaic, anticipates the rich abstract decoration which, though never used to detract from the basic architectural concept of a building, was to become such a feature of Islamic architecture. In 785 Islamic architects built what was probably the most brilliant and sophisticated building yet seen in western Europe, the Great Mosque in Córdova, constructed by Syrian builders in a style already tried out in Damascus. The main part of the building was built off the tops of a forest of salvaged classical marble columns. As the columns nowhere matched the height of interior required, the arches they supported were raised on 'stilts', and still more height was gained by making the crown of the arches in one direction into the springing-line of arches in the transverse direction. This simple functional approach provided a great fluidity and variety of form which is further enriched by the introduction of domes at certain points and by the variety of surface decoration. All over the Islamic world, unlike that of Christendom, the approach to architecture was remarkably consistent, largely due to the universal acceptance of the Qur'ān as a guide to all the questions of life, including those of building design. As a result, certain basic features emerged: an essential similarity between both religious and secular buildings, for there was no sharp distinction between spiritual and everyday life; a rejection of monumentality in favour of a small, human scale; and buildings which were essentially low and horizontal in conception.

Although this was in contrast to the way in which western architecture evolved, in one respect Islamic architecture had great influence. The Qur'ān forbade representational art in a religious context: painting and sculpture on the western pattern were rare, but abstract applied art became highly developed, especially in the surface decoration of buildings, using abstractions of natural forms and forms developed from Arabic calligraphy. The Arabs were accomplished mathematicians, and their designs were carried out in a stylised, mathematical way which enhanced their perception of building geometry. The accuracy and geometrical ingenuity of Islamic building became a permanent lesson to architects in the west.

In 800, Charlemagne (768–814) was crowned Holy Roman Emperor by Pope Leo III. Energetic, brutal and a brilliant politician, he turned the Frankish kingdom into the strongest political unit in western Europe since the fall of Rome. He established sensible, defensible boundaries to the kingdom, and developed Europe's trade both with the eastern Empire and with Caliph Haroun al Raschid in Baghdad. His

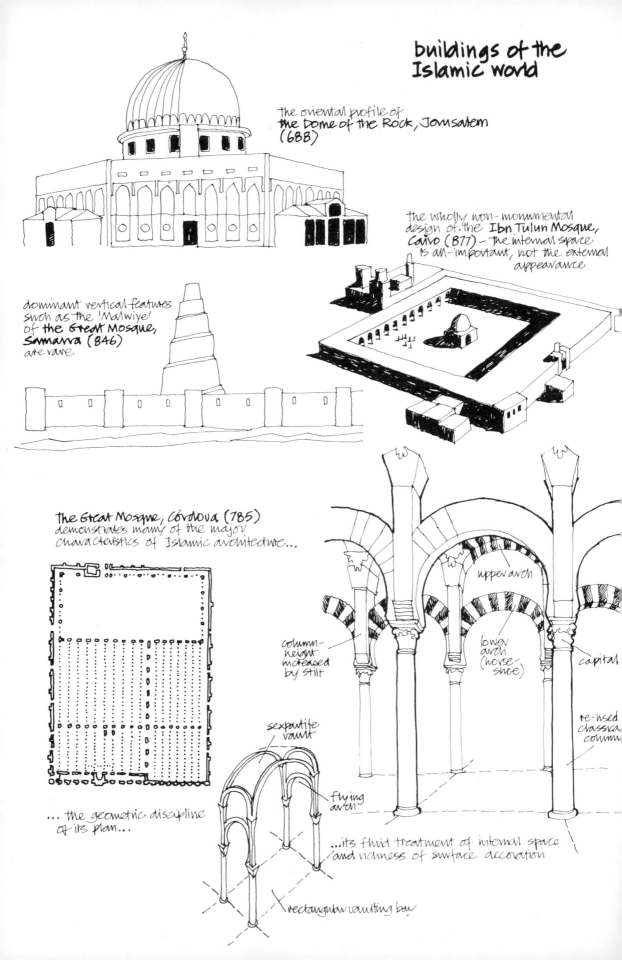

buildings of the Islamic world

the oriental profile of **the Dome of the Rock, Jerusalem (688)**

the wholly non-monumental design of the **Ibn Tulun Mosque, Cairo (877)** – the internal space is all-important, not the external appearance

dominant vertical features such as the 'Malwiye' of **the Great Mosque, Samarra (846)** are rare.

The Great Mosque, Córdova (785) demonstrates many of the major characteristics of Islamic architecture...

column-height increased by stilt

upper arch

lower arch (horse-shoe)

capital

re-used classical column

sexpartite vault

flying arch

... the geometric discipline of its plan...

...its fluid treatment of internal space and richness of surface decoration

rectangular vaulting bay

delicate relationship with Leo, also a powerful figure, gave rise to a continuing conflict between emperor and Pope. Significantly, Charlemagne chose Aachen for his capital, not Rome. Here he could establish his own institutions, free from the influence of Rome. For a time there was a return to strong central government. An uneducated man himself, he presided, with the help of the intellectuals he gathered round him (men such as Alcuin of York), over a revival of arts and learning. From his brief, meteoric reign came the establishment of the 'Carolingian minuscule' as the standard medieval script, the establishment of the secular Palace Schools of grammar, rhetoric and logic alongside those of the church, the production of beautiful books and psalters, a golden age in the development of Gregorian chant, and new achievements in the crafting of jewellery and metalwork.

In Carolingian Europe the feudal system reached maturity. Social relationships were no longer those of kinship, as in the tribal 'extended family', but were now based on a complex set of reciprocal obligations between different classes of society. Tribalism had not encouraged the division of labour: the man who had tilled the field had also, when necessary, taken up arms to defend it. But now agricultural production and military power belonged to different classes, and the relationship between them, their rights and mutual obligations, were strictly defined.

The basis of the system was the manor, a large estate owned by a lord and tended by the tenants who lived on it. The tenants enjoyed the lord's protection in times of trouble and in return owed him their labour. In his turn, the lord owned the estate by authority of the king or emperor and owed him military service in return. Estates were usually in three sections, the 'demesne' belonging exclusively to the lord, the 'mansi' or holdings of the tenants, and the common land over which everyone had certain defined rights. Tenants were usually obliged to work on the demesne for three days a week, and might also owe the lord extra obligations. Possibly the most significant feature of the feudal system was its lack of mobility: a tenant was not only imprisoned within his class but also tied to the land. Attempts to escape from the system incurred severe punishment. Feudal landlords might be abbots or bishops, knights or barons. The emergence of this powerful class to challenge the supremacy of kings and emperors was to be one of the main political issues of the early Middle Ages.

Carolingian Europe was not wealthy: it still had an agricultural economy and a relatively decentralised administrative system. It could not produce buildings to match those of Byzantium and Córdova, but nevertheless a remarkable upsurge in building activity did take place. Charlemagne's wealth, like that of his Roman predecessors, depended on taxation, and his form of government was just strong enough to ensure the supply of sufficient funds to enable him to demonstrate in building form the heights of his imperial ambition.

The complex of buildings at Aachen demonstrates this. Though much altered and added to, it still contains his original Palatine Chapel (792), a small polygonal building with a central dome originally intended as his mausoleum and destined to become the scene of the coronation of successive Holy Roman emperors. The building obviously derives from the Byzantine church of San Vitale of Ostrogothic Ravenna: it has the same double-storey colonnade supporting the dome, outside which lies a surrounding aisle. If less subtle than San Vitale, it is nevertheless a remarkably elegant building for its time, and though small by Byzantine standards, its construction was a great technical achievement. Its architects, versed in the

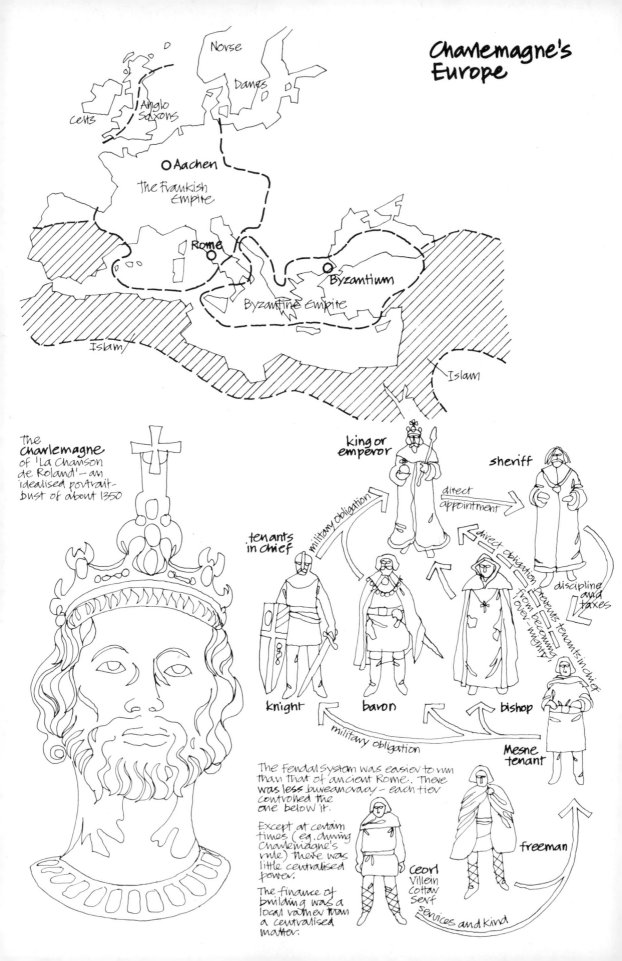

Charlemagne's Europe

Norse

Danes

Celts

Anglo Saxons

O Aachen

The Frankish Empire

Rome

Byzantium

Byzantine Empire

Islam

Islam

The Charlemagne of 'La Chanson de Roland' – an idealised portrait-bust of about 1350

king or emperor

sheriff

direct appointment

military obligation

tenants in chief

direct obligation prevents tenants in chief from becoming 'over-mighty'

discipline and taxes

knight

baron

bishop

military obligation

Mesne tenant

The Feudal System was easier to run than that of ancient Rome. There was less bureaucracy – each tier controlled the one below it.

Except at certain times (eg. during Charlemagne's rule) there was little centralised power.

The finance of building was a local rather than a centralised matter.

ceorl
Villein
Cottar
Serf

freeman

services and kind

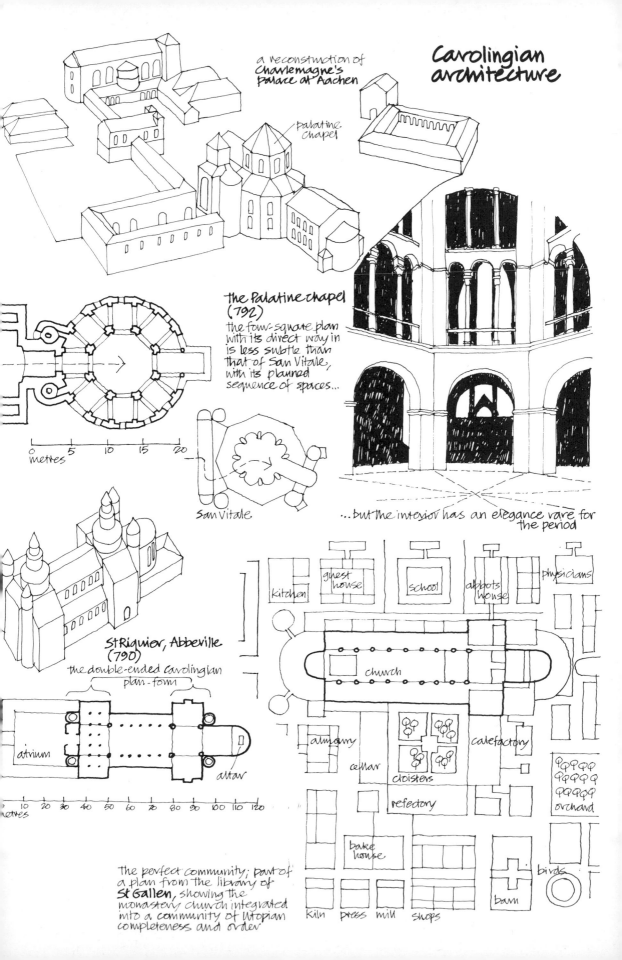

a reconstruction of **Charlemagne's Palace at Aachen**

Palatine chapel

Carolingian architecture

the Palatine chapel (792)

the four-square plan with its direct way in is less subtle than that of San Vitale, with its planned sequence of spaces...

0 5 10 15 20
metres

San Vitale

...but the interior has an elegance rare for the period

St Riquier, Abbeville (790)
the double-ended Carolingian plan-form

atrium

altar

0 10 20 30 40 50 60 70 80 90 100 110 120
metres

kitchen

guest house

school

abbots house

physicians

church

almonry

cellar

cloisters

refectory

calefactory

orchard

bake house

barn

birds

kiln press mill shops

the perfect community; part of a plan from the library of **St Gallen**, showing the monastery church integrated into a community of utopian completeness and order

Byzantine tradition, were nevertheless imbued with that barbaric vigour and inventiveness from which medieval architecture was to develop. An original feature is the ceremonial west end forming a strong architectural counterpoint to the sanctuary at the east end. Containing the emperor's throne, the west end was intended to demonstrate Charlemagne's role as Christ on earth. Wherever he travelled, his abbeys and cathedrals were provided with a 'Palace Chapel' in which the emperor could sit at the west end in opposition to God at the east. Typical examples are the church of St Riquier, Abbeville (790), which has a fully-fledged tower, crossing and transepts at each end of a squarish nave, and the abbey church of Fulda (802) which has an apse at each end of a basilican plan.

The Carolingian building that had the most lasting influence was the Benedictine monastery of St Gallen in Switzerland (820). It is notable less for what was built than for the complete plan prepared by Charlemagne's architect, Eginhardt, which crystallised the Benedictine design theories of the time and became the prototype for other monasteries for centuries to come. The plan shows a typical Carolingian double-ended church, of the type that was to remain popular, particularly in Germany, into the 11th and 12th centuries. More interestingly it shows a preferred layout for the numerous supporting facilities of which a monastery then consisted, giving some idea of its importance as a social centre: school, infirmary, guest-house, farm, mill, barn and threshing floor in addition to the religious apartments.

The Carolingian renaissance ended with Charlemagne's death. In 843, the Treaty of Verdun divided the great empire, according to Frankish custom, among his three sons, and Europe descended once more into political uncertainty. Magyar incursions from the east and Viking raids all along the northern seaboard from Ireland to Russia broke the fragile peace; trade between western Europe and the eastern Mediterranean ceased almost completely. The Vikings spread into Poland and Russia, France, Normandy and Britain, dominating much of northern Europe. Only Spain, most remote from the invaders in the north and east, seems to have produced significant buildings. The churches of Santa Maria de Naranco, Oviedo (848), Santa Cristina de Lena (c. 900) and San Miguel de Escalada, León (913), all show a development of a barrel-vaulted Romanesque style, with, at León, particularly strong Islamic features reminiscent of Córdova. The quality of Spanish workmanship at this time, even in small buildings, far surpassed that generally found in contemporary buildings of northern Europe. Moslem domination had left behind trained craftsmen capable of setting out buildings squarely and of producing a fair brick wall or a geometric arch.

In the rest of Europe, during the late 9th century, with trade at a standstill and society torn either by invasion or by the political struggles of local barons, creative cultural activity might have seemed a thing of the past. Yet out of this situation grew, during the 10th century, a series of developments which set the scene for a cultural renaissance to dwarf that of Charlemagne and rival imperial Rome.

The stringent economic situation of the 9th century had forced a number of trading cities on the edge of western Europe to forge strong links with Byzantium and Islam in order to survive. Naples, Ravenna, Milan, Amalfi, Pisa, Pavia and above all Venice were thus, during the 9th and 10th centuries, working their way to the economic forefront of Europe. In addition, Viking domination of the northern coasts had linked northern Europe, from Britain to Russia, by trade routes. From these two developments would eventually emerge the two main trading systems of medieval

the growth of the city, 400-1200

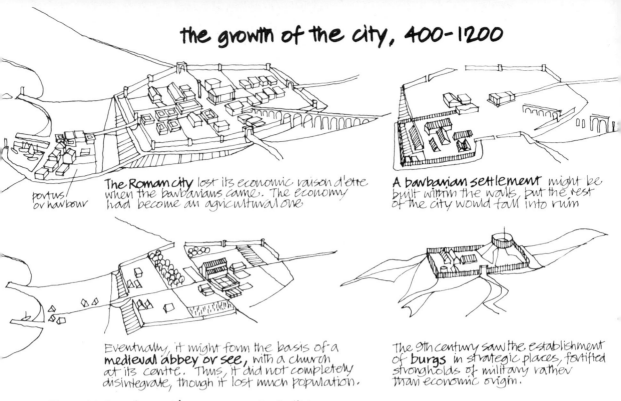

portus or harbour

The Roman city lost its economic raison d'etre when the barbarians came. The economy had become an agricultural one.

A barbarian settlement might be built within the walls, but the rest of the city would fall into ruin

Eventually, it might form the basis of a **medieval abbey or see,** with a church at its centre. Thus, it did not completely disintegrate, though it lost much population.

The 9th century saw the establishment of **burgs** in strategic places, fortified strongholds of military rather than economic origin.

s yet, neither **bishopric** nor **burg** was a real city: ither had an independent economic life and neither ngaged in commerce or industry except to provide its own mediate needs. Both were based on the feudal system nd lived off the surrounding countryside.

faubourg

portus or commercial centre

When cities revived in the 11th and 12th centuries, they expanded. Much of the land inside the old walls might be owned by the church, so a **portus** of commerce might grow up outside.

A burg at the centre of a similar commercial growth might develop a business area or **faubourg** outside the fortified centre

t first, neither **portus** nor **faubourg** was fortified. As ompetition for wealth grew, fear of attack increased. It was also mportant to protect the 'free' citizens inside the city from the eudal world outside. So where the citizens could afford it, assive outer lines of defence were built.

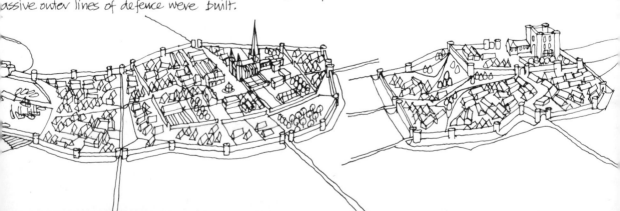

the emergence of Romanesque

Cluny II (981) the archetype of the 'parallel-chapel' plan-forms

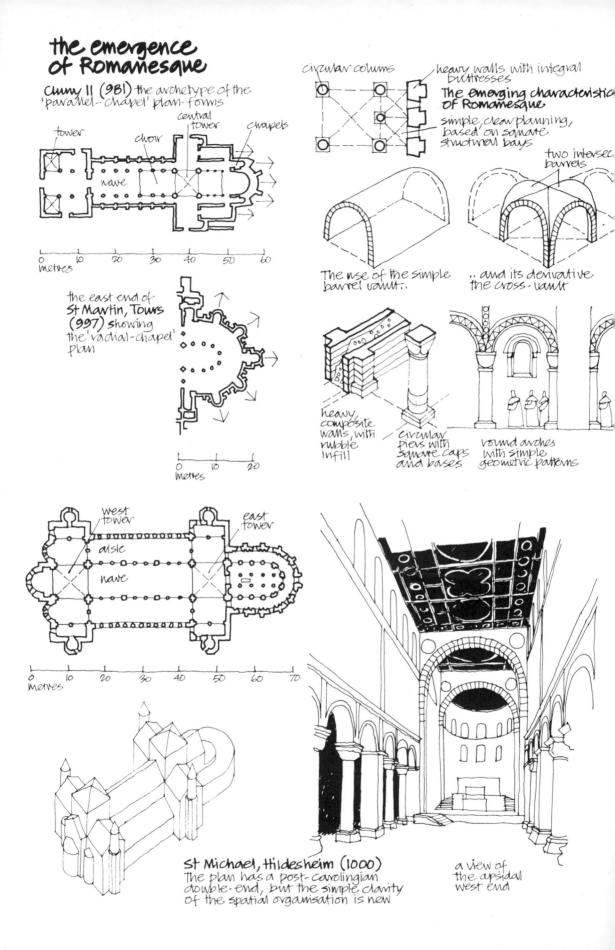

tower

choir

central tower

chapels

nave

0 10 20 30 40 50 60
metres

the east end of St Martin, Tours (997) showing the 'radial-chapel' plan

0 10 20
metres

circular columns

heavy walls with integral buttresses

The emerging characteristics of Romanesque

simple, clean planning, based on square structural bays

two intersecting barrels

The use of the simple barrel vault..

.. and its derivative the cross-vault

heavy composite walls, with rubble infill

circular piers with square caps and bases

round arches with simple geometric patterns

west tower

east tower

aisle

nave

0 10 20 30 40 50 60 70
metres

St Michael, Hildesheim (1000)
The plan has a post-Carolingian double-end, but the simple clarity of the spatial organisation is new

a view of the apsidal west end

Europe, based on the Lombardic league of Italian trading towns in the south and on the Hanse in the north.

At the same time, with the gradual expansion of northern agriculture, it was now possible to support a greater number of people. Population increased and towns, which had been in a state of decline since the late Roman empire, began slowly to revive. The feudal system and general economic uncertainty had made the countryside the basis for economic life. Few western towns still existed as trading centres of any importance. Some had been converted into tribal homesteads; others had been chosen as the seats of bishops or as sites for abbeys, retaining the outward appearance of urban communities but with no economic significance. Urban populations were much smaller than in Roman times, many old buildings had been used as quarries for building stone, and large areas of cultivated land now lay within the old city boundaries. But the gradual migration of people from the countryside into the cities changed their character. From the start, urban people could claim freedom from feudal ties, so towns became centres of freedom of thought and action, of progress and radicalism, the spearheads of an eventual revolution in the social order.

The feudal system, when not firmly controlled at the top, had resulted in ambitious, 'over-mighty' barons, with consequent political instability. After a succession of weak rulers, Otto the Great (936–73) in Germany and Hugh Capet (987–96) in France re-established strong central government, and cultural developments could once more take place. Similar anarchy had prevailed in the church; for many rich land-owning bishops and abbots, corrupt practices such as simony had become a way of life. The Cluniac movement now sought to purify the church by the strict application of Benedict's Rule. The emperor Otto III (d. 1002) saw Cluny as a force to help unify the empire; his support for it established a new era of co-operation between the empire and the church.

The centre of the reform was Cluny in Burgundy, where the abbot Majeul authorised the rebuilding of the Abbey Church. 'Cluny II' as it is known, consecrated in 981, represented not only monastic reform but also a new architectural era, the birth of the romanesque style. Not only at Cluny but also at St Martin, Tours (997), and at St Michael's, Hildesheim (1000), the rigorous spirit of Cluniac reform was interpreted in architecture of great quality. The builders were masons and carpenters, but the designers were no doubt monks seeking to express their religious ideals. These buildings are no longer re-workings of half-remembered styles of the past. They are large, simple, functional, and above all have a completeness of conception, an ordered relationship between one part and another, which represents a new approach. Most remarkable in the French churches were the many chapels which the liturgy now required for all the priests to say mass every day. The chapels, parallel at Cluny and radial at St Martin, opened off ambulatories behind the high altar. These new additions were conceived as part of an overall design. St Michael's shows the same completeness, developing the double-ended design of the Carolingian churches into a well-ordered geometric design.

The 'millennial' theory of medieval history – that intellectual effort in the 10th century was stifled because so many people thought the world would end in the year 1000 – does not fit the facts. The papacy and the empire were emerging as great political powers, population was increasing, towns were growing, a new religious spirit was in the air and a social and technical movement had begun which would in 200 years culminate in the greatest achievements of European architecture.

The triumph of Christian feudalism

The 11th and 12th centuries

> Therefore, after the above-mentioned year of the millennium, now about three years past, there occurred, throughout the world, especially in Italy and Gaul, a rebuilding of church basilicas ... each Christian people strove against the others to erect nobler ones. It was as if the whole earth, having cast off the old by shaking itself, were clothing itself everywhere in the white robe of the Church.

Raoul Glaber, a Cluniac monk and chronicler, wrote this enthusiastic passage in 1003. We are so used to thinking of architectural development as a matter of one style succeeding another that it is easy to overlook changes of a more basic kind. Even more remarkable than the development of the romanesque style itself, with its new-found clarity of thought, was the number of buildings and, above all, their great size. During the 11th century, all over western Europe and particularly in Italy, France, Spain and Britain, new buildings were appearing whose size and height, for the first time in eight or more centuries, rivalled those of ancient Rome.

The upsurge in activity reflects the increasing wealth and political stability of the times, but the great size of the buildings suggests something more: an ability to organise, to plan and budget for large-scale works, to transport materials and to put together teams of workers. The early Middle Ages had seen the gradual emergence from disunity of an ordered social system, which by the 11th century had reached a plateau of development. In control were two wealthy social groups: on the one hand a feudal hierarchy of emperors, kings and aristocracy, and on the other the church. Both groups now had an established place in society and had developed that degree of internal organisation which makes them recognisable as classes. They were classes, moreover, with an increasingly European rather than merely local background, and their buildings, as expressions of class strength, began to develop identifiable European characteristics.

Representative of the powerful class of feudal landlords, and archetypal of the progressive spirit of their time, were the Normans. Three or four generations earlier they had been Viking invaders – 'Norman' means 'north-man'. Now they had established Normandy as a small, dynamic feudal state which the kings of France, technically their overlords, had great difficulty in controlling. During the 11th century Norman political and cultural influence spread through Europe, to England in 1066, to Italy and Sicily in 1071, and in 1084 to Rome itself. Their expansion, at a time of growing cultural unity in Europe, ensured especially that the development of England would henceforward be linked with that of the mainland, instead of with Scandinavia as hitherto. The story of the conquest of England is related visually in the famous Bayeux Tapestry. There is also a written account by Master Wace, a troubadour at the court of Henry II. As soon as the invaders landed,

> ... they consulted together and sought for a good spot to place a strong fort upon. Then they cast out of the ships the materials and drew them to land, all

36

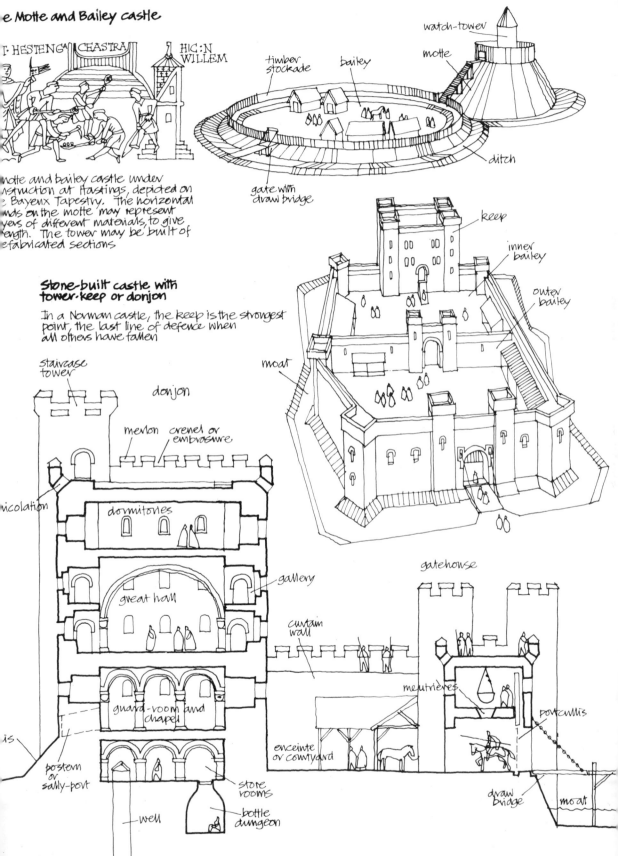

the Norman castle

the Motte and Bailey castle

T·HESTENGA CEASTRA HIC:N WILLEM

motte and bailey castle under construction at Hastings, depicted on the Bayeux Tapestry. The horizontal bands on the motte may represent layers of different materials, to give strength. The tower may be built of prefabricated sections

watch-tower
motte
timber stockade
bailey
ditch
gate with draw bridge

Stone-built castle with tower-keep or donjon

In a Norman castle, the keep is the strongest point, the last line of defence when all others have fallen

keep
inner bailey
outer bailey
moat

staircase tower
donjon
merlon
crenel or embrasure
machicolation
dormitories
gallery
great hall
guard-room and chapel
glacis
postern or sally-port
store rooms
well
bottle dungeon

gatehouse
curtain wall
meutrières
portcullis
enceinte or courtyard
draw bridge
moat

shaped, framed and pierced to receive the pins which they had brought, cut and ready in long barrels; so that before evening had well set in, they had finished a fort.

A similar fort is shown in the Tapestry itself, a version of what we now know as the 'motte and bailey' castle. The bailey was a compound, protected by ditch and stockade and sheltering a group of dwellings and storehouses. The motte was the strong-point of the castle, an artificial mound, also protected by a ditch and surmounted by a palisade or a wooden tower. The concept of the castle had developed in Europe in the 9th century, when Charlemagne and Charles the Bald had defended key border points by establishing block-houses in strategic places, which later became the dwelling places of feudal lords. Edward the Confessor had introduced the castle to England in the early 11th century, but it was the Normans who developed the definitive form. There are many surviving motte and bailey castles, most of them altered by subsequent improvements. Thetford in Norfolk has one of the largest, 25 metres in height, and Dromore in Northern Ireland (1180) one of the most intact.

Duke William of Normandy (d. 1087) became William I of England. He ruled with great efficiency, and his exhaustive survey of the country's economic resources, the Domesday Book (1081), formed an important part of his plan for complete control of the country through universal taxation. He saw that the key to this was by local control through his feudal barons: so he began a programme of castle building to provide them with bases for tax gathering and from which to mount punitive raids on the restless Anglo-Saxon people. During the twenty-one years of William's reign, fifty baronial castles were built. But it was also William's style to keep firm control in his own hands. He appointed commissioners and sheriffs to oversee the barons' activities. He kept large tracts of land for himself, to ensure a firm economic base for the crown, and built himself no less than forty-nine castles all over the country from which he and his sheriffs could oversee the workings of his local policies.

During the Conquest, castles were built in wood for speed and convenience, but the establishment of a permanent site demanded, for greater safety, a castle of stone. The tested motte and bailey principle was used at first, but with the new material came certain innovations. The defensive stockade around the bailey was replaced by a stone wall and, where feasible, the palisade on the motte by a squat circular defensive tower of stone now known as a 'shell keep'. Often, though, a hastily thrown-up motte might not be consolidated enough to carry a shell keep of any size, and so to replace both motte and keep, the 'donjon' was developed. This was a large, square tower, several storeys in height, containing guardrooms, a living-floor, sleeping quarters for the lord's family, and possibly cells for prisoners. The base was often a 'glacis', splayed to keep sappers at a distance from the walls and to cause offensive missiles dropped from above to ricochet among the attackers. An entrance high up in the wall discouraged the use of battering rams.

At intervals along the outer bailey, projecting towers were built to allow defenders to cover the walls by flanking arrow-fire, and the main entrance to the bailey, easier to storm than the donjon, often had a gatehouse with a portcullis, and sometimes a separate forward defensive tower, known as a barbican, for extra protection. Besiegers reaching the portcullis would find themselves under attack from *meurtrières* ('murder holes') in the stonework above.

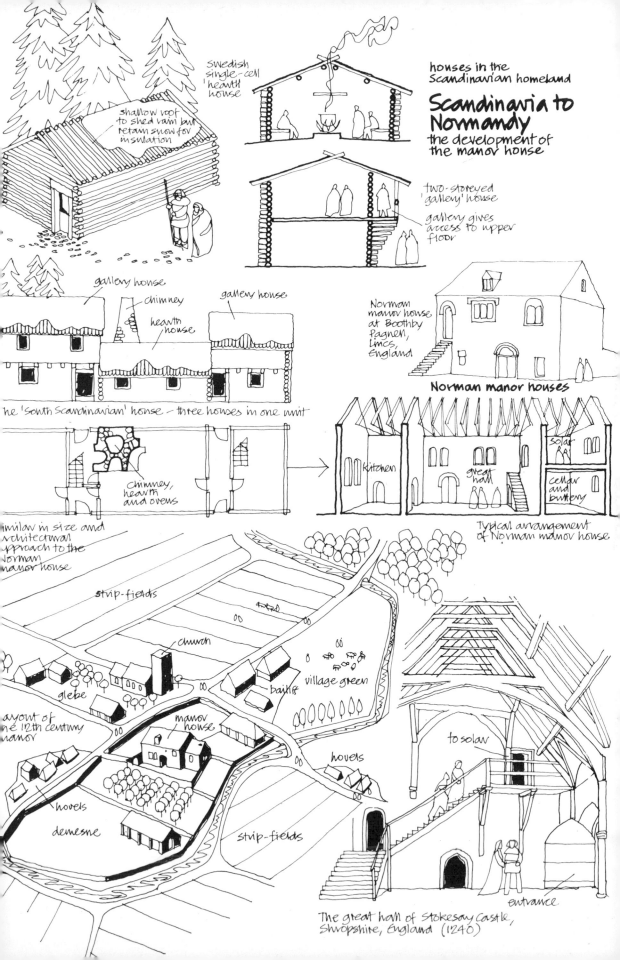

swedish single-cell 'hearth' house

shallow roof to shed rain but retain snow for insulation

houses in the Scandinavian homeland

Scandinavia to Normandy
the development of the manor house

two-storeyed 'gallery' house

gallery gives access to upper floor

gallery house

chimney

hearth house

gallery house

Norman manor house at Boothby Pagnell, Lincs, England

Norman manor houses

the 'South Scandinavian' house – three houses in one unit

chimney, hearth and ovens

kitchen

great hall

solar

cellar and buttery

Typical arrangement of Norman manor house

similar in size and architectural approach to the Norman manor house

strip-fields

church

village green

glebe

bailiff

layout of the 12th century manor

manor house

hovels

demesne

hovels

strip-fields

to solar

hovels

entrance

The great hall of Stokesay Castle, Shropshire, England (1240)

Shell keeps still exist at Carisbrooke (1140) and Windsor Castle (1170), but the greatest castles of the period were of the donjon type. Finest of all were the White Tower at the Tower of London, begun in 1086, and the Château Gaillard in France (1196). The former is a square building, 30 metres in height with a tower at each corner, one of which is enlarged to accommodate the unique little chapel of St John. The latter, built by Richard I of England on a strategic site at Les Andelys in Normandy, was a massive construction protected by three successive lines of earth-works and towers.

A castle originally had a strategic role: like the Roman camp it enabled a strong central authority to defend its borders from an outside enemy. As time went on, however, tensions began to develop within the feudal system. Castles continued to be built to defend borders and mountain passes, but now they were also built to control the local population.

The immense strength of the great castles of the 11th and 12th centuries enabled them to be successfully defended by very small garrisons, often of only twenty or thirty men; but this strength must also have had an intimidating psychological effect – perhaps deliberately – on the local people. Ironically, the castles were often built by the serfs themselves, pressed into service, usually without payment, by their feudal landlord. A castle, though used as a dwelling-place by its lord and often the centre of a large feudal manor, was primarily a military installation, belonging exclusively to a specialist military elite. Just as membership of the elite was in the gift of the king, so was the construction of a castle, which required a royal 'license to crenellate'.

For tenants of more lowly status, the typical dwelling was the manor-house, a group of buildings consisting of dwelling, byres and store houses, usually round a fortified courtyard. The main building was the lord's house, consisting of a large central hall for meals and daily activities, adjoining kitchens, butteries and pantries, and an upper retiring chamber, the solar or 'sun-room', for sleeping. The origins of the manor-house can be seen in the houses of the Normans' Scandinavian homeland. For centuries the simplest Swedish, Norwegian and Danish house had been a single-cell building with a pitched roof. The walls consisted of long, straight baulks of softwood laid horizontally, notched together at the corners in 'log-cabin' style. Unlike the barbarians, the Northmen did not share buildings with their animals, which were housed separately. A more advanced style of living had led them in the early Middle Ages to develop two-storeyed and multi-roomed houses, which set the pattern for the manor-houses they built in France and England. These too were usually of timber, but the best surviving examples are of stone, built in a simple, straightforward style like that of contemporary churches. None survive from the 11th century, but the 12th-century English houses at Boothby Pagnell, Lincolnshire, at St Mary's Guild in Lincoln, and at Christchurch, Hampshire, are typical of the style.

Europe's growing political order temporarily re-energised the feudal system, to the great benefit of the land-owners; not only the barons, but also the church, which by this time also owned large estates. Foremost among the economic powers of the time were the monasteries, which benefited from the generosity of kings seeking their moral support and of rich laymen in search of spiritual justification. If a rich man entered monastic life, the Rule forbade him his personal wealth, which became instead the property of the community. By the 11th century, the monasteries owned money and property equivalent, it is estimated, to one-sixth of the entire wealth of Europe. Their economic power was matched by their spiritual influence, and it is important to remember that they were originally founded in protest against the church establishment. A gap remained between, on the one hand, the monastic or 'religious' orders, and on the other, the Pope, his bishops and priests, or 'secular' clergy. The monasteries, concentrating on spiritual and social matters, remained largely untainted by the political intrigues which in the preceding centuries had so reduced papal authority. They gave Europe a spiritual leadership in which the example of Cluny was particularly dominant: the great Cluniac abbots such as St Odilo (994–1049) or St Hugh (1049–1109) spoke with more spiritual authority than the Pope himself. The movement was also expanding, and during the 11th century two more orders were founded, the Carthusians at Grenoble in 1086 and the Cistercians at Cîteaux and Clairvaux in 1098.

In church building too, monastic influence was strong: designing a complex building required education, a commodity of which the monasteries still had a monopoly. The masons and carpenters were often serfs, though the more fortunate might have gained their freedom and received some sort of education. The masters, however, who designed the buildings, would all have been educated men – usually monks, but sometimes (and increasingly after the 10th century) educated laymen. The building boom of the 11th century was largely due to the monastic houses investing their wealth not only to the glory of God but also to the enlargement of their own prestige. One of the contradictions of monastic building is that, while seeking to express the notion of church unity, it also fostered a divisive kind of local pride.

The prestige of the secular church was relatively small, but growing, and the papacy itself was subjected to a Cluniac reformation in 1046. One feature of the church's development was the growth to maturity, all over Europe, of the parochial system. Parishes had three main features: a geographical boundary, often based on the boundaries of the feudal estates, a parish priest, appointed as a 'cure of souls' to the local population, and a church building.

Continental parishes, in France and the Netherlands for example, typically were large, with church buildings appropriately large and splendid. English parishes were small and numerous, the churches consequently smaller and, with a few exceptions, architecturally less remarkable.

The significant difference between a parish church and one of monastic origin was one of function: in a monastic church the nave, for the lay worshippers, was subordinate to the choir in which the monks worshipped; in a parish church the nave, like that of a cathedral, had to be larger. Existing monastic churches were sometimes adapted to secular use by the addition of a nave, but normally a parish church was purpose-built, appearing in an identifiably secular form from about the 9th century onwards. Pre-conquest churches in Britain include Worth in Sussex, a simple cruciform plan in which the nave undoubtedly dominates, and Earls Barton in Northamptonshire with its 'long-and-short-work' tower. In France, the church of St Philibert Tournus in Burgundy (950 and later) began as the abbey church of a Benedictine monastery. Its nave is spanned by diaphragm arches which carry a series of transverse barrel-vaults.

It is likely that many early parish churches were not wholly secular in provenance, and that monastic finance and monastic building ability helped to create them. The design of church buildings had for so long been a monastic prerogative that secular society was only gradually developing the necessary skills. Nevertheless, a growing vigour and unity of expression was seen in great church buildings, both monastic and

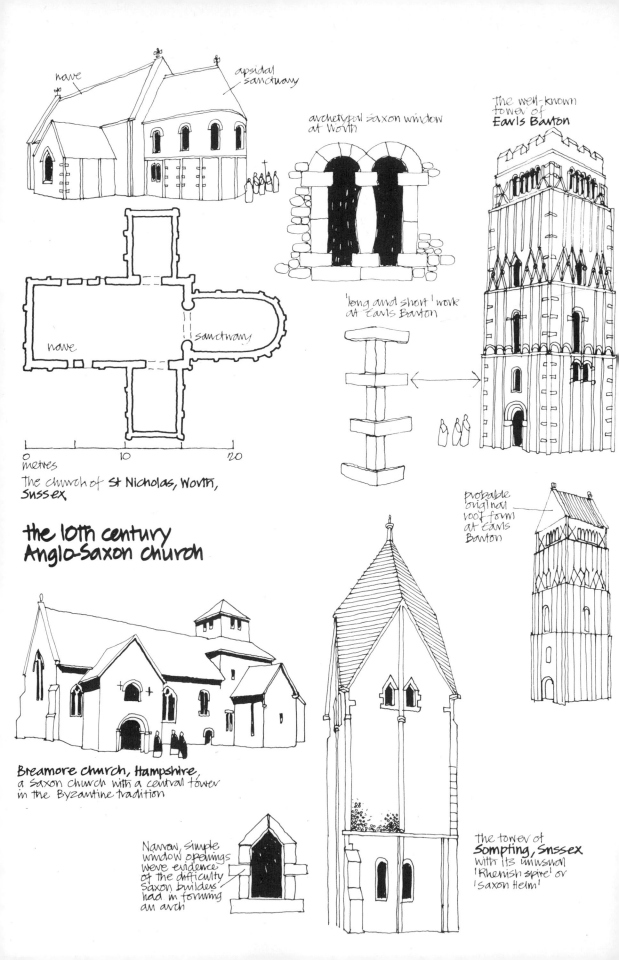

nave

apsidal sanctuary

archetypal saxon window at Worth

the well-known tower of **Earls Barton**

nave

sanctuary

'long and short' work at Earls Barton

0 metres 10 20

The church of **St Nicholas, Worth, Sussex**

the 10th century Anglo-Saxon church

probable original roof form at Earls Barton

Breamore church, Hampshire, a Saxon church with a central tower in the Byzantine tradition

Narrow, simple window openings were evidence of the difficulty Saxon builders had in forming an arch

the tower of **Sompting, Sussex** with its unusual 'Rhenish spire' or 'Saxon Helm'

secular, all over Europe, and even buildings on the geographical fringes, where outside influences were strongest, began to display identifiable romanesque features.

The only major exception to this is the church of San Marco in Venice (1063), a *tour-de-force* which owes much less to western Europe than to Byzantium. Built to replace an earlier basilican church burnt down in 976, it has a Greek-cross plan with a main central dome on pendentives carried on four great piers, and smaller domes over the narthex, transepts and sanctuary. It is a building *sui generis*; its unique location near the Grand Canal, and its highly individual decorative features, added to over the centuries to celebrate the city's rise to power, have no equal elsewhere, and it lies outside the mainstream of European architectural development of the time.

The beautiful church of San Miniato al Monte, Florence (1018), appears from the outside to be a straightforward basilica in the Roman tradition, but the interior shows some romanesque innovations, in particular the division of the long straight nave by piers and transverse semi-circular diaphragm arches into three basic compartments, which reflect the current preoccupation with spatial organisation and anticipate the concept of vaulting in bays.

The Cathedral of Pisa (1063) forms the centrepiece of the celebrated group which also contains the later Baptistery and Campanile. Like San Miniato, it is basically a basilican building, with rows of columns supporting a clerestorey on semi-circular arches and a double aisle on each side, but the formation of a crossing by the addition of transepts relates the plan-form to contemporary development in north-western Europe. In new buildings everywhere the basilican plan of the Roman tradition was being synthesised with the centralised Greek-cross plan of Byzantium. Re-interpreted in the rigorous romanesque idiom, the result was the Latin-cross plan, the first truly indigenous church plan of north-west Europe, and the basis for the planning of almost all later medieval cathedrals. The relationship between the churches of Rome and Byzantium had been decaying during the 9th and 10th centuries. By the middle of the 11th century the rift was almost complete, and though the indirect influence of the east was still felt in cities with strong trade links, the cultural development of Europe as a whole was taking on a more western aspect.

Norman church-building is an example. La Trinité in Caen (1062), known as the Abbaye-aux-Dames, is one of the earliest of the great Norman churches with nave, transepts and square crossing-tower establishing the basic formal arrangement used time and again in succeeding centuries. The roof is vaulted, with early and slightly crude sexpartite vaulting. The sister-church of St Etienne in Caen (1068), the Abbaye-aux-Hommes, though subsequently altered, originally featured the charac-teristic *chevet* east end of Cluny II. The sexpartite vaults of La Trinité are developed in a more confident way and two other features used in later centuries are intro-duced: the west end with twin towers surmounted by spires is an early prototype for later, gothic façades, and the outward thrust of the nave vault is contained on each side by a continuous, half barrel-vault built against it – a concept anticipating the flying buttress.

Norman architectural influence had been felt in Britain some years before the Conquest, the most celebrated example being Edward the Confessor's original Westminster Abbey (1055), then a continental monastery in the Cluniac tradition. But the style reached its peak of development in the great churches built by the Normans themselves.

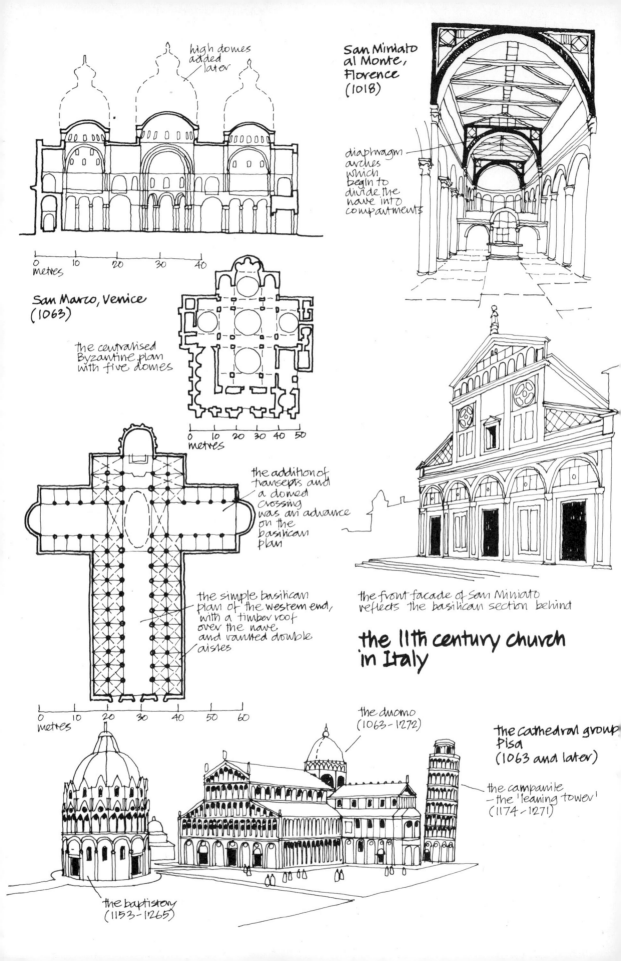

high domes added later

San Miniato al Monte, Florence (1018)

diaphragm arches which begin to divide the nave into compartments

0 10 20 30 40 metres

San Marco, Venice (1063)

the centralised Byzantine plan with five domes

0 10 20 30 40 50 metres

the addition of transepts and a domed crossing was an advance on the basilican plan

the simple basilican plan of the western end, with a timber roof over the nave, and vaulted double aisles

0 10 20 30 40 50 60 metres

the front facade of San Miniato reflects the basilican section behind

the 11th century church in Italy

the duomo (1063 - 1272)

the Cathedral group Pisa (1063 and later)

the campanile - the 'leaning tower' (1174 - 1271)

the baptistery (1153 - 1265)

Most English cathedrals had a monastic origin. Many retain their cloisters and ancillary buildings, now adapted to other uses. The ruins of the great abbeys of Rievaulx (1132), Fountains (1135) and Kirkstall (1152) give a clearer picture of what a Norman abbey was like in its day. Fountains is dominated by the ruins of a late medieval tower, but its cruciform church, with its unusual 'chapel of the nine altars', is mid-12th century. On the south side is a cloister garth, flanked on one side by a 90-metre-long block which housed the refectory and dormitory of the lay brethren. Nearby were the monks' dormitory and refectory, chapter-house, kitchens, infirmary, abbot's house and stores.

Seventeen English cathedrals still retain substantial examples of Norman work, including the naves of Ely, Chichester and St Albans, the choirs of Gloucester and Winchester, and the twin transept-towers of Exeter. The most complete examples, however, are Peterborough (1117) with its fine interior and original decorative timber roof, Norwich (1096) with its long nave and *chevet*-type choir with radial chapels and, above all, Durham.

Durham Cathedral (1093 and later) is built on a great rock above the River Wear. It is a dramatic location, suitable for a castle, and the building has an appropriate masculine quality. The long, tall nave has massive circular piers supporting triforium and clerestory, but their effect, though sober, is airy rather than oppressive, lightened by simple but delicately carved abstract decoration, flutings and zig-zags. The choir, finished in 1104, has one of the earliest examples of rib-vaulting known in Europe, a feature of the greatest importance in the subsequent development of stone-built roofing. The nave vaulting, finished in 1130, is taken even further, for here the pointed arch is introduced in order to allow its apex to be brought in line with the top of rounded arches of greater span, a feature which would be brought to its logical conclusion in gothic buildings two and three centuries later.

One of the main functional impulses behind the architecture of the 11th century was the search for roofs capable of spanning larger and larger spaces. These could, of course, be of timber, but the use of candles and rushes for lighting made the risk of fire ever-present. The Romans had used barrel-vaults and groined-vaults over wide spans, but the 11th century did not have Roman concrete; a barrel-vault in stone alone has a high weight-to-strength ratio which limits its span. This was changed by the development of the rib-vault: here the ribs alone were structural, and could be infilled with relatively lightweight panels of stone, allowing wider spans. Further-more, the ribs concentrated the stresses onto localised points where they could be carried on columns, rather than on the continuous wall implied by the barrel-vault. The rib-vaulting at Durham, clearly demonstrating the lines of stress, gave the interior a tense, lively appearance and presaged the great gothic interiors of the 12th and 13th centuries.

Though seldom as structurally dynamic as Durham, church designs all over Europe were beginning to show a similar concern for articulation, for the clear expression of structural elements and the division of internal space into bays and compartments. The church of Sant' Ambrogio in Milan (1080 and later) was an ancient foundation, begun by St Ambrose himself in the 4th century and still retaining archaic features such as an entrance atrium and an eastern apse, but its rebuilding in the late 11th and early 12th centuries incorporated new ideas. The severe and majestic nave is divided by diaphragm arches into bays, each vaulted with round-arched rib-vaults. Like those at Durham, the rib-vaults are among the

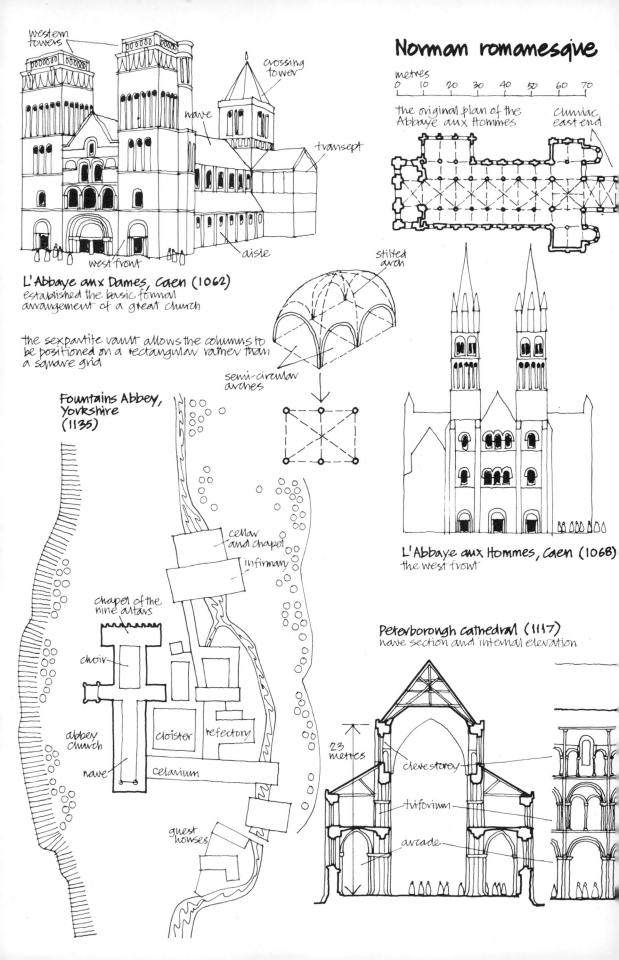

western towers

crossing tower

nave

transept

west front

aisle

Norman romanesque

metres

0 10 20 30 40 50 60 70

the original plan of the Abbaye aux Hommes

Cluniac east end

L'Abbaye aux Dames, Caen (1062)

established the basic formal arrangement of a great church

the sexpartite vault allows the columns to be positioned on a rectangular rather than a square grid

stilted arch

semi-circular arches

Fountains Abbey, Yorkshire (1135)

cellar and chapel

infirmary

chapel of the nine altars

choir

abbey church

cloister

refectory

nave

cellarium

guest houses

L'Abbaye aux Hommes, Caen (1068)

the west front

Peterborough cathedral (1117)

nave section and internal elevation

23 metres

clerestorey

triforium

arcade

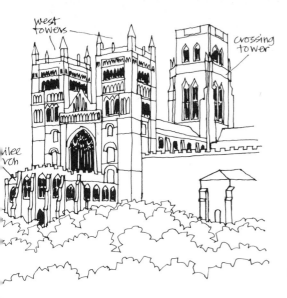

west towers

crossing tower

galilee rch

chapel of the nine altars

altar

choir

tower

rib-vaulted nave

galilee porch

cloister garth

monastic buildings

0 20 40 60 80 100
metres

Durham and the rib-vault

e Romans had used mple barrel vaults, fteed to reduce eir weight...

... and had also developed the groined or cross-vault which introduced the concept of vaulting in compartments

repetitive bay or compartment

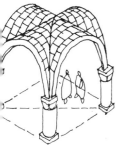

e Normans were able to use avy, stone groined vaults, inly in undercrofts and crypts

groin

One of the weakest aspects of the groined vault was the groin itself, liable to failure. Another problem was the continuous, all-over support which the groined vault needed during construction.

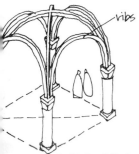

ribs

is changed with the 12thC velopment of the rib-vault. nly the ribs themselves required pport during construction, and...

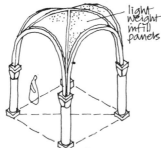

light weight infill panels

..the panels in between could be filled afterwards with light-weight stone, allowing the size of the supports to be reduced

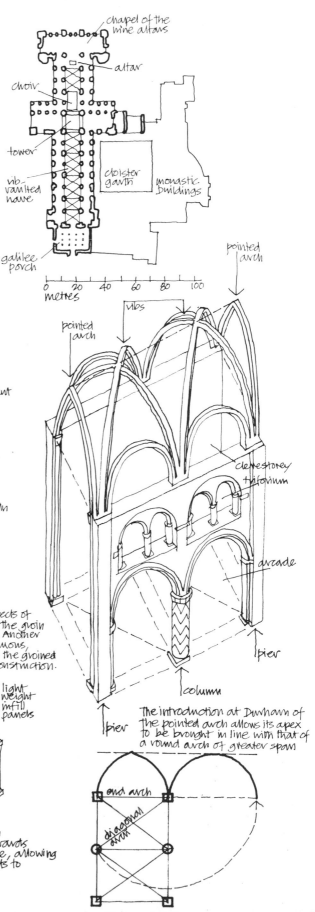

pointed arch

ribs

pointed arch

clerestorey

triforium

arcade

pier

column

pier

The introduction at Durham of the pointed arch allows its apex to be brought in line with that of a round arch of greater span

end arch

diagonal arch

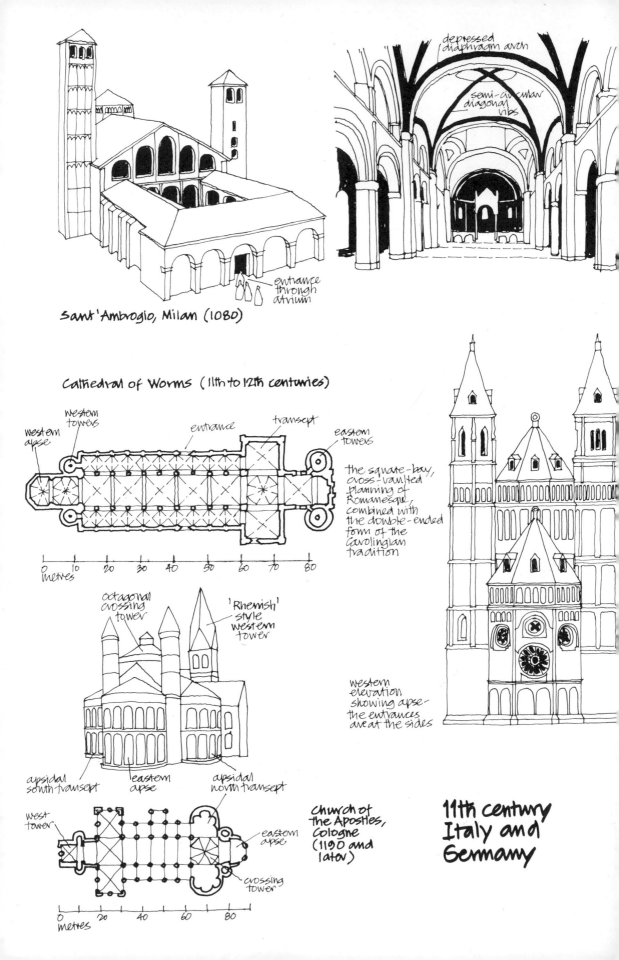

depressed
diaphragm arch

semi-circular
diagonal
ribs

entrance
through
atrium

Sant'Ambrogio, Milan (1080)

Cathedral of Worms (11th to 12th centuries)

western apse

western towers

entrance

transept

eastern towers

0 10 20 30 40 50 60 70 80
metres

the square-bay,
cross-vaulted
planning of
Romanesque,
combined with
the double-ended
form of the
Carolingian
tradition

octagonal
crossing
tower

'Rhenish'
style
western
tower

western
elevation
showing apse-
the entrances
are at the sides

apsidal
south transept

eastern
apse

apsidal
north transept

west
tower

eastern
apse

Church of
the Apostles,
Cologne
(1190 and
later)

crossing
tower

0 20 40 60 80
metres

11th century
Italy and
Germany

earliest in Europe and the pattern for subsequent imitations, notably at San Michele, Pavia (1100).

Contemporary churches in north Germany still retained Carolingian elements but here, too, new ideas appeared. Maria Laach abbey (1093), south of Cologne, has an apse at the west end, recollecting Charlemagne's Palace Chapels, but the three eastern apses and the multiplicity of towers are more reminiscent of Cluny. The 11th-century cathedral of Worms, a major monument of the period, also has a western apse but with the addition of transepts and a crossing-tower and, as well as two eastern towers, a further pair of flanking towers at the west end. Nave and aisles are roofed by stone cross-vaults on square compartments. The later Church of the Apostles, Cologne (1190), has an eastern transept with apsidal ends over which is an octagonal crossing-tower. The west end is given prominence by a single tall tower on the axis of the nave.

Ste Madeleine at Vézelay in Burgundy (1104) presents a different aspect of romanesque architecture. Like Durham, it is a large building on a commanding hill-top site. It has an aisled nave, a transept, double towers at the west end and a *chevet* at the east. Its structure is less adventurous than that of Durham, consisting basically of a series of semi-circular groined vaults, the vaulting compartments articulated by great transverse arches. It is remarkable, however, for less tangible reasons: the elegance of its proportions, the rightness of its balance between structural simplicity and decorative richness, and above all, the contrast between the subdued lighting of the nave with its high clerestories and the transparent luminosity of the east end.

Farther south in France, Byzantine influences were still felt. The cathedral of Angoulême (1105), though undoubtedly a romanesque building in the clarity of its Latin-cross plan and the multiplicity of its eastern chapels, both radial and parallel, is roofed with a series of shallow domes on pendentives. The great church of St Front at Périgueux (1120) also has a mixed parentage. It has almost exactly the layout of San Marco, Venice, with its Greek-cross plan and five domes, but whereas San Marco glows with Byzantine mosaic, St Front has a severe stone interior, a model of romanesque sobriety.

One facet of the growing European identity was the ideological importance of Spain, which Islamic occupation had made the subject of universal Christian ambition. For political as well as religious reasons, much interest was shown in the shrine of St James at Compostela and the pilgrimage route to it. Great churches were built along the route at Tours, Limoges, Conques and Toulouse. At Compostela itself, the symbolic importance of the cathedral of Santiago (1075 and later) made it the focus of much international effort and therefore of current European design ideas. It has a cruciform plan with a crossing-tower and barrel-vaulted nave and transepts. At the sides are aisles with galleries above; the gallery roofs are a half barrel-vault, as at St Etienne, buttressing the nave vault. The east end has an ambulatory with radiating chapels on the pattern already established at St Martin, Tours. The whole building is a mature and accomplished achievement, its success being heightened by the fine detail design, of which the Portico de la Gloria (1168) is the supreme example.

Though not directly inspired by Cluny II, the pilgrimage churches were certainly a result of Cluniac influence. In 1088, the abbey church of Cluny itself was rebuilt yet again, and with its length of nearly 140 metres became the largest and most splendid

12th century France

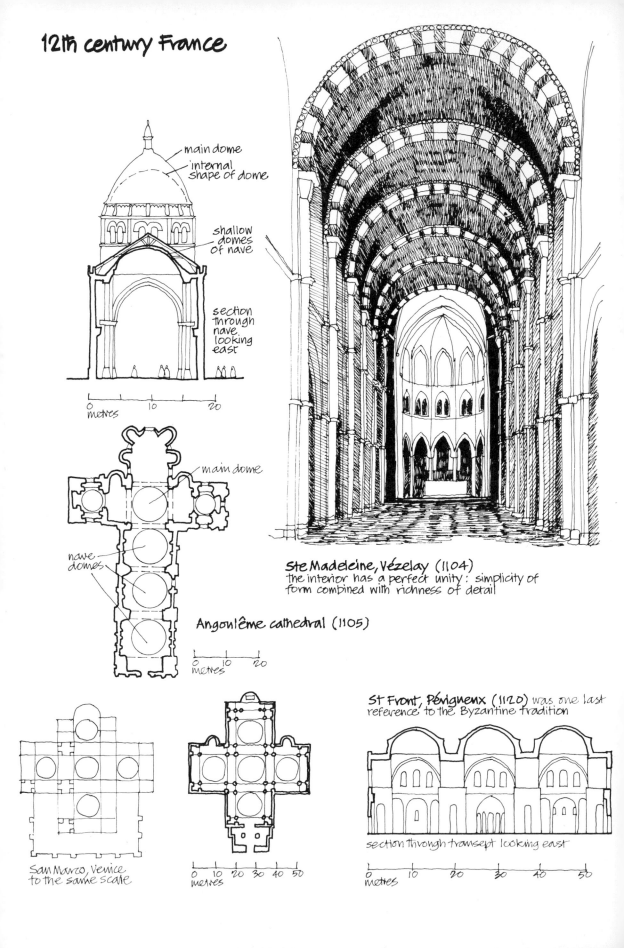

main dome

internal shape of dome

shallow domes of nave

section through nave looking east

0   10   20
metres

main dome

nave domes

Angoulême cathedral (1105)

0   10   20
metres

Ste Madeleine, Vézelay (1104)
the interior has a perfect unity: simplicity of
form combined with richness of detail

St Front, Périgueux (1120) was one last
reference to the Byzantine tradition

San Marco, Venice
to the same scale

0 10 20 30 40 50
metres

section through transept looking east

0   10   20   30   40   50
metres

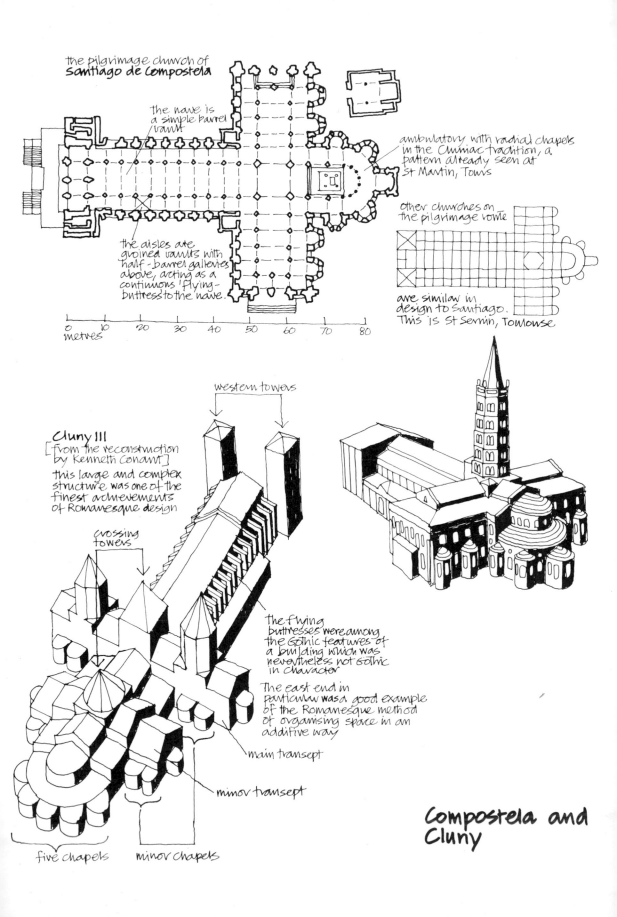

the pilgrimage church of
Santiago de Compostela

the nave is
a simple barrel
vault

ambulatory with radial chapels
in the Cluniac tradition, a
pattern already seen at
St Martin, Tours

the aisles are
groined vaults with
half-barrel galleries
above, acting as a
continuous 'flying-
buttress to the nave.

other churches on
the pilgrimage route

are similar in
design to Santiago.
This is St Sernin, Toulouse

0 10 20 30 40 50 60 70 80
metres

western towers

Cluny III
[from the reconstruction
by Kenneth Conant]
this large and complex
structure was one of the
finest achievements
of Romanesque design

crossing
towers

the flying
buttresses were among
the Gothic features of
a building which was
nevertheless not Gothic
in character

The east end in
particular was a good example
of the Romanesque method
of organising space in an
additive way

main transept

minor transept

five chapels   minor chapels

Compostela and Cluny

building in France. Most of this building, Cluny III, has been destroyed, which has tended to obscure its importance in the history of architecture. It was a complex building with a long double-aisled nave, two transepts, each with towers over the crossing, and a multiplicity of chapels at the east end. Its great size presented a structural problem, and for the first time rows of fully-developed flying buttresses were used, above the aisles, to contain the thrust of the nave roof. This structural device was to become a major feature of architectural development for the next three centuries. At Cluny, in the late 11th century, it was a celebration of virtuosity, an expression of the growing confidence of its builders. The development of architectural knowledge and building skill was part of a general re-awakening, not only in the arts but in all branches of knowledge.

Cultural progress is not necessarily a reflection of general social progress: greater knowledge provides the opportunity for social improvement – it does not guarantee it. The increased architectural ability of the 11th century did not, for example, improve the living conditions of the serf. Indeed, cultural development depended in some degree on inequality and exploitation: a cultural elite could develop only if society relieved it of the responsibility of supporting itself by primary labour. An architectural achievement such as a great church depended still more on the existence of wealth and power in the hands of a few; though possibly conceived and certainly presented as a symbol of unity and fellowship, its very existence was an indication of a divided society.

Most people in 11th-century Europe still lived in primitive huts, similar to those of the 5th-century barbarian. Except in barren, rocky districts where stone rubble was more common, timber was the most typical structural material. Roofs were still covered in heather or reed thatch or turf, with low walls of wattle or mud. The homes of the peasants – and of the poorest townspeople – were mainly single-room dwellings, with a central hearth from which smoke filtered out through cracks in the roof. A second room under the same roof might provide shelter for the animals. One or two 'wind-eyes' – unglazed openings in the outside walls – provided extra light and ventilation.

Hovels like these, probably built by the owner for a generation's occupation, were not made to last long. The few medieval houses which remain today are those of the rural freeman or richer urban merchant, built in more enduring materials. Characteristic of the Anglo-Saxon world was the use of heavy hardwood framing for walls and roof, often using a form of construction known as 'crucks': opposed pairs of curved timbers spanning from ground to ridge formed a basic frame onto which subsidiary timbers, walls and rafters, were fixed. Cruck construction was used in both single-storey and two-storey buildings and was in common use for better-class houses until about 1600. Occasionally, the house of a very rich owner would be built in dressed stone. Not many remain today, but the 'Jew's House' (c. 1160) of Aaron of Lincoln, the wealthiest man in the city and benefactor of many abbeys is a simple but very fine two-storey building with round-headed romanesque windows and doorway.

The expansion of the European economy was given great impetus by the First Crusade. By the late 11th century, Byzantine military power had declined, and the eastern emperor Alexis became vulnerable to attack from the Seljuk Turks who then dominated the Islamic world.

It was in the interests of the west to keep Byzantium as a buffer-state: so western

honses and hovels

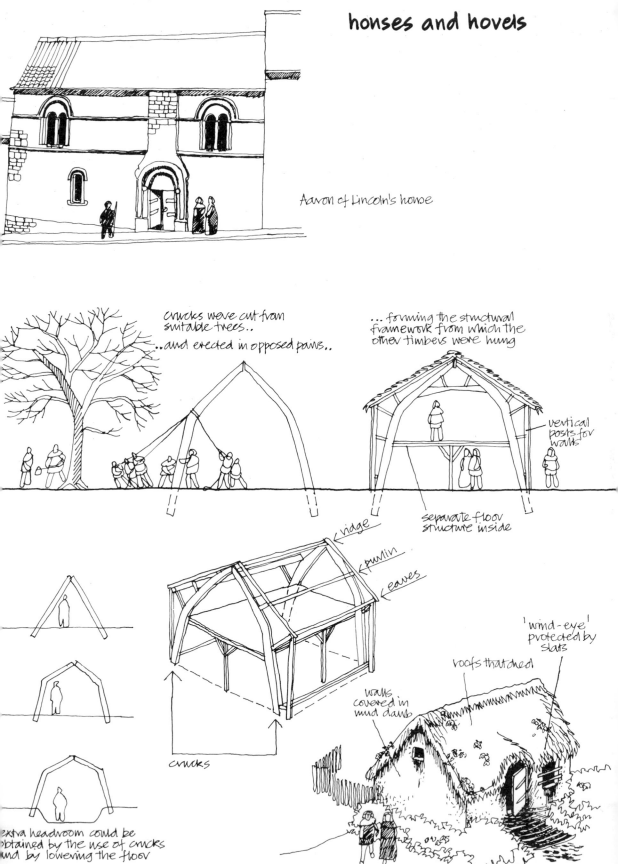

Aaron of Lincoln's honse

cruicks were cut from suitable trees..

..and erected in opposed pairs..

... forming the structural framework from which the other timbers were hung

vertical posts for walls

separate floor structure inside

ridge

purlin

eaves

'wind-eye' protected by slats

roofs thatched

walls covered in mud daub

cruicks

extra headroom could be obtained by the use of cruicks and by lowering the floor

rulers readily agreed to a joint attack on Turkish holdings in the Holy Land. Pope Urban II, in his famous call to arms at Clermont in 1095, represented it as a religious mission:

> Go forth and fight boldly for the Cause of God. Christ himself will be your leader as, more valiant than the Israelites of old, you fight for *your* Jerusalem . . . let the words *Deus vult* resound from every side.

Coming during an especially productive phase in Islamic scholarship, science and poetry, the age of Nizam-al-Mulk and of Omar Khayyám, the Crusade brought many thousands of westerners into direct contact with an advanced civilisation. Whether the Crusade had been initiated for political or for religious reasons, there is no doubt that the most significant gains to the west were economic and cultural. The Crusaders, in a campaign notable for both chivalry and brutality, captured Jerusalem in 1099 and established a western feudal state in Palestine. The military orders were set up to protect pilgrimage routes to Jerusalem, and with their support European trade began to dominate the eastern Mediterranean and to open routes into Asia Minor. Captured Turkish craftsmen brought their superior skills into Europe, looted artefacts provided patterns for western craftsmen to copy, and acquired books helped to spread Arabic ideas and knowledge. Thus, as the Arabs' political power declined, their cultural influence grew, and eastern textiles, cutlery and glassware, as well as agricultural and banking methods, mathematical and medical knowledge, and building techniques, began to find their way westwards.

Among the first beneficiaries were the Crusaders themselves, who had seen Islamic military architecture at first hand. In Spain, the castle of Loarre (1070) with its curtain wall and defensive towers, and the town fortifications of Avila in Castile (1088), a remarkable $2\frac{1}{2}$-kilometre wall with eighty-six towers and ten gates, already showed a certain Islamic influence. However, when the Templars, the Hospitallers and the Teutonic Knights came to build defences for the newly-won territory and pilgrim-routes in the east, they adopted Saracenic ideas wholesale, changing the pattern of western castle-building. The Crusader castles were immensely strong, suitable for a protracted war of attrition, and proof against all but the most persistent of sieges. They were also very large, for though many of them were built within sight of each other and able to exchange signals for help, each had to hold a big garrison consisting largely of mercenaries and enough stores for a long siege. Many castles were built with inner strong-points for defence, not only from the enemy outside the walls, but also in case the mercenaries mutinied.

Crusader castles were concentric in form: the inner strong-point was defended by two or more complete circles of curtain-walls punctuated by towers, which were usually cylindrical to provide more resistance to missiles; and most castles, in addition to the natural advantages of a well-chosen site, had wide moats, cuttings or earth-works for extra protection. The Château de Saone in present-day Syria (1120 and after) sits on a triangular outcrop of rock, protected on two sides by natural slopes and on the third by a rock-cut ditch 20 metres wide. It has a square keep in the European style but also some of the first circular towers to be built by the Crusaders. The famous Krak des Chevaliers, developed by the Hospitallers from 1142 onwards, is the most redoubtable fortress. It has a commanding hill-top position, protected on three sides by steeply sloping terrain. An inner keep of three clustered towers stands in an inner bailey whose curtain-wall is protected by a gigantic glacis. An outer ward

the concentric castle

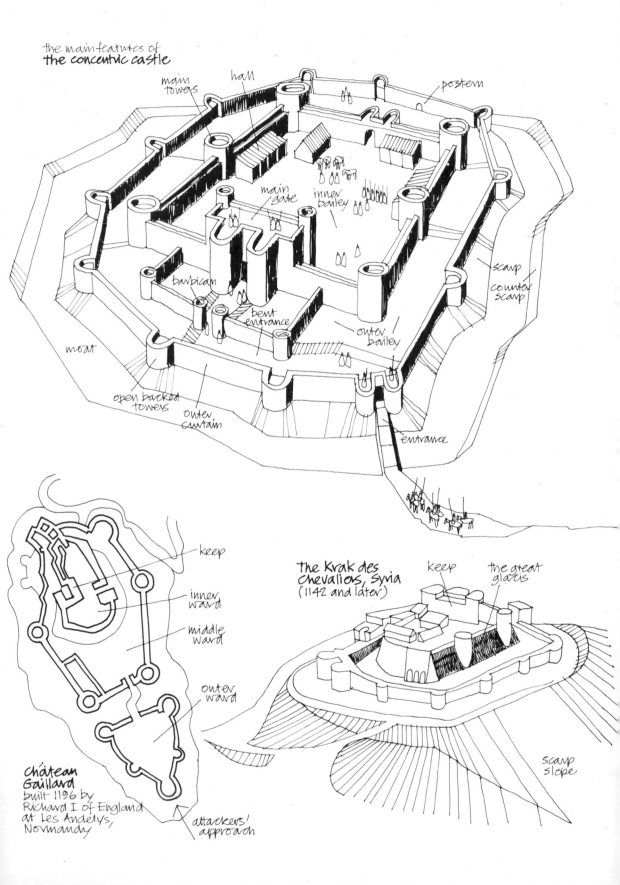

the main features of
the concentric castle

main towers

hall

postern

main gate

inner bailey

scarp

counter scarp

barbican

bent entrance

outer bailey

moat

open backed towers

outer curtain

entrance

keep

inner ward

middle ward

outer ward

The Krak des chevaliers, Syria (1142 and later)

keep

the great glacis

château Gaillard
built 1196 by
Richard I of England
at Les Andelys,
Normandy

attackers' approach

scarp slope

is encircled by a curtain-wall topped with offensive machicolations and punctuated with cylindrical towers. The main gatehouse gives access to a characteristic 'bent entrance', adopted from Moslem town fortifications and consisting of a sloping, twisting and confined route designed to restrict the movements and split up the forces of an attacking enemy. The Krak was attacked or besieged twelve times without success; but on the thirteenth, in 1271, it fell to the Moslems, in whose hands it has remained ever since, the finest monument to both the destructiveness and the creativity of the Crusaders.

the monastic orders

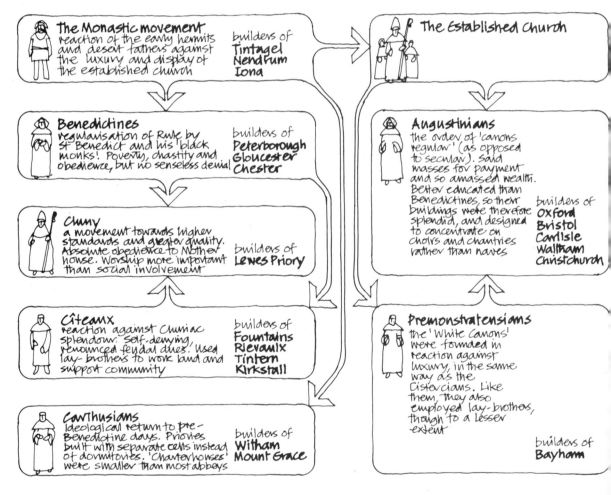

The Monastic movement
reaction of the early hermits and desert fathers against the luxury and display of the established church
builders of **Tintagel Nendrum Iona**

The Established Church

Benedictines
regularisation of Rule by St Benedict and his 'black monks'. Poverty, chastity and obedience, but no senseless denial
builders of **Peterborough Gloucester Chester**

Augustinians
the order of 'canons regular' (as opposed to secular). Said masses for payment and so amassed wealth. Better educated than Benedictines, so their buildings were therefore splendid, and designed to concentrate on choirs and chantries rather than naves
builders of **Oxford Bristol Carlisle Waltham Christchurch**

Cluny
a movement towards higher standards and greater quality. Absolute obedience to Mother house. Worship more important than social involvement
builders of **Lewes Priory**

Cîteaux
reaction against Cluniac splendour. Self-denying, renounced feudal dues. Used lay-brothers to work land and support community
builders of **Fountains Rievaulx Tintern Kirkstall**

Premonstratensians
the 'White Canons' were founded in reaction against luxury, in the same way as the Cistercians. Like them, they also employed lay-brothers, though to a lesser extent
builders of **Bayham**

Carthusians
Ideological return to pre-Benedictine days. Priories built with separate cells instead of dormitories. 'Charterhouses' were smaller than most abbeys
builders of **Witham Mount Grace**

The greatest of centuries

The 13th century

The colonial expansionism of which the Crusaders were part was a symptom of the changing western society. As population grew, the changing economic structure brought to the fore new classes and institutions to challenge the old. The knight and his code of chivalry were being replaced by a class of professional soldiers, to whom fighting was more of a business than a duty. The new monastic orders, the Franciscans and the Dominicans, were primarily intellectual, occupying a less practical and more peripheral place in the church's activities. Increasingly, the church's wealth, investment and building activities lay in the hands of the secular church rather than the monasteries.

Above all, urban growth was gradually eroding the feudal system. In a town, a one-time serf could escape feudal obligations and rise in the social hierarchy. It became increasingly difficult to tie serfs to the land: in 1100, they were still the largest class numerically, but enough were escaping to the towns to create a labour shortage in the country. In feudal Europe the sole source of wealth was the ownership of land, which at that time had no market value and did not, as it does today, form a basis for credit. When the growing merchant class began to demand building-sites, placing for the first time a commercial value on urban land, there was at first no accepted way of transferring ownership from feudal barons or the church. Tensions grew between old and new populations. The greatest resistance to change came from the church, whose long-standing legal authority seemed threatened and for whom many aspects of commerce were morally unacceptable. The new middle classes, seeing the church as a barrier to commercial freedom, broke free by proclaiming communes or negotiating various degrees of self-government, and were joined by many landed aristocrats who welcomed the opportunity for commercial enterprise. The rigid social stratification of feudalism, supported by ethical codes based on Christian virtue and knightly chivalry, began to yield to a world in which commercial success was the sole distinction. The merchants, endeavouring to ensure their own survival, set up local governments, levied taxes – in particular for the upkeep of the city walls on which security depended, enforced the keeping of the peace, controlled entry into the city, and negotiated rights of passage through the countryside to safeguard trade outlets.

Towns began to form trade associations with each other, and the Lombardic League and Hanseatic League came into being. Within each town, craft-guilds were set up to protect trade by controlling the quality of goods and by fixing prices, especially of the food on which survival depended. The artists and craftsmen involved in building, however, developed their guilds rather more slowly than the traders and manufacturers, owing to the dominance between the 12th and 15th centuries of an alternative organisation peculiar to the building industry known as the 'lodge'.

Building before the 12th century had been a feudal enterprise, dominated by the church and the aristocracy. The designers of the great abbeys had often been monks

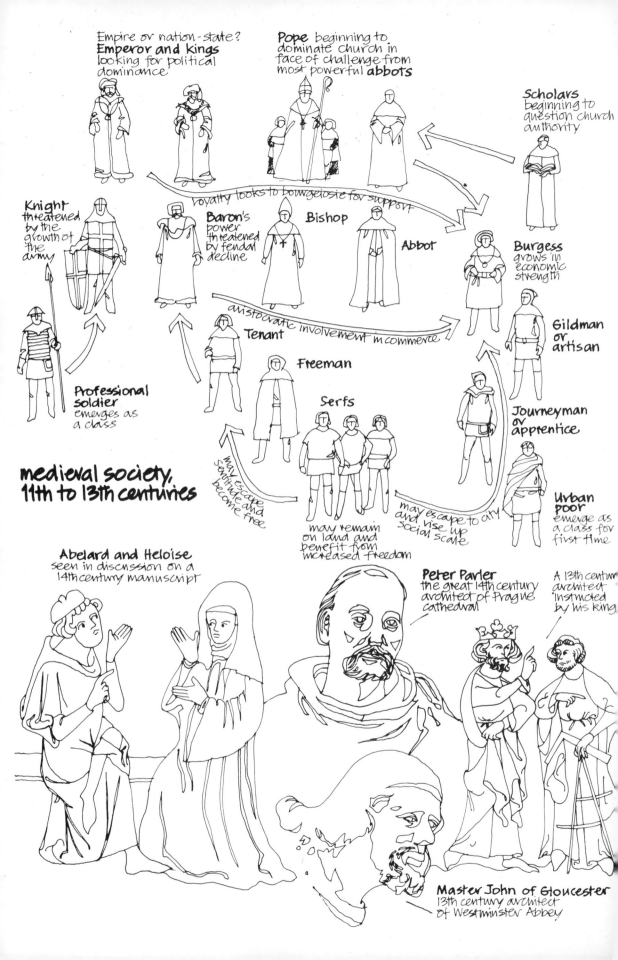

Empire or nation-state? **Emperor and kings** looking for political dominance

Pope beginning to dominate church in face of challenge from most powerful **abbots**

Scholars beginning to question church authority

royalty looks to bourgeoisie for support

Knight threatened by the growth of the army

Baron's power threatened by feudal decline

Bishop

Abbot

Burgess grows in economic strength

Professional soldier emerges as a class

aristocratic involvement in commerce

Tenant

Freeman

Serfs

Gildman or artisan

Journeyman or apprentice

Urban poor emerge as a class for first time

medieval society, 11th to 13th centuries

may escape, seritude and become free

may remain on land and benefit from increased freedom

may escape to city and rise up social scale

Abelard and Heloïse seen in discussion on a 14th century manuscript

Peter Parler the great 14th century architect of Prague cathedral

A 13th century architect instructed by his king

Master John of Gloucester 13th century architect of Westminster Abbey

and the craftsmen who built them had the status of serfs – which allowed for little contact or exchange of ideas with outsiders but a high degree of local involvement and identification with the work.

The coming of the secular, urban society of the 12th century changed this pattern. Free from feudal ties, weavers, dyers, butchers, bakers and chandlers were forming guilds for self-protection, and it was logical that the building industry should do something similar. However, the logistics of a major building project differed from other commercial activities: instead of a number of craftsmen following the same trade it involved a team made up of diverse trades; and so lodges were formed, hierarchical groups of designers, masons, carpenters, carvers, glaziers, painters and their journeymen and apprentices. A lodge was formed for a specific building project; when the work was finished it would break up and re-form elsewhere. By its nature it was marked out as different from the rest of the town: the masons' carefully preserved freedom of movement gave them independence and allowed an unprecedented opportunity for exchanging ideas and techniques, but it also brought the mistrust of the townspeople. As a result, the lodges tended to develop a self-sufficient attitude, building up a protective tradition of hospitalty to new masons against the hostility of the town.

In Britain, 120 new towns were established between the mid-11th and late 13th centuries, including Ludlow, Windsor, Bury St Edmunds, Portsmouth, Liverpool and Harwich. In France 300 were established in the century or so before 1350, and in Germany even more, including Lübeck (1134), Berlin (1230) and Prague (1348). A distinguishing feature of these new towns was their regular layout, often a rectangular grid. Most were fortified with walls and ditches, and the fortifications of the great French *bastides* of Aigues-Mortes, Carcassonne and Avignon still remain today.

Generally, medieval towns were built for people on foot, their narrow streets and small-scale buildings making few concessions to wheeled traffic; individual houses with workshops and small courtyards were more important than any niceties of street layout. Towns depended for their livelihood on craft-work and small-scale industry, and most houses were built for or by the craftsmen themselves, with work-places on the ground floor and living-space and storage above. The Shambles in York and the Fuggerei in Augsburg give a good idea of the small-scale, narrow-fronted medieval building pattern. Many towns functioned as a market for the agricultural produce of the surrounding area: often an old market-place already existed. With the growth of local industry, another market-place, a 'new-market', would be set up as a trading centre for crafted goods. Medieval towns were not large by modern standards; as late as the 14th century a typical big town such as Milan, Venice, Ghent, London or Bruges had 40,000–50,000 inhabitants. Only exceptional towns were larger, such as Avignon which, on becoming a papal seat in 1309, grew to 120,000.

The main building material of medieval towns, especially in the north, was still timber. Simple framed houses of the cruck type remained in general use but were gradually superseded by better forms of construction. By about 1500 the box-frame building had become usual for all except the poorest houses. A plinth of brick or rubble supported a framework of vertical posts or studs on which horizontal beams were placed to carry the walls and roof. Studs set closely together – as they were when oak was plentiful – were infilled with plastered hurdle, giving the external walls the characteristic black-and-white appearance known in England as half-timbering.

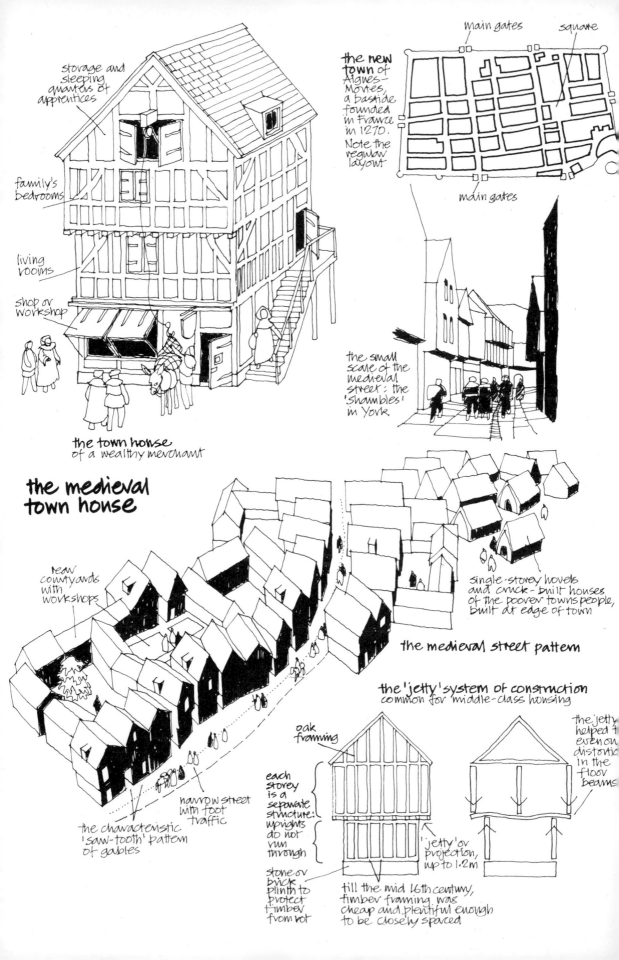

storage and sleeping quarters of apprentices

family's bedrooms

living rooms

shop or workshop

the town house of a wealthy merchant

the medieval town house

the new town of Aigues-Mortes, a bastide founded in France in 1270. Note the regular layout

main gates

square

main gates

the small scale of the medieval street: the 'shambles' in York

rear courtyards with workshops

single-storey hovels and cruck-built houses of the poorer townspeople, built at edge of town

the medieval street pattern

the characteristic 'saw-tooth' pattern of gables

narrow street with foot traffic

the 'jetty' system of construction
common for middle-class housing

oak framing

the jetty helped t even ou distortio in the floor beams

each storey is a separate structure: uprights do not run through

'jetty' or projection, up to 1.2m

stone or brick plinth to protect timber from rot

till the mid 16th century, timber framing was cheap and plentiful enough to be closely spaced

The studs were discontinuous from one storey to another: often the upper floors were projected out over the lower ones in the form of 'jetties'. Roofs were thatched or covered in timber shingles; and windows, at first without glass, were protected by wooden lattices with shutters which could be closed for extra protection.

Gradually jettied construction was overtaken by a simpler kind of box-frame known as the balloon-frame system. Here the studs were continuous from ground floor to roof, avoiding the over-hang of the jetty. Though studding was more widely-spaced as timber became scarcer, the continuity of structure increased the stability of the buildings. Infill panels were still wattle hurdles fixed in place and plastered over: sometimes the whole wall, oak frame and all, would be covered.

Local variations in building style depended on materials. In rocky areas, stone rubble might be used instead of timber-framing. Timber buildings were relatively easy to extend by the addition of another storey, but stone buildings would usually be extended sideways, resulting in the characteristic 'long-house' of the more rugged parts of Europe. In particularly poor areas, the only viable material might be mud. The 'cob' of south-west England consisted of mud, chalk and a binding agent such as reed or straw and was reasonably long-lasting if protected by a good thickness of lime-wash.

The growth of the towns was not the only phenomenon to reduce the power of the barons; a tendency towards strong central government was also hastening the end of feudalism. The powerful and shrewd Frederick Barbarossa (1152–90) challenged the authority of barons and bishops through a central bureaucracy of *ministeriales*, and his 'Magdeburg Law', allowing many northern European towns self-government, encouraged the rise of the bourgeoisie. Similar results came from the rule of Henry II of England (1154–89), who established 'scutage' or money payments as an alternative to feudal services, enriching the central treasury and in the process striking a further blow at feudalism. In France, a bureaucratic system similar to Germany's was set up under the direction of Louis VI (1108–37) and his great minister Suger (1081–1151).

Suger was an ecclesiastic and a politician. In 1140 he rebuilt the choir of the Abbey of St Denis, near Paris, a symbolic enhancement of the royalty through the improvement of its time-honoured burial-place, in which religious and political significance were combined. This building marks the appearance of the gothic style – not because it contained recognisably 'gothic' features (rib-vaults had already appeared at Durham and elsewhere, flying buttresses at Cluny, and pointed arches had many precedents), nor merely because they were for the first time combined into a unified design, though that is striking enough; but rather because their unique combination allowed the opportunity for a subtle change in the approach to the ordering of spaces. Though the romanesque designers divided spaces into ordered compartments, the designers of the 12th century and onwards increasingly blurred spatial divisions; columns became lighter, dividing walls less substantial, roofs freer in shape, allowing space to flow from one area into another.

The development of architecture had reached the point at which great buildings needed a specialist designer; St Denis is not the work of an amateur, in any sense, and Abbot Suger's two 'little books', which describe in glowing terms the improvements to the building without once mentioning the name of an architect, should not be taken as an indication that such a man did not exist. They suggest, instead, a man whose humble status and lay origin made his name not worth mentioning. The building itself indicates a man of intellect and capability, and points to a growing phenomenon of the 12th century: the educated and cultured but secular mind playing an increasingly dominant part in intellectual life. Western philosophy owed a great deal to its contacts with the east. The Second and Third Crusades in 1149 and 1190 ended in failure, but at least continued the traffic in ideas. Under the influence of Arab scholars and those Greek and Latin classics which had been translated from Arabic versions, reason became a major element in philosophy. Doubt and dissent replaced blind faith. The intellectual tension of the day is epitomised by the struggle between the orthodoxy of St Bernard of Clairvaux (1091–1153) and the progressive ideas of Peter Abelard (1079–1142) as expressed in his inquiring treatise *Sic et Non*. We think of 'the Renaissance' as a phenomenon of 15th-century Italy, yet many of its characteristic movements and institutions were already alive in the 12th century, not only in Italy but all over Europe.

Confronted today by the sheer power of gothic architecture, we tend to argue *a posteriori* that it must have been the product of a uniquely religious society. The physical dominance of the buildings themselves leads us further to imagine that only the collective efforts of the whole community could have been capable of such achievements. Yet we misunderstand gothic architecture if we fail to see it, at least in part, as the product of an increasingly secular society, and of a small section of society, at that. A great cathedral was without doubt built to the glory of God by religious men, yet paradoxically its construction depended on the money of the bourgeoisie, a class in moral conflict with the church, on non-Christian mathematical and building knowledge and on the talents of a master-mason whose education and experience now lay outside the confines of the church. An enthusiastic description, written by Abbot Haimon in 1145, of the people of Chartres banding together to rebuild their cathedral, has helped spread the myth that a gothic building was the outpouring of medieval society's collective unconscious, yet the fact is that its design and construction lay in the hands of a highly skilled team of specialist craftsmen who approached their work in a cool and analytical way.

Gothic buildings stand at a crucial transition-point in history, between the church-dominated early Middle Ages and the free, secular world of the Renaissance. It is perhaps this very fact which makes them arguably the finest achievements in the history of western architecture; they are the perfect expression of the dialectical tension between two worlds: between religious faith and analytical reason, between the serene, closed monastic society of the old order and the dynamic expansionism of the new.

An early insight into the mind of a master-mason is given by the monk Gervase, writing in about 1200 of the destruction by fire, twenty-six years earlier, of the choir of Canterbury cathedral. Among the eminent French and English masons called in, offering a babel of contradictory advice, there was

> ... a certain William of Sens, a man active and ready, and ... a workman most skilful in both wood and stone. Him, therefore, they retained, on account of his lively genius and good reputation, and dismissed the others. And to him, and to the providence of God, was the execution of the work committed.

William emerges as both resourceful and inventive, dedicated to his work and independent of spirit. He brings stone over from France by ship, devising ingenious machines for loading and unloading it. He provides his sculptors with templates to

St Denis and Canterbury
The birth of the Gothic style

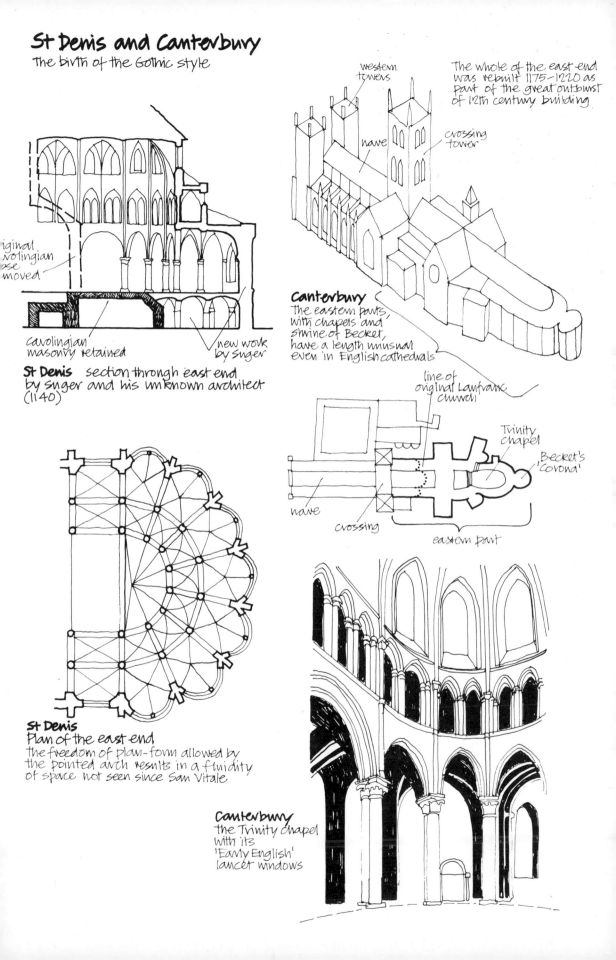

western towers

nave

crossing tower

The whole of the east-end was rebuilt 1175–1220 as part of the great outburst of 12th century building

original Carolingian ose moved

Carolingian masonry retained

new work by Suger

St Denis section through east end by Suger and his unknown architect (1140)

Canterbury
The eastern parts, with chapels and shrine of Becket, have a length unusual even in English cathedrals

line of original Lanfranc church

Trinity chapel

Becket's 'Corona'

nave

crossing

eastern part

St Denis
Plan of the east end
the freedom of plan-form allowed by the pointed arch results in a fluidity of space not seen since San Vitale

Canterbury
the Trinity chapel with its 'Early English' lancet windows

medieval building

An ordinary house..

...could be financed and even built by the owner himself...

..helped perhaps by a local carpenter and roofer using their own simple tools.

A building like a great church was more complex

The church provided the finance..

assisted by the burgesses of the city

The Dean might act as building manager..

..on behalf of the chapter

He would own the machinery and tools, hiring smiths to maintain them..

..and be responsible for quarrying the stone, cutting the timber and getting them to the site

In this he had the help and advice of his most important appointee, the master mason

It was the master's job to draw plans for the work, set out the building and hire masons to build it

the masons were craftsmen, mostly from outside the city

During construction they built a lodge, where they lived and where they laid out a tracing floor on which to draw templates for the work

A building with complex timber work would justify the appointment of a master carpenter to oversee the work of the craftsmen carpenters

Masons worked long hours, usually those of daylight

They therefore earned more in summer than in winter

unskilled labour would be got locally

There were two types of mason

The setters and wallers were skilled in heavy ashlar work..

As outsiders they were suspected by the townspeople

and the freemasons were decorative carvers

they were therefore hospitable to new masons

close-knit and powerful they were capable of taking up tools and leaving the job

features of the gothic style 1

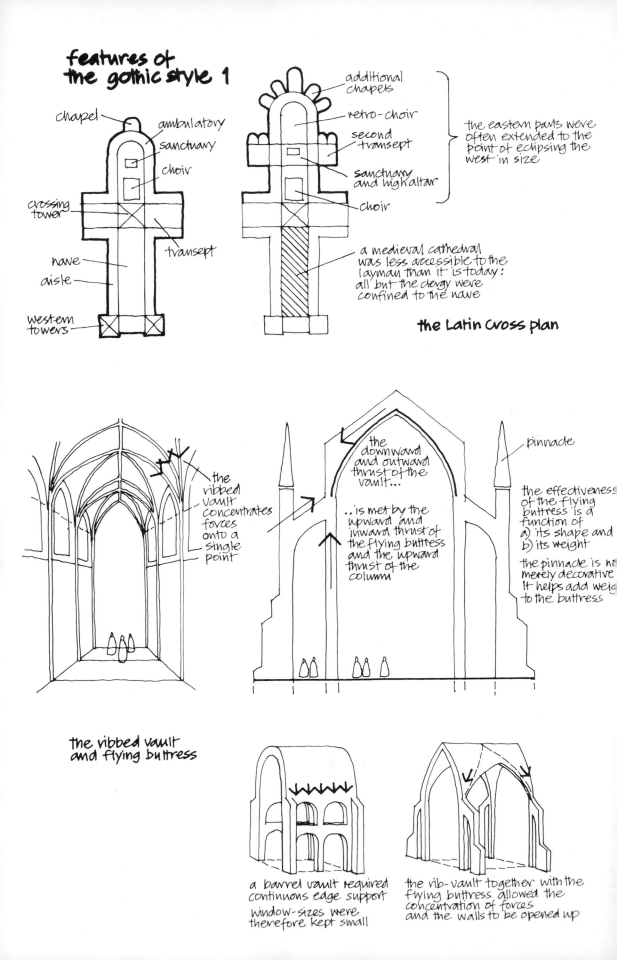

chapel
ambulatory
sanctuary
choir
crossing tower
transept
nave
aisle
western towers

additional chapels
retro-choir
second transept
sanctuary and high altar
choir

the eastern parts were often extended to the point of eclipsing the west in size

a medieval cathedral was less accessible to the layman than it is today: all but the clergy were confined to the nave

the Latin cross plan

the ribbed vault concentrates forces onto a single point

the downward and outward thrust of the vault...

...is met by the upward and inward thrust of the flying buttress and the upward thrust of the column

pinnacle

the effectiveness of the flying buttress is a function of
a) its shape and
b) its weight

the pinnacle is not merely decorative. It helps add weight to the buttress

the ribbed vault and flying buttress

a barrel vault required continuous edge support

window-sizes were therefore kept small

the rib-vault together with the flying buttress allowed the concentration of forces and the walls to be opened up

features of the gothic style 2

the pointed arch

apex of diagonal ribs higher than sides

diagonal ribs same height as sides but structurally unsound

cross-vault with semi-circular arches on sides and diagonals

cross-vault with depressed diagonal ribs

the pointed arch offered the freedom to depart from the square bay

all ribs same height but stilts unsightly

stilt

cross-vault with all arches semi-circular, with side arches stilted

ribbed vault constructed with pointed arches : structurally sound, consonant in height and visually satisfactory

the development of the timber roof

rafters

collars

trusses

purlins

timber roofs were often used above stone vaults to carry the weathering

all simple roof consists entirely of rafters

pairs of rafters linked with collars for extra strength

collared rafters acting as trusses to support rafters on purlins

trussed rafters

tie beam

smaller buildings, trussed roofs were often used for their own decorative effect

an alternative treatment was the cladding of the trusses with a decorative wood ceiling: known as a barrel roof

a collar lowered to eaves-level became a tie-beam, structurally very sound

king post

before the tie-beam roof, the king-post truss obscured the roof-shape

the tie-beam roof, often highly decorated, was appropriate to a low-pitched roof

the arch-braced roof-truss was a step towards the construction of...

...the wide-span hammer-beam roof truss, probably the highest form of medieval roof design

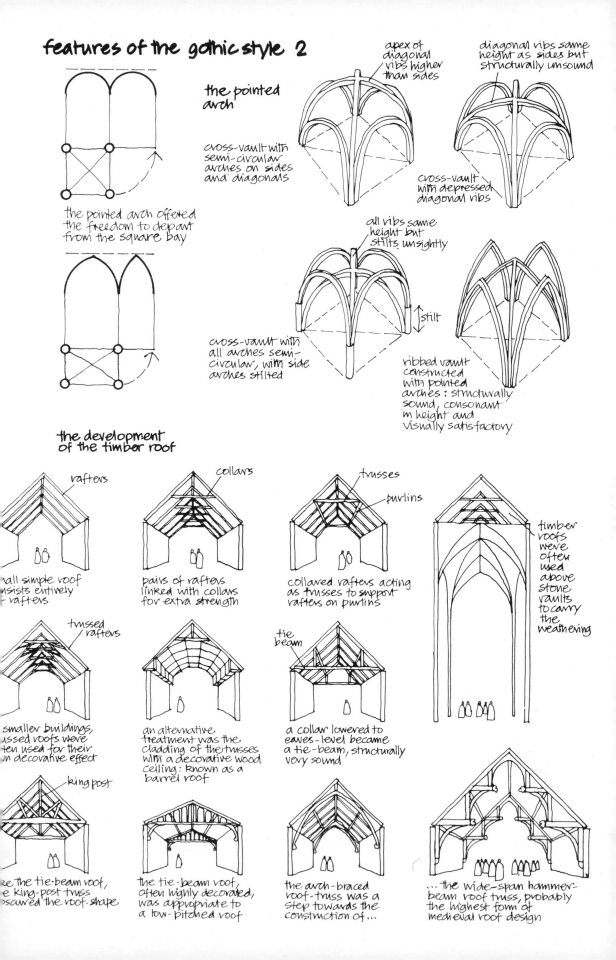

guide their carving, but also directs their work himself. And when after four years, with the work well advanced, he falls from a high scaffold and is badly injured, he continues supervision from a stretcher.

At length, Gervase tells us, 'the master, perceiving that he derived no benefit from the physicians, gave up the work and crossing the sea, returned to his home in France', leaving behind, on the foundations of the ruined Norman choir, an enlarged choir which, with its pointed arches and rib-vaults, was Britain's first gothic building, as significant in its way as St Denis in France.

During the remainder of the 12th century and for most of the 13th, Europe was an open society with few political barriers to travel and trade. The easy passage of master-masons from one place to another encouraged the spread of architectural ideas and expertise, and from its beginnings on the Ile-de-France the gothic style developed rapidly everywhere. A common vocabulary was evolved, of both form and content: a basic pattern which allowed a thousand local variations. Essential to cathedral building was the Latin-cross plan which formed a sequential development of space from the nave at the west, through the crossing, to the choir and sanctuary in the east. The people were confined to the nave only; the eastern parts, ever-increasing in size with the addition of retro-choirs, ambulatories and chapels, almost matching the length of the nave, were for the clergy alone. Also typical of the style were the great stone rib-vaulted roofs, their outward thrust counter-balanced by flying buttresses. Rib-vaults permitted the concentration of forces onto localised points along the wall; so larger and larger openings could be made in the spaces between, and during the 12th century this allowed the phenomenal development of the art of stained glass. Today, we tend to think of medieval churches as essays in grey, functional stonework, but in the Middle Ages their interiors were covered with symbolic wall-paintings and carvings and lit by the glorious colours of windows telling the stories of prophets and martyrs to the illiterate poor. The pointed arch allowed great freedom of plan-form: the semi-circular arch tends to demand a square structural bay, which limited romanesque planning, but since pointed arches of similar height can easily be adjusted to varying spans, gothic planning had much greater freedom. Rectangular structural bays became common, resulting in planning flexibility, structural economy and more subtle spatial effects.

Archetypal among the great French cathedrals, Notre Dame de Paris (1163 and later) is also one of the earliest. The great internal height of its rib-vaulted nave, 32 metres to the top of the arches, is characteristic of many subsequent buildings. So too is the sideways extension of the nave by double aisles, which threaten at ground-level, though not spatially, to submerge the short transepts. The transepts themselves occur about half-way along the building: the eastern parts with their *chevet*-end and numerous chapels are almost as large as the western. The height demands three levels of flying buttresses all round, the lowest contained within the aisle roofs. The west end has twin towers flanking a central entrance with a great wheel window above: equally typical in France, the crossing has no tower but a single tall *flèche*. The interior and exterior are both sober and majestic, enlivened at key points with intricate and humanistic carvings. Notre Dame was followed by Laon (1170), Bourges (1192), Chartres (1195), Reims (1211), Amiens (1220), the Sainte Chapelle in Paris (1243) and Beauvais (1247).

Laon is notable for the magnificent west front, similar in outline to that of Notre Dame but with entrance-porches which emphasise their function by projecting boldly. The twin towers have a new plasticity of form, changing in plan from square at the bottom to octagonal above, and are enriched by fantastic corner-turrets in the form of carved oxen. The plan of Bourges is very similar to that of Notre Dame, but the complete absence of transepts gives both interior and exterior an impressively single-minded uniformity. The west front, too, with its strongly projecting buttresses at every junction, is monumental rather than attractive.

Chartres is perhaps the most appealing of French gothic cathedrals, both in the profusion and richness of its decorative sculpture and in the unsurpassed beauty of its copper-red and cobalt-blue glass. Spires are unusual in France, but Chartres has two, above its two western towers. The southern one is earlier, lower and simpler; the northern, an early 16th-century rebuild, is higher and magnificently decorative. Together they give the building a unique skyline which dominates the town and the countryside around but is nevertheless informal and humane.

The Sainte Chapelle in Paris, though small, is a characteristic gothic structure. Apart from an entrance porch it consists of a single rectangular space with an apsidal east end. External buttresses allow the reduction of supporting wall to a minimum; large areas of coloured glass play a crucial part in the design of the decorative interior, and permit a dramatic effect of insubstantiality.

The cathedral of Reims develops the pattern of Notre Dame. The plan-form is similar, though Reims, the setting for the crowning of several French kings, has widened and deepened transepts to accommodate a coronation theatre. The impressive interior is a move towards greater internal height – 42 metres to the top of the intersecting roof-vault; and the west front, in the basic form of both Notre Dame and Laon, is a mass of finely-sculptured detail which yet does not obscure the harmonious proportions of the whole. Amiens, on the same pattern, is equally decorative both externally and internally, and of similar internal height.

Higher still is Beauvais, an amazing 48 metres to the apex of its roof-vault, the highest cathedral in Europe and the most ambitious of all gothic buildings. What we see today, vast though it is, is no more than the choir and transept of a building never completed. The projected nave was not even begun, and an enormously high crossing-tower, 150 metres to the top, collapsed in the 16th century. What remains is held together by tie-rods and a double row of gigantic flying buttresses. The Middle Ages had no theory of structures: the stability of a building could not be predicted beforehand but only tested in practice, testimony in itself to the daring of the builders. At Beauvais the striving for greater extremes of height obviously overstepped the bounds of medieval technology.

Gothic buildings were built all over Europe – in Italy, Germany, Spain and the Low Countries – but it was primarily in England that this French invention was pursued with greatest vigour. The choir of Canterbury was a distinctly French building, but English Gothic soon began to develop a character of its own. One reason for this was the monastic origin of many English cathedrals. Typically, a French cathedral stands in the middle of a town with the houses clustering around, and an English one, with its attached cloisters and out-buildings, in the seclusion of a monastic close. One result of this difference is the relative importance given in French designs to the western entrances, framed by great porches and opening on to the town square. Like French cathedrals, English ones were paid for by secular wealth, but the designs were more constrained by monastic simplicity: less dramatic, more severe and rectangular. The buildings were often much longer but also lower,

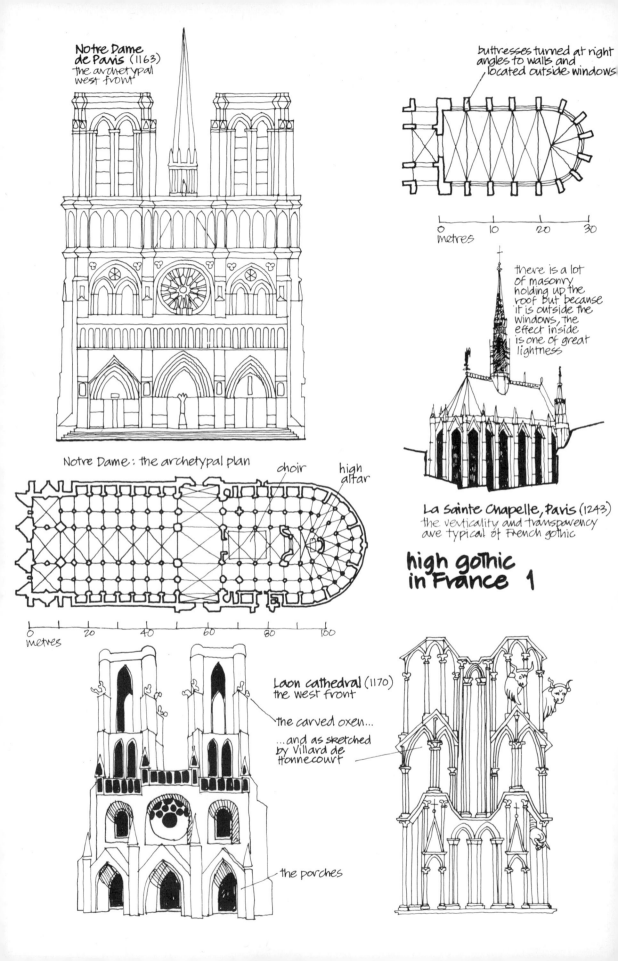

Notre Dame de Paris (1163)
the archetypal west front

buttresses turned at right angles to walls and located outside windows

0 10 20 30
metres

there is a lot of masonry holding up the roof but because it is outside the windows, the effect inside is one of great lightness

Notre Dame: the archetypal plan

choir

high altar

0 20 40 60 80 100
metres

La Sainte Chapelle, Paris (1243)
the verticality and transparency are typical of French gothic

high gothic in France 1

Laon cathedral (1170)
the west front

the carved oxen...

...and as sketched by Villard de Honnecourt

the porches

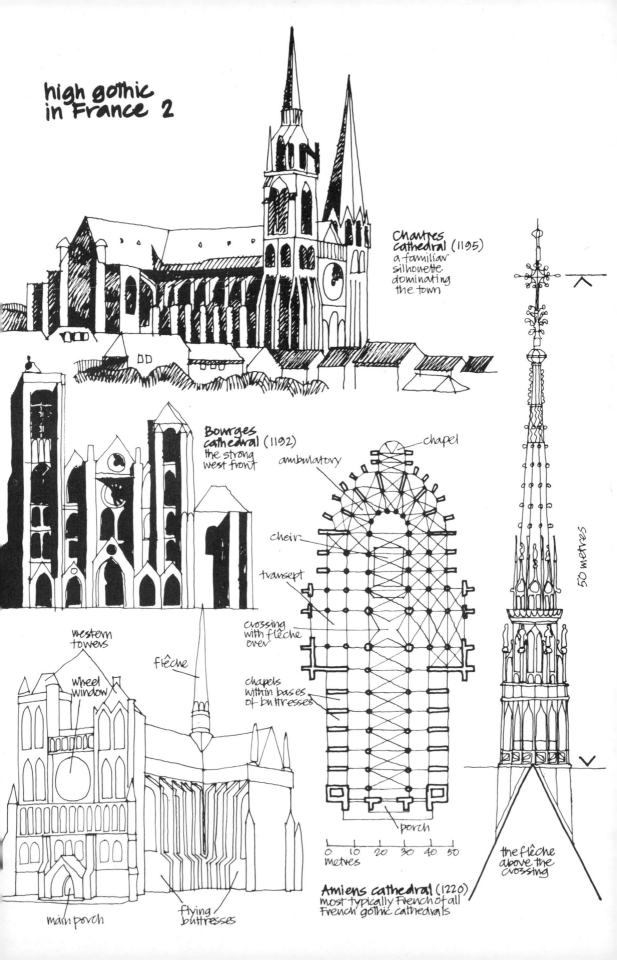

high gothic in France 2

Chartres cathedral (1195)
a familiar silhouette dominating the town

Bourges cathedral (1192)
the strong west front

chapel

ambulatory

choir

transept

crossing with flèche over

chapels within bases of buttresses

porch

```
0  10  20  30  40  50
metres
```

Amiens cathedral (1220)
most typically French of all French gothic cathedrals

western towers

wheel window

flèche

main porch

flying buttresses

50 metres

the flèche above the crossing

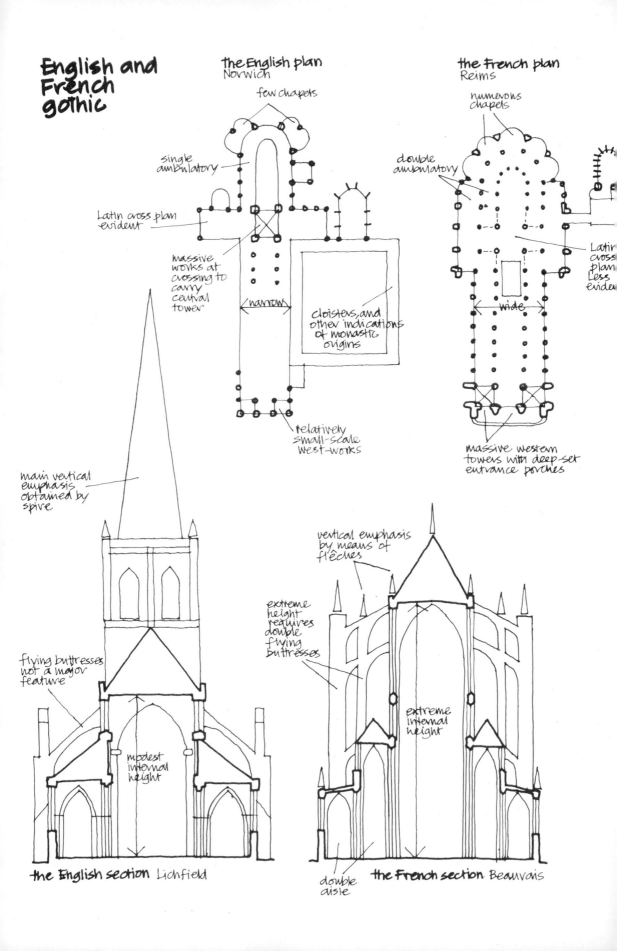

English and French gothic

the English plan Norwich

few chapels

single ambulatory

Latin cross plan evident

massive works at crossing to carry central tower

narrow

cloisters, and other indications of monastic origins

relatively small-scale west-works

the French plan Reims

numerous chapels

double ambulatory

Latin cross plan less evident

wide

massive western towers with deep-set entrance porches

main vertical emphasis obtained by spire

flying buttresses not a major feature

modest internal height

the English section Lichfield

vertical emphasis by means of flèches

extreme height requires double flying buttresses

extreme internal height

double aisle

the French section Beauvais

with less need for dramatic structural devices like flying buttresses, though the lack of height was often offset by the construction of tall towers and spires; two western towers with a crossing-tower was a common pattern. Perhaps, being less pre-occupied than France with dramatic structural feats, England was able to carry its less ambitious structures to a greater degree of perfection; and the development of both stone rib-vaulting and complex timber roofing are among its finest achievements.

The western facades of English cathedrals, though often sculpturally and decora-tively impressive, seldom reached the quality of the best French ones. Too often, as at Lincoln, they are static screens, quite unrelated to the dynamic architecture behind. Among the best is that of Peterborough (1193), whose three gigantic arched recesses reflect to some extent the Norman nave and aisles beyond. The tall, simple outlines of the 'lancet' arches, reminiscent of knife-blades, are typical of this phase of English Gothic, known as 'Early English'.

Salisbury, the most characteristic of Early English cathedrals, begun in 1220 by the master Nicholas of Ely and largely completed by 1258, displays great consistency of style. It has a long but not very high nave, double transepts with a crossing-tower over the larger, and monastic cloisters and chapter-house adjoining the south aisle. The plan-form is simple and rectangular, including the eastern parts which contrast strongly with the fluidity of the typical French equivalent at, say, Amiens.

Similar in character is Lincoln, begun in the late 12th century by the master Alexander. His choir and lesser transept of 1192 are the first Early English work known to us, and the style was continued in the larger transept, the crossing-tower, the entrance-porch and chapter-house of 1209. One of Alexander's successors, Simon of Thirsk, greatly increased the length of the building in 1256 by the addition of a retro-choir at the east end. Length was as English a feature as internal height was French, and is demonstrated best at Winchester, where the completion of a large retro-choir in 1235 gave it a total length of 170 metres, more than any other medieval cathedral in Europe.

One of the finest achievements of Early English Gothic is at Wells, begun in 1180, particularly the west front of 1206–42, a composition similar to Bourges and with the same robustness, but enriched with fine decoration by the architect Thomas Norreys and his sculptor master Simon.

For political as well as architectural reasons, the most important medieval site in England, the centre of English political life for almost 1000 years, is Westminster. Like Charlemagne's Aachen, it combined the seats of both temporal and spiritual power: the secular Palace of Westminster was combined in a single building complex with the great abbey, a symbol of the unity of monarchy and church. Founded in 960 by St Dunstan on the site of a 7th-century church, the abbey was largely rebuilt in 1055 during the reign of Edward the Confessor, and again on a grand scale in the 13th century, from which time most of the present church dates. The eastern part, the single main transept and the eastern bays of the nave were built between 1245 and 1269 in Early English style – also used, in conscious imitation, when the nave was extended westwards in the late 14th century. The choir was pulled westwards into the nave to leave the crossing free, as at Reims, for use as a coronation theatre.

The building retains many original monastic features, including cloisters and outbuildings, but in other ways is untypical of English cathedrals of the time: its great height, its complex of flying buttresses, its twin-towered west front and lack of a

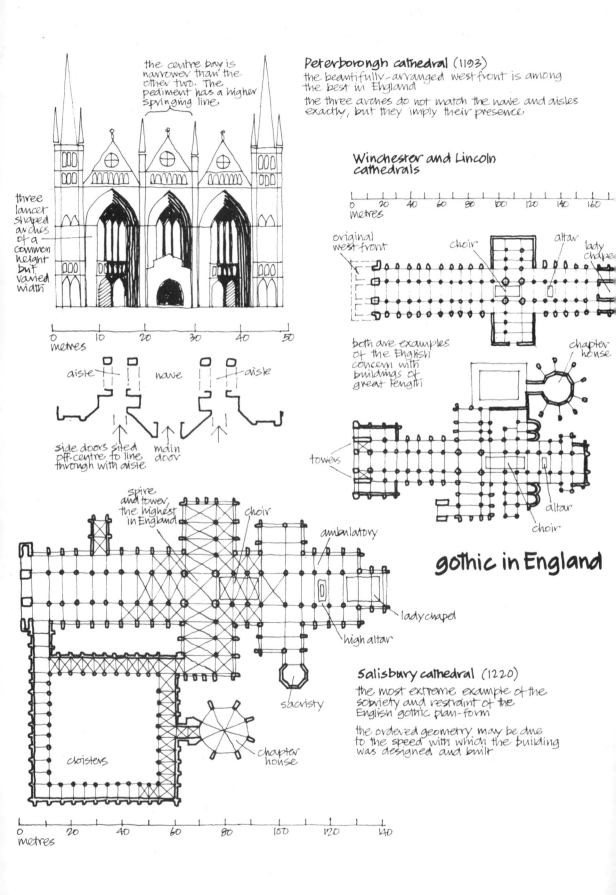

the centre bay is narrower than the other two. The pediment has a higher springing line.

three lancet shaped arches of a common height but varied width

aisle   nave   aisle

side doors sited off-centre to line through with aisle

main door

0 metres 10 20 30 40 50

Peterborough cathedral (1193)

the beautifully-arranged west front is among the best in England

the three arches do not match the nave and aisles exactly, but they imply their presence

Winchester and Lincoln cathedrals

0 metres 20 40 60 80 100 120 140 160

original west-front   choir   altar   lady chapel

both are examples of the English concern with buildings of great length

chapter house

towers   altar   choir

gothic in England

spire and tower, the highest in England

choir

ambulatory

lady chapel

high altar

sacristy

chapter house

cloisters

0 metres 20 40 60 80 100 120 140

Salisbury cathedral (1220)

the most extreme example of the sobriety and restraint of the English gothic plan-form

the ordered geometry may be due to the speed with which the building was designed and built

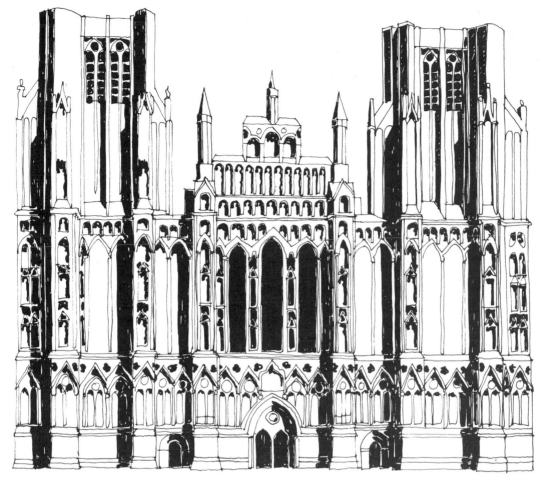

Wells cathedral (1180 and later)

The west front, rich with decoration and sculpture, yet with a strong underlying form, is one of the finest in England

gothic in England 2

Westminster Abbey with its great internal height, prominent flying buttresses and chevet-type plan is one of the most French of English churches

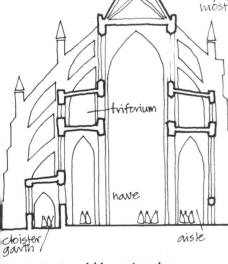

triforium

nave

aisle

cloister garth

Westminster Abbey, London
(largely 13th century)

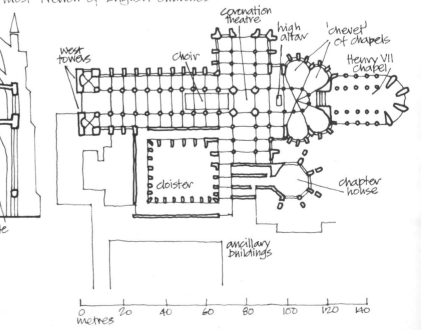

west towers

choir

coronation theatre

high altar

'chevet' of chapels

Henry VII chapel

cloister

chapter house

ancillary buildings

```
0    20    40    60    80    100   120   140
metres
```

crossing-tower, its *chevet*-type east end, the only complete example in England, mark its design as French, paradoxical in a building so wholly identified with English public life. It is a further paradox that the building of this great church, outwardly demonstrating the enduring power of king and archbishop, came at a time when the rise of the middle classes had already begun.

In the early Middle Ages much of northern Europe's culture had come from Scandinavia, but by the 12th century the emphasis had shifted. Constructional knowledge for the more grandiose building projects of Norway, Denmark and Sweden now came from France and, especially, England: the church at Trondheim (1190) was contemporary with, and very similar in design to, Lincoln cathedral; Uppsala cathedral (1273) was begun in an English style and completed in a French one; the nave of Linköping cathedral (1240) was built by a team of English masons. But none of these importations compared in quality with the contemporary 'stave' churches in which the local, old-established timber techniques now reached their highest level. The earliest known example was at Hemse in Gotland, a simple rectangular building with a pitched roof. The walls were of staves, split logs, plain on the inside and rounded on the outside, butted together side by side and driven into the ground. Sancta Maria Minor, Lund (1020), is the earliest surviving example, and the nave of Greensted church in Essex, almost contemporary, obviously derives from the same design source. A structural frame incorporating a ground-beam to carry the staves and prevent their rotting had by now been introduced. The buildings were often intricately decorated; the surface carving in the Celtic tradition at Urnes church, Sogne Fiord, Bergen (1125), is a famous example. Urnes also demonstrated a new two-tier structure in which a high, central space, defined by a timber colonnade, was surrounded by a lower aisle. This reached its culmination at Hoprekstad, at Lom and above all at Borgund (1150). Here the plan was centralised in the Byzantine tradition. Both the main space and the surrounding aisles were multi-tiered: the drama of the exterior and the spatial richness of the interior were comparable in mood with a gothic cathedral.

Through direct French influence, gothic architecture also developed early in Spain: the cathedral of Avila, with its *chevet*-type plan was started in 1160. Arabic influences persisted, and Spanish Gothic is remarkable for its intricate geometric decoration. A particular feature was a pierced screen of decorative stonework, firmly in the Arabic tradition but adapted to Christian uses. It appears in the cathedral of Burgos (1220 and later) in the form of elaborate internal screen-walls at triforium level and externally on the richly decorative crossing-tower and western towers, the latter crowned with delicate open-work stone spires. The French plan-form is discernible, with its *chevet*-type east end, but other more Spanish features were perhaps demanded by a more elaborate liturgy. The profusion and considerable size of the side chapels is remarkable; so too is the location of the choir which, typically in a Spanish cathedral – as at Reims and Westminster – is located in the eastern nave, leaving the crossing free for rituals and reducing the western nave almost to a narthex.

The cathedrals of Barcelona (1298 and later) and Toledo (1227 and later) are also based on French plans, with Spanish adaptations. Barcelona has a fully-developed *chevet* of nine chapels, with several more outside the main aisles, contained between the great buttresses of the main roof. Toledo's plan strongly resembles Paris or Bourges, with double aisles continuing round the apsidal east end. By comparison

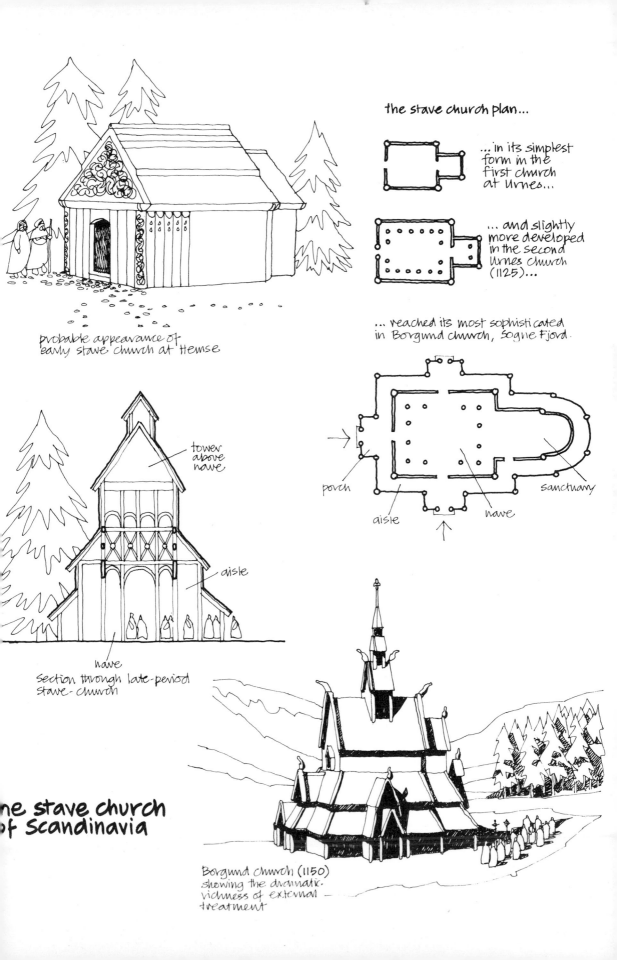

probable appearance of
early stave church at Hemse.

... in its simplest
form in the
first church
at Urnes...

... and slightly
more developed
in the second
Urnes church
(1125)...

... reached its most sophisticated
in Borgund church, Sogne Fjord.

tower
above
nave

aisle

nave

porch

aisle

nave

sanctuary

nave

Section through late-period
stave-church

the stave church
of Scandinavia

Borgund church (1150)
showing the dramatic
richness of external
treatment

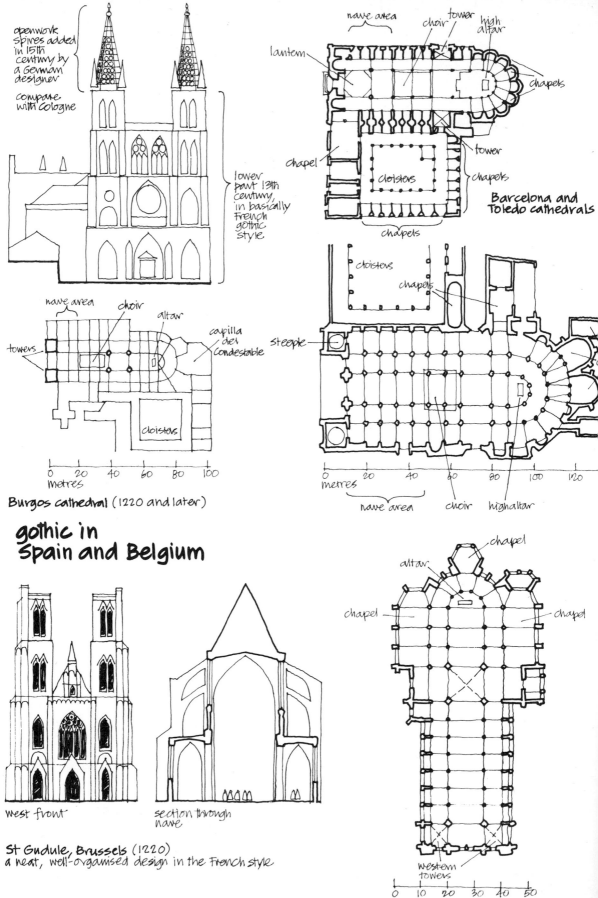

openwork spires added in 15th century by a German designer

compare with Cologne

lower part 13th century, in basically French gothic style

nave area

choir

tower

high altar

lantern

chapels

chapel

tower

cloisters

chapels

chapels

Barcelona and Toledo cathedrals

cloisters

chapels

nave area

choir

altar

capilla del Condestable

towers

cloisters

steeple

0 20 40 60 80 100
metres

Burgos cathedral (1220 and later)

0 20 40 60 80 100 120
metres

nave area

choir

highaltar

gothic in Spain and Belgium

west front

section through nave

chapel

altar

chapel

chapel

western towers

0 10 20 30 40 50
metres

St Gudule, Brussels (1220)
a neat, well-organised design in the French style

with England, cathedrals in France were wide in relation to their length; Toledo, over 60 metres wide, takes this feature to its ultimate: it is a grand and monumental building, enlivened by a richly carved interior and fine stained glass.

In central and northern Europe, with strong Carolingian and romanesque traditions, the gothic style developed slowly and laboriously. The earliest gothic building in the Netherlands was probably the church of St Gudule, Brussels (1220). Romanesque features are still present in the detail design, but the plan-form and twin-towered western façade are in the French Gothic style. The cathedral of Utrecht (1254) is a fully-developed French Gothic building reminiscent of Amiens. Its single great western tower is an important indigenous feature, prototypical of many in Holland and Belgium. In Germany, the Liebfrauenkirche in Trier (1242), with its round and pointed arches, represents a gradual transition from Romanesque to Gothic, as does the church of St Elisabeth, Marburg (1257), which, though it has traditional features such as the markedly apsidal transept and east end, is identifiably a gothic building.

Early Gothic in Germany reached a high development in the cathedral of Cologne (1257 and later) and its derivatives Freiburg (1250) and Regensburg (1275), though none of them realised the full integration of form and content displayed by, say, Reims or Wells. Cologne, largest of all north European cathedrals, is remarkable for its size alone: double aisles give it great internal width, its internal height approaches that of Beauvais, and its most striking features are its massive western towers with spires rising some 150 metres above the flat plain of the Rhine. In the Netherlands, the counterpart of Cologne was perhaps the cathedral of Antwerp (1352 and later), a building of no great height but of great width; the basic plan-form is French – designed by the master Amel of Boulogne – but characteristic Belgian features, including the monumental north-western tower, are recognisable.

By the 13th century, the Hanseatic League dominated the trade of north Europe. Lübeck and Hamburg formed an association in 1241, and other towns soon followed; a single main trade-route was established to Bruges and London in the west and through Danzig and Riga to Novgorod in the east. Cologne, near the geographical centre, profited most, but many other northern towns benefited from the growing trade in wool, metal, timber, furs and manufactured goods of all kinds including cloth. Town halls, guild halls and customs houses were built to cater for the trade. Notable were those of the Netherlands; the great cloth halls at Bruges (1282), with a tower rivalling that of Antwerp cathedral, and at Ypres (1202), a magnificent building of monumental simplicity, were the finest secular buildings of the 13th century, approaching the size and splendour of cathedrals and demonstrating that commerce now rivalled religion as a central fact of life.

This was most true in Italy which, through its links with the east, was able to satisfy the demand all over Europe for imported goods such as silk and spices. Mediterranean trade was increasingly secure, and the co-operation of Pisa, Genoa and Venice with the Crusaders gained trading concessions in the middle east and the establishment of Italian *fondachi* or warehouses in Syria and Egypt.

In northern Europe, the church's onslaught on money-lending and usury successfully hampered commercial development, but in Italy, with its cosmopolitan traditions, church control was weaker: at first Syrians, Byzantines and Jews, but later Christians too, were free to develop their banking techniques. By the end of the 13th century, Siena, Piacenza, Lucca and Florence had become the banking centres of

German and Flemish gothic

0 10 20 30 40
metres

a traditional plan given a gothic form

open work spires

the aisles are raised to give a 'hall-church' section

St Elisabeth, Marburg (1257)

Cologne cathedral (1257)
the monumental west front

the great north-west tower

section

West front

Antwerp cathedral
the tall nave is flanked by triple aisles -
the total width is over 50 metres

0 10 20 30 40 50 60
metres

1282
Cloth Hall, Bruges

The cloth-halls give a cathedral-like dignity to a secular institution

Cloth Hall, Ypres (1202)

Europe, introducing non-negotiable bills of exchange, the offering of credit and a system of double-entry book-keeping.

Two major political events of the 13th century further increased Italian dominance. In the Fourth Crusade of 1204, when the Crusaders were persuaded to turn aside from the Holy Land to sack Constantinople, Venice gained control of the eastern Mediterranean. And the massive expansion of the Mongol empire, which by the 1240s united most of Asia under one rule, gave Italian merchants free access to India and China. Inspired by Marco Polo, they made the most of the opportunity.

The north-European barons generally remained aloof from commerce, continuing to get their income from their rural estates. Their Italian counterparts, with a stronger tradition of city dwelling, were the first of the European aristocracy to become active in urban commercial life. Primitive capitalism was competitive and brutal, and its architecture had to be both defensive and aggressive. A rich man's house in a congested, high-density Italian town was obviously a very different building from a feudal castle or manor-house, but it shared with them two important design features: the defence of the owner's property from robbers and rivals, and an aggressive expression of wealth and power. The Torre Asinelli (1109), the Torre Garisenda (1100), both in Bologna, and the thirteen towers which still remain of the reputed seventy-two built in San Gimignano between the 10th and 14th centuries, are good examples. The strongholds of feuding families, their grim and featureless elevations were obviously built for defence, but their height, 70 metres and more in some cases, can only partly have been for functional reasons such as the congested nature of the sites or the need for high look-out positions; it must also have been an attempt to express the family's importance in the town. So it may well have been for political reasons as well as for safety that the municipalities gradually introduced height limits.

The urban *palazzo* of the 12th and 13th centuries was a solid block-like building of five or so storeys in heavily rusticated stone. For protection, the windows on the lower floors were much smaller than those above, and battlements, machicolations and watch-towers, at least partly functional, made up a characteristic skyline. Some, like the fine Palazzo Vecchio, Florence (1298), were family strongholds. Others, like the Torre del Comune, Verona (1172) and the Palazzo Pubblico, Siena (1289), were municipal buildings which could serve as places of public refuge in time of trouble.

Of all the medieval *palazzi*, that of the Doge in Venice (1309–1424) is the most splendid. Its architectural relationship with the cathedral of San Marco, like the juxtaposition of Palace and Abbey at Westminster, publicly brought together the secular and spiritual powers. The Doge was the chief examining magistrate of the Venetian republic and symbol of that rule of law on which the city's commerce was inevitably based. By contrast with the forbidding Palazzo Vecchio, the design of his palace implies public accessibility. Instead of external grimness there is richness of colour and texture. The lower storeys present to the passer-by a double-storey open colonnade of gothic arches and plate tracery, and the offensive roof-top crenellations of the fortress-house are transmuted into a crest of delicate stone lace-work of Arabic character. The architects, Giovanni and Bartolomeo Buon, also designed the Ca d'Oro in Venice (1424) which in a smaller-scale, more informal way displays many of the same characteristics, including the arcaded ground floor, the gothic plate tracery, the Arabic skyline and the same lightness of texture and coloration.

The buildings of Venice imply a closer relationship between municipality and

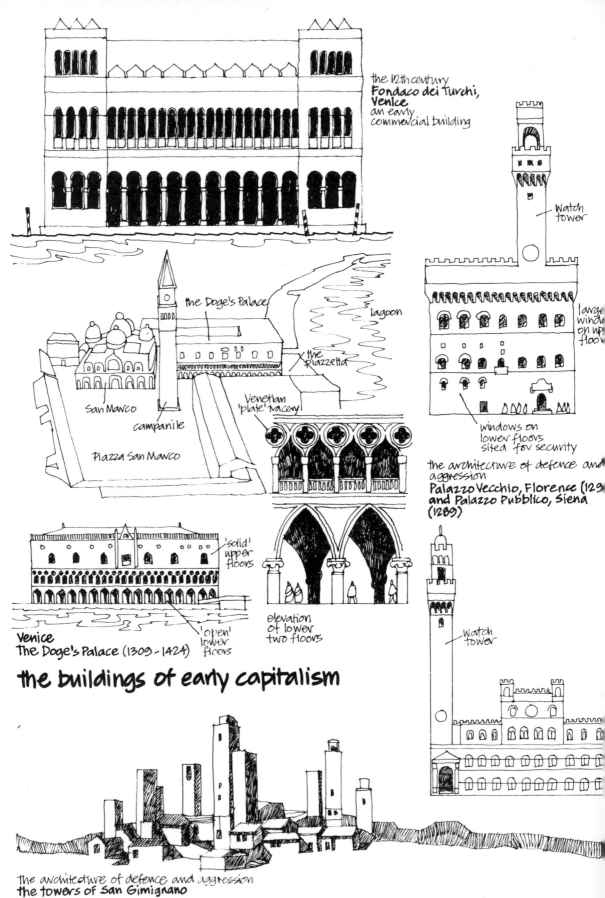

the 12th century
Fondaco dei Turchi, Venice
an early commercial building

the Doge's Palace

lagoon

the Piazzetta

San Marco

campanile

Piazza San Marco

Venetian 'plate' tracery

Watch tower

large windows on upper floors

windows on lower floors sited for security

the architecture of defence and aggression
**Palazzo Vecchio, Florence (129...
and Palazzo Pubblico, Siena (1289)**

'solid' upper floors

'open' lower floors

elevation of lower two floors

**Venice
The Doge's Palace (1309 - 1424)**

the buildings of early capitalism

Watch tower

the architecture of defence and aggression
the towers of San Gimignano

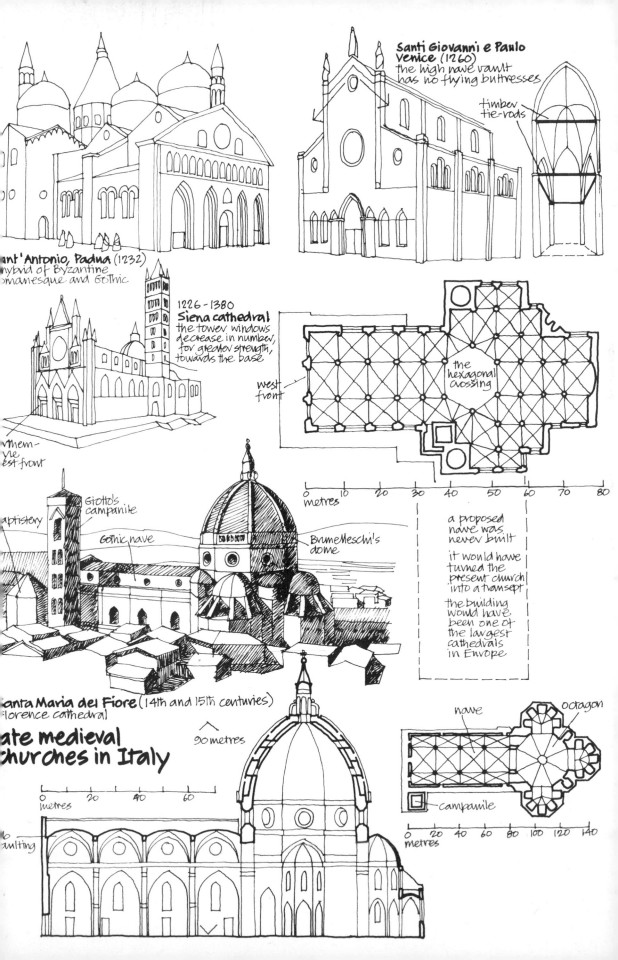

Santi Giovanni e Paulo
Venice (1260)
the high nave vault
has no flying buttresses

timber
tie-rods

Sant'Antonio, Padua (1232)
hybrid of Byzantine
Romanesque and Gothic

1226 - 1380
Siena cathedral
the tower windows
decrease in number,
for greater strength,
towards the base

west
front

the
hexagonal
crossing

0 10 20 30 40 50 60 70 80
metres

them-
vle
est front

Baptistery

Giotto's
campanile

Gothic nave

Brunelleschi's
dome

a proposed
nave was
never built

it would have
turned the
present church
into a transept

the building
would have
been one of
the largest
cathedrals
in Europe

Santa Maria del Fiore (14th and 15th centuries)
Florence cathedral

ate medieval
churches in Italy

90 metres

nave

octagon

0 20 40 60
metres

campanile

0 20 40 60 80 100 120 140
metres

vaulting

church than actually existed: both authorities were inevitably suspicious of each other but generally did what they could to enlist each other's support. The municipality of Florence, with sound commercial instinct, came to terms with the papacy by becoming the official collector of papal taxes, to the financial benefit of both parties. A town council could obtain church support by financing religious buildings, and the construction of many magnificent Italian churches from the 12th century onwards owes more to this than to any popular upsurge of religious feeling.

The Romano-Byzantine tradition persisted in Italian church architecture, though geographical location often encouraged other influences. In the south, Islamic influences were stronger; the cathedral of Palermo (1170) has a basilican plan with decidedly Moorish elevations. In the north, Venetian influences were strong. The pilgrimage church of Sant' Antonio, Padua (1232), though equipped with a *chevet* of chapels in the contemporary French manner, is roofed with seven domes similar in arrangement to San Marco.

In general, though some north-European features appeared in Italy during the 12th, 13th and 14th centuries, there were few wholly gothic buildings: the continuity of Mediterranean traditions was too strong for that. Though the plan-forms of the Venetian churches of Santi Giovanni e Paulo (1260) and Santa Maria Gloriosa (1250) are of a northern, Latin-cross type with transeptal chapels and apsidal east ends, the square vaulting-bays and the use of tie-beams in the nave instead of flying buttresses place the buildings firmly in the Roman tradition. In the great pilgrimage church of San Francesco, Assisi (1228), pointed rib-vaults and tentative flying buttresses are used, but the building as a whole, part of a vast monastic complex on a hill-top site, has a romanesque simplicity and grandeur.

One of the most ambitious projects of the 13th century was the building of Siena cathedral (1226–1380), a grand essay in civic pride. Its ornate west front is north European Gothic but is literally a façade, bearing little relationship to the magnificent and original building behind, a rich composition of semi-circular and pointed vaulting centred on a hexagonal crossing carrying a dome and lantern.

Florence too was investing hugely in building, not only in the churches of Santa Maria Novella (1278) and Santa Croce (1294), though these were fine enough, but particularly in the great complex of buildings forming the cathedral of Santa Maria del Fiore. As at Siena, the cathedral was paid for by the city council in an outpouring of civic ambition, and its construction occupied a succession of Florentine designers over a period of 200 years. Under the circumstances, the design is remarkably unified and the building itself very simple. Arnolfo di Cambio began the construction in 1296. The main design element is the east end, in the form of a Greek cross, centred on an octagonal crossing 43 metres wide. Three of the arms, forming sanctuary and transepts, are short apses ringed with chapels, but the fourth is a long rectangular nave of four square vaulted bays lined with aisles. A few gothic elements were used, but the structural system is less adventurous than Chartres or Reims, with none of their dynamic spatial effects internally, and no flying buttresses or pinnacles to disturb the tranquil outline. An important external feature is the simple rectangular campanile, 84 metres high, designed by Giotto and begun in 1334. But the major element both internally and externally, the centre of the whole design, is the octagonal crossing-dome built nearly a hundred years later by Brunelleschi – a conscious rejection of structural expression in favour of surface symmetry that was to become a significant contribution to the architectural philosophy of Europe.

The growth of capitalism
The 14th and 15th centuries

During the 14th century the national monarchs of Europe, recognising the growing influence of the urban middle class, formed alliances with them and began to dominate Europe politically and economically, at the expense of the church and the aristocracy. Between them, kings and bourgeoisie were now responsible for most of the investment in building. One of the most dramatic examples of this is Edward I's castle-building programme – the largest ever undertaken – during his pacification of Wales in the late 13th century. The death of the Welsh prince Llywelyn the Last in 1282 was Edward's opportunity to create a strong military presence in Wales and, more important, to re-mould its economy. Not only were the great castles built, but many of them were supported by new towns which encouraged the replacement of the Welsh pastoral way of life by an urban one. These Edwardian *bastides* included Flint, Conwy, Caernarvon, Beaumaris, Ludlow and Chepstow, whose regularity of layout resembled that of purpose-built new towns everywhere.

Edward's great castles were the final development of the Crusader castle in western Europe. The concentric curtain walls of the Krak des Chevaliers or the Château Gaillard were a major feature of Edwardian design, but the keep was no longer placed inside. Instead, the outer wall became the strongest line of defence and the keep (the living quarters) was replaced by an enormously strong gatehouse, located aggressively at the front. The outer wall was invariably defended by escarpments or ditches and often by a low concentric spur wall which kept attackers at a distance from its base. Numerous round towers, to provide flanking fire, punctuated its length and served to divide the upper rampart into sections so that any section to which an enemy gained access could be isolated. Conwy and Caernarvon (both begun in 1283) are the largest, strongest and grandest; Harlech and Beaumaris (also 1283) and Caerphilly (1267) the most systematic, ordered and symmetrical. During the 14th century, the advent of gunpowder strengthened the position of kings and towns, the only two institutions rich and organised enough to manufacture explosives and weapons on a large scale. By the end of the 14th century, warfare had changed in character and Welsh castles, no longer impregnable, had already had their day. In the Wars of the Roses and the Civil War they were held by small garrisons against difficult odds before being breached and overthrown, but they fulfilled only for a short time their original role as unassailable defences against medieval hand-weapons and siege machines. A change of role was inevitable, and several medieval castles, such as Kenilworth – originally built by the Normans – and Raglan (1430) were adapted for living in. Apartment blocks were added and windows enlarged, reducing their strength but increasing their comfort.

The same is true of other European castles of the period. The Château de Pierrefonds (1390), though well-fortified by its cliff-like walls and eight circular towers on a rocky outcrop, was a luxurious dwelling for its day. The Dauphin's two châteaux at Loches and Chinon each had an outer *enceinte* enclosing a large complex of buildings, including both a fortified area and more gracious living quarters.

85

Conwy (1283)

barbican

outer ward

inner ward

great hall

barbican

inner bailey

the short distance between inner & outer curtains allowed defenders to fire simultaneously

inner bailey

outer bailey

barbican

gatehouse (residence)

Harlech (1283)

main gatehouse

inner curtain

barbican

outer curtain

the castle in the 13th and 14th centuries

Pierrefonds (1390)

main wall

towers

Palace of the Popes, Avignon (1316)

By the beginning of the 14th century the 500-year struggle between empire and papacy was almost over: the Emperor's power was broken and his claims over Europe and the Pope ended. The papacy was in no position to assume political power, however: a succession of weak or corrupt popes and a church confused by the increasing worldliness of society contrasted sharply with the growing ambitions of the nation-states and their kings. In 1309, Philip IV of France secured the appointment of a French pope, setting him up in a palace in Avignon where for seventy years the papacy underwent a 'Babylonian captivity', subservient to France, worldly, corrupt and powerless. The great papal palace, towering above the city on its cliff-like podium with arched buttresses, looked like a veritable fortress but to its incumbent must also have seemed a prison.

In 1378 two rival popes were elected, one in Avignon and the other in Rome, resulting in the 'Great Schism' which brought papal authority to its lowest point and sorely divided the church. Revolutionaries within the church, such as John Wycliffe, challenged its right to own secular possessions and condemned many of its dogmas; Johann Huss tried to promote a return to the Bible as the basis of Christian life; other Christians, following Meister Eckhardt, turned to mysticism in an effort to purify the faith. Paradoxically, amid all this turmoil, the 14th century saw some of the church's greatest architectural achievements. Royal or bourgeois patronage was playing an increasingly important part in church building. Relatively few new cathedrals were built, but everywhere existing ones were being enhanced and in almost every town and village parish churches were re-modelled or new ones were built. Germany and Italy were politically unstable; so it was in France, the Netherlands and England, where monarchy and national government were making most headway, that kingly architecture flourished.

Philip IV of France (1285–1314), recognising the power of wealth, increased taxes, confiscated the property of Jews, befriended the rich bourgeoisie and, in a bitter war, annexed the property of the Knights Templar, who after the fall of the Holy Land had settled in France. One of his main building projects was the enhancement of Reims cathedral, the place of royal coronations. A symbolic sculptured group of the coronation of the Virgin (1290) above the main west door gave implicit assent to the divine right of kings, and the fine west towers (started 1305) added grandeur to the composition. The richly decorative style of late French Gothic, with its curving, flame-like lines, is known as 'flamboyant'. It is seen inside the otherwise stern and fortress-like Albi cathedral (1282 and later), on the fine south transept front of Beauvais cathedral, in the church of La Trinité, Vendôme and the magnificently decorative church of St Ouen at Rouen (1318 and later).

However, growing royal controls in France, backed by a strong bureaucracy, had begun to anger not only the feudal lords but also the townspeople. When in 1337 Philip VI tried to annex Aquitaine at the beginning of a protracted struggle for land with the kings of England, he found himself without popular support. The first phase of the Hundred Years' War brought England victory at Crécy in 1346 and Poitiers in 1356. The credibility of the French monarchy was left in ruins, and royal patronage of building works suffered a setback. In the early 13th century France had led the world in architectural invention, but the last part of the 13th and the first half of the 14th were dominated by England.

The turn of the century saw the beginning of a new and more confident phase in English Gothic. At first geometrically regular, it gradually developed sinuous curves and rich decoration. Between 1261 and 1324 the nave and chapter-house and the richly decorative west front of York Minster were built, and during the 14th century its fine stained glass was installed. In 1307 the square crossing-tower was added to Lincoln cathedral, at 82 metres the highest in England, and in 1325 a great circular window with flowing tracery. In 1321 a similar central tower was built at Wells. The added stress placed by the tower on the structure below was taken up by four huge extra arches inserted between the main piers of the crossing; they are unique in medieval architecture and illustrate the artistic imagination of their builders in coping with what they assumed – for they had no means of knowing for certain – to be structural necessity.

Typical of the new splendour of English architecture was Ely cathedral, in particular its Lady Chapel (1321) and the rebuilt nave crossing (1323). The Lady Chapel is about 30×14 metres, its rectangular plan the only simple feature. Its walls are formed by arcades of serpentine or 'ogee' arches rising like tree-trunks to branch out into a ceiling of decorative rib-vaulting, and the whole is covered in carved foliage of great luxuriance. The nave-crossing is an undeniable achievement of 14th-century architecture. Built by the master mason John Attegrene to replace a collapsed tower, it stylishly departs from the simple rectangularity of the rest of the building and forms a high octagonal space. A vast octagonal lantern by the king's carpenter William Hurley, set at an angle to the angles of the stone octagon below, further increases the richness of the spatial effect.

The finest example of a complete building in 14th-century 'decorated' style is Exeter cathedral. Each of the decorative piers has an engaged pilaster running vertically up past the triforium to branch into a multiplicity of roof-ribs spreading inwards like palm-fronds to meet the ridge, in a composition of great consistency and imagination. It was a short step from this 'palm' vaulting to the decorative vaulting of Gloucester cathedral, where each group of ribs was designed to the same length, so defining an arc around each support and describing the fan-shape which gives this system its name. Fan-vaulting was not a new structural departure, but mainly a decorative feature; it was adopted by the king's mason Henry Yevele in rebuilding the nave of Canterbury cathedral in 1379, and was to reach its peak of development in the royal chapels of the 15th century.

Possibly the best example of royal patronage and the finest single creation of any medieval craftsman was Westminster Hall, built in 1397 for Richard II (1377–99), an energetic promoter of the arts. For him the Wilton Diptych was painted, and Chaucer is thought to have entertained his court with 'The Canterbury Tales'; and for him Hugh Herland the master carpenter rebuilt the roof of the great hall at the Palace of Westminster. Like the best of gothic building, the great oak roof, covering an area of over 70×20 metres, is a perfect synthesis of structural and artistic expression, deriving its aesthetic directly from the way in which the mechanical problems were solved. In order to reduce the great span down to a manageable size, horizontal hammer-beams, supported by curved struts from below, were canti-levered from the walls and their ends became the springing points of the arched roof trusses which seem to hang daringly in space. The decorative treatment followed the function of each element: the big curved arches, springing across the central space, are sinewy with carved fluting and the heavy hammer-beams static with rich decoration.

In the 200 years since the 12th century, the master-craftsman had become a

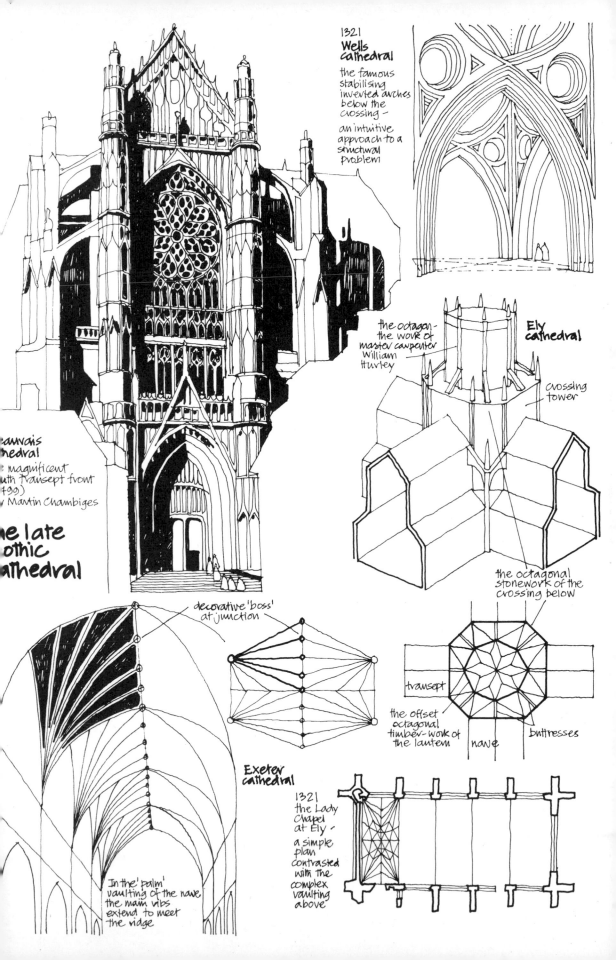

1321
Wells cathedral

the famous stabilising inverted arches below the crossing —

an intuitive approach to a structural problem

the octagon-the work of master carpenter William Hurley

Ely cathedral

crossing tower

the octagonal stonework of the crossing below

...auvais
...hedral

...magnificent
...th transept front
...799)
...Martin Chambiges

**he late
othic
athedral**

decorative 'boss' at junction

the offset octagonal timber-work of the lantern

transept

nave

buttresses

In the 'palm' vaulting of the nave, the main ribs extend to meet the ridge

Exeter cathedral

1321
the Lady Chapel at Ely — a simple plan contrasted with the complex vaulting above

different man. William of Sens and the unknown master of St Denis, though respected for their ability, had occupied a lowly place in society, but the 14th-century craftsman's increasing economic power gave him a high status. He or his sons might now be educated at a university or marry into the nobility. For a long time the activity of building had been remote, through its technical sophistication, from the everyday life of the common man: now it was becoming socially removed as well.

Gothic architecture in 14th-century Europe did not generally reach the standard set by England. In Germany, the 13th-century pattern continued: the Frauenkirche in Nuremburg (1354), with one large roof covering nave and aisles, was a hall-church in the local tradition, and the cathedral of Ulm (1377 and later) an intricate but uninspired building with one high western spire similar to Freiburg. Among the best buildings was the cathedral of Prague (1344), designed by the French master Mathieu of Arras. Its plan-form with a *chevet* east end and its flying buttresses are typically French and its detail design, taken over in 1353 by Peter Parler, another master with French connections, was continued in the same style with its own enrichments. The gothic architect's knowledge of structural theory was still very limited, and even achievements like Beauvais or Westminster Hall owed more to experience and guesswork than to any precise analysis of the loads and forces involved. Gothic roof-trusses often contained superfluous members of no structural significance. In late Gothic architecture, such elements were used more and more, becoming a kind of mannerism. Buttresses at Prague were decorated with 'blind' window tracery; roof-vaults had free-flying ribs added, through which the true ribs could be seen; pendent vaults were built, hanging like stalactites, with no real purpose other than that of surprise and ambiguity.

In the early 14th century, old and new institutions co-existed in a peculiar kind of transitional society. Italy, often with church connivance at a process which was actually eroding the old medieval Christian ethic, was pioneering modern commerce, while northern Europe was manufacturing goods from the raw materials which Italy did not have. The high level of co-operation between the towns of the Hanseatic League contrasted strongly with the cut-throat competition between Italian cities. In England, wool production flourished; though manufactured goods were inferior to those of Flanders, the trade itself was more vigorously pursued and its success was one of the economic prodigies of the 14th and 15th centuries. As production increased, the advantages of a captive labour-force became apparent, and the gradual liberalisation of feudalism was suddenly arrested. Payment for labour ceased as feudal landlords, in both town and country, tried to hold onto their labour-force. As the peasants' condition and status declined, the gap between rich and poor grew wider.

Then in the mid-14th century a cataclysmic event left its mark on almost every aspect of society. An outbreak of bubonic plague, the 'Black Death', spread along the caravan routes from the far east in 1346, through the Crimea into southern Europe in 1348 and to the north in 1350. Between a quarter and a third of the people died in affected areas, with devastating results for Europe: harvests went ungathered and trading ceased. But the longer-term effects were catalytic, even positive. The previous trend towards humanism in the arts, exemplified by the painting of Giotto (1276–1337) and the poetry of Dante (1265–1321), was intensified: in some, a feeling of pessimism and despair produced a pre-occupation with death; to others came an attitude of defiance towards accepted religious tenets. Whether stimulated by the

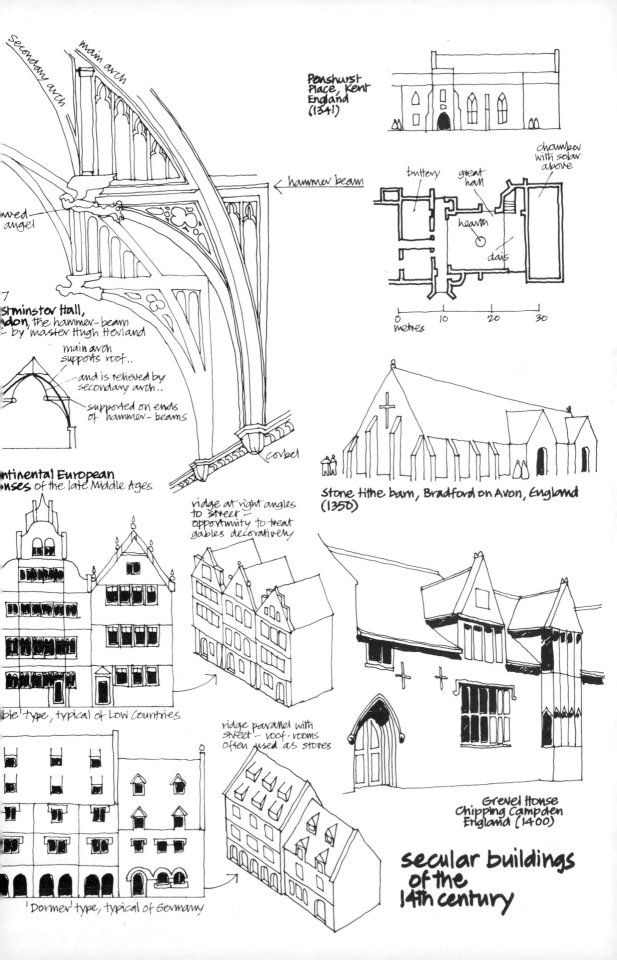

secondary arch

main arch

hammer beam

...wed
angel

Penshurst
Place, Kent
England
(1341)

buttery   great
hall

chamber
with solar
above

hearth

dais

0   10   20   30
metres

7
...stminster Hall,
...don, the hammer-beam
... by 'master Hugh Herland'

main arch
supports roof...

...and is relieved by
secondary arch...

...supported on ends
of hammer-beams

corbel

...ntinental European
...uses of the late Middle Ages

Stone tithe barn, Bradford on Avon, England
(1350)

ridge at right angles
to street =
opportunity to treat
gables decoratively

...ble' type, typical of Low Countries

ridge parallel with
street - roof rooms
often used as stores

Grevel House
Chipping Campden
England (1400)

'Dormer' type, typical of Germany

**secular buildings
of the
14th century**

plague or not, philosophical, artistic and architectural achievements in the ensuing century were of a high calibre.

The Black Death also intensified the economic contradictions in society since, with the labour-force decimated, land-owners tried to place even stricter controls on those that remained. The workers, seeing their labour at a premium, increased their demands for better conditions, and the inherent tensions present in both city and countryside came to the surface. The Hundred Years' War dragged on, and the growing discontent of the ordinary people gave rise to the rebellions of the *Jacqueries* in France in 1358 and the English peasants' revolts of the 1380s. In London, city workers and peasants, led by Wat Tyler and John Ball and inspired by the idealism of Wycliffe and his 'Lollard' followers, opposed the primitive capitalism of the property-owners with their own primitive communism.

Their efforts, however, were premature; crushed by the forces of the crown the peasants fell back, left behind by the developments of the 14th century. Certainly they had evidence enough that others than they were prospering: Henry Despenser, the avenging bishop of Norwich, for example, to whose fine manor house at South Elmham the first of the Lollard martyrs, William Sawtry, was brought for torture in 1399; or Sir John de Poulteney, the rich London merchant who built Penshurst Place in Kent (1341). By 14th-century standards, Penshurst was a luxurious place to live. Based on the design of the Norman manor house and built in stone, with decorated tracery in the windows, it had a great hall with kitchen and buttery on one side and a withdrawing-chamber on the other, with solar above: a stark contrast with the hovels of the countryside around. Another type of building that presented a perpetual reminder of servility was the tithe-barn. The church's preoccupation with tithes – taxes in the form of goods – was quite marked by the 14th century, and the tithe-barn, often located near the church, was a dominant feature of the landscape.

Cities, too, presented a contrast, between the well-built town-houses of the merchants and the huts and shelters of the poor. Typical of the more substantial English houses was the Grevel House, Chipping Campden (late 14th-century), a translation into stone of forms already familiar in timber, with main ground storey, steeply-pitched roof storey and prominent gabled dormers. Medieval house frontages generally varied between 4.5 and 6 metres, with the ridges of the pitched roofs running at right angles to the streets. The richest merchants could combine two or more plots, forming a wide-fronted property with the ridge parallel to the street. Large houses of this kind were built in Germany. Some, in Braunschweig, Nuremburg and elsewhere, had three or more roof storeys, each lit with a line of dormers. Narrow-fronted houses in which the front gable was made a decorative feature were also built in Germany but were more common in Holland and Belgium. Old houses at Ghent, Liège, Middelburg, Utrecht and Malines still survive.

With the growth of capitalism, the Middle Ages in Europe came to an end: the inherent tensions that accompanied the new system – between nation-states and between the classes within them – are features of the modern world. One casualty was the medieval system of scholastic philosophy, that long search begun in Charlemagne's Palace Schools to reconcile reason with religious faith. In its place, many thinkers outside both church and university, and untramelled by their traditions, were developing a new humanistic attitude. In literature, the works of Boccaccio, Petrarch, Froissart, Chaucer, Langland and Villon were dealing with people and their lives rather than with weighty abstractions, and the paintings of Fra Angelico,

Milan cathedral
(1385)

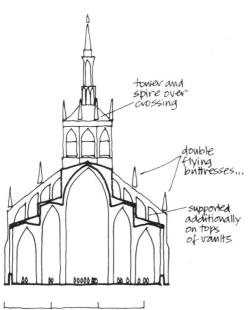

tower and spire over crossing

double flying buttresses...

supported additionally on tops of vaults

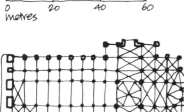

Milan —
the richly ornate
window in the eastern apse

Seville cathedral
(begun 1402)

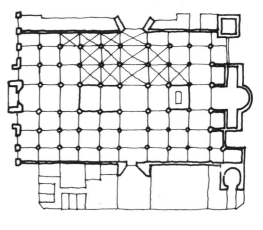

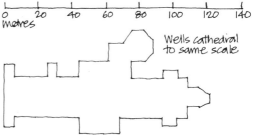

Wells cathedral to same scale

late gothic in Italy and Spain

Salamanca cathedral
(1512)

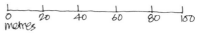

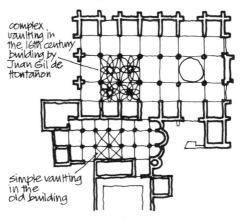

complex vaulting in the 16th century building by Juan Gil de Hontañon

simple vaulting in the old building

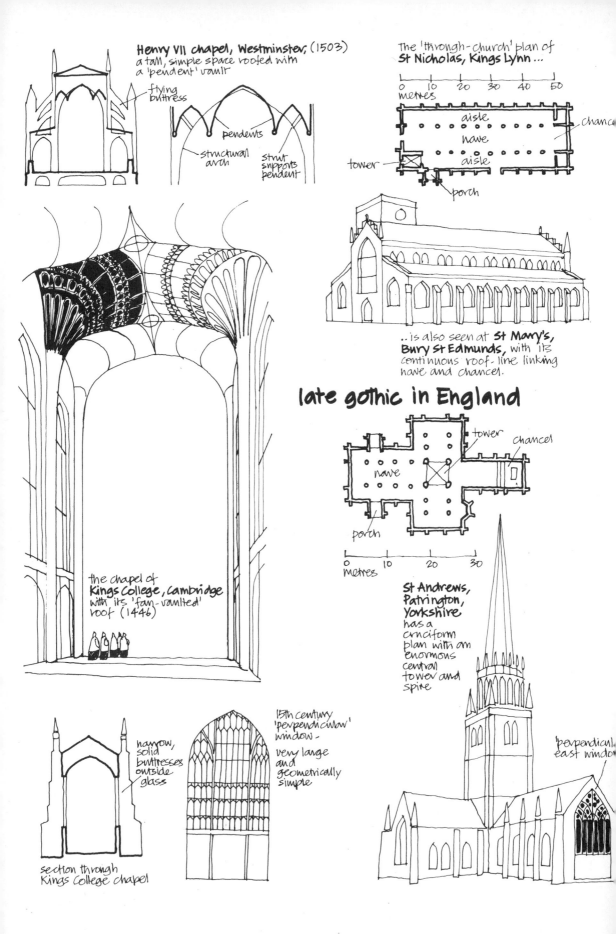

Henry VII chapel, Westminster, (1503)
a tall, simple space roofed with a 'pendent' vault

flying buttress

pendents

structural arch

strut supports pendent

The 'through-church' plan of **St Nicholas, Kings Lynn** ...

0   10   20   30   40   50
metres

aisle
nave
aisle
chancel

tower

porch

.. is also seen at **St Mary's, Bury St Edmunds,** with its continuous roof-line linking nave and chancel.

the chapel of **Kings College, Cambridge** with its 'fan-vaulted' roof (1446)

late gothic in England

tower

chancel

nave

porch

0   10   20   30
metres

St Andrews, Patrington, Yorkshire has a cruciform plan with an enormous central tower and spire

narrow, solid buttresses outside glass

15th century 'perpendicular' window - very large and geometrically simple

section through Kings College chapel

'perpendicular' east window

Masaccio, Fra Lippo Lippi, della Robbia and Van Eyck were setting aside medieval symbolism in favour of characterisation. Inevitably, a comparable attitude developed in architectural design.

In most of Europe it took the form of a late flowering of gothic architecture, craftsmanship and sculpture. A spectacular example is Milan cathedral, begun in 1385 and developed during the 15th century into one of the largest and most decorative cathedrals in the world. Its size and richness reflected the wealth of its sponsor, Visconti, Duke of Milan; its design came from the experience of fifty or more designers from north of the Alps and the result was a combination of Italian, French, and German influences. The nave, with French double aisles, terminates in an apsidal east end, not in the *chevet* form but surrounded instead by a polygonal German aisle. The great height of the main side-aisles effectively reduced the opportunity for a clerestory: the internal effect is dark and solemn like a German hall church, contrasting with the bright, Italian marble exterior, a mass of lacy buttresses, pinnacles and statuary. Finest of all are the three main windows of the apse, with their asymmetrical flowing tracery.

Similar in concept though very different in execution is the cathedral of Seville, the largest of all medieval churches. Begun in 1402, it was not completed till 1520. Its great size and unusually rectangular plan came from the re-use of the foundations of a former mosque, parts of which, notably the elegant minaret, were incorporated into the final design. The nave, with double aisles and side chapels of great width, is roofed with massive yet intricate rib-vaulting. The exterior, with triple flying buttresses, is gothic in general character and outline but Moorish in detail.

More consistent in style than Milan or Seville, 15th-century English churches were among the finest achievements of late gothic design. Many large projects, some begun centuries earlier, were reaching completion: the magnificent west front of Beverley Minster was built c. 1400, and about the same time a spire was added to Norwich cathedral. Fine crossing-towers were added to Durham (1465) and Canterbury (1490). In addition, several important royal chapels were built, among them Henry VI's chapels at Eton College (1440) and at King's College, Cambridge (1446), the chapel of St George at Windsor Castle begun by Henry VII in 1481, and the Henry VII chapel at Westminster Abbey, built in 1503 by his son Henry VIII. The architectural style of these amazing buildings, known as 'perpendicular', has no parallel outside England. The name derives from the simple regularity of the window-tracery, in contrast to the richness of English decorated and French flamboyant. This feature has led to theories about a dearth of adequate craftsmen in the years following the Black Death; in fact 15th-century buildings in general, and perpendicular in particular, demonstrate medieval craftsmanship at its most technically accomplished.

If King's College chapel lacks anything, it is the ambiguous spatial variety of early Gothic, which so added to the mystery and excitement, and which has no place in this rational, almost materialistic, building. A simple box, 88 metres long, 12 metres wide and 24 high, its only internal division is a timber choir-screen. The brilliance of the effect comes from the enormous, repetitive windows with their simple tracery, alternating with tall piers whose vertical flutings emphasise their height and continue up to branch into master John Wastell's richest and most intricate fan-vaulting. The vaulting ribs were no longer lines of structural stress, but had become decorative features carved onto the surface of the stone shell built up from a mosaic of panels. This retreat from structural 'expression' culminated in the Vertue brothers' fantastic stone roof of Henry VII's chapel at Westminster, where the real structural arches are almost submerged in an effusion of intricate stone pendent vaults.

Royal sponsorship of church building had its parallel in villages and towns throughout Britain, where the local bourgeoisie, many of them enriched by the sudden growth of the wool industry, were following suit. Some churches retained traditional or local forms, but generally the perpendicular style was used, in light, airy churches of great size.

Strong definition between nave and chancel was rejected in favour of 'through churches', with a high, continuous roof linking nave and chancel into one main space separated only by a decorative rood-screen; St Mary's, Bury St Edmunds, is a good example. Many great churches were newly-built in the perpendicular style; others had new features added, such as the big east window at Patrington, Yorkshire, or the enormous tower of Boston in Lincolnshire. Finest of all were the timber roofs: the depressed tie-beam type, as at St Cuthbert's, Wells, was used on low-pitched lead roofs, and on steeper pitches a variety of types including the magnificent double hammer-beam, as at March in Cambridgeshire.

The rich and fanciful church designs of England had their counterparts all over Europe, in a last outburst of gothic imagination, from the Church of the Jerónimos at Belém, Portugal (1500), the cathedrals of Salamanca (1512) and Segovia (1522), to the west front at Rouen (1509) and the church of St James at Brno (1495). Though clearly gothic in spirit, all these designs were strikingly individual. The growing identity of national culture and the increasing autonomy of the individual designer had taken architecture a long way since the days, three centuries before, when European Gothic had recognisably been that of the Ile de France. A common European tradition based on skills and experience handed down through practice rather than theory had yet allowed local styles to emerge and individual talent to flourish; and by the end of the 16th century, though local methods of construction would persist in humble buildings, this tradition was a thing of the past. The lodge system had broken down in favour of the guild system: big buildings were built less by integrated multi-skill teams than by collections of craftsmen of different trades. A designer was often a man of considerable status, separated by education and class from the craftsmen on the site, whose skill was more intellectual than practical; he became increasingly remote from the building process itself while seeking to control it more and more. The autonomy of the individual craftsman diminished as he was allowed to make fewer and fewer design decisions of his own.

Three developments gave these trends further impetus. The first was the invention by Johann Gutenberg (1400–68) of the moveable-type printing-press, which revolutionised written communication and enabled a rapid increase in the transmission of ideas in written form: the medieval tradition of communicating building knowledge by practical example was superseded by the spread of theoretical ideas.

The second was the gradual discovery by the Italians of their imperial Roman history. Encouraged by growing secularism, interest in classical pagan authors led to a revived interest in the buildings of ancient Rome. Medieval Italy had remained strangely unaware of its legacy of ancient buildings, except as symbols of a barbaric past and quarries for building materials. The 5th-century baptistery at Florence, converted in the 11th century, was vaguely thought to be a Roman building; elsewhere genuine Roman buildings lay half-ruined or, like the Colosseum, provided living-space for squatters. Gothic architecture had never taken hold in Italy to the extent that it had in the north, and the 15th century saw an unequivocal return to the architectural forms of ancient Rome. Inspiration came not only from the ruins themselves but also from the writings of Vitruvius, a 1st-century Roman architect, whose somewhat suspect and pedantic theories were given the reverence due to a sole authority.

The biggest impetus for the movement usually described as 'the Renaissance' came from the existence in Italy of a unique new class, a merchant aristocracy of unprecedented wealth and power which had drawn into its ranks many of the old feudal nobility and had assumed their education and refinement of life-style. These new merchant princes, in the fragmented society of 15th-century Italy, were able to command positions of absolute power, unchallenged by the petits-bourgeois and artisans whose status was gradually degenerating into wage-slavery. The changes took place more quickly in Italy than anywhere else. Northern merchants were slower to usurp the power of the hereditary aristocracy, and the strength of the northern guilds protected the status of the lower middle classes and artisans, but in Italy the merchant-princes and their families ruled supreme. Despite the Black Death, trade and production were growing and capital formation increased rapidly. No merchant specialised; his activities were spread over banking, money-lending, mining and manufacturing, importing and exporting, building, real-estate and art-dealing. To replace the medieval institutions and now outmoded republicanism of Venice and Genoa came the oligarchic city-states of Milan under the Visconti and the Sforza and Florence under the Medici; through skilful diplomacy and the exercise of great wealth, they each attained the power and influence of much larger states. Painting and sculpture flourished as a result of the patronage offered by these great families to artists like Ghiberti, Donatello, Botticelli and Leonardo, and investment in building dramatically increased.

The medieval architect, invariably a stone-mason or carpenter and consequently a serf, might be prized by the ruling classes for his abilities but despised as a manual labourer. Even in 15th-century Florence architecture was still not a profession in its own right. The usual approach to it was through one of the associated crafts – jewellery or silver-smithing, painting or sculpture, masonry or carpentry – all of which still carried the social stigma of manual labour. But with feudalism at an end, status was no longer automatically inherited; it had to be attained. Some artists and architects went to great lengths in fighting for recognition of their special status. Some refrained from manual work: purely intellectual pursuits like philosophy and natural science were socially more acceptable. Others achieved high positions in society through wealth or by marrying into noble families, becoming, in the words of William Morris, 'the great architect, carefully kept for the purpose and guarded from the common troubles of common man'.

High status gave the artist or architect greater freedom to develop his modes of expression. At the same time, something was lost, for greater independence gradually increased alienation. The static nature of feudal society, for all its limitations on personal development, had at least ensured that a building was the product of a well-defined and close relationship between designer and user. As capitalism developed, society became more fluid and relationships not only more complex and less easily defined but also less close. In 15th-century Florence, however, with capitalism in its infancy, this alienation was not yet far advanced. Moreover, the

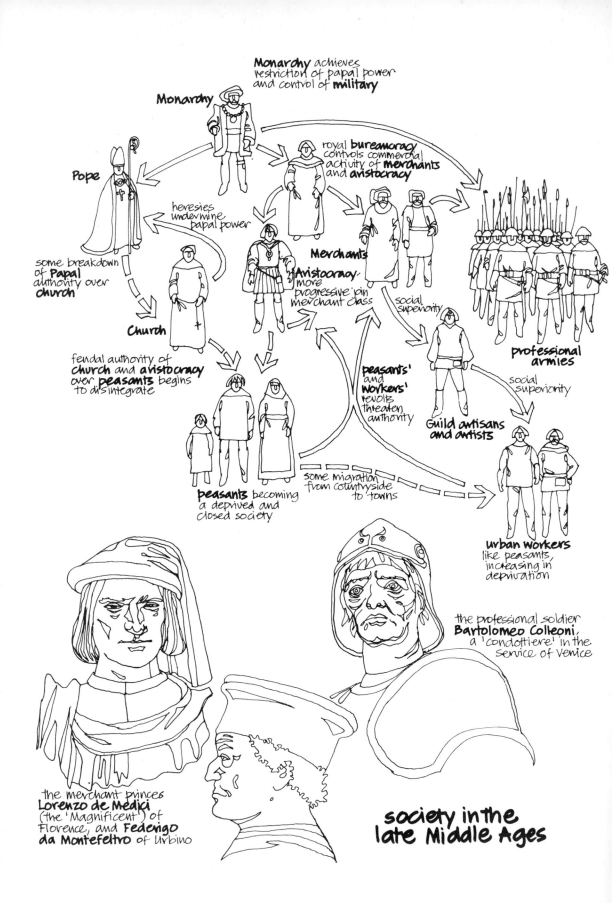

Monarchy achieves restriction of papal power and control of **military**

Monarchy

royal **bureaucracy** controls commercial activity of **merchants** and **aristocracy**

Pope

heresies undermine papal power

some breakdown of **Papal** authority over **church**

Merchants

Aristocracy more progressive join merchant class

social superiority

Church

feudal authority of **church** and **aristocracy** over **peasants** begins to disintegrate

peasants' and **workers'** revolts threaten authority

professional armies

social superiority

Guild artisans and artists

some migration from countryside to towns

peasants becoming a deprived and closed society

urban workers like peasants, increasing in deprivation

the merchant princes **Lorenzo de Medici** (the 'Magnificent') of Florence, and **Federigo da Montefeltro** of Urbino

the professional soldier **Bartolomeo Colleoni,** a 'condottiere' in the service of Venice

society in the late Middle Ages

social milieu within which the architect worked was extremely stimulating: the new bourgeoisie was still an active and revolutionary force with generous and expansive ideas. At this stage, the architect's new-found independence, stimulated by the merchant-prince's wealth and dynamism, ensured a great outburst of architectural achievement.

Among the foremost Florentine achievements were those of Filippo Brunelleschi (1377–1446). Starting as a goldsmith and sculptor, he demonstrated his great skill as early as 1401 in a competition entry for the bronze doors of the Baptistery. Gradually he became interested in architecture and by 1410 had already designed a few buildings and visited Rome, where he had measured and drawn the monuments. In 1418 he won a competition for the completion of the cathedral of Santa Maria del Fiore, Florence's most important building. His aim was to construct a dome over the crossing, according to Arnolfo's original intention but without using formwork; to prove his ability to a sceptical Board of Works, he tried out his method on a smaller dome at the church of San Jacopo Oltrarno. The great dome itself was begun in 1420 and substantially complete by 1436. The ingenuity of its box-rib structure, covered with inner and outer skins, together with the incomparable serenity of its outline, won universal admiration. 'Who could be so harsh or envious', asked Alberti, 'as not to praise our architect Pippo who has built so great a structure high into the sky, so huge as to overshadow all the people of Tuscany?'

During the building of the Florence dome Brunelleschi was able to devote himself to several other major buildings, an indication in itself of the way the architect's role had changed. In 1421 he was directing the building of a loggia at the Ospedale degl'Innocenti, a simple arcaded cloister carrying an enclosed upper storey and standing on a stepped podium. Much of the detail, including the round columns with their composite capitals and the simple groined vaulting, were Roman in origin, and the elegance of the detail has much in common with the romanesque of San Miniato. However, the whole concept was so clear and unified that it went well beyond its Roman and romanesque antecedents. The intellectual life of renaissance Italy was the product of the most progressive minds of the day, engaged in a search for an underlying order in a tumultuous world. Just as the painter was beginning to investigate the geometry of perspective and the sculptor was discovering the structure of human anatomy, the architect was becoming interested in the harmony imparted to a building by the choice of mathematically related dimensions. One of the best examples of this is the church of San Lorenzo (1421), a basilican building with a high nave and groin-vaulted aisles, with the sanctuary flanked by two sacristies. The Sacristia Vecchia (1428) on the north side is one of the masterpieces of Italian architecture. Brunelleschi designed this small room as a cube, over which he placed a hemispherical dome. To one side, for the altar, is a small *absidiola*, a double cube with its own small dome. All the wall and ceiling surfaces are white plaster, on which the dark grey of pilasters, arches and applied medallions stand out, emphasising the geometry of the room with great clarity. The effect of liveliness is nevertheless firmly controlled, though in a creative rather than a pedantic way.

The chapel Brunelleschi built for Andrea Pazzi at the church of Santa Croce in 1430 is a development of his work at San Lorenzo. A small building, with a ribbed dome over a rectangular space, it displays the same interest in the use of simple geometric shapes, again expressed in terms of grey stone ribs against a white background. A particular achievement is the beautifully organised front elevation

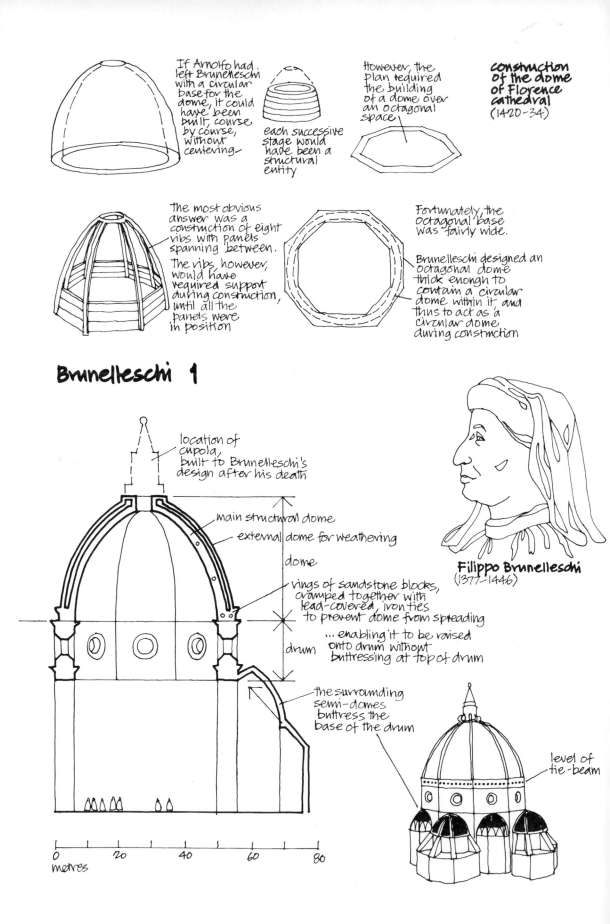

If Arnolfo had left Brunelleschi with a circular base for the dome, it could have been built, course by course, without centering.

each successive stage would have been a structural entity

However, the plan required the building of a dome over an octagonal space

construction of the dome of Florence cathedral (1420-34)

The most obvious answer was a construction of eight ribs with panels spanning between.

The ribs, however, would have required support during construction, until all the panels were in position

Fortunately, the octagonal base was fairly wide.

Brunelleschi designed an octagonal dome thick enough to contain a circular dome within it and thus to act as a circular dome during construction

Brunelleschi 1

location of cupola, built to Brunelleschi's design after his death

main structural dome

external dome for weathering

dome

rings of sandstone blocks, cramped together with lead-covered, iron ties to prevent dome from spreading

...enabling it to be raised onto drum without buttressing at top of drum

drum

the surrounding semi-domes buttress the base of the drum

Filippo Brunelleschi (1377-1446)

0   20   40   60   80
metres

level of tie-beam

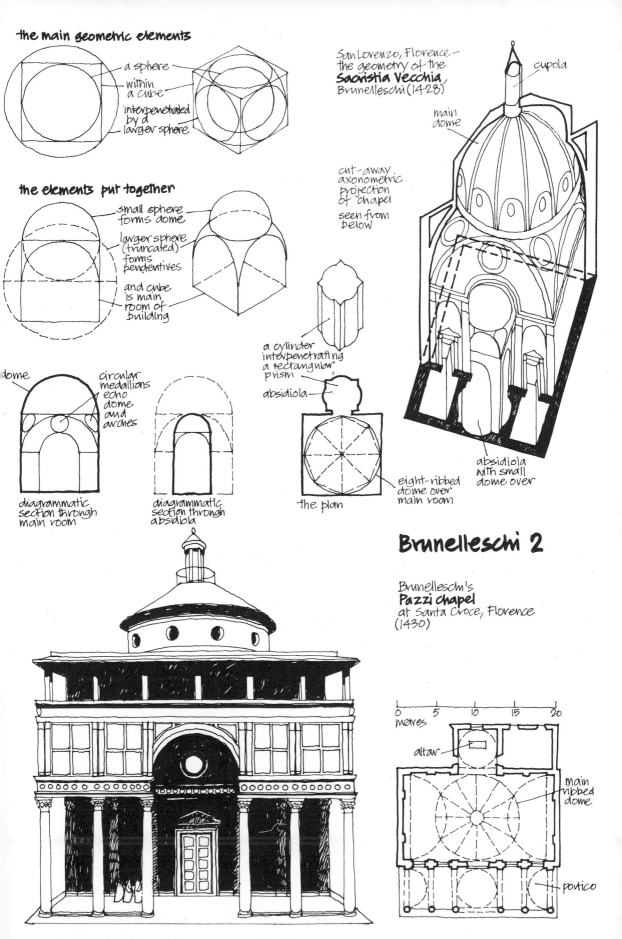

the main geometric elements

a sphere

within a cube

interpenetrated by a larger sphere

the elements put together

small sphere forms dome

larger sphere (truncated) forms pendentives

and cube is main room of building

dome

circular medallions echo dome and arches

diagrammatic section through main room

diagrammatic section through absidiola

a cylinder interpenetrating a rectangular prism

absidiola

the plan

eight-ribbed dome over main room

San Lorenzo, Florence.— the geometry of the **Sacristia Vecchia,** Brunelleschi (1428)

cupola

main dome

cut-away axonometric projection of chapel seen from below

absidiola with small dome over

Brunelleschi 2

Brunelleschi's **Pazzi chapel** at Santa Croce, Florence (1430)

0   5   10   15   20
metres

altar

main ribbed dome

portico

with its projecting portico, the architrave broken by a semi-circular arch echoing the shape of the dome above.

Brunelleschi is sometimes credited with having been the first to analyse the laws of perspective, which allowed painters accurately to represent three dimensions on a flat canvas, and architects to investigate spatial effects before they were built. At their best, Brunelleschi's buildings certainly bear this out: his most mature works display a richness of spatial effect which could only have come from meticulous pre-planning. In 1436 he designed the church of Santo Spirito, a large Latin-cross building which went beyond the simplicity of the basilican San Lorenzo. Tall, arched colonnades separate nave and aisles and are seen against further colonnades formed by the engaged columns which divide the side chapels.

Brunelleschi was an eclectic, deriving his architectural vocabulary from classical, romanesque and even gothic sources with equal readiness. Soon, however, increasing reliance was placed on ancient Rome as the source of architectural inspiration. This was partly due to the influence of Leon Battista Alberti (1404–72), a writer and academic interested in the study of classical literature. His book *De Re Aedificatoria* was published in 1485, the first architectural book to be printed by the Gutenberg method, and the first attempt to lay down a set of theoretical design rules since those of Vitruvius, on which it was largely based. Alberti also designed buildings. In his west façade for Santa Maria Novella in Florence, the decorative flanking 'scrolls' joining nave and aisles, which were to become a feature of church design, made an appearance. And in the Palazzo Rucellai (1451) he brought a modest development of style to the building-form which had begun with the Palazzo Vecchio and been developed and humanised by Brunelleschi in his Palazzo Pitti (1435) and by Michelozzi in the Palazzo Riccardi (1444). Alberti adorned his three-storey elevation with three tiers of superimposed orders, a direct reference to the Colosseum of ancient Rome. The Palazzo Strozzi by Majano and Cronaca (1495) is a typical Florentine palace of the time, a solid block-like building with reasonably large and attractive windows on the two upper floors and a massive Roman cornice. Typically, the *palazzo* was planned around a central *cortile* or courtyard which gave light and ventilation to the interior.

In 1446, a design by Alberti was used for re-modelling the west front of San Francesco in Rimini as a monument to Sigismondo Malatesta, a rich merchant. It was a suitably grandiose design, based partly on the arch of Augustus in Rimini. Alberti was perhaps not typical of the architects of the time, being more academic and theoretical than most, but he did not even stay to see the design executed; instead he sent detail drawings by letter to the resident engineer as work progressed. Alberti's best work was the church of Sant' Andrea in Mantua, begun in 1472, just before his death, and completed forty years later. A massive, Latin-cross type building without aisles and with a crossing-dome on pendentives, it has a grand, Roman character, emphasised by a west front in the form of a triumphal arch.

The three orders appear again in the inner *cortile* of the Palazzo Ducale at Urbino, designed in 1465 by Laurana for the Montefeltro family. This building is also remarkable for its elegant interior, which includes the famous wall-panel, possibly by Piero della Francesca, showing an imaginary renaissance town drawn in accurate parallel-perspective. Florentine ideas were gradually spreading. The church of the Certosa at Pavia (1453 and later) is essentially a gothic building in character, but the west front designed and sculpted by Giovanni Amadeo, though medieval in spirit, is

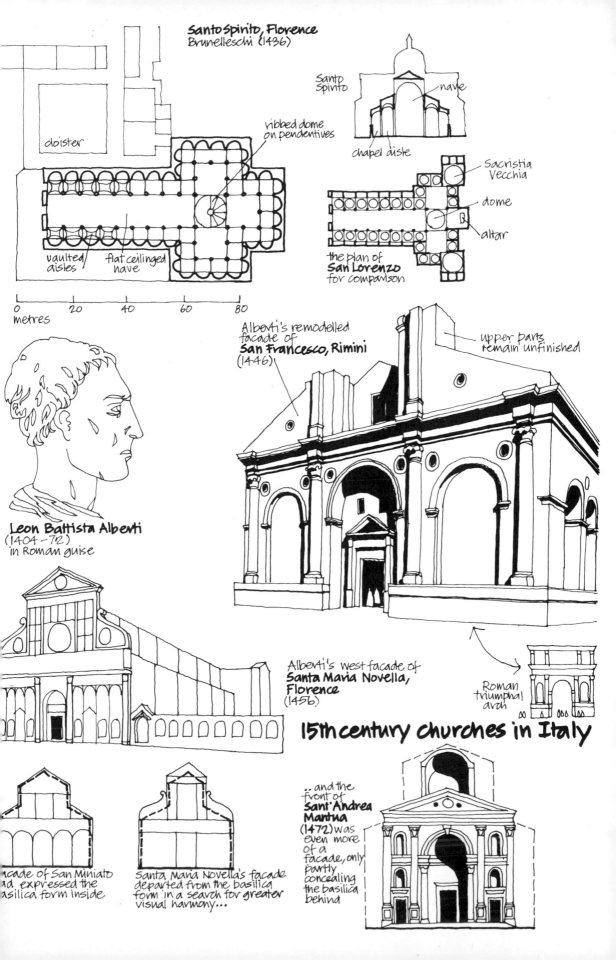

Santo Spirito, Florence
Brunelleschi (1436)

cloister

ribbed dome
on pendentives

vaulted
aisles

flat ceilinged
nave

0   20   40   60   80
metres

Santo
Spirito

nave

chapel aisle

Sacristia
Vecchia

dome

altar

the plan of
San Lorenzo
for comparison

Leon Battista Alberti
(1404–72)
in Roman guise

Alberti's remodelled
facade of
San Francesco, Rimini
(1446)

upper parts
remain unfinished

Alberti's west facade of
**Santa Maria Novella,
Florence**
(1456)

Roman
triumphal
arch

15th century churches in Italy

...acade of San Miniato
...nd expressed the
...asilica form inside

Santa Maria Novella's facade
departed from the basilica
form in a search for greater
visual harmony...

.. and the
front of
**Sant'Andrea
Mantua**
(1472) was
even more
of a
facade, only
partly
concealing
the basilica
behind

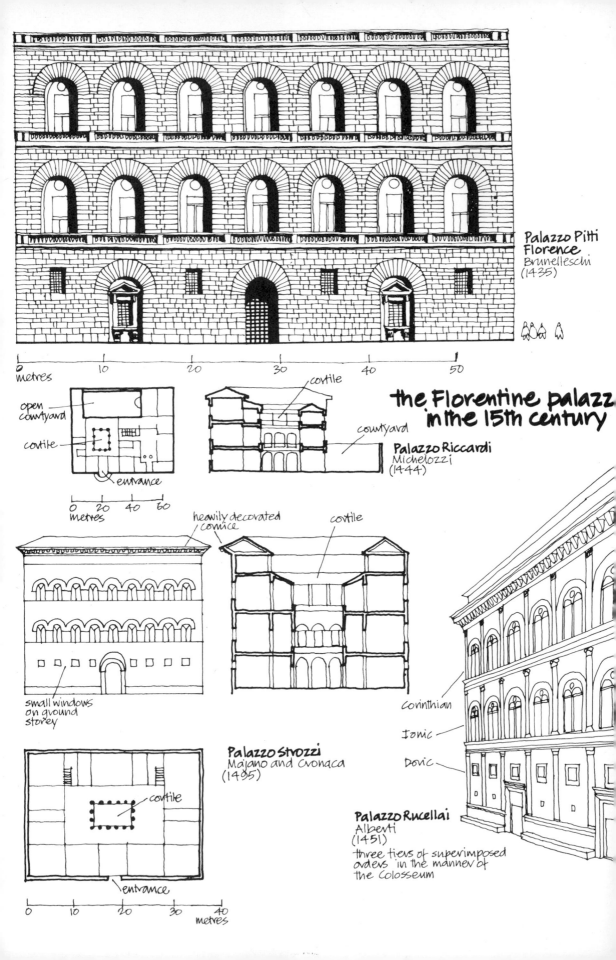

Palazzo Pitti
Florence
Brunelleschi
(1435)

the Florentine palazz
in the 15th century

open
courtyard

cortile

entrance

0 20 40 60
metres

cortile

courtyard

Palazzo Riccardi
Michelozzi
(1444)

heavily decorated
cornice

cortile

small windows
on ground
storey

Palazzo Strozzi
Majano and Cronaca
(1495)

cortile

entrance

0   10   20   30   40
                    metres

Corinthian

Ionic

Doric

Palazzo Rucellai
Alberti
(1451)
three tiers of superimposed
orders in the manner of
the Colosseum

0   10   20   30   40   50
metres

classical in detail. The Venetian architect Pietro Lombardo introduced the new ideas into Venice. His design for Santa Maria dei Miracoli (1480), beautifully crafted in marble in the Veneto-Byzantine tradition, has a two-tier elevational treatment.

It was in Rome, however, that the new ideas were pursued with the greatest enthusiasm. As the papacy's spiritual influence declined its wealth grew. In this final century before the Reformation, it could at least use its wealth to make an unparalleled outward demonstration, in building form, of the spiritual influence it was losing. Its main agent was Donato Bramante (1444–1514). Though from a poor background, Bramante's talents enabled him to train as a painter in Urbino and to develop into an architect occupying in Rome the position that Brunelleschi did in Florence. By the time he had seriously begun work in Rome in 1499, he had already completed several important works in Milan, including in 1492 a magnificent domed east end to the medieval abbey church of Santa Maria delle Grazie. He may have been associated with the building of the Palazzo della Cancelleria in Rome, though it was largely completed by the time he lived there permanently. This fine building, a further development of the Florentine *palazzo* style, was the first big renaissance building in Rome: built for the wealthy Cardinal Riario, it was a three-storey palace with inner *cortile*, incorporating into one of its wings the whole of the ancient basilican church of San Lorenzo in Damaso.

It was to be expected that in Rome, with its papal ambitions to relive the days of imperial power and with many ancient buildings to serve as models, architecture would develop away from the eclecticism of Brunelleschi towards a historically correct re-creation of the Roman design method. Bramante's work certainly took it in this direction, and led to the so-called 'High Renaissance' period when discovery and experiment were over and architects worked within an accepted framework of conventional knowledge and set formulae. Lesser designers than Bramante made this an excuse for undistinguished buildings, but his Tempietto di San Pietro di Montorio in Rome (1502) is a minor masterpiece. Built to mark the place where St Peter was martyred, it is in the form of a small circular Roman temple, only 4.5 metres across internally, surrounded by a Doric peristyle and surmounted by a drum and dome. Perfect in proportion and form, it was a dignified tribute by the 16th century to its Roman past.

We do not know for certain how medieval churches were used, but it seems likely that the design of the buildings reflected the symbolism of the mass: the Host being prepared in the sanctuary while the people waited in the nave, and the two coming together at the crossing, the symbolic heart of the building. During the 15th and 16th centuries, architects began to look for new meanings. A more grandiose and more abstract conception evolved, of the church building as representative of the cosmos, the most perfect symbol of which was the circle. Alberti in *De Re Aedificatoria* identified nine ideal plan-forms for a church: the circle, and eight polygons deriving from it. For justification he pointed to nature's predilection for spherical forms – the world and the stars – and for precedent to the Roman Pantheon. The adoption of this form raised liturgical and architectural problems, hardly significant in such a special building as the Tempietto, but more so in a parish church. The circular plan, reinforced in its effect by a centrally placed dome, implied a central location for the altar and the sacrament. However ideal in symbolic terms, this was often unsatisfactory in practice – where for example should the priest and congregation stand? On

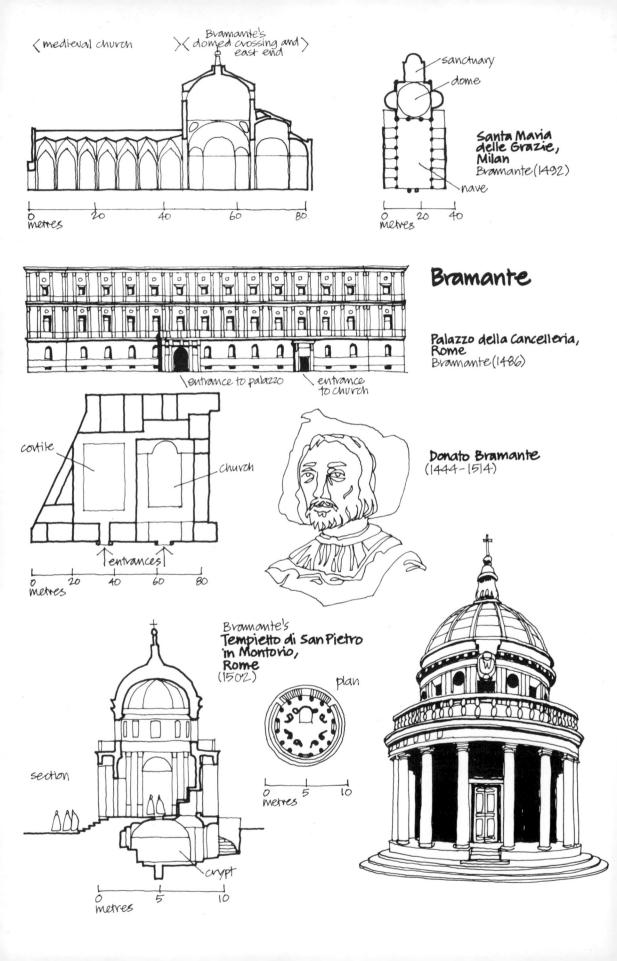

‹ medieval church ›‹ Bramante's domed crossing and east end ›

sanctuary

dome

nave

Santa Maria delle Grazie, Milan
Bramante (1492)

0 20 40 60 80.
metres

0 20 40
metres

Bramante

Palazzo della Cancelleria, Rome
Bramante (1486)

entrance to palazzo

entrance to church

cortile

church

Donato Bramante
(1444-1514)

entrances

0 20 40 60 80
metres

Bramante's
Tempietto di San Pietro in Montorio, Rome
(1502)

plan

section

0 5 10
metres

crypt

0 5 10
metres

the other hand, an altar in a niche at the side, leaving room for the people under the dome, appeared to banish the most important spiritual element to a subordinate position. Nevertheless, for some time the circular form had considerable currency. Bramante's Tempietto was only one of thirty or more important centrally-planned churches built in Italy during the 15th and 16th centuries.

The architectural ideas of Florence and Rome were slow to spread beyond the Alps. Apart from the powerful dukedom of Burgundy, France was becoming a unified nation, thanks largely to the politics of Louis XI (1461–83), but in the aftermath of the Hundred Years' War social and economic reconstruction was more important than building. England too was becoming unified, but having suffered the Hundred Years' War and the Wars of the Roses, the country had been in no state for economic progress. Richard III was an able administrator but his death in 1485 brought the cunning and ambitious House of Tudor to the throne and Henry VII immediately began to strengthen the monarchy by strict control of the country. The way was open in both France and England for cultural and economic expansion. But richest and most expansive of all the northern countries were the Netherlands. Antwerp in particular had a rich bourgeoisie whose success was based on thriving trade with Italy, Germany, France and England, and it was here that the architectural ideas of Italy spread first.

In Spain and Portugal, in the meantime, events were taking place which would be of great importance to the Europe of the future. The marriage in 1469 between Ferdinand of Aragon and Isabella of Castile had united their two countries and created modern Spain. Immediately they set about creating a national identity, in a spirit of aggressive expansionism. The aristocracy was firmly controlled, Moslems and Jews were expelled from the country and Torquemada's Inquisition visited on any non-believer who remained. The search for new trade, backed by the development of the armed ocean-going ship suitable for both trade and piracy, encouraged a number of epic journeys of exploration. The Portuguese prince Henry the Navigator prompted the exploration of the West African coast, Bernal Diaz reached the Cape of Good Hope, and Vasco da Gama rounded the Cape to India. Christopher Columbus, sponsored by Ferdinand and Isabella, set sail westwards in 1492 in search of another route to India and unexpectedly discovered a new continent. The future development of western culture would no longer be that of Europe alone.

Europe's exploration of the world was stimulated originally by the capitalist classes, looking for new ways to India and China to break Italy's monopoly of the eastern trade routes. But undreamed-of lands were discovered and their colonisation pushed India and China into the background of men's minds. Conflict arose over possession of the new lands. Suddenly increased sources of silver and gold brought inflation and price increases to Europe as a whole, the middle-class merchants prospered, and the poor fell even farther behind, setting the pattern for the economy and class-system of the later industrial age.

Scientific discovery also flourished, though technology did not necessarily benefit. Science had for so long been a branch of philosophy, while technology was the province only of the artisan, that the two did not meet immediately. Technological developments continued in the medieval pattern: gradual, pragmatic shifts towards mastery of techniques, still unsupported by general theories. However, man's pursuit of discovery for its own sake was insatiable, and facts were indefatigably catalogued in a way which would allow scientific theories to emerge in the future.

The age of discovery
The 16th and 17th centuries

'It is a poor disciple', wrote Leonardo da Vinci, 'that does not excel his master.' The new horizons opening up around him had greatly widened man's potential for expanding his mind and skills and for using them with greater confidence and freedom. However, by the beginning of the 16th century it was plain to some that although the old medieval system might be collapsing, an oligarchy of a different kind was developing in its place. If some freedoms were gained, others were lost as everywhere the 'new princes' of the capitalist world climbed to power and began to dominate political life. Niccolo Machiavelli (1469–1527) recognised this. His treatise *Il Principe*, published in 1513, was written specifically to further his own political career at the Medici court, but its realistic analysis of contemporary political life and its practical advice on how to gain and to retain power made it relevant to all such 'new princes'. Its lack of scruple caused some shocks, and the author's name became synonymous with evil.

Tudor England, whose rulers were as ruthless as any advocated by Machiavelli, had freedom neither of worship nor of speech, nor even, in the case of Thomas More – executed in 1535 for holding unacceptable opinions which yet he had kept to himself – of thought. To a man of Christian principle like More the Tudor court was a waking nightmare, and in reaction against it he wrote *Utopia* (1516), the description of an imaginary country in which he propounded in detail his view of the ideal human society. The Middle Ages had neither admitted nor needed any Utopias: the only ideal society, like that of St Augustine's 'City of God', had been a heavenly one, for which earthly life was no more than a preparation. But as man's reliance on heaven gradually declined, and interest in his own world grew, it became apparent that life on earth, far from being irrelevant, merited serious attention and improvement. Maybe poverty and oppression were not pre-ordained states but capable of being altered. Maybe the same moral freedom which allowed the rise of unprincipled tyrants would permit those opposed to tyranny to seek a world in which it did not exist – and in which the sanity of man's institutions could be reflected in the order of his cities and their buildings. *Il Principe* and *Utopia* are different aspects of the same phenomenon, opposing views which continue to recur in European thought: that society's mental and physical resources can be used either to enhance the power of the few or to benefit society as a whole.

As long as society is dominated by a privileged class, the first of these attitudes will almost inevitably predominate, and will be reflected in the architecture of the time. The cathedrals of the Middle Ages, though in many respects the expression of their sponsors' personal ambition, had also had the glorification of God as a justification for the enormous wealth expended on them. But post-medieval society needed no such excuses: in the more secular ethos that had developed, great buildings could be undisguised expressions of their owners' wealth and power, and 16th-century palaces attracted the kind of investment and architectural effort which in the 13th century had been given only to God.

Foremost among these were the châteaux of the Loire Valley in France. Like many royal courts of the day, the house of Valois spent much of its time travelling from one place to another, and a chain of great palaces was built to accommodate it. When the food and wine were gone and the cess-pits full, the court would move on, leaving the resident household to clear up afterwards. The great days of the Loire châteaux lasted from the reign of Charles VII in the mid-15th century to that of Henri III, last of the Valois, at the end of the 16th. During this time they developed from medieval *châteaux forts*, built for protection, into magnificent places of comfort and display. The medieval castle of Blois was extended with a grand courtyard of new buildings centred round the wing of François I (1515), with its spiral processional staircase. At Chenonceaux in 1515 and Azay-le-Rideau in 1518 two ornate châteaux were begun whose picturesque medieval silhouettes were enhanced by their waterside settings. Most magnificent and famous of all, Chambord (1519), though classical in many of its details, was still essentially medieval, its plan-form deriving from that of the concentric castle and its vertically-designed elevations and exuberant roofline from the gothic cathedral.

In 1556, an extension to Chenonceaux was built out on a five-arched bridge over the river Cher, by the master of the king's works, Philibert de l'Orme (1515–70), the first great French architect in the post-medieval sense. An enthusiast for Vitruvius, he had visited Italy in 1533, returning imbued with the spirit of classicism which he celebrated in his two books *Le Premier Tome de l'Architecture* and *Nouvelles Inventions pour bien Bastir*. But neither his books nor his buildings conveyed a dry academicism, for his was an essentially practical mind with an understanding of building materials. The château of Anet (1547) used Vitruvian motifs, but adapted them in an individual way. The chapel, though using classical detail, was a highly original composition of bold geometric forms. But de l'Orme's main contribution belongs more to the mainstream of French architectural development. The classical influences brought into France by returning French designers or expatriate Italians did not develop in quite the same way as in Italy. The Italians' primary inspiration, the buildings of the Romans, were few and far between in France, and the tradition of gothic craftsmanship too strong to die easily. So throughout the 16th century, French architects gradually assimilated the new influences and evolved both from them and from medieval traditions an indigenous French style, in which de l'Orme's distinctive way of ordering a façade played an important part. His extension at Chenonceaux and his designs for Anet, Fontainebleau, Villers-Cotterets and the Château de Boulogne with their elegant, even severe lower storeys and steeply pitched hipped roofs with decorative dormers, set a pattern for the future which dominated French domestic architecture for about three centuries, equally adaptable to middle-class urban housing, as in the Place des Vosges in Paris by Claude Chastillon (1605), and to the royal palaces of the Tuileries and the Louvre.

The Tuileries, on the bank of the Seine in Paris, was begun in 1564 by de l'Orme for Catherine de Médicis, and in the next century was added to successively by Bullant, du Cerceau and Le Vau. The projected plan of three large courtyards was never achieved, but the single group of blocks which was built remained the main residence of French kings and emperors till its destruction in 1871. Linked to the Tuileries and its gardens into one vast formal composition was the Louvre, begun in the reign of François I on the site of an old medieval château, and gradually built up by a succession of architects into one of the largest palaces in European history.

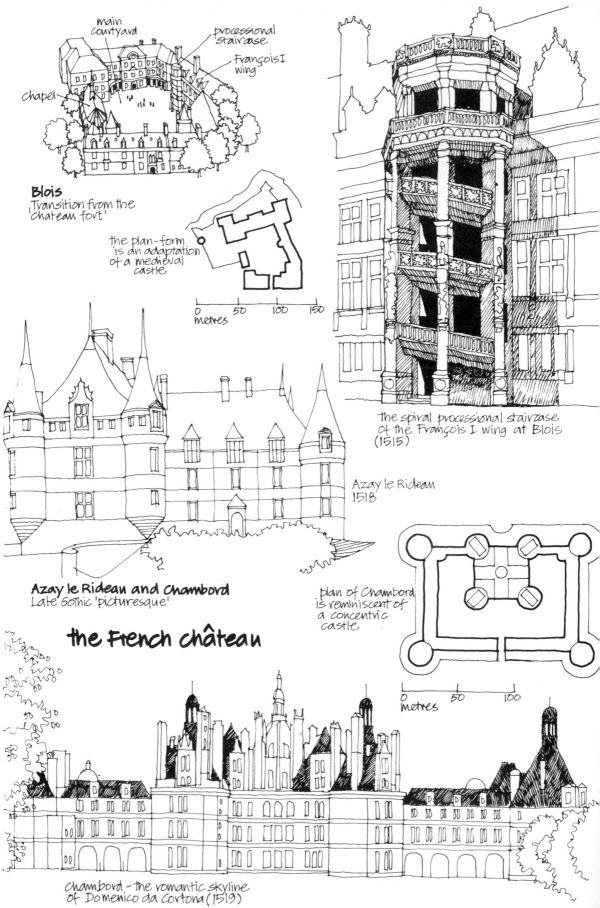

chapel

main courtyard

processional staircase

François I wing

Blois
'Transition from the chateau fort'

the plan-form is an adaptation of a medieval castle

0   50   100   150
metres

the spiral processional staircase of the François I wing at Blois (1515)

Azay le Rideau 1518

Azay le Rideau and Chambord
Late Gothic 'picturesque!'

the French château

plan of Chambord is reminiscent of a concentric castle

0   50   100
metres

Chambord - the romantic skyline of Domenico da Cortona (1519)

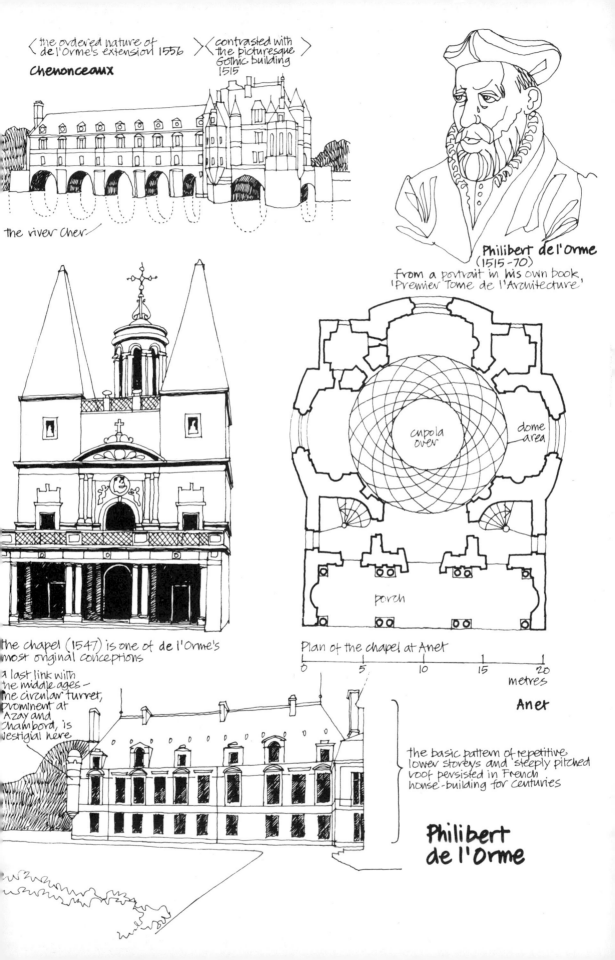

⟨ the ordered nature of de l'Orme's extension 1556 ⟩ ⟨ contrasted with the picturesque Gothic building 1515 ⟩

Chenonceaux

the river Cher

Philibert de l'Orme
(1515–70)
from a portrait in his own book, 'Premier Tome de l'Architecture'

the chapel (1547) is one of de l'Orme's most original conceptions

a last link with the middle ages — the circular turret, prominent at Azay and Chambord, is vestigial here

cupola over

dome area

porch

Plan of the chapel at Anet

0   5   10   15   20
                                metres

Anet

the basic pattern of repetitive lower storeys and steeply pitched roof persisted in French house-building for centuries

Philibert de l'Orme

But the products of royal patronage in France, fine as they were, did not attain the heights of those of papal and bourgeois patronage in Italy, where the 16th century saw much inventive architecture. Among the grandest was the Belvedere courtyard at the Vatican, built in 1503 by Bramante for Julius II and containing a Roman-scale three-storey triumphal feature, a gigantic semi-domed open-air niche, whose only purpose was architectural effect. Of comparable splendour was the Palazzo Farnese (1515), finest of the urban *palazzi* of the time, designed by Antonio da Sangallo, a pupil of Bramante, as a three-storey block in stuccoed masonry enclosing a fine 25-metre square *cortile*. Respect for the legacy of ancient Rome did not prevent the builders from pillaging stones from the Colosseum for the travertine dressings round the windows.

Among the most splendid of Rome's high renaissance buildings was another Palazzo Farnese, built at nearby Caprarola in 1547 by Giacomo da Vignola, a theoretician those scholarly book *Regola delli Cinque Ordini d'Architettura* was to have great influence in France, and a capable architect. The plan of the Palazzo is pentagonal, 46 metres to each face, enclosing a circular *cortile*. The whole composition with its external staircases, ramps and terraces arranged about the hill-top on which the building stands, is highly monumental.

As time went on, the imagination of designers began to go beyond the Vitruvian rules which inspired Bramante and his circle. A search for new means of expression gave rise to impatience with the rule-book and even with the principles of building construction. Significantly, perhaps, much of the impetus came not from a conventionally-trained architect or craftsman but from a painter and sculptor. The first important manifestation of this 'mannerist' approach was the chapel at San Lorenzo in Florence, designed in 1521 by Michelangelo (1475–1564) to contain the tombs of Giuliano and the younger Lorenzo de Medici. The chapel is the counterpart of Brunelleschi's Sacristia Vecchia but is radically different in mood. Instead of Brunelleschi's lively, essentially architectural logic, Michelangelo's is that of the sculptor. The architecture is intense and distorted, in keeping with the dramatic character of the monumental figures it contains. The interest of the design is centred about 4 metres up on the two opposing walls, where the seated figures of the two dukes brood over their sarcophagi below. Around these two points, the architectural detail is complex and unconventional. The composition includes pairs of Corinthian pilasters with no entablature whose only function is visually to frame the sculpted figures.

This feature was developed further in the ante-room to the nearby Laurentian Library, designed by Michelangelo in 1524 and built by others in 1559. The curiously free form of the triple staircase and the bizarre treatment of the double columns, which instead of standing on a solid base are cantilevered from the walls on consoles, are part of Michelangelo's unconventional treatment.

A similar impatience with classical precedent can be seen in the work of Giulio Romano (1492–1546), another who came to architecture from painting. His Palazzo del Tè in Mantua, a pleasure resort built for the Gonzaga family in 1525, is a solid, rusticated building with applied Doric pilasters used in a very unacademic manner.

Venice, to whom classical architecture had come relatively late, had not yet rejected it; but her architects were transmuting Roman forms into a highly personal Venetian style, often richly decorative as at the Library of San Marco by Sansovino (1536) or the Palazzo Grimani by San Michele (1556). Foremost among the Vene-

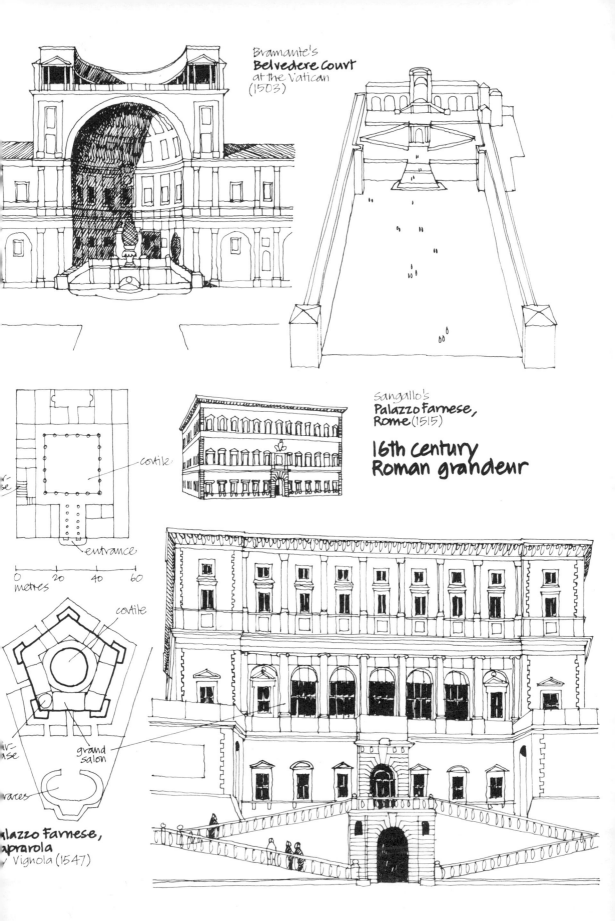

Bramante's
Belvedere Court
at the Vatican
(1503)

Sangallo's
**Palazzo Farnese,
Rome** (1515)

16th century
Roman grandeur

covile

entrance

0   20   40   60
metres

covile

grand
salon

...lazzo Farnese,
...prarola
/ Vignola (1547)

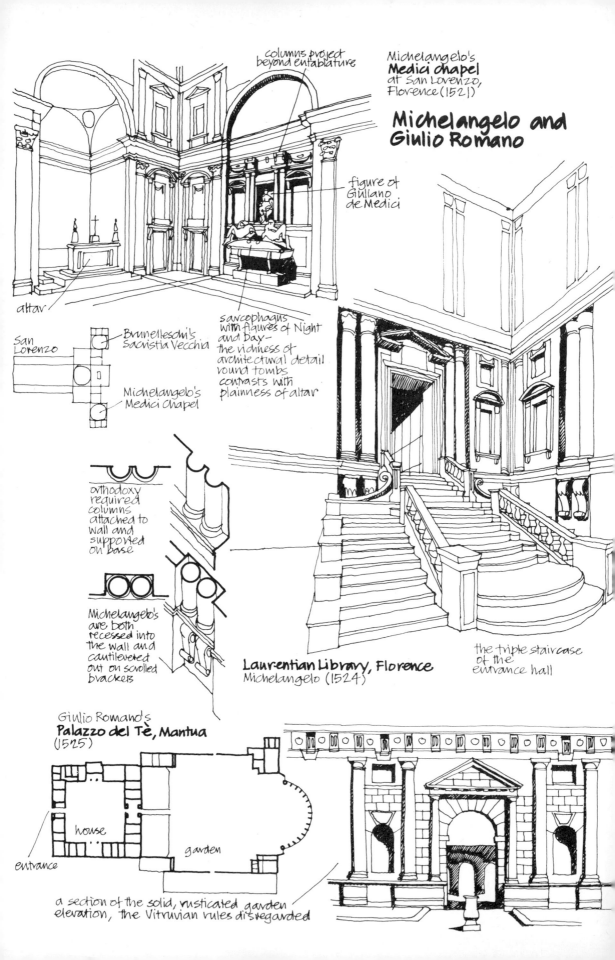

columns project
beyond entablature

Michelangelo's
Medici chapel
at San Lorenzo,
Florence (1521)

Michelangelo and
Giulio Romano

figure of
Giuliano
de Medici

altar

San
Lorenzo

Brunelleschi's
Sacristia Vecchia

Michelangelo's
Medici Chapel

sarcophagus
with figures of Night
and Day—
the richness of
architectural detail
round tombs
contrasts with
plainness of altar

orthodoxy
required
columns
attached to
wall and
supported
on base

Michelangelo's
are both
recessed into
the wall and
cantilevered
out on scrolled
brackets

Laurentian Library, Florence
Michelangelo (1524)

the triple staircase
of the
entrance hall

Giulio Romano's
Palazzo del Tè, Mantua
(1525)

house

garden

entrance

a section of the solid, rusticated garden
elevation, the Vitruvian rules disregarded

tian architects and possibly, for his subsequent influence, one of the most important in Europe, was Andrea Palladio (1508–80). Unlike Michelangelo and Giulio he did not reject classicism, but he did temper it with his own imaginative approach. His adopted home-town of Vicenza is now a monument to his own particular blend of academicism and originality. The Palazzo Chiericati (1550) is a characteristic building, unsensational, harmoniously proportioned, classical in spirit yet sufficiently original in the treatment of its main façade, with its contrast between solid and void, to be highly memorable. Palladio also gave an architectural form to the country houses which rich merchants increasingly preferred to congested urban *palazzi*. Unlike the *palazzo*, the Palladian 'villa' was designed to be seen as part of a landscape and from all sides. Archetypal is the Villa Capra at Vicenza (1552), a square building with a columnar portico on each face and surmounted by a shallow dome, a revolutionary departure which inspired several imitations.

Palladio's great influence on architectural design lay chiefly with the publication of his famous *I quattro libri dell' Architettura*. It was printed in every European country from 1570 onwards, and did much to publicise his concern with classical form and proportion. As he wisely included pictures of his own buildings, it did much to publicise them, too.

Palladio's least pretentious buildings are often his most successful. A mason by training, he understood the properties of materials, and though all his buildings display this to some extent, it is often the smaller ones that demonstrate with the greatest simplicity and directness his mastery of colour and texture and of the use of humble brick and stucco.

Another aspect of his work is seen best in the two Venetian churches of San Giorgio Maggiore (1565) and Il Redentore – 'the Redeemer' – (1577). Each is basilican but with a domed crossing which gives a Greek-cross aspect to the east end. The treatment of the western elevation in each case emphasises the basilican form behind, with single-height pilasters on the ends of the side-aisles and giant double-height engaged columns on the nave, reflecting the respective heights of the spaces. These 'giant orders' are a distinctive feature of several of Palladio's larger buildings and evoke a feeling of considerable grandeur.

The fine self-confidence of Italian architecture in the 16th century was in strong contrast to the crisis the papacy was undergoing. The growing reliance of philosophers on reason rather than dogma turned many minds away from traditional forms of faith, and there was almost universal disillusion about the corruption of many of the church's practices. In 1517, the German priest Martin Luther (1483–1546), who taught that the Bible, not the Church, should be the supreme Christian authority, published his 'Ninety-five Theses' as a head-on challenge to the power of the Pope. Luther was supported by many Electors who sensed that a collapse of church authority could mean the final removal of obstacles to the free development of capitalism.

Amid much conflict, Luther's Reformation gained ground. Protestantism spread through Germany and, by the efforts of Zwingli and Calvin, to Switzerland, Scotland, England and France. The Catholic church retaliated. A revival of the inquisition in Spain and in Italy began to stamp out open heresy, and this counter-reformation was reinforced by Loyola's new 'Society of Jesus', a fierce monastic order dedicated to intellectual attainment and the conversion of the unbeliever. The Reformation and its consequences left Europe split between a

Palladio

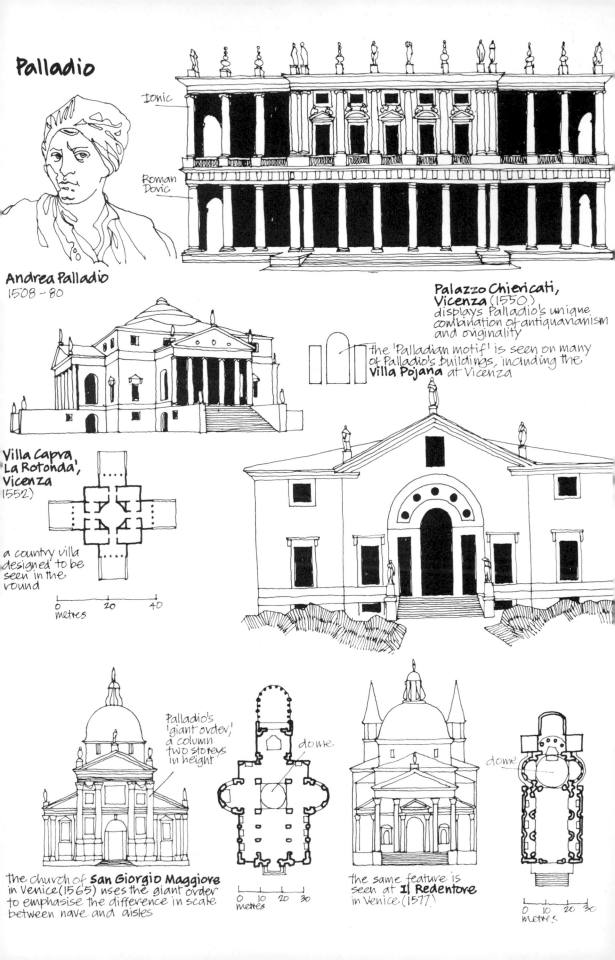

Ionic

Roman Doric

Andrea Palladio
1508 – 80

Palazzo Chiericati, Vicenza (1550)
displays Palladio's unique combination of antiquarianism and originality

the 'Palladian motif' is seen on many of Palladio's buildings, including the **Villa Pojana** at Vicenza

Villa Capra, 'La Rotonda', Vicenza (1552)

a country villa designed to be seen in the round

0   20   40
metres

Palladio's 'giant order', a column two storeys in height

dome

dome

the church of **San Giorgio Maggiore** in Venice (1565) uses the giant order to emphasise the difference in scale between nave and aisles

0 10 20 30
metres

the same feature is seen at **Il Redentore** in Venice. (1577)

0 10 20 30
metres

Protestant north and a Catholic south, and brought four destructive wars of religious freedom and political emancipation: within Germany, between Holland and Spain, between Catholics and Huguenots in France and between Spain and England. National unity and self-determination increased, and with them the wealth of the kings and bourgeoisie. Church exemptions from taxes and from civil law were ended, capitalism was boosted as the church's moral sanctions were removed, and the royal treasuries filled with confiscated gold.

But there seems to be no hint in the papal architecture of the mid-16th century of the church's political problems, except, perhaps by way of reaction, its even greater display of confidence. The Villa Giulia, a country pleasure-resort for Pope Julius III designed by Vignola in 1550, is a model of serenity, with its calm, ordered front façade and a sweeping semi-circular courtyard at the rear which develops into a long succession of terraces, staircases and walled gardens.

Vignola's great church of Il Gesù, designed in 1568 for the Society of Jesus, is another affirmation of confidence. In form it is a more self-assured version of Alberti's Sant' Andrea at Mantua. Its domed, centralised east end was extended into a Latin cross by a lengthened western arm, which foreshadowed a general move in subsequent church planning away from a totally centralised plan. The interior, completed by a succession of later architects, is of great decorative richness, and the exterior features a west façade which is also a development of Alberti, a basilican elevation complete with the linking scrolls of Santa Maria Novella.

During the whole of the 16th century, while the church was torn apart, the biggest building project of all was proclaiming Christian unity to the world. It began in 1505 with the desire of Julius II to build himself a mausoleum in Rome, which involved the demolition of Constantine's ancient basilica of St Peter. A competition was won by Bramante, whose scheme for a vast Greek-cross church with a central dome was begun in 1506. In 1513, Raphael revised the design, with the intention of changing the plan-form to a Latin cross, but the church's recurrent political crises, a shortage of funds and the changing ideas of successive architects slowed the work drastically, till in 1546, amid a period of militant confidence, it was taken over by the ageing Michelangelo. The construction of his new Greek-cross design proceeded steadily till his death in 1564, when the building was complete as far as the drum of the dome. From models left by him, the dome and cupola were built in 1585, and at the turn of the century Carlo Maderna reverted to a Latin-cross plan, pulling the nave forward and adding a majestic west front. Eventually, in the mid-17th century, Bernini's colonnade completed the composition by forming a wide ceremonial piazza at the front; after some 160 years and the efforts of twelve important architects, Julius' memorial was complete.

It is easy to say that St Peter's lacks architectural unity – under the circumstances of its creation, it could hardly be otherwise – and the most criticised feature of this enormous building is the fact that external views of the dome, the centre of the whole design, are obscured by the extreme length and height of the nave. But the building is enormously impressive; not only its size but also its decorative richness give it an appropriate air of solemn grandeur. Bramante's dome would have been low and shallow, like that of his Tempietto, but Michelangelo's is tall and soaring, some 140 metres to the top, supported on four gigantic piers and bound internally by tension chains to prevent collapse. Appropriately, the high altar, with its fine *baldacchino* designed by Bernini, is placed over the supposed tomb of St Peter, and both are

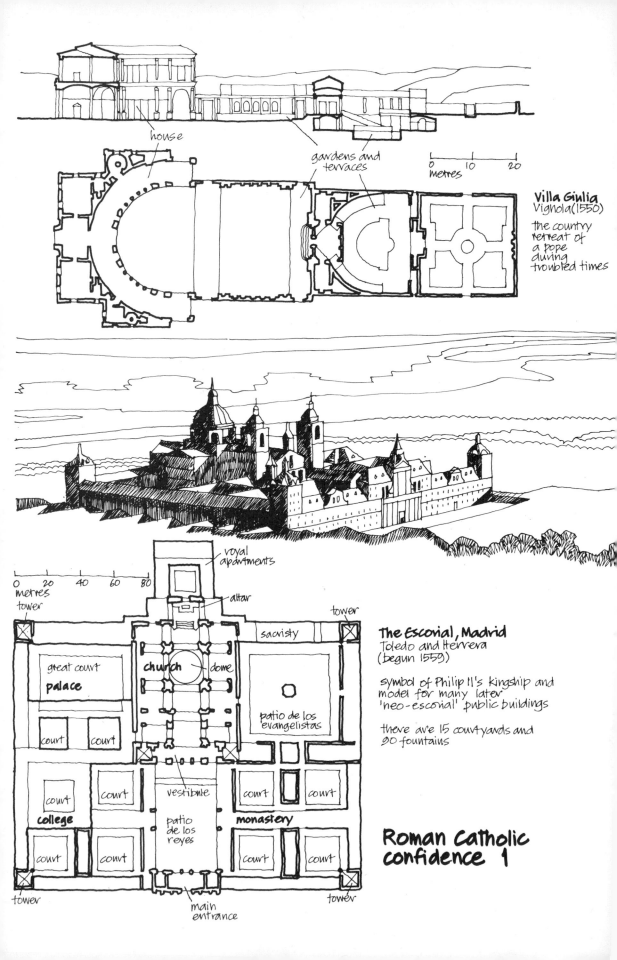

house

gardens and
terraces

0   10   20
metres

Villa Giulia
Vignola (1550)

the country
retreat of
a pope
during
troubled times

royal
apartments

altar

0   20   40   60   80
metres
tower

tower

sacristy

great court
palace

church — dome

patio de los
evangelistas

court   court

court   court

vestibule

court   court

college

patio
de los
reyes

monastery

court   court

tower

main
entrance

tower

The Escorial, Madrid
Toledo and Herrera
(begun 1559)

symbol of Philip II's kingship and
model for many later
'neo-escorial' public buildings

there are 15 courtyards and
90 fountains

**Roman Catholic
confidence 1**

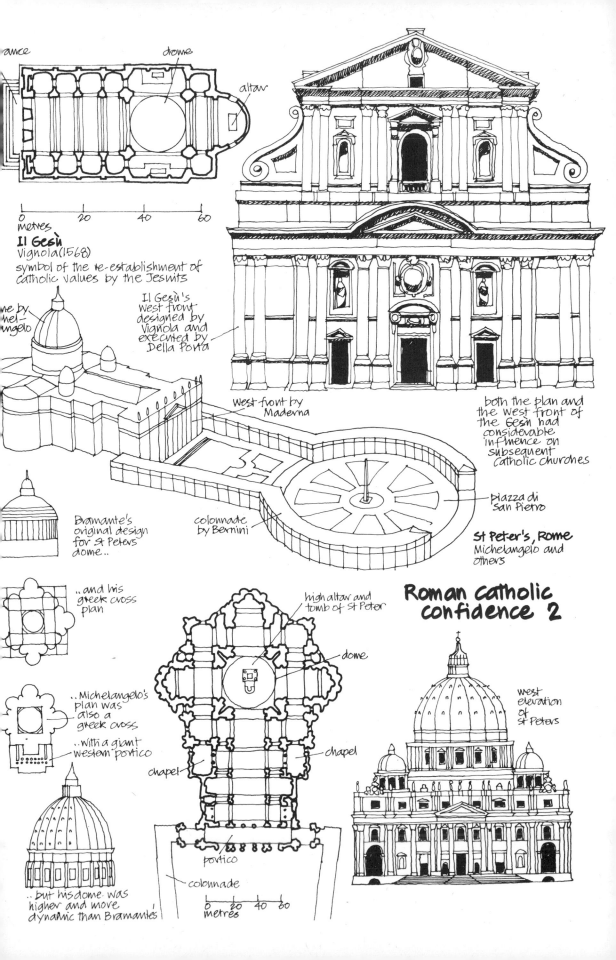

ance

dome

altar

0   20   40   60
metres

Il Gesù
Vignola (1568)
symbol of the re-establishment of
Catholic values by the Jesuits

Il Gesù's
West front
designed by
Vignola and
executed by
Della Porta

me by
Mel-
angelo

West front by
Maderna

both the plan and
the West front of
the Gesù had
considerable
influence on
subsequent
Catholic churches

Bramante's
original design
for St Peters
dome..

colonnade
by Bernini

piazza di
San Pietro

St Peter's, Rome
Michelangelo and
others

..and his
greek cross
plan

high altar and
tomb of St Peter

Roman Catholic
confidence 2

dome

..Michelangelo's
plan was
also a
greek cross

..with a giant
western portico

chapel

chapel

West
elevation
of
St Peters

portico

colonnade

0   20   40   60
metres

..but his dome was
higher and more
dynamic than Bramantes

located in the exact centre of the dome area, the symbolic focus of the whole composition.

The Pope's main allies in Europe were the catholic kings of Spain, leaders of the 16th century's most powerful empire. Charles V (1519–56) became Holy Roman Emperor in 1520 and ruled over Spain, Sicily, Naples, Sardinia, Austria, Luxembourg and Holland as well as the colonies which his Conquistadors were assembling in central America. To the New World the Spanish took gunpowder, the horse and the Bible; from it, they brought a seemingly unending supply of gold and silver which enriched the Spanish treasury – though without stimulating the economy. Inflation began to run high, the balance of trade was poor and spending lavish. Among the great buildings of the early 16th century was Granada cathedral (1528 and later), in size and shape comparable with Seville, both Gothic and classical in spirit, and richly ornate in detail. It belongs to a period known as 'plateresque' – *plateria* means silverware – thought to have been inspired by the intricacy of the precious metalwork being brought back by explorers. Gradually Italian architectural influences grew stronger. By 1527 Pedro Machuca had begun a great palace for Charles V adjoining the 14th-century Moorish Alhambra in Granada; a two-tier, 60-metre-square block with a circular central courtyard, it was an assimilation of the spirit of Bramante, straightforwardly classical in character, grand and monumental. The Tavera Hospital by Bustamente (1542 and later), with its elegant two-tier arched courtyard, was equally Italianate.

Philip II came to the Spanish throne in 1556 and ruled for the rest of the century. He saw the forcible establishment of Catholicism throughout Europe and the Spanish empire as the best means of achieving a political unity over which he and the Pope would preside. But he was destined to fail. Corruption within his own bureaucracy undermined his strength at home, and his dream of a united Europe was ended by the Dutch protestants' fierce struggle for independence under William the Silent. The means of achieving dominance finally came to an end in 1588 when the English destroyed his entire fleet. The severe, dedicated existence of this troubled king is expressed in the vast Escorial Palace near Madrid, begun in 1599 by Juan Bautista de Toledo and continued by Juan de Herrera. An extensive complex of buildings some 200 metres square on a lonely mountainous site, it contained all the necessities for Philip's austerely religious kingship: a central courtyard, dominated by a domed church and flanked by a monastery on one side and a religious college and royal apartments on the other, grand, monastic and austere to the point of grimness.

Monastic severity was not the style of the Tudor monarchs of England. Henry VII established more than just a new dynasty: through rigid control of barons and parliament he established a strong rule, stabilising the political life of England and encouraging trade. His son Henry VIII (1509–47) broke from the Pope, creating a national church with himself as the head, and dissolved the catholic monasteries, seizing their wealth. The firm establishment of the new Anglican church was completed by his daughter Elizabeth I (1558–1603). Her sea-power became pre-eminent in the world, stimulating overseas exploration and colonisation, expanding trade and steadily increasing the country's wealth. Henry and Elizabeth presided over a sequence of cultural achievements including those of Tallis, Byrd, Spenser and Shakespeare.

In contrast to the Escorial, Henry VIII's palace of Nonsuch in Surrey was a pleasure garden, built around two courtyards, on which the collective abilities of

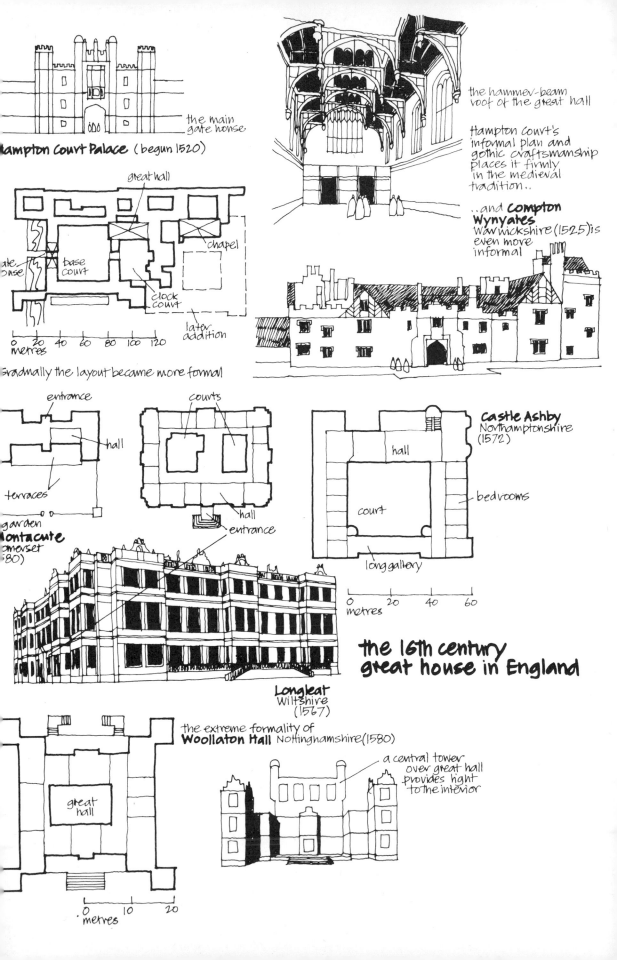

Hampton Court Palace (begun 1520)

the main gate house.

the hammer-beam roof of the great hall

Hampton Court's informal plan and gothic craftsmanship places it firmly in the medieval tradition..

..and **Compton Wynyates** Warwickshire (1525) is even more informal

great hall

chapel

gate house

base court

clock court

later addition

0 20 40 60 80 100 120
metres

Gradually the layout became more formal

entrance

hall

terraces

garden

Montacute Somerset (1580)

courts

hall

entrance

Castle Ashby Northamptonshire (1572)

hall

court

bedrooms

long gallery

0 20 40 60
metres

the 16th century great house in England

Longleat Wiltshire (1567)

the extreme formality of **Woollaton Hall** Nottinghamshire (1580)

a central tower over great hall provides light to the interior

great hall

0 10 20
metres

craftsmen from Italy, France, Holland and England were lavished. Nonsuch was pulled down in the 17th century, but contemporary descriptions reveal it as having been five storeys high with many towers, pinnacles and statues. The ground storey was stone and the upper ones timber-framed with decorative panelling covered in gilt. There was a three-storey-high banqueting-hall and numerous formal gardens and walks.

However, Henry soon tired of his great palace in favour of an even grander one being erected by his Chancellor, Cardinal Wolsey, at Hampton Court. Built by native-born craftsmen, it depended heavily on the gothic tradition. It is a rambling, informal building, mainly in decorative brickwork, built around four courtyards of different sizes, with many fine features: ornate gatehouses, a chapel, and a Great Hall with a hammer-beam roof by James Nedeham. The work was begun in 1520, and by 1526 Henry's envy was so great that Wolsey had no option but to bestow the palace on his king.

During the 16th century there was a great demand for fine houses by the rich aristocracy and aspiring merchants of England, and a characteristic style was established. Most house plans were arranged around a great hall, developed from the Norman manor but now elaborately panelled in oak, with a decorative timber roof or elaborate plaster ceiling and a large fireplace and chimney. The hall was the main room of the house and also the main circulation space: a grand staircase at one end gave access to the upper rooms, which included the main withdrawing-room, developed from the Norman 'solar', and that 16th-century innovation, the long gallery. This covered walkway joining all the upper rooms was gradually widened, lengthened and improved as time went on to become an art gallery, a place of recreation and an object of wonder. The late-medieval informality of the early 16th century, seen at Compton Wynyates (1525), gave way to a strongly geometric plan, including perhaps a square internal courtyard, and also to a rectilinear external appearance in which large, mullioned windows, often in projecting bays, played an important part. Large houses were usually built in the limestone and sandstone of central and south-west England, and include Longleat (1567), Castle Ashby (1572), Woollaton Hall and Montacute (both 1580). Considerable use was made, in lesser manor-houses, of timber-framed construction and Moreton Old Hall in Cheshire (1559) and Pitchford in Shropshire (1560) are fine examples of Elizabethan 'black-and-white' building.

The richness of these aristocratic and wealthy bourgeois houses, with their lavish use of timber, is a contrast to the cottages and farmhouses of the period. By the late 16th century a drastic shortage of timber in Europe jeopardised economic expansion. Wood had always been used in considerable quantities for building and ship-building, but the rapid growth of towns and trade were making ever-greater inroads into the forests. In addition, timber had always been used as an energy source. The 16th century, like the Middle Ages, depended largely on water and wind power, and considerable advances were made in the improvement of water- and wind-mills. However, the growing metallurgical industry, in particular, relied on timber for fuel and helped to precipitate a crisis which was not fully resolved until the development of alternative energy sources in the industrial revolution of the 18th century. In some parts of Europe, timber prices rose during the 16th century by 1200 per cent. Added impetus was given to the development of brick construction, and timber was used much more sparingly, especially in cheaper buildings. The typical farmhouse or

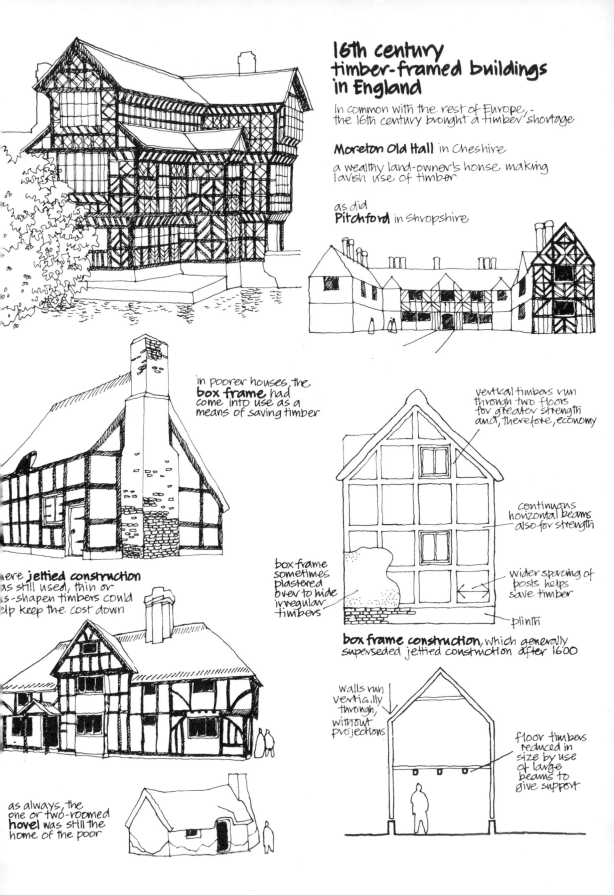

16th century timber-framed buildings in England

In common with the rest of Europe, the 16th century brought a timber shortage

Moreton Old Hall in Cheshire

a wealthy land-owner's house making lavish use of timber

as did
Pitchford in Shropshire

in poorer houses, the **box frame** had come into use as a means of saving timber

...ere **jettied construction** ...s still used, thin or ...s-shapen timbers could ...lp keep the cost down

as always, the one or two-roomed **hovel** was still the home of the poor

vertical timbers run through two floors for greater strength and, therefore, economy

continuous horizontal beams also for strength

box frame sometimes plastered over to hide irregular timbers

wider spacing of posts helps save timber

plinth

box frame construction, which generally superseded jettied construction after 1600

walls run vertically through, without projections

floor timbers reduced in size by use of large beams to give support

cottage of the time had its framing timbers widely spaced, and more use was made of inferior or mis-shapen wood.

Rural 16th-century England was the scene of a fundamental social change. In a general move towards the establishment of private property, the old medieval fields were being enclosed – by the landlords – with hedges and ditches, the peasants dispossessed and their hovels pulled down. Added to the thousands of estate workers thrown out of their jobs by the dissolution of the monasteries, the peasants created an enormous unemployment problem, only partly solved by the growth of manufacturing industry. This too was beginning to change rapidly: the wool trade of the 15th century had developed into a thriving cloth industry, requiring factories and a new class of wage-labourers to work them. As the peasants everywhere declined in numbers, society became polarised between the capitalist property-owners and a working class who owned literally nothing but their ability to work – assuming that they could find employment.

'Faith', Luther had said, 'as it makes man a believer, so also it makes his works good.' Now that Protestantism was spreading through Europe, there was less emphasis on monastic contemplativeness than on the development of man's practical talents. Those who embraced the new faith – and many who did not – were happy to use it to justify the pursuit of industry and commerce. The steady economic growth of north European countries during the 17th century, especially Britain and Holland, was due at least in part to their capitalists imbibing the protestant ethic. There were more solid reasons too, notably that their wealth was based firmly on manufacturing industry, unlike Italy's which relied on commerce and Spain's which derived mainly from its store of captured gold. So the 17th century saw a rapid build-up of the sea-routes carrying British and Dutch trade to and from their colonies, while Italy and Spain were left in the past.

Great wealth still existed in both countries, however, particularly in Italy. As a result of the Reformation, the papacy had suffered a drastic financial setback as its sources of income dried up, but the loyalty of the remaining catholic countries, and increased taxes, helped to keep the coffers full. Churches and palaces were still built and Italian architecture entered a magnificent autumnal phase. Under the influence of the architects Carlo Maderna (1556–1629), Francesco Borromini (1599–1667) and the great Giovanni Bernini (1598–1680) a style was developed, rich, bold and powerful, which though still using the Roman vocabulary, broke entirely from the restraints of classicism into an effusion of curving, plastic shapes. The word *barocco* is a jeweller's term to describe a rough pearl or uncut stone, and so the lack of classical refinement in the style of Maderna and his successors has given us 'baroque'. Maderna was the architect of the nave and west front of St Peter's, a monumental essay in the Corinthian order, with columns almost 30 metres in height, impressive for its great size rather than its originality. His church of Santa Susanna in Rome (1597) is less grandiose but more imaginative. Its façade has a rich display of decorative features, groups of orders clustered together, repeated pediments and projecting bays, which build up to emphasise the central entrance.

Bernini, like Michelangelo, was also a sculptor, and had a similar disregard for architectural rules, which he subordinated to sculptural effects. The sweeping curves and false perspective of his colonnade at St Peter's, though out of character with the building itself, are baroque town design at its finest, as, at the other end of the scale, is his tiny church of Sant' Andrea del Quirinale in Rome (1658). It is simple and elliptical on plan, surmounted by a dome. Its front façade, ordered and pedimented, has a semi-circular porch on a stepped podium which projects forward and, together with a curved pair of wing walls, integrates the building with the public space in front. The Scala Regia (1663) is Bernini's famous staircase linking the Vatican with the portico of St Peter's. Given a restricted, tapering site he made a virtue out of necessity, and the diminishing perspective and unusual lighting effects of this long indoor space give it great dignity. Bernini's spatial effects were essentially theatrical, designed to draw the viewer into the composition and involve him totally. In the Medici chapel Michelangelo designed the architecture around the sculpture; Bernini, in the Santa Teresa chapel (1646) at Santa Maria della Vittoria in Rome, went further: the architecture, with its clustered orders and 'broken' pediment, frames the focal point like a proscenium in which the ecstatic St Teresa and the angel are depicted with stunning realism.

Bernini, for all his theatricality, obtained his rich effects by simple means. The architecture of Borromini, his pupil, is by contrast complex and intense. It is typified by the church of San Carlo alle Quattro Fontane in Rome (1638 and later), which though similar in size and shape to Bernini's Sant' Andrea, and roofed with a similar elliptical dome, has a much more complex plan-form. Its main facade, too, is arranged along an undulating plane which gives a dramatic and restless effect.

By the time baroque architecture spread to the rest of Italy, building activity had considerably died down, but there is one major building in Venice by Baldassare Longhena, a contemporary of Bernini, which can stand comparison with those of Rome. This is the church of Santa Maria della Salute (1631), a fantastic, centrally planned building, octagonal on plan, with a high dome mounted on a drum supported by sixteen scrolled buttresses. A second, lower dome over the sanctuary, flanked by minaret-like towers, gives an almost oriental richness to the skyline. Two other northern architects of outstanding ability, who brought new inspiration to Italian architecture at a time when Rome's was beginning to decline, were Guarino Guarini (1624–83) and Filippo Juvarra (1678–1736). Guarini's two great church buildings, San Lorenzo in Turin (1668) and the chapel of the Holy Shroud in Turin cathedral (1667) are very complex spatially, built up out of overlapping ovoid or circular volumes and with domes constructed in complicated intersecting vaulting. Juvarra's work, by contrast, is simple and grand, typified by the Superga in Turin (1717), a church and convent on a hill-top site in which the contrasting treatment of the simple, repetitive convent building and the magnificent domed church at the front complement each other to great effect.

If some of the southern European towns were entering a period of slow decline, those in the north continued to grow, and ornate town halls in Antwerp (1561) – with its nearby guild houses – Cologne (1569), Ypres (1575) and Ghent (1595), picturesque in character and rich in classical detail, are indicative of expanding wealth.

By now, most towns had a considerable number of factories and workshops, but industry was not yet a predominantly urban activity. As long as wind or water power and adequate transport were available, many processes, including the all-important cloth-making, could be carried out in country-cottage workshops where the raw material was easy to obtain. The 17th-century industrialist was often a rural land-owner too. The richness of Jacobean country houses demonstrates that though England's income came immediately from the trade of the towns, it was dependent ultimately on the wealth and productivity of country estates. Hatfield House (1607)

Italian baroque 1
Bernini

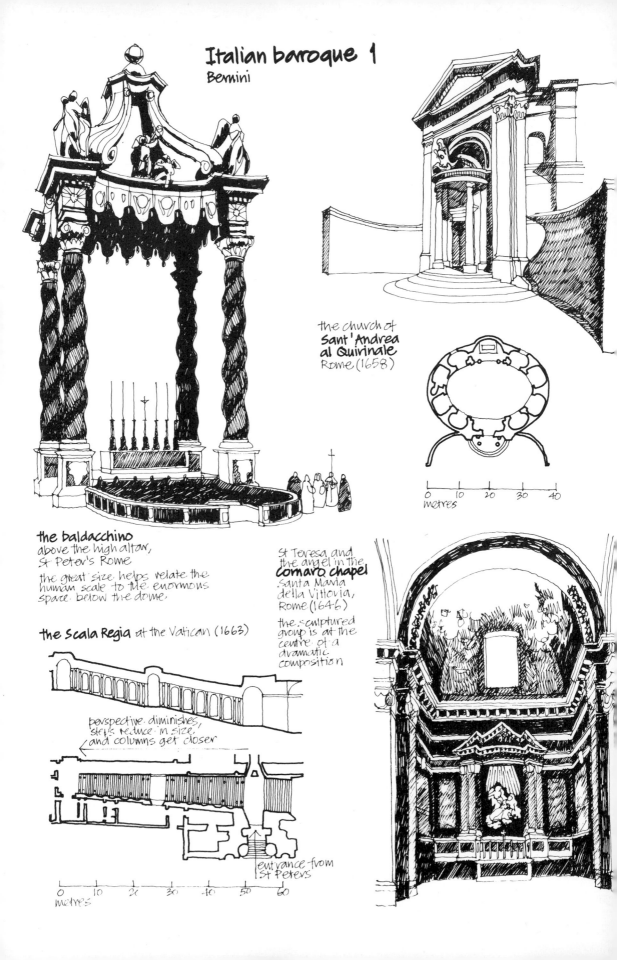

the church of
**Sant'Andrea
al Quirinale**
Rome (1658)

0   10   20   30   40
metres

the baldacchino
above the high altar,
St Peter's Rome

the great size helps relate the
human scale to the enormous
space below the dome.

the Scala Regia at the Vatican (1663)

perspective diminishes,
steps reduce in size,
and columns get closer

entrance from
St Peters

0   10   20   30   40   50   60
metres

St Teresa and
the angel in the
Cornaro chapel
Santa Maria
della Vittoria,
Rome (1646)

the sculptured
group is at the
centre of a
dramatic
composition

Italian baroque 2

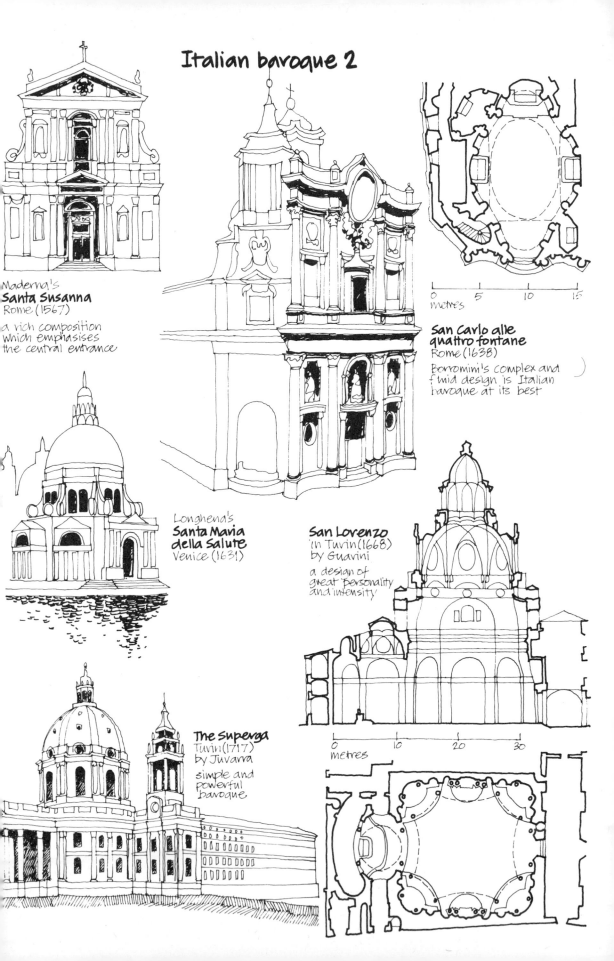

Maderna's
Santa Susanna
Rome (1567)

a rich composition
which emphasises
the central entrance

**San Carlo alle
quattro fontane**
Rome (1638)

Borromini's complex and
fluid design is Italian
baroque at its best

Longhena's
**Santa Maria
della Salute**
Venice (1631)

San Lorenzo
in Turin (1668)
by Guarini

a design of
great personality
and intensity

The Superga
Turin (1717)
by Juvarra

simple and
powerful
baroque.

0   5   10   15
metres

0   10   20   30
metres

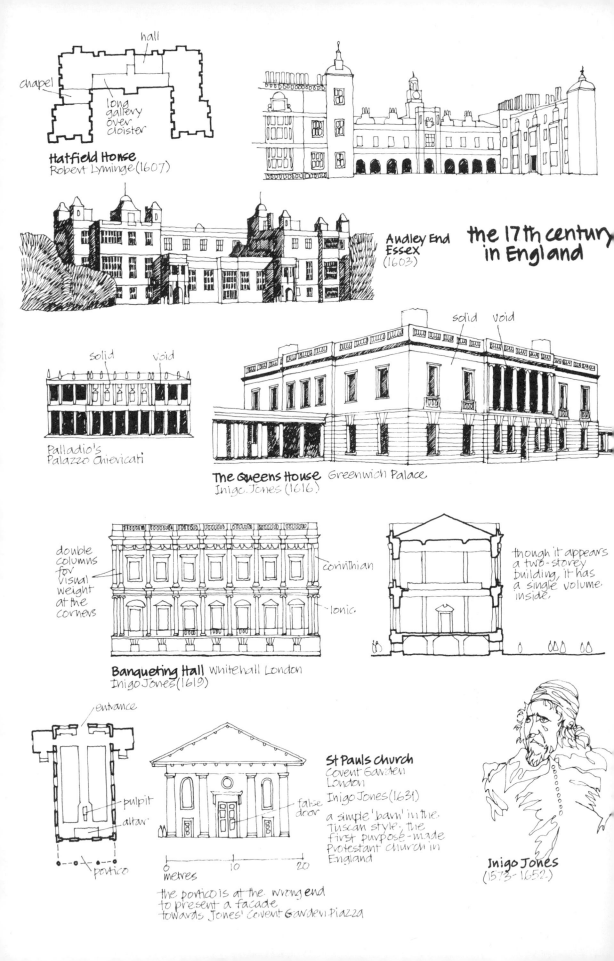

Hatfield House
Robert Lyminge (1607)

chapel

hall

long gallery over cloister

Audley End Essex (1603)

the 17th century in England

solid   void

Palladio's Palazzo Chievicati

solid   void

The Queens House Greenwich Palace
Inigo Jones (1616)

double columns for visual weight at the corners

corinthian

Ionic

Banqueting Hall Whitehall London
Inigo Jones (1619)

though it appears a two-storey building, it has a single volume inside.

entrance

pulpit

altar

portico

false door

0   10   20
metres

St Pauls church
Covent Garden
London
Inigo Jones (1631)
a simple 'barn' in the Tuscan style, the first purpose-made Protestant church in England

the portico is at the wrong end to present a facade towards Jones' Covent Garden Piazza

Inigo Jones
(1573-1652)

by Robert Lyminge for the Earl of Salisbury is among the finest, combining simplicity of conception with richness of detail. The fine craftsmanship of its brick and stone façades, its picturesque skylines and the ordered formality of its layout extending into the landscape around, have their counterparts at Knole (1605) and Audley End (1603).

The early 17th century was a dramatic turning-point for the English kings. The Tudors, though despotic, had preserved a relationship with parliament, but their Stuart successors were more ambitious. The words of James I (1603–25), 'a Deo rex, a rege lex' (the king comes from God, the law from the king), expressed his desire to rule absolutely and were echoed by other monarchs of the time. James's catholicism in a now-protestant state, his autocracy, his self-indulgence and nepotism were resented, but his successor Charles I (1625–49) went even further. He tried to levy personal taxes on his subjects and when parliament intervened he dissolved it, ruling autocratically, collecting taxes illegally, appointing the catholic William Laud as archbishop and jailing anyone who protested.

The career of the great Inigo Jones (1573–1652) almost exactly spanned the reigns of the first two Stuart kings. Ironically, the architectural expression he gave to this precarious monarchy was one of great serenity. His career began in earnest as a stage and costume designer for lavish royal entertainments and he soon progressed to the position of Surveyor of the King's Works, the most important architectural post in the country at the time. He brought to his work a consuming interest in classical architecture and design, which he had studied in Italy at first hand. Classical details had been copiously used in English buildings since Tudor times, but never as part of an integrated philosophy of design. This, however, was what Jones introduced, causing a minor artistic revolution.

For the first time, the English saw what had been seen in France since de l'Orme and in Italy since Brunelleschi: a style of architecture in which every element, and its relationship with every other element, was carefully considered. From the first it was Palladio, with his well-mannered blend of academicism and originality, who appealed most to the English, and Jones's first major English building demonstrated his debt. The elegant Queen's House at Greenwich (1616), built for the wife of James I, is a two-storey stone building with a double-height entrance hall. The lower storey is rusticated and the upper one plain stonework, finished with a cornice and stone balustrade. The south elevation makes more than a passing reference to the Palazzo Chiericati, echoing the proportion and the general mood and simply reversing Palladio's pattern of solid and void.

Jones's other important Italianate building was the Banqueting Hall at the royal palace of Whitehall in London (1619), the only completed part of an ambitious rebuilding project. The Hall stands on a rusticated stone base and has finely-proportioned two-tier elevations enclosing a single large volume inside. The elevations have superimposed Ionic and Corinthian orders, doubled at the corners for visual strength. The Banqueting Hall was built for the performance of court masques, but in 1649 it became the scene of a grimmer entertainment: Charles I, defeated in a civil war by Cromwell's army of parliamentarians, was publicly executed on the balcony. Jones, who never concealed his esteem for his king, was arrested as a collaborator by Cromwell's men and, though later released, survived Charles by only four years.

In central Europe the struggle for religious freedom and political power was even

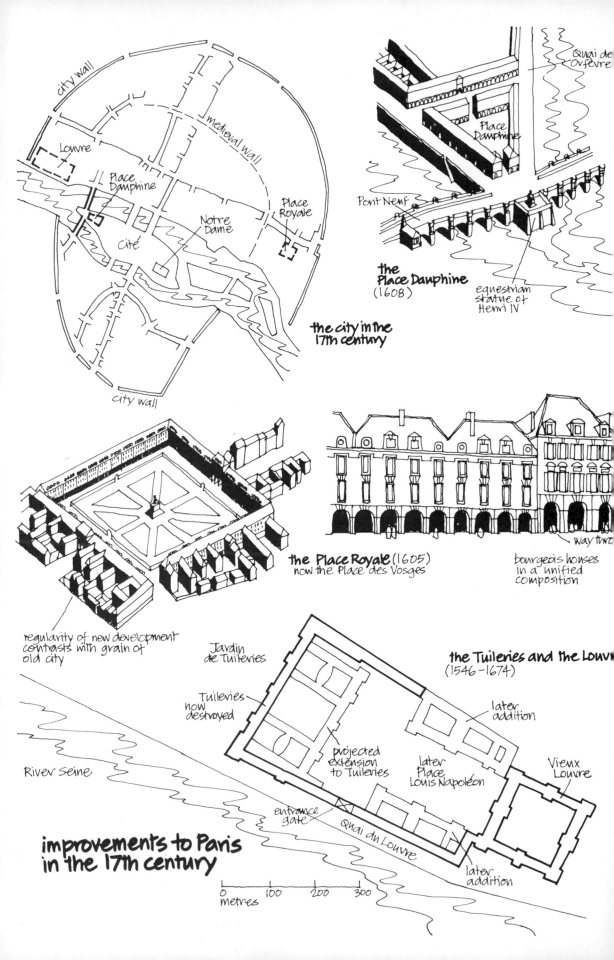

city wall

medieval wall

Louvre

Place Dauphine

Notre Dame

Cité

Place Royale

the city in the 17th century

city wall

Quai de Orfèvre

Place Dauphine

Pont Neuf

the Place Dauphine (1608)

equestrian statue of Henri IV

the Place Royale (1605) now the Place des Vosges

Way traz

bourgeois houses in a unified composition

regularity of new development contrasts with grain of old city

Jardin de Tuileries

Tuileries now destroyed

River Seine

entrance gate

Quai du Louvre

projected extension to Tuileries

the Tuileries and the Louvre (1546–1674)

later addition

later Place Louis Napoléon

Vieux Louvre

later addition

improvements to Paris in the 17th century

0   100   200   300
metres

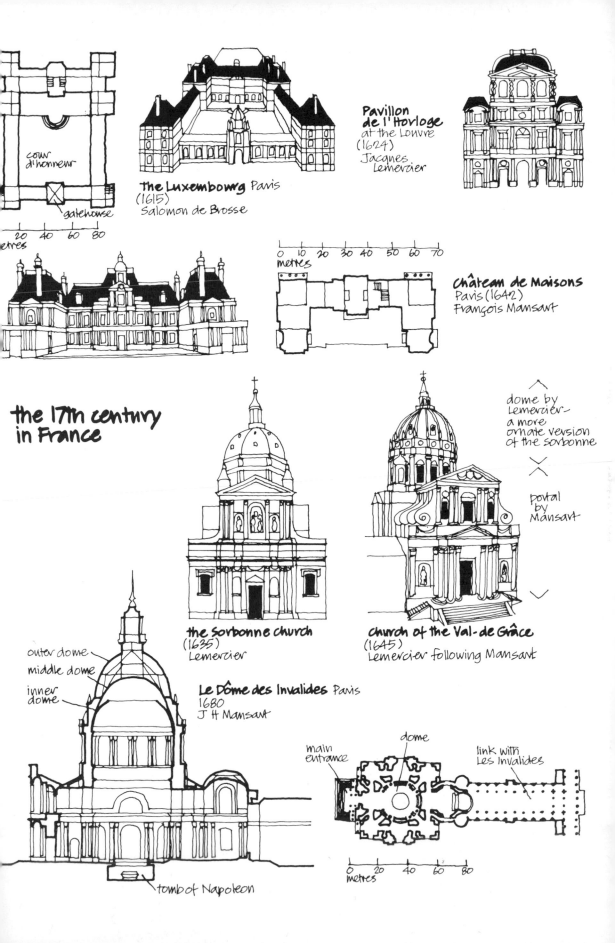

cour d'honneur

gatehouse

20 40 60 80
metres

the Luxembourg Paris
(1615)
Salomon de Brosse

Pavillon de l'Horloge
at the Louvre
(1624)
Jacques Lemercier

0 10 20 30 40 50 60 70
metres

château de Maisons
Paris (1642)
François Mansart

the 17th century in France

dome by Lemercier—
a more ornate version
of the sorbonne

portal by Mansart

the Sorbonne church
(1635)
Lemercier

church of the Val-de-Grâce
(1645)
Lemercier following Mansart

outer dome
middle dome
inner dome

Le Dôme des Invalides Paris
1680
J H Mansart

tomb of Napoleon

main entrance

dome

link with Les Invalides

0 20 40 60 80
metres

greater than in England. The Thirty Years' War began in Germany in 1618 with protestant demands for religious toleration. After involving Bohemia, France, Sweden, Denmark and Holland in what had become a struggle for the domination of Europe, it ended in 1648 with the Empire crushed and vast areas of land devastated and depopulated, but having at least ensured German protestantism. Protestantism in France was less assured. The new Bourbon monarchy, in the person of Henri IV (1589–1610) aided by his minister Sully, had issued the Edict of Nantes in a spirit of religious toleration which had united the country, increased royal revenues by reducing the extravagant palace-building of the Valois, and improved agriculture and foreign trade. But his successor Louis XIII (1610–43), guided by the formidable Cardinal Richelieu, had a less progressive attitude. He crushed opposition wherever he saw or suspected it, destroying the fortified châteaux of the nobles, subjecting both them and the bourgeoisie to rigorous control, and removing many of the rights of the Huguenots.

The reign of Henri IV had seen many royal public works and works of capitalist enterprise, including the improvement of Paris by civic-design schemes which brought an air of formality and bourgeois affluence to the medieval city. The Place Royale (1605) – now the Place des Vosges – is a square surrounded by the regular façades of *hôtels*, terraced houses built round courtyards with a colonnaded ground storey, two upper storeys and a steeply pitched roof with dormers. The Place Dauphine (1608), on the west end of the Ile de la Cité, is triangular, linked at one end to the Pont Neuf, centred on a formal statue of Henri IV.

As Louis and Richelieu gradually engineered a move back to catholicism and royal absolutism, investment was once again directed towards the building of churches and royal palaces. The Palais de Luxembourg in Paris (1615) was built by Salomon de Brosse for Henri's widow Marie de Médicis. A front *porte-cochère* gives access to a *cour d'honneur* around which the three-storey house is arranged. The treatment is bold and classically simple. Smaller, but more elegant and refined, is the Château de Maisons near Paris (1642), a symmetrical composition with a decorative central pavilion and side wings, designed by François Mansart (1598–1666). Mansart was the greatest French architect of the period. Though wilful and difficult in his dealings with others, a factor which cost him many aristocratic commissions, he created buildings which are models of restraint and clarity and did much to establish the grave and elegant French classical style of the 17th century. Maisons was designed for a wealthy merchant whose purse and patience were elastic enough to allow the building to be pulled down during construction to enable Mansart to revise the design. The result was his masterpiece and shows his ability to achieve rich effects without recourse to elaborate decoration. The Château de Richelieu (1631) by Lemercier was by contrast enormous, though nothing of it now remains; but the equally impressive Vaux-le-Vicomte (1657) by Louis Le Vau is still intact. It has no *cour d'honneur*; instead, the main rooms, including a big, elliptical salon, look out onto a vast formal garden designed by Le Nôtre.

The church of the Sorbonne in Paris (1635), designed for Richelieu by Lemercier, is formal and classical, with a simple two-tier elevation and an elegant, high, central dome. Richer in effect is the church of the Val-de-Grâce in Paris (1654) by Lemercier in succession to François Mansart. It is similar in outline to the Sorbonne church, but the supporting consoles round the drum of the dome and the scrolls on the entrance façade are part of a more vigorously decorative approach. Most impressive of all is the church of the Hôtel des Invalides (1680) designed by J. H. Mansart. It has a Greek-cross plan with a tall, central dome almost 30 metres across, built off a drum with external buttresses in the form of a colonnade of paired orders. To obtain the right appearance externally, Mansart made the external dome considerably higher than the one visible inside. The latter is in effect two domes: a lower one with a central opening through which a decorative upper one is seen.

Richelieu's efforts on behalf of Louis XIII were continued for his successor Louis XIV (1643–1715) by Mazarin and Colbert. They built up the royal treasury through monetary reforms, and during his long reign of seventy-two years Louis reached a position of unprecedented power. 'L'état, c'est moi', he said, and it was no idle boast: parliament was not called into session once during his reign, and political life centred entirely on his court. He took charge of the collection and spending of all taxes, making of laws, dispensing of justice and waging of war. The colonies expanded, culture was encouraged, and French manners – as reflected in the plays of Corneille, Molière and Racine, the music of Lully and Rameau, and the painting of Poussin – were copied by all Europe's high society.

Louis rejected Paris as his capital; instead he built a new one at Versailles, some miles out of the city, housing all the functions of government and his entire court in a single vast building where he could keep his eye on them. The Palace of Versailles is perhaps the most spectacular monument to absolute kingship ever seen in Europe. Built mainly between 1661 and 1756 by Le Vau and J. H. Mansart, it has a front *cour d'honneur* enclosed on three sides by the building. Stretching away on both sides are wings which together add up to a garden façade some 400 metres in length, treated repetitively with an order of giant pilasters on the main storey. The 70-metre-long Galérie des Glaces, designed by Mansart and panelled with mirrors, is the main feature of the luxurious interior, but finest of all are the vast formal gardens of Le Nôtre (1613–1700) which influence the environment for miles around.

The intention was to provide recreation for the palace's hundreds of inhabitants and guests. Close to the building, the woods were cleared to form a wide axial vista in which formal pathways and terraces, decorated with statuary and pools, were set between *parterres*, low ornamental shrub-beds laid out in geometric patterns. At the end a wide canal led apparently endlessly into the distance and on either side formal avenues for riding and driving cut their way into the forests, leading to artificial grottoes and temples, open-air theatres and small lakes, to surprise and delight the jaded aristocratic eye. Other avenues radiated out into the surrounding landscape or, from the front of the palace, into the town, symbolically extending the king's domain to the horizon.

The 'grand manner' of Le Nôtre influenced not only garden design but also city planning. From the 17th century onward, the artistic and philosophical ideas which accompanied the rebuilding of many European city centres, or the founding of new ones in colonies overseas, were to find expression through his architectural vocabulary: the straight avenue forming a vista, the radial or grid layout of routes and the *rond-point* or square where the routes met.

In 1685, Louis revoked the Edict of Nantes and established catholicism as the supreme religion. Many Huguenots left France, taking with them their skills as craftsmen and entrepreneurs. The economy was further weakened by Louis's extravagances at home and his costly and disastrous military exploits abroad, and taxes were steadily increased. The magnificence of his reign, of which Versailles is

133

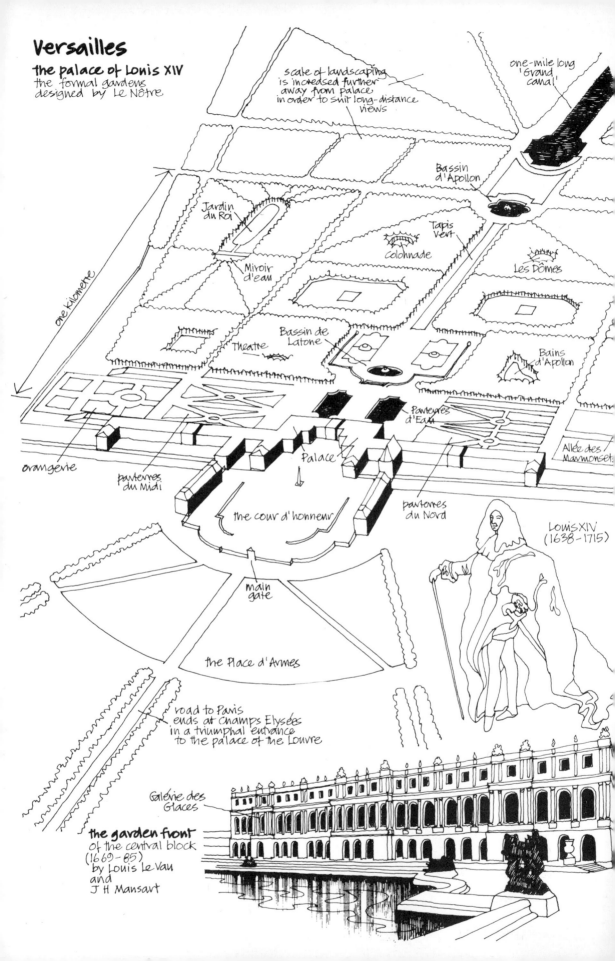

Versailles
the palace of Louis XIV
the formal gardens
designed by Le Nôtre

scale of landscaping
is increased further
away from palace
in order to suit long-distance
views

one-mile long
'Grand canal'

Bassin d'Apollon

Jardin du Roi

Tapis Vert

Colonnade

Les Dômes

one kilometre

Miroir d'eau

Theatre

Bassin de Latone

Bains d'Apollon

Parterres d'Eau

Allée des Marmousets

orangerie

parterres du Midi

Palace

parterres du Nord

the cour d'honneur

Louis XIV (1638 - 1715)

main gate

the Place d'Armes

road to Paris
ends at Champs Elysées
in a triumphal entrance
to the palace of the Louvre

Galérie des Glaces

the garden front
of the central block
(1669 - 85)
by Louis Le Vau
and
J H Mansart

the ultimate expression, eventually resulted in France's decline as a world power and in the growing discontent of the middle classes.

The aftermath of the Thirty Years' War brought renewed confidence to northern and eastern Europe. In some areas, notably the Low Countries and north Germany, protestantism was firmly established. Holland, having thrown off Spanish domination, was prospering, and Amsterdam and The Hague were overtaking Antwerp as the main outlets for north European trade. The royal household and the merchants were the main patrons and Jacob van Campen their architect. His Mauritshuis in The Hague (1633) for Prince Maurice of Nassau is a rich and well-proportioned adaptation of the Palladian style to Dutch tastes, and his Town Hall in Amsterdam (1648), later the royal palace, is a large stone building, also Palladian in content, with the four main storeys divided into pairs and treated with giant pilasters. A large cupola over the central, pedimented portico is an indigenous feature. His New Church at Haarlem (1645) with its centralised plan and prominently located pulpit represents a search for a form for protestant worship. Among the finest buildings in 17th-century Belgium were the Guild Houses of the Grand' Place, Brussels (1691 and later), magnificently ornate with classical detail, and with a picturesque skyline reminiscent of earlier ones in Antwerp.

The Thirty Years' War left the Empire powerless and Germany in a confusion of small states, each with cultural and religious autonomy. Catholicism remained prominent in Bavaria, Austria and Bohemia, and strong architectural influences came from Italy and France. These would reach fruition in the fantastic late-baroque churches of the 18th century, but in the 17th a more sober style prevailed. The Theatine church in Munich (1663), by Barelli and Zuccali, is Italian baroque in conception, with two west towers added to a façade not unlike Vignola's Gesú. The Troja Palace in Prague (1679), by the Frenchman J.-B. Mathey, is Bohemian baroque at its finest, a well-ordered design held together by the use of giant pilasters.

In Russia, the unchallenged power of the monarchy was reaching a peak. The firm foundation given to it by Ivan III and Ivan the Terrible in the 16th century was built on by Peter the Great in the 17th. His policy of opening 'windows to the west' was based on a view of western Europe, in particular France, as a model for progress. During his reign (1682–1725) he opened the ice-free ports of the Baltic to western trade, brought the Greek Orthodox church in Russia under Russian control, built schools and hospitals, developed printing and introduced western-style clothing to his medieval Tsardom. He also built a new capital, Petersburg, and employed western architects to design its buildings in a grand, western style. The first was Domenico Tressini who was responsible for the Peter-and-Paul fortress and for the cathedral, both on the island in the Neva where the new city began.

In England, absolute monarchy had died with Charles I. The Civil War had been more than a religious conflict: it was essentially a struggle for power between the puritan bourgeoisie on the one hand and the king and aristocracy on the other. The old feudal powers undoubtedly lost, but as yet the bourgeoisie had not completely triumphed: Oliver Cromwell had dissolved parliament in 1653 and ruled as a religious and military dictator. Bourgeois democracy was thus still denied, though trade, industry and Britain's sea-power were on the ascendant, and building activity continued unabated.

On Cromwell's death, parliament returned and reinstated the catholic Stuart kings. Charles II (1660–85) tried to strip the puritan ministers of their power, but

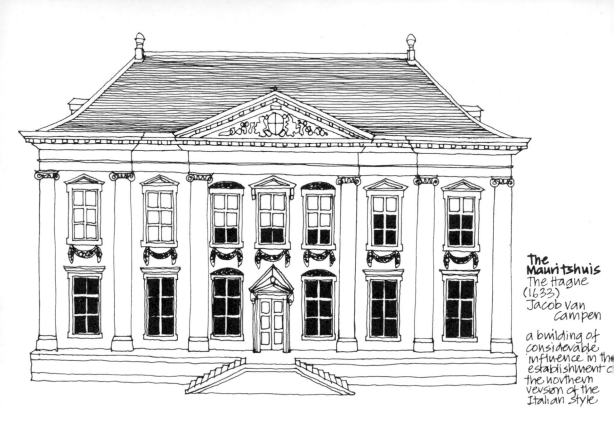

The Mauritshuis
The Hague
(1633)
Jacob van Campen

a building of considerable influence in the establishment of the northern version of the Italian style

the New Church
Haarlem (1645)
by van Campen

a Greek-cross-in-a-square plan which set a trend for Protestant churches

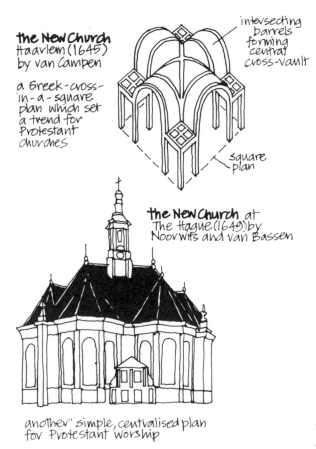

intersecting barrels forming central cross-vault

square plan

the New Church at The Hague (1649) by Noorwits and van Bassen

another simple, centralised plan for Protestant worship

Guild Houses at Grand' Place, Brussels (1690)

similar in character to late Gothic examples like these in Antwerp (1561)

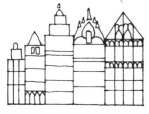

the 17th century in the Low Countries

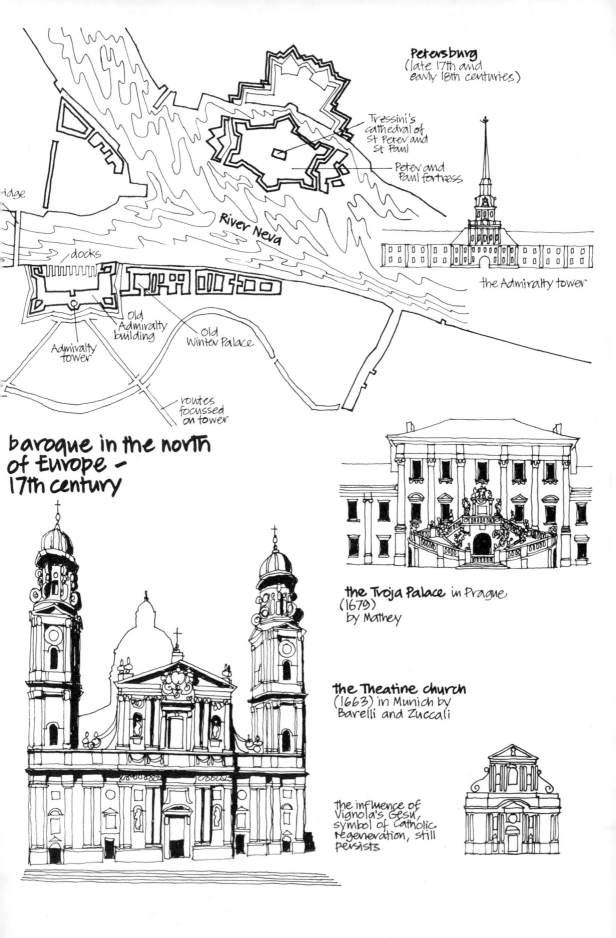

Petersburg
(late 17th and
early 18th centuries)

Tressini's
cathedral of
St Peter and
St Paul

Peter and
Paul fortress

...idge

River Neva

the Admiralty tower

docks

Old
Admiralty
building

Old
Winter Palace

Admiralty
tower

routes
focussed
on tower

baroque in the north
of Europe –
17th century

the **Troja Palace** in Prague
(1679)
by Mathey

the **Theatine church**
(1663) in Munich by
Barelli and Zuccali

the influence of
Vignola's Gesù,
symbol of Catholic
regeneration, still
persists

parliament countered by limiting his own, through the Habeas Corpus Act (1679). James II's short reign (1685–8), marked by continuous struggles with parliament, ended prematurely when William and Mary of the protestant House of Orange were invited to the throne in 1688, on parliament's terms: supremacy of parliament over the king and an assured future for protestantism. A bourgeois 'English Revolution' had taken place, just as a French one would a century later. One side-effect of protestantism was its indirect encouragement of scientific research: faith in the written word had greatly encouraged the spread of literacy, and with it the universal spread of ideas, including scientific ones. Science at that time consisted of observing the natural world and recording and classifying it; using the methodology developed by Descartes and Bacon, scientists were now able to construct theories based on observable fact. Galileo, Kepler and above all Newton were able to extend dramatically man's view of himself in relation to his world. In the years to come, science would vastly increase man's technological powers, but in the 17th century science and technology were only just beginning to come together, presided over by the Royal Society, founded in 1645 by a group of wealthy dilettanti insatiable for knowledge on every subject from language to astronomy. Bacon, Boyle and Newton were members, and so was Christopher Wren (1632–1723).

By education this greatest of English architects was not an architect at all, but a classicist, mathematician and astronomer. Early in his career he wrote that 'mathematical Demonstrations being built upon the impregnable foundations of Geometry and Arithmetick, are the only Truths, that can sink into the mind of man, void of all uncertainty', and he brought this precision to the solving of structural and spatial problems. Coming from a family of royalist sympathisers, he did not progress till after the restoration of Charles II. The brilliance of his mind, his uncommon ability to solve practical problems – such as his ingenious roof for the Sheldonian Theatre in Oxford – and a shared interest in astronomy, soon attracted the attention of the king. In 1666 a disastrous fire swept through the City of London destroying the old gothic cathedral of St Paul, scores of parish churches and hundreds of homes, and Wren was put in charge of the reconstruction.

He had visited France the previous year, where he had met François Mansart and the ageing Bernini – then sixty-seven – who was there on a commission, and seen Maisons, Versailles and the Louvre, and the churches of the Sorbonne and Val-de-Grâce. His education as an architect was founded on this short visit, on the authors he had read – Vitruvius, Alberti, Serlio and Palladio among them – and on such classical buildings as Jones and his pupils had already built in England. His plan for the city, a 'grand manner' exercise of radial routes and *ronds-points*, would have transformed it, but cost, expediency and indecision prevented it from being carried out. St Paul's and the city churches, however, are among the finest achievements of English architecture.

Fifty city churches were rebuilt between 1670 and the mid-1680s. All were different and all show the ingenuity with which Wren solved the problems of designing for cramped urban sites. He was breaking new ground, for designing a protestant parish church was almost unprecedented: the only existing examples known to Wren were one by Jones in Covent Garden and one in Charenton by de Brosse. Wren's approach was to design a church as capacious as possible in which everyone could see the pulpit and hear what was said from it. Generally, this suggested a square rather than longitudinal plan and often two tiers of seating. The

Christopher Wren

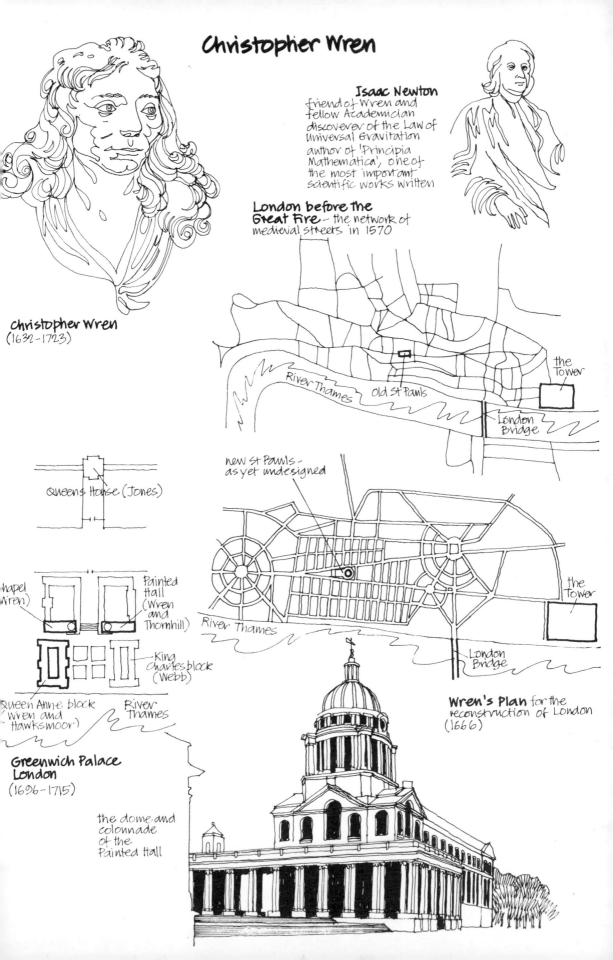

Christopher Wren
(1632-1723)

Isaac Newton
friend of Wren and
fellow Academician
discoverer of the Law of
Universal Gravitation
author of 'Principia
Mathematica', one of
the most important
scientific works written

**London before the
Great Fire** - the network of
medieval streets in 1570

River Thames

Old St Pauls

the Tower

London Bridge

Queens House (Jones)

Chapel
(Wren)

Painted
Hall
(Wren
and
Thornhill)

King
Charles block
(Webb)

Queen Anne block
(Wren and
Hawksmoor)

River
Thames

**Greenwich Palace
London**
(1696-1715)

the dome and
colonnade
of the
Painted Hall

new St Pauls -
as yet undesigned

River Thames

the
Tower

London
Bridge

Wren's Plan for the
reconstruction of London
(1666)

Wren's City churches
the plan form

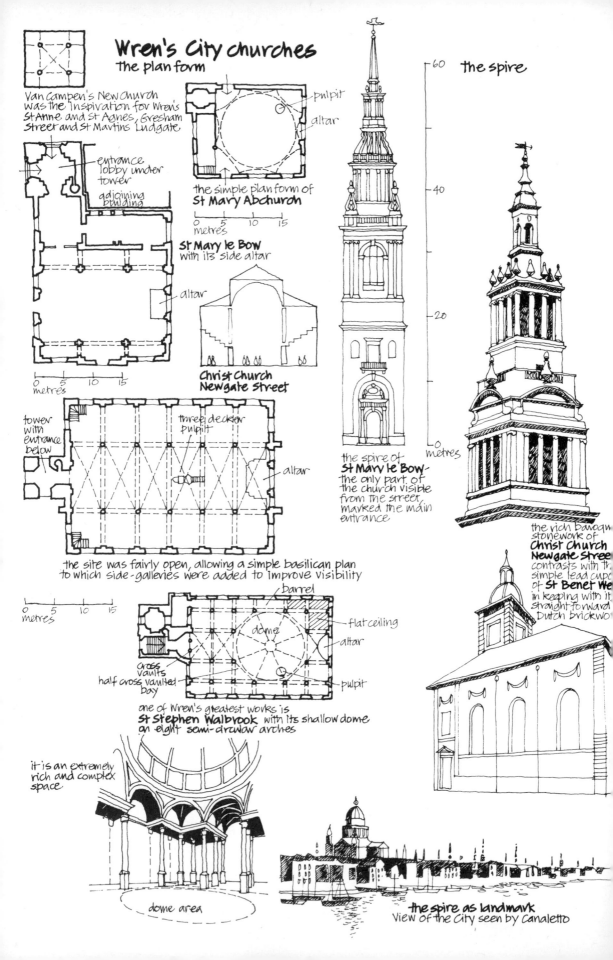

Van Campen's New Church was the inspiration for Wren's St Anne and St Agnes, Gresham Street and St Martins Ludgate.

entrance lobby under tower

adjoining building

altar

0 5 10 15
metres

the simple plan form of **St Mary Abchurch**

0 5 10 15
metres

pulpit
altar

St Mary le Bow with its side altar

altar

Christ Church Newgate Street

tower with entrance below

three decker pulpit

altar

the site was fairly open, allowing a simple basilican plan to which side-galleries were added to improve visibility

0 5 10 15
metres

barrel

dome

flat ceiling

altar

cross vaults

half cross vaulted bay

pulpit

one of Wren's greatest works is **St Stephen Walbrook** with its shallow dome an eight semi-circular arches

it is an extremely rich and complex space

dome area

the spire

60

40

20

0
metres

the spire of **St Mary le Bow** — the only part of the church visible from the street marked the main entrance

the rich baroque stonework of **Christ Church Newgate Street** contrasts with the simple lead cupola of **St Benet We** in keeping with it straight forward Dutch brickwo

the spire as landmark View of the City seen by Canaletto

St Paul's Cathedral
London (1675-1710)

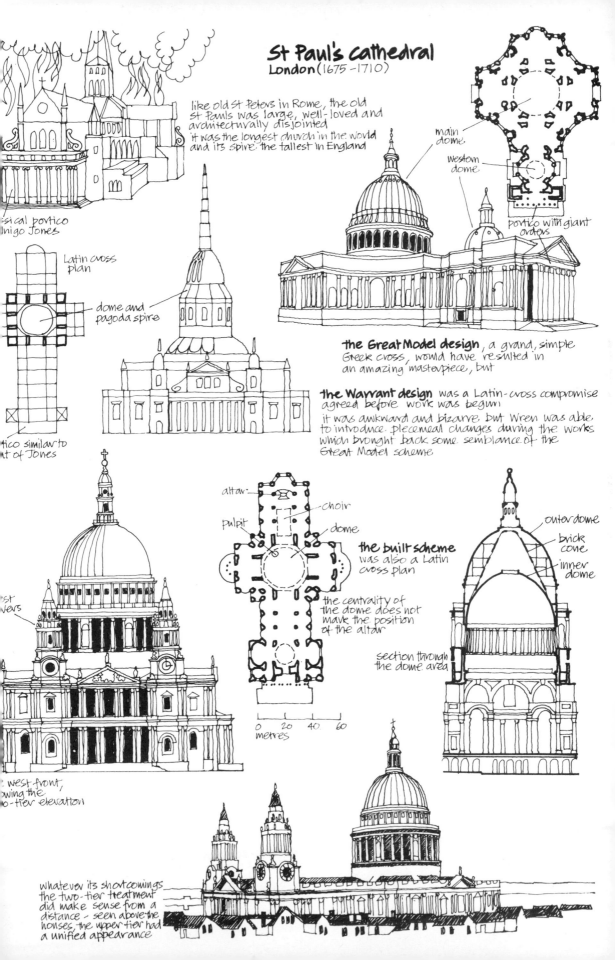

like old St Peters in Rome, the old
St Pauls was large, well-loved and
architecturally disjointed
it was the longest church in the world
and its spire the tallest in England

main dome

western dome

portico with giant orders

...ssical portico
...nigo Jones

Latin cross plan

dome and pagoda spire

...tico similar to
...t of Jones

the Great Model design, a grand, simple
Greek cross, would have resulted in
an amazing masterpiece, but

the Warrant design was a Latin-cross compromise
agreed before work was begun

it was awkward and bizarre, but Wren was able
to introduce piecemeal changes during the works
which brought back some semblance of the
Great Model scheme

altar

choir

pulpit

dome

the built scheme
was also a Latin
cross plan

the centrality of
the dome does not
mark the position
of the altar

0 20 40 60
metres

outer dome

brick cone

inner dome

section through
the dome area

...st
...ers

... west front,
...wing the
...o-tier elevation

whatever its shortcomings
the two-tier treatment
did make sense from a
distance - seen above the
houses, the upper tier had
a unified appearance

pulpit was tall and prominent and, as the Word held sway over the Mass, the altar was located out of the way against a side or end wall.

In the densely built-up city, church towers helped to identify the building from a distance. Wren's designs for them were boundless in their imagination and ranged from simple lead-covered cupolas to elaborate stone spires. The steeple of St Mary-le-Bow, almost 70 metres high, is among the finest, as are those of Christchurch and St Stephen, Walbrook. The plan-form of St Mary-le-Bow is a good example of ingenuity on a restricted site, and Christchurch shows the assurance with which Wren adapted a basilican plan to accommodate a gallery. The interior treatments ranged from the whitewash and panelling of St Benet Welsh to the rich plasterwork and wood-carving of St Clement Danes. Among the simplest plan-forms was that of St Mary Abchurch, a dome over a square room, and the richest spatially was St Stephen, Walbrook, with a coffered dome rising off eight semi-circular arches.

Stimulated by the domed churches he had seen in France, Wren had long been pre-occupied by the idea of a dome on eight arches for St Paul's. In 1673, after many abortive sketches and models, he produced the design from which the 6-metre-long 'Great Model' was made, a magnificent Greek-cross plan with a lengthened western arm and a central dome only slightly smaller than that of St Peter's. Regrettably, the establishment found it too revolutionary and demanded a Latin-cross plan. The result (1675–1710), though one of England's finest buildings, is a compromise.

The interior is grave and elegant, flooded with clear light through the plain glass windows which Wren preferred. At the centre of gravity is the dome though, unlike St Peter's, the altar is placed farther east, in the chancel. The dome, on its eight huge piers, is as wide as nave and aisles together – a reference perhaps to the octagon at Ely, which Wren knew well. Internally, the dome is a hemisphere and above it is a structural brick cone supporting the cupola. The outer dome, framed in timber and sheathed in lead, is raised high on a colonnaded drum, at the base of which an iron chain prevents spreading.

The external silhouette of the dome is calm, classical and very beautiful, but the lower parts of the façade are less inspired. A two-tier elevation runs all round the upper tier, with blank windows, acting as a screen wall to conceal the flying buttresses which the gothic plan-form made necessary. Wren abandoned his west portico of giant orders in favour of the weaker-looking design built, but the two west towers are among his finest inspirations, rich, baroque and very un-English.

As the king's architect, Wren was called upon to fulfil many large-scale commissions during his long life, and his output was enormous. His last great work (1696–1715) was his improvement of Greenwich Palace, bringing together a number of disparate elements by other architects into a unified, sober and beautifully ordered design. Wren is important not only for his buildings but also for the way in which he looked at architectural problems. The designer of St Paul's had far fewer resources at his disposal than had those who built St Peter's, but his flexible, scientific way of thinking enabled him to find solutions much more quickly. Since Galileo's death in 1642 the science of statics had been developing, and Wren's knowledge, together with his great mathematical ability, probably enabled him to predict with more certainty the stresses in his structures than any architect hitherto. Science and technology were coming together and were to cause great changes in society. At the forefront of these changes would be the men most ready to grasp what a science-based technology had to offer.

The dual revolution

The 18th century

'Descartes', the writer Boileau said, 'has cut the throat of poetry', and there is no doubt that during the period in which Cartesian thought dominated Europe, the late 17th and early 18th centuries, a marked intellectual change was taking place. Politics were now less dominated by religion and as a result public life was becoming less idealistic, less dogmatic and much more pragmatic, encouraging compromise in all things including, to Boileau's evident disgust, artistic expression. In 18th-century architecture, manifestations of the baroque spirit lay tangential to the general direction of development.

Society was in a kind of equilibrium, dominated by bureaucrats and professionals. Europe's energies were now being channelled elsewhere: by the mid-17th century exploration had almost ceased and the exploitation of the new colonies, their minerals, crops, animals and people, had begun in earnest. The products of plantations and mines in central America, of herding in America, Australia and South Africa and of trapping in Canada and Asia flowed into northern Europe.

Colonial societies, though similar in some ways to those of Europe, differed in an important respect: shortage of labour inevitably made them rigid and authoritarian. Some, like the West Indies, depended on slavery; others, like New England, became harshly egalitarian. Sometimes, as in Spanish America, the culture of the mother country was firmly imposed from above: rigid control by church and bureaucracy kept the Indians in cultural sterility until the end of the 18th century, when an indigenous middle class began to challenge the old Spanish aristocracy. In north America, by contrast, things were more complicated. There were no cultural achievements to rival those of the strong Spanish-American upper class in central America – as late as 1800, Mexico City was still the finest city in the whole continent – but there was an inbuilt strength in the society which came from its diversity: close-knit puritan groups in the New England states, a European merchant class which dominated the eastern seaports, and a freer, frontier society farther west. Political liberty, freedom of thought in general – including religious belief – and the freedom to move up the social ladder existed here in a way only dreamed of in Europe.

Mexico City cathedral, completed in the mid-17th century, is a very grand building in the tradition of Seville and Valladolid, covering some 60 metres by 120. Its west front, with twin towers and central portico, is very like Valladolid in design. In general, the detail treatment is classical and restrained, in marked contrast to many Spanish-American churches in which plateresque decoration found its way home again. Among these is the pilgrimage shrine at Ocotlán in Mexico, of the early 18th century, a confection of white stucco and ceramic tiles by the native-born sculptor Francisco Miguel.

North American architecture was much more restrained, not only because the society was largely puritan but also because the contemporary north-European architecture from which it derived was itself entering a period of rational under-

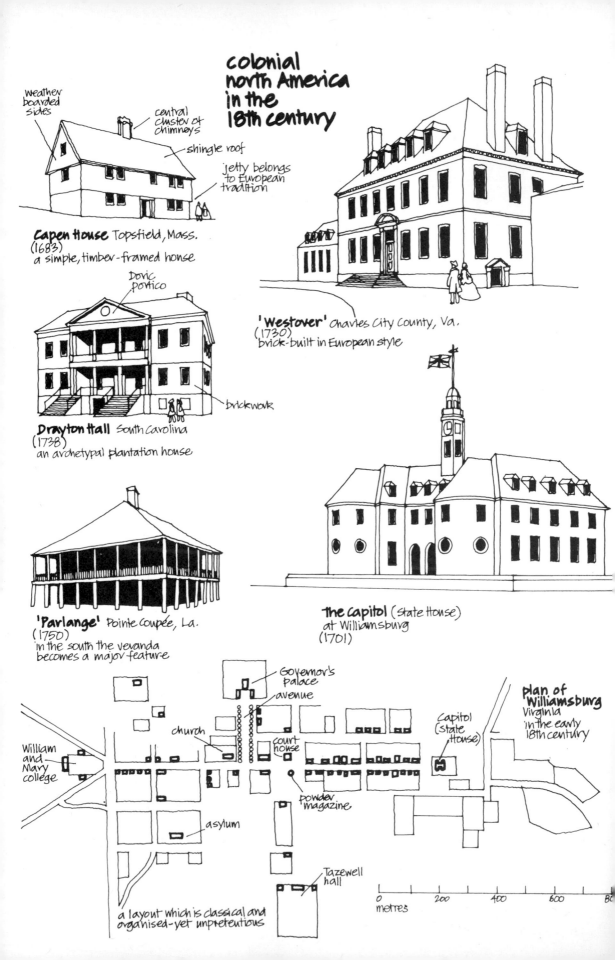

colonial north America in the 18th century

weather boarded sides

central cluster of chimneys

shingle roof

jetty belongs to European tradition

Capen House Topsfield, Mass.
(1683)
a simple, timber-framed house

Doric portico

brickwork

Drayton Hall South Carolina
(1738)
an archetypal plantation house

'Westover' Charles City County, Va.
(1730)
brick-built in European style

'Parlange' Pointe Coupée, La.
(1750)
in the south the veranda becomes a major feature

the Capitol (State House)
at Williamsburg
(1701)

Governor's Palace

avenue

church

court house

plan of Williamsburg
Virginia
in the early 18th century

Capitol (State House)

William and Mary college

powder magazine

asylum

Tazewell hall

a layout which is classical and organised—yet unpretentious

0   200   400   600   8[0]
metres

statement. In the north-eastern states, the pattern was late 17th-century English or Dutch architecture, though often translated into timber forms. Capen House, Topsfield, Mass. (1683) is representative of many such timber-framed, weather-boarded and shingle-clad small houses. Larger houses might be built in brick and one of the best examples is Westover in Charles City County, Va. (1730), a fine formal building with two storeys and a hipped roof with dormers, equal in both design and craftsmanship to the English Georgian houses it resembles. Farther south, the north-European style had to be adapted to the sub-tropical climate. Drayton Hall in South Carolina (1738) is basically English Georgian but with the addition of a double-height portico for use as a veranda in hot weather. Farther south still, the veranda became the main feature of the house: in Parlange at Pointe Coupée, La. (1750) a two-storey open gallery runs all round the house giving access and direct ventilation to the rooms.

Many of the most original ideas in colonial architecture are demonstrated in its public buildings. Protestant churches tended to derive from those of Wren and his successors, but often, like St Michael's Church, Charleston, sc (1752), they are imaginative re-workings of Wren's vocabulary in terms of timber rather than stone. Williamsburg, Va., a colonial town now preserved largely intact as a living museum, has several fine examples, including William and Mary College (1695) consisting of a central pavilion with two side wings, the Governor's Palace (1706), and the fine Capitol building (1701), H-shaped on plan with a slim central clock-tower. Finest of all, however, was State House, Philadelphia (1731), a dignified civic complex in brickwork with stone dressings with a central pavilion surmounted by a magnificent original clock tower and open cupola.

As the Indians were gradually pacified and the French in Canada defeated (1756–63), the presence in the north American colonies of English troops became a burden and the taxes paid to London anomalous. Attempts by the ruling Tory party in Westminster to assert English authority met with increasing resentment, and progressive thinkers on both sides of the Atlantic began the first truly international revolutionary movement; the middle classes of the world were uniting to put an end to the old aristocratic regime.

The *ancien régime* seemed nowhere stronger than in France where Louis XIV's court exercised its apparent domination of Europe. Culturally at least Europe had not been so unified since the 13th century. A state of political equilibrium had been reached: it was as if the old regime, determined not to lose its constitutional power, had had to find a workable formula in order to retain the *status quo*. Even the Bourbons, most absolute of kings, depended for support on a number of monolithic institutions, governed by bureaucratic procedures, which served to stabilise society and stave off the revolution which England had already undergone. In art, a kind of unadventurous classicism reflected this era of pragmatism, typified perhaps by the Petit Trianon at Versailles, a small detached house built in the gardens in 1762 by the architect Gabriel for Louis XV. It is a classical three-storey block built in honey-coloured stone, restrained in detail, sedate in mood and beautifully executed. Slightly richer in detail but equally restrained in character is a contemporary civic design scheme for the centre of the town of Nancy. By the architects Boffrand and de Corny, it was completed in 1757 and consists of three linked squares of different sizes and shapes flanked by public buildings of simple design.

Typical of the late 17th and early 18th century in France was the rich bourgeois

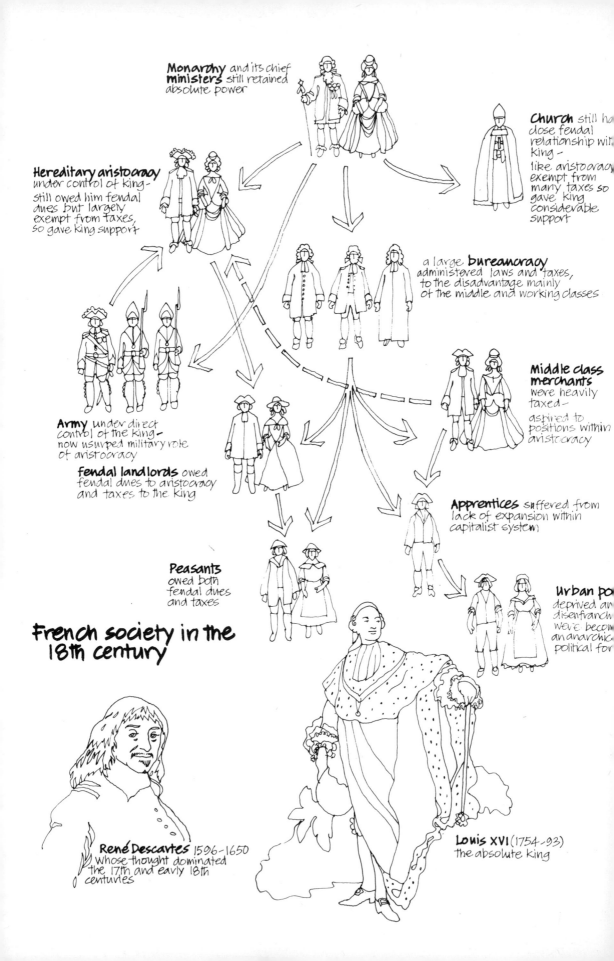

Monarchy and its chief **ministers** still retained absolute power

Church still ha[s] close feudal relationship wit[h] king — like aristocracy exempt from many taxes so gave king considerable support

Hereditary aristocracy under control of king — still owed him feudal dues but largely exempt from taxes, so gave king support

a large **bureaucracy** administered laws and taxes, to the disadvantage mainly of the middle and working classes

Middle class merchants were heavily taxed — aspired to positions within aristocracy

Army under direct control of the king — now usurped military role of aristocracy

feudal landlords owed feudal dues to aristocracy and taxes to the king

Apprentices suffered from lack of expansion within capitalist system

Peasants owed both feudal dues and taxes

Urban po[or] deprived an[d] disenfranch[ised] were becom[ing] an anarchic political for[ce]

French society in the 18th century

René Descartes 1596-1650 whose thought dominated the 17th and early 18th centuries

Louis XVI (1754-93) the absolute king

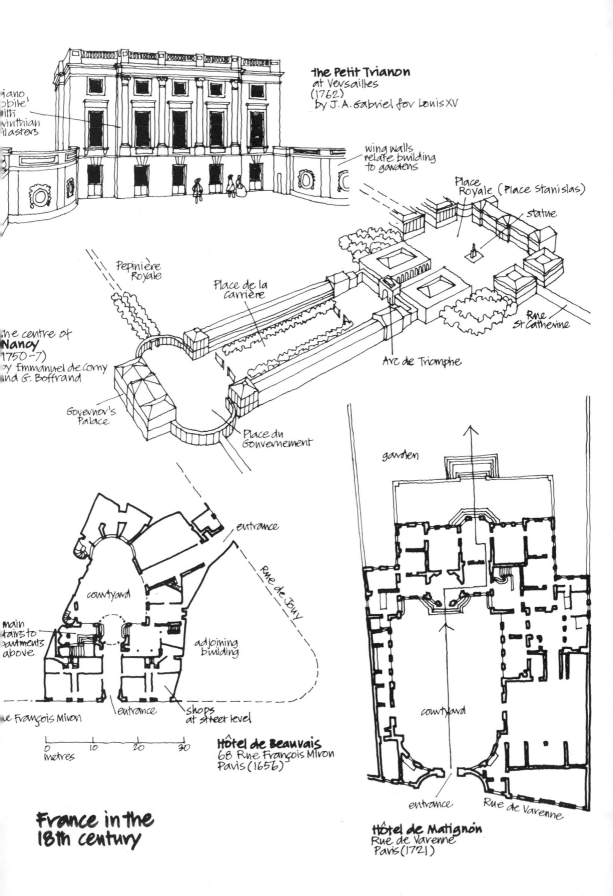

the Petit Trianon
at Versailles
(1762)
by J. A. Gabriel for Louis XV

'piano
nobile'
with
Corinthian
pilasters

wing walls
relate building
to gardens

Place
Royale (Place Stanislas)

statue

Pepinière
Royale

Place de la
Carrière

the centre of
Nancy
(1750-7)
by Emmanuel de Corny
and G. Boffrand

Rue
St Catherine

Arc de Triomphe

Governor's
Palace

Place du
Gouvernement

entrance

Rue de Jouy

courtyard

garden

main
stairs to
apartments
above

adjoining
building

Rue François Miron

entrance

shops
at street level

0   10   20   30
metres

Hôtel de Beauvais
68 Rue François Miron
Paris (1656)

courtyard

entrance

Rue de Varenne

**France in the
18th century**

Hôtel de Matignon
Rue de Varenne
Paris (1721)

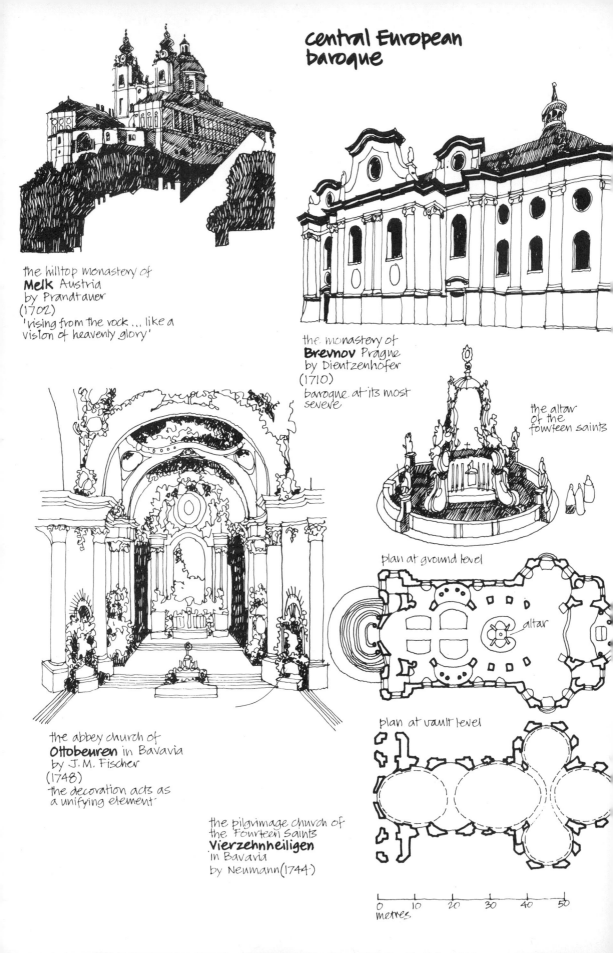

central European baroque

the hilltop monastery of
Melk Austria
by Prandtauer
(1702)
'rising from the rock ... like a
vision of heavenly glory'

the monastery of
Brevnov Prague
by Dientzenhofer
(1710)
baroque at its most
severe

the altar
of the
fourteen saints

plan at ground level

altar

the abbey church of
Ottobeuren in Bavaria
by J. M. Fischer
(1748)
the decoration acts as
a unifying element·

plan at vault level

the pilgrimage church of
the fourteen saints
Vierzehnheiligen
in Bavaria
by Neumann (1744·)

0   10   20   30   40   50
metres

town-house or *hôtel*. Often built on restricted sites in densely built-up areas, they have an ingenuity of planning which was not necessary in contemporary English houses. In the Hôtel de Beauvais, Paris (1656), a central entrance flanked by shop units leads to a rear courtyard, a development of the grander *cour d'honneur* of earlier days, around which the main residence is tightly packed. A later and larger version, the Hôtel de Matignon, Paris (1721), has space for a rear garden as well as a front court. The awkwardness of the site places the garden front on a different axis to the front entrance, but the change of direction is managed neatly in the internal planning.

House interiors of the period were often decorated with the spiky ornamentation known as *rocaille*, from which comes the word 'rococo'. Gilded plasterwork in abstract, asymmetrical scrolls and swags, built-in mirrors and delicately-painted walls and ceilings were combined to create an impression of elegance and lightness. Boffrand's interiors for the Hôtel de Soubise in Paris (1706) and Verberckt's decorations in Louis XV's apartments at Versailles (1753) were typically rococo; the bold drama of the baroque style had been transmuted into something politer and more restrained.

In the electorates and dukedoms of Germany, French manners were followed at court, but other influences were exerted on the architecture. Particularly in the south, where contact with Italy was greater, the 18th century saw an outburst of late-baroque building which had more in common with Guarini than with Gabriel. The hill-top monastery of Melk (1702) by Jacob Prandtauer is a richly-designed domed and twin-towered building of almost Spanish character, and Brevnov monastery in Prague (1710) by Christoph Dientzenhofer is a strong, curvilinear building of distinctive baroque character despite its spareness of decoration. Contemporary churches in Bavaria show less restraint. Still recognisably baroque, with their curvilinear forms and interpenetrating spaces, they are lavishly decorated with rococo ornament and painted designs in an almost overwhelming profusion. St Paulin in Trier (1732) by Balthasar Neumann, and St Johann-Nepomuk in Munich (1733) by the brothers Asam, are highly decorative but spatially fairly simple. However, in the abbey church of Ottobeuren (1748) by J. M. Fischer and the pilgrimage church of the Vierzehnheiligen (1744) by Neumann, spatial complexity and decorative richness are combined. In Vierzehnheiligen, the nave consists of a double interconnecting oval and the sanctuary of a single one; at the side are vestigial circular transepts. The crossing – the focal space in a centralised church – is therefore no more than the joint between four spaces, with the focus of the church, the elaborate altar of the fourteen saints, located in the nave. The interior is alive with rococo decoration – vegetation, fruit, shells, asymmetrical scrolls and swags – which ignores the discipline of the architecture, flowing freely over columns and cornices and linking the building, its statuary and its ceiling paintings into a unified whole.

In Russia, the French influence on the Tsar's court and the upper classes extended to its architecture. The palace of Peterhof (1747) was built for Peter the Great by the French architect Le Blond and extended by the Italian Rastrelli. A central three-storey block with a wing on either side emulates Versailles, and its magnificent garden makes spectacular use of fountains and cascades. Rastrelli had studied in France and his buildings for the empress Elizabeth are strongly reminiscent of Versailles in treatment, with added decorative detail in a Russian style. The summertime Ekaterininsky Palace (1749) at Tsarskoe Seloe or 'Tsar's village', and

imperial Petersburg

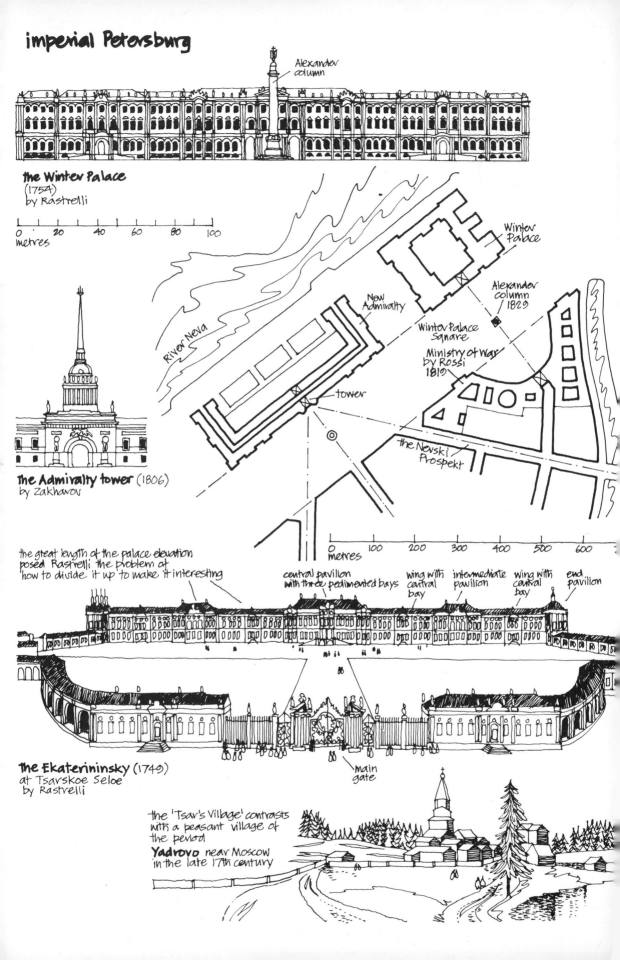

Alexander column

the Winter Palace
(1754)
by Rastrelli

0   20   40   60   80   100
metres

the Admiralty tower

River Neva

New Admiralty

Winter Palace

Alexander column 1829

Winter Palace Square

Ministry of War by Rossi 1819

tower

the Nevski Prospekt

the Admiralty tower (1806)
by Zakharov

0   100   200   300   400   500   600
metres

the great length of the palace elevation posed Rastrelli the problem of how to divide it up to make it interesting

central pavilion with three pedimented bays

wing with central bay

intermediate pavilion

wing with central bay

end pavilion

main gate

the Ekaterininsky (1749)
at Tsarskoe Seloe
by Rastrelli

the 'Tsar's Village' contrasts with a peasant village of the period
Yadrovo near Moscow in the late 17th century

the Winter Palace on the Neva in Petersburg (1754) are his two greatest buildings. Both make use of giant orders as the main feature of their long façades – the former is 300 metres long – and both are enlivened with bright colour and decorative detail.

During the 18th century, four great powers were beginning to dominate Europe politically. Three of them were authoritarian monarchies: Russia under the Romanovs, pushing her way into Finland, Poland and the Crimea; the Prussian state led by the Hohenzollerns, beginning to dominate Austria and the rest of Germany; Bourbon France, retaining her power in Europe and developing her colonies overseas.

The fourth power was England. The English Revolution had firmly established parliament on the political stage, confirming the rights of bourgeois property-owners to make political decisions. France's bourgeoisie, dominated by the Bourbon court, or those in countries still dominated by the church, looked enviously at the middle classes in Britain. The parliamentary system was much more capable of responding to people's needs than was the rigid bureaucracy of France. In practice, the needs to which it responded were those of the middle class, the planters, the slavers, the farming landlords and the cotton magnates; so in Britain middle-class power and prestige were correspondingly higher than elsewhere. In France, entering the aristocracy was the ambition of the successful merchant, but in Britain the reverse was true: the aristocracy, as in Renaissance Italy, were only too glad to enter commerce. In France the spendthrift, idle nobility were dispersing capital, but in England it was being conserved and accumulated. In consequence, British economic growth during the 17th and 18th centuries was prodigious and her position as a great power and the strength of her institutions at home were ensured. The major building works of the 17th century – such as Greenwich – had been royal commissions, and the tax that paid for St Paul's and the city churches had been levied by the king. Now a new group of patrons came to the fore; the palaces of the 18th century were those of great land-owners and successful businessmen.

Blenheim Palace, Oxfordshire (1704), was the gift of a grateful nation to one of its military heroes, the first Duke of Marlborough. The architect, John Vanbrugh (1664–1726), was already engaged on another palace, Castle Howard in Yorkshire (1699), a commission he had obtained through his social connections. He had no architectural training – his early success had come from writing plays – but he had great architectural imagination, which was given direction when he was appointed to assist Wren as royal surveyor. Blenheim, Castle Howard and his later Seaton Delaval in Northumberland (1720) fell into no current architectural pattern. Large, powerful and dramatic, heavy and grossly proportioned, deliberately discordant, they shocked the classical purists of the day. They are in fact among the few achievements of English baroque, highly personal in style and owing little to precedent – except perhaps that their general conformation around a *cour d'honneur* resembles the great French houses of the 17th century.

Vanbrugh stood quite outside the prevailing architectural thought of the time. The conventional wisdom was in favour of an understated, sedate Palladianism of an almost antiquarian correctness. Mereworth Castle, Kent (1722), by Colen Campbell, is virtually a reproduction of Palladio's Villa Capra, attractive, but inappropriate in the English climate. It has a square plan with a classical portico on each front, and is surmounted by a dome above a central circular hall. Very similar is Chiswick House, London (1725), by Lord Burlington and William Kent, though

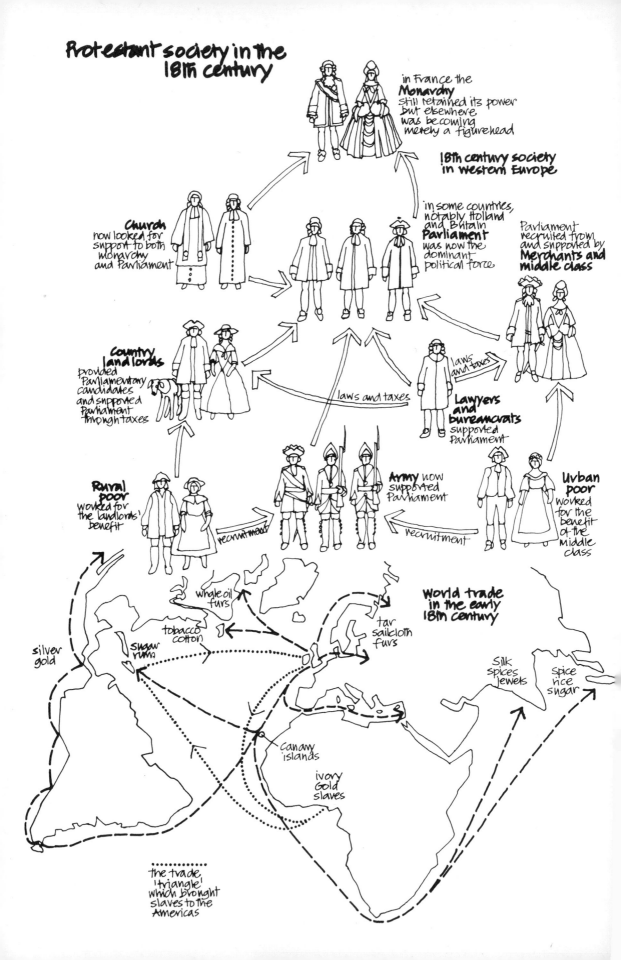

Protestant society in the 18th century

in France the **Monarchy** still retained its power but elsewhere was becoming merely a figurehead

18th century society in western Europe

Church now looked for support to both monarchy and Parliament

in some countries, notably Holland and Britain **Parliament** was now the dominant political force

Parliament recruited from and supported by **Merchants and middle class**

Country landlords provided Parliamentary candidates and supported Parliament through taxes

laws and taxes

Lawyers and bureaucrats supported Parliament

laws and taxes

Rural poor worked for the landlords' benefit

recruitment

Army now supported Parliament

recruitment

Urban poor worked for the benefit of the middle class

World trade in the early 18th century

whale oil furs

tobacco cotton

tar sailcloth furs

silver gold

sugar rums

silk spices jewels

spice rice sugar

canary islands

ivory gold slaves

············ the trade 'triangle' which brought slaves to the Americas

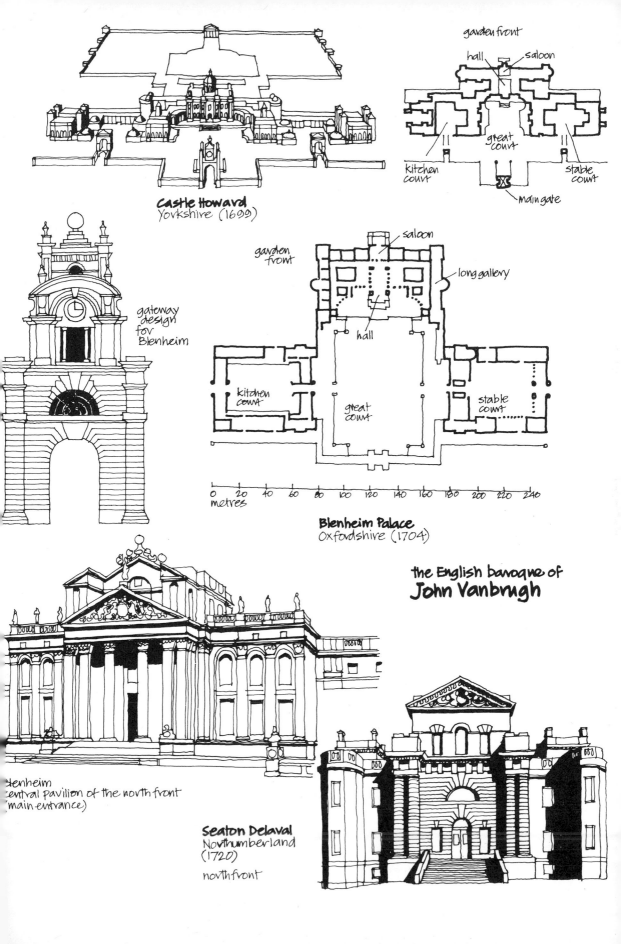

Castle Howard
Yorkshire (1699)

garden front

hall   saloon

great
court

kitchen
court

stable
court

main gate

gateway
design
for
Blenheim

garden
front

saloon

long gallery

hall

kitchen
court

great
court

stable
court

0 20 40 60 80 100 120 140 160 180 200 220 240
metres

Blenheim Palace
Oxfordshire (1704)

the English baroque of
John Vanbrugh

Blenheim
central pavilion of the north front
(main entrance)

Seaton Delaval
Northumberland
(1720)

north front

here the dome is raised on a drum through which the hall is lit by clerestories, and the porticos are reduced to one.

An integral part of the design of the grand Palladian house was its garden. The characteristic style of the English 18th-century garden was developed first by William Kent and continued by his assistant Lancelot 'Capability' Brown (1716–83). It was the exact opposite of the style of Le Nôtre; in place of a strongly-imposed discipline on nature came an artful, informal approach, designed to improve and enhance the natural landscape rather than to re-structure it. Expanses of lawn, dark clumps of deciduous trees, curving routes and natural-looking lakes provided a setting for ornamental bridges, temples and follies. No formal terrace or *parterre* separated the house from its park; instead the informal landscape came up to the very walls. The distinction between the park and the natural landscape beyond was likewise blurred, so that everything the eye could see seemed part of the same composition. Kent's finest landscape, on which Brown also worked, was at Stowe House, Buckinghamshire, and displays these characteristics perfectly. Brown's own work included the gardens at Croome Court (1751) and Ashburnham (1767). His garden at Vanbrugh's Blenheim (1765), where he swept away much of the original formal landscape, includes a lake which he enlarged to match in scale the bridge which Vanbrugh had built over it.

The Palladian style offered a good workaday solution to the design of the many public buildings being put up, and though not all rose above the merely mechanical, there were some notable exceptions. The Senate House in Cambridge (1722) by James Gibbs, a pupil of Wren, a formal classical block with a central pedimented bay, dignified by the use of giant Corinthian orders, and the Horse Guards building in London (1750) by Kent, are successful adaptations of the style. Finest of all, perhaps, is Somerset House in the Strand (1776), a large complex built round a central courtyard by William Chambers (1723–96). It has a long, dignified river frontage of 200 metres, broken up into sections, and a central feature surmounted by a small dome. Similar in character is the fine Customs House in Dublin (1781) by James Gandon.

In church building, the influence of Wren persisted well into the 18th century, and the pattern set by him of a short, squarish plan, with galleries and a prominent pulpit, was taken up by James Gibbs, designer of St Mary-le-Strand (1714) and St Martin-in-the-Fields (1722), both in London – the former Italianate and rather baroque, the latter consciously Palladian. More flamboyant were the churches of Thomas Archer: St Philip's, Birmingham (1709), has a powerful front tower with concave sides, and St Paul's, Deptford (1712), and St John's, Smith Square (1714), both in London, have centralised plans, the former with a single western spire and a semi-circular portico, the latter with four circular towers flanked with detached columns.

The only English architect to stand comparison with Wren and Vanbrugh, however, was Nicholas Hawksmoor (1666–1730). Unlike them, Hawksmoor was trained as an architect, and seldom can there have been such professional dedication. If Wren represented a new attitude in architecture, the scientific discovery of the most appropriate design, then Hawksmoor provided the corollary. His method was to analyse rigorously every detail in a building and, leaving nothing to chance, to describe it to the builder by copious drawings. He worked with Wren in the royal Office of Works till 1718 when both were dismissed in favour of mediocre but

Palladianism in England

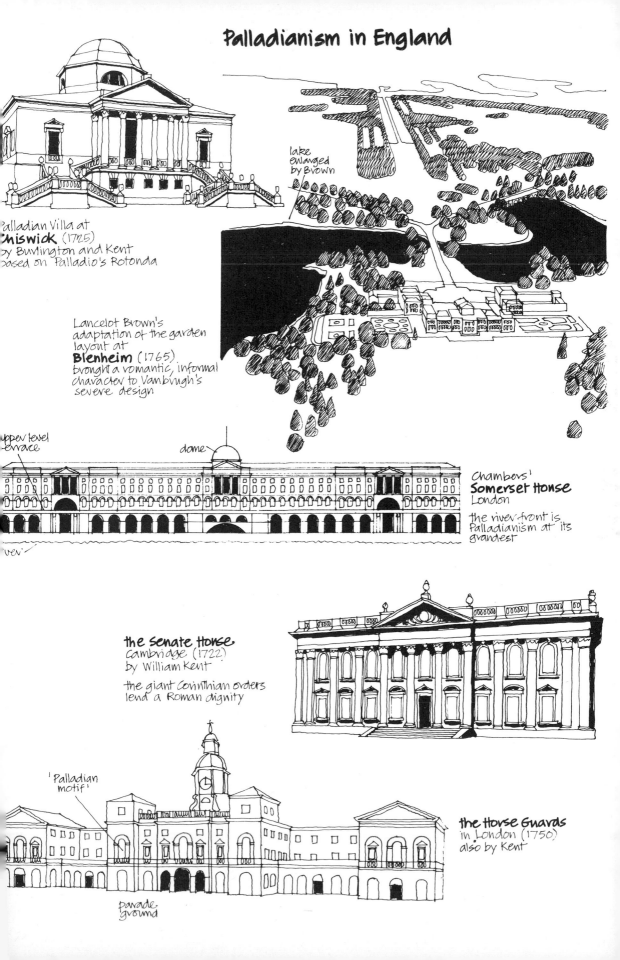

Palladian Villa at
Chiswick (1725)
by Burlington and Kent
based on Palladio's Rotonda

lake
enlarged
by Brown

Lancelot Brown's
adaptation of the garden
layout at
Blenheim (1765)
brought a romantic, informal
character to Vanbrugh's
severe design

upper level
terrace

dome

river

Chambers'
Somerset House
London

the river-front is
Palladianism at its
grandest

the Senate House,
Cambridge (1722)
by William Kent

the giant Corinthian orders
lend a Roman dignity

'Palladian
motif'

the Horse Guards
in London (1750)
also by Kent

parade
ground

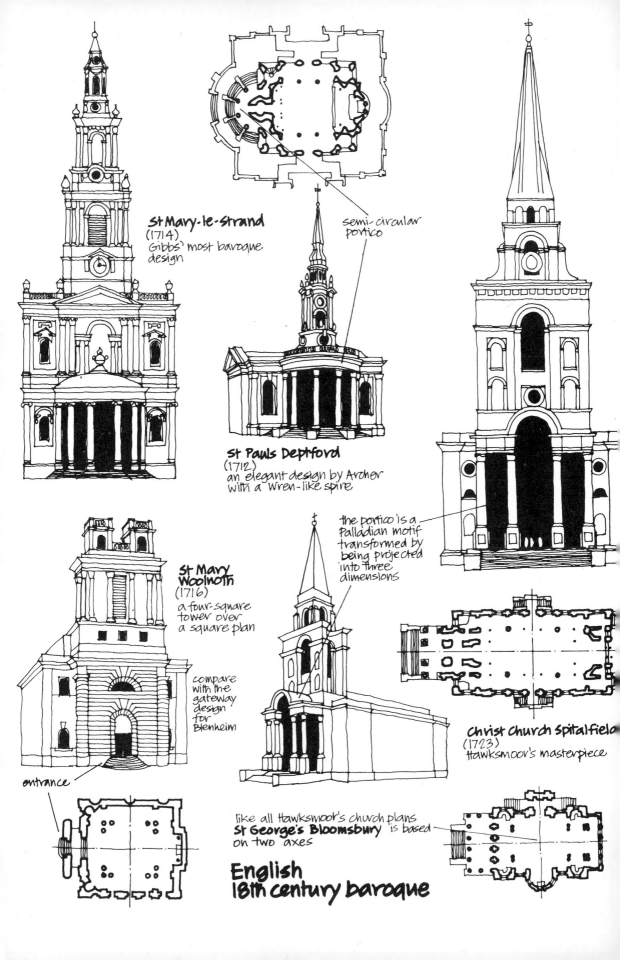

St Mary-le-Strand
(1714)
Gibbs' most baroque design

semi-circular portico

St Pauls Deptford
(1712)
an elegant design by Archer with a Wren-like spire

the portico is a Palladian motif transformed by being projected into three dimensions

St Mary Woolnoth
(1716)
a four-square tower over a square plan

compare with the gateway design for Blenheim

entrance

Christ Church Spitalfield
(1723)
Hawksmoor's masterpiece

like all Hawksmoor's church plans
St George's Bloomsbury is based on two axes

English
18th century baroque

politically acceptable competitors. He shares with Wren much of the credit for Greenwich, and with Vanbrugh he worked on Castle Howard and Blenheim. There is much of the baroque spirit of both Wren and Vanbrugh in his work, though his spare, rugged style is undoubtedly his own.

Among his masterpieces were six London parish churches built as a result of an Act of Parliament in 1711. The first two, St Alphege, Greenwich and St Anne, Limehouse, were begun in 1712, followed by St George-in-the-East (1715), St Mary Woolnoth (1716), St George, Bloomsbury (1720) and Christchurch, Spitalfields (1723). Each is different in detail though each displays the same pre-occupations with rich spatial effects internally and dramatic, powerful statements externally. St Mary Woolnoth has a strange rectangular rusticated tower surmounted by two square turrets, St Anne's tower is strong, geometrical baroque in diminishing tiers, and Christchurch, finest of all, has a pointed spire of almost romanesque character above a square tower with two concave sides and a barrel-vaulted portico. The combination of such disparate elements into an 'incorrect' but brilliantly organic whole did not impress his Palladian critics.

The influence of Palladianism was far-reaching, affecting the design of small houses as well as grand ones. By the end of the 17th century, a distinctive style had been evolved for the country houses of the well-to-do middle class, partly from the style of Jones, partly from ideas imported from 17th-century Holland, both adapted to English use. The houses of Sir Roger Pratt, notably Coleshill in Berkshire (1662 – now destroyed), typify the style. Coleshill was a compact, two-storey house with a central doorway and vertical sash-windows, Palladian in style, in the manner of the Queen's House. Above the heavy cornice-line, however, instead of Jones's apparent flat roof was a heavy hipped roof, reminiscent of Van Campen's Mauritshuis. This feature, with added dormers and chimneys, became an accepted – and appropriate – method of adapting Jones's style to the English climate and in the hands of master-builders and local craftsmen it was reproduced up and down the country.

In the towns, the middle classes – merchants, lawyers, agents and clerks – were increasing in number, and the growing need for houses somewhere in standard between a mansion and a worker's hovel was supplied by the development of speculative building. Speculators acquired what land they could, often from the estates of commercially-minded aristocrats, and laid out housing developments. Some, often the landlords themselves acting as developers, realised that an attractive layout including shops and open space would be more commercial, and the Earl of Southampton's development of Bloomsbury in the 17th century set a pattern, with its related streets, squares and open spaces, for the higher-class estate. Others were interested in obtaining as many houses as possible on their land in closely packed streets.

In both cases, the basic architectural form was the terraced house, arranged in geometric rows and designed along classical lines. The form evolved had a basement, an entry floor forming a podium and approached through an ornate street door, a tall upper floor with the main rooms and further upper floors diminishing in height towards the top. Household servants were accommodated in basements or attics. The elevations were arranged according to the Palladian canon; the proportions of doors and windows, their relationship to one another, their diminution towards the top of the building, were set down in pattern books, like those of the carpenter Batty Langley which enjoyed a considerable currency in the early 18th century and which

157

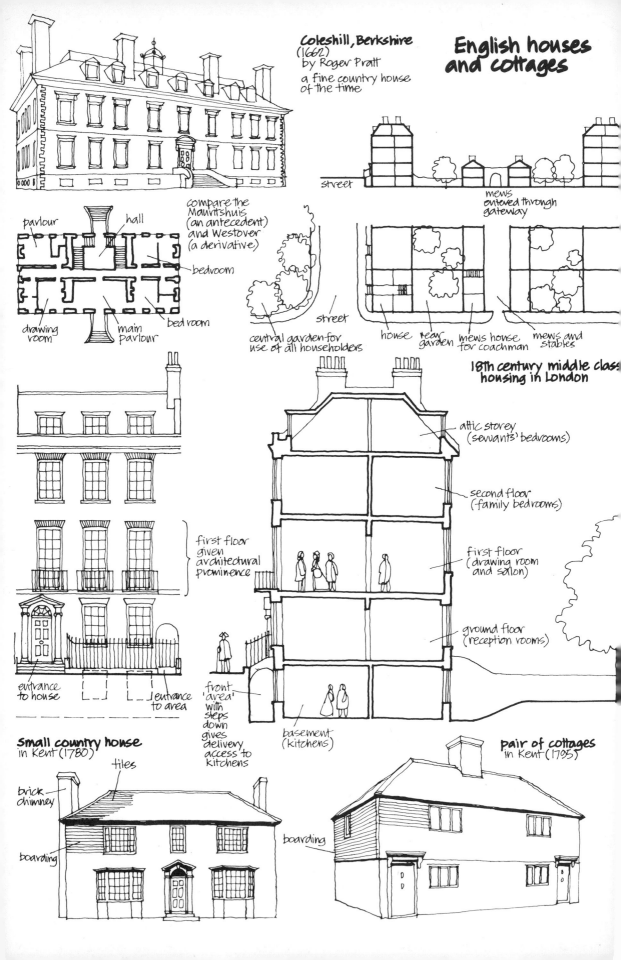

Coleshill, Berkshire
(1662)
by Roger Pratt
a fine country house
of the time

English houses and cottages

street

mews entered through gateway

parlour

hall

bedroom

compare the Mauritshuis (an antecedent) and Westover (a derivative)

drawing room

main parlour

bed room

central garden for use of all householders

street

house

rear garden

mews house for coachman

mews and stables

18th century middle class housing in London

attic storey (servants' bedrooms)

second floor (family bedrooms)

first floor given architectural prominence

first floor (drawing room and salon)

ground floor (reception rooms)

entrance to house

entrance to area

front 'area' with steps down gives delivery access to kitchens

basement (kitchens)

small country house
in Kent (1780)

tiles

brick chimney

boarding

pair of cottages
in Kent (1795)

boarding

boarding

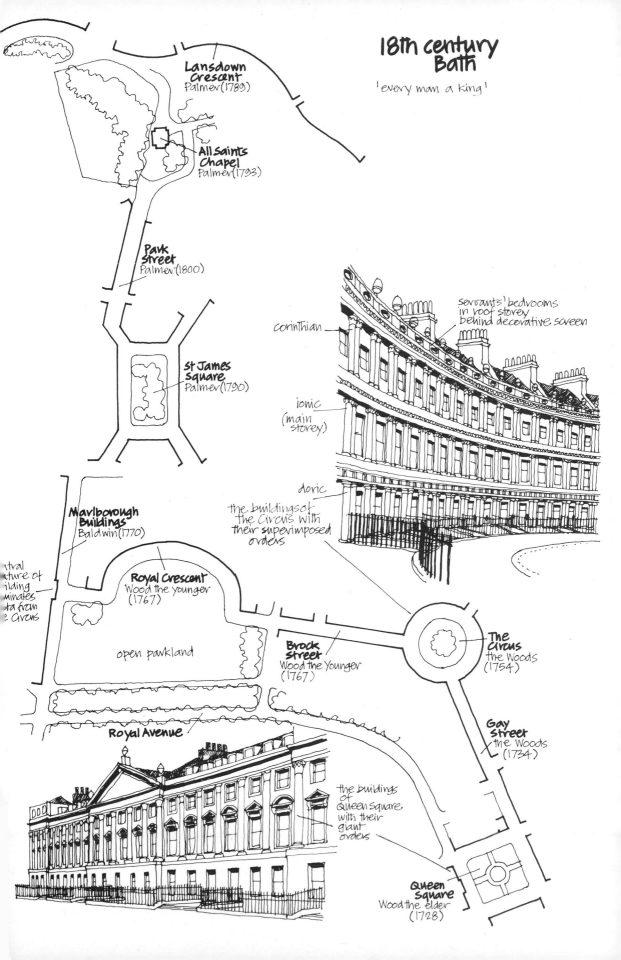

18th century Bath

'every man a king'

Lansdown Crescent
Palmer (1789)

All Saints Chapel
Palmer (1793)

Park Street
Palmer (1800)

St James Square
Palmer (1790)

corinthian

servants' bedrooms in roof storey behind decorative screen

ionic
(main storey)

doric

the buildings of the Circus with their superimposed orders

Marlborough Buildings
Baldwin (1770)

...tral ...ture of ...ilding ...minates ...ta from ...e Circus

Royal Crescent
Wood the Younger (1767)

open parkland

Brock Street
Wood the Younger (1767)

The Circus
the Woods (1754)

Gay Street
the Woods (1734)

Royal Avenue

the buildings of Queen Square with their giant orders

Queen Square
Wood the elder (1728)

enabled small speculative builders everywhere to put up tolerably stylish buildings. The whole side of a square could be made into more than the sum of its parts if the centre house were designed as a main central block and the end two as pavilions. Each house plan was the same but the owners had the satisfaction of appearing to live in a palace. Large areas of London, Dublin and Edinburgh were built in this way, but the finest example was the small English town of Bath. Known to the Romans for its medicinal water, Bath was re-discovered around 1720 by fashionable society, and the job of re-planning the town to meet the needs of large numbers of wealthy hypochondriacs fell to the two John Woods, father and son. Using the local sandstone, they built three groups of majestic terrace houses, linked together as part of a sequence of spaces: Queen's Square (1728), The Circus and the Royal Crescent (1754). The buildings in The Circus, three curved blocks forming a circular space, are designed with three main storeys treated, like the Colosseum, with superimposed orders. The Queen's Square houses have a rusticated ground storey as a podium, with the two upper floors bound together by giant orders. A central pedimented bay and two end pavilions lend a palatial aspect, and the whole is capped by a heavy pediment which largely conceals the servants' rooms in the roof space.

Though the poor were not deliberately included in the improvements that were taking place in society, they did benefit in some ways. Improved crops, fewer wars, better transport, gradually-acquired immunity to disease and better medicine were enough to raise their expectation of life, if not their wealth. Most workers still lived in a single-storey dwelling, built in local materials, with a thatched roof. It might have no more than two rooms, one of which contained a brick-built chimney-stack. The water-supply might be far from the house and – though this was almost true of the upper classes as well – sanitation was non-existent. The better cottages, built not by the tenants themselves but by local builders, perhaps for top estate workers, were more varied. Typically two-storeyed, they might be timber-framed and weather-boarded, though as bricks and tiles became more common a greater constructional variety was possible. A steeply-pitched roof might contain the top-floor bedrooms, lit with small dormer windows. Perhaps the most significant feature of the 18th-century cottage was its external regularity. The central, hooded doorway, with glazed sash-windows placed symmetrically on either side show, if only faintly, the extent of Palladio's influence.

Eventually, the developments of the 18th century brought other influences to bear on design. A German shoemaker's son called Johann Winckelmann, a poet, classical scholar and Vatican bureaucrat was in Naples in 1748 when engineers working for the King of Naples uncovered the first wall-paintings in the buried town of Pompeii. His published description of the amazing finds as they gradually came to light awoke a wide interest in antiquity. This interest was given a romantic direction by the artist Giovanni Battista Piranesi (1720–78) whose views of Pompeii, Herculaneum and the monuments of Rome, ivy-covered and decaying, and of terrifying, imaginary prison-scenes – the celebrated *Carceri* – were widely published and assimilated. The growing passion for the past was not confined to Rome but extended to Etruria, Greece, the far east and to Europe's own medieval heritage. Langley's *Gothic Architecture Improved* (1742), Chambers' *Design of Chinese Buildings* (1757) and Stuart and Revett's *Antiquities of Athens* (1762) were books which had considerable influence.

The Scottish architect Robert Adam (1728–92) studied in Italy and Paris, visited

Rome where he measured the monuments and met Piranesi, and returned to England to start a practice with his brothers James and John. Robert's design ability and the business acumen of the other two brought them great success, not only in numerous re-modellings of old houses for wealthy clients, but also in full-blooded ventures into property speculation. The Adelphi development in London (1768) between the Strand and the river was the most impressive, a multi-level complex of warehouses, stables, offices and residences which turned a derelict riverside mud-flat into a fashionable area. Robert was by training a Palladian designer but his anti-quarian studies had given his work an eclectic aspect. In his travels he had seen Diocletian's Palace at Split, and the riverside frontage of the palatial Adelphi development was a conscious borrowing. A wharf at water level gave access to a vast vaulted basement storage area which formed a visual and actual podium for the development at road level above. A network of narrow streets ran directly in from the Strand and gave access to the upper-level terraces. The style of building was elegant and formal, dressed in painted stucco and giant pilasters which were enlivened by Robert's characteristic low-relief decoration. The colours and patterns chosen are strongly reminiscent of plasterwork and frescoes Robert must have seen at Pompeii. They appear again and again in his interior designs for large houses, at Kedleston (1760), Osterley (1761), Syon (1762) and Kenwood (1767), where rich Roman colour and delicate Hellenistic ornament are used in the most artful way. In his finest works, Robert Adam is also a master of internal spatial effects, both in the way he organises a sequence of spaces of different sizes and shapes and in the way he divides spaces by free-standing columns and beams, or extends them with alcoves, to obtain lively and subtle effects.

At the same time, other architects were exploring the opportunities offered by the Greek and gothic styles. James Wyatt's Radcliffe Observatory, Oxford (1772) was based on the Tower of the Winds in Athens; and among the best-known essays in 18th-century Gothic were Strawberry Hill (1750), a cottage owned by Horace Walpole which he rebuilt in an elegant and delicate medieval style, and Fonthill Abbey, a vast house built by Wyatt in 1795. An octagonal tower 85 metres high, a great hall and an elevation some 90 metres in length were features of this extra-ordinary building. As in most buildings of the Gothic revival, its medievalism was superficial rather than essential – though its tower did emulate several medieval predecessors by collapsing in a storm in 1807.

The thinkers of the 18th century saw the past as of more than antiquarian interest; to some, rather more fundamentally, it was one of the keys to man's future. The French *philosophes* and their German counterparts differed among themselves over many things; the religious and political attitudes of Rousseau were not those of Voltaire and Diderot, nor Kant's those of Goethe. Among Anglo-Saxon economists and social reformers there were also differences: between Smith and Hume, Gibbon and Bentham, Hobbes and Locke, Jefferson and Franklin. However, they held many basic ideas in common. They were generally hostile to 'revealed' religion, in particu-lar to the church's medieval doctrine of original sin, and looked back with favour on the pre-catholic era of history when men had a greater dignity. They sought for a rational explanation of existence and, believing that human understanding was capable of coming to terms with the problems of the world, looked forward to a better future. Their idea of progress, to be based on values which somehow had been lost, offered an unprecedented intellectual challenge to contemporary society.

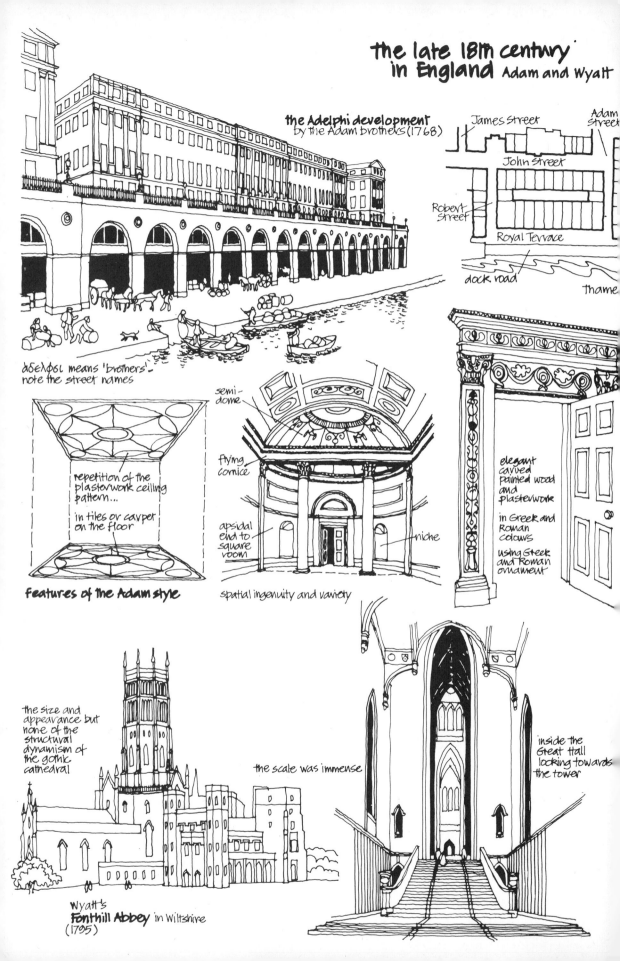

the late 18th century in England Adam and Wyatt

the Adelphi development
by the Adam brothers (1768)

James Street

Adam Street

John Street

Robert Street

Royal Terrace

dock road

Thame

δδελφοι means 'brothers'.
note the street names

semi-dome

flying cornice

apsidal end to square room

niche

features of the Adam style

repetition of the plasterwork ceiling pattern...

in tiles or carpet on the floor

spatial ingenuity and variety

elegant carved painted wood and plasterwork

in Greek and Roman colours

using Greek and Roman ornament

the size and appearance but none of the structural dynamism of the gothic cathedral

the scale was immense

inside the Great Hall looking towards the tower

Wyatt's
Fonthill Abbey in Wiltshire
(1795)

Architectural theorists of the late 18th century were caught up by the dynamism of the *philosophes*. Buildings, it was thought, should express the essential grandeur of man both by their sublimity and by their reference to his dignified past. Sublimity was capable of analysis: buildings should be large, simple, sombre, cavernous and mysterious in a way typified, perhaps, by Piranesi's *Carceri*. The two greatest exponents of this approach were Étienne Louis Boullée (1728–99) and Claude Nicolas Ledoux (1736–1806). Both designed and theorised much more than they built, and the reputation of Boullée at least depends on his drawings, which include designs for an enormous national library, museums, cemeteries and a monument to Isaac Newton, the symbol of the new age, which was to be a vast hollow sphere, 150 metres or more in diameter, representing the universe. As social awareness increased, new building-types were required; everywhere architects were inventing forms for buildings designed to promote health, welfare and social responsibility: hospitals, prisons, schools, model factories, housing estates, monuments and Temples of the Moral Values. Among Ledoux's finest built works was the model industrial estate built in 1775 for the chemical works of La Saline near Besançon, a complex of factories and laboratories with a nearby residential quarter. The style was robust and consciously primitive, using the Tuscan order and heavily rusticated walls. The same features appeared on the *barrières* or toll-gates of Paris, built in a ring around the inner city in 1785. Only four of the original forty-five now survive, but La Villette with its heavy rotunda and L'Enfer with its strongly rusticated columns represent the geometric qualities of them all.

John Soane (1753–1837) in England and Friedrich Gilly (1772–1800) in Germany were the counterparts of Boullée and Ledoux. Soane's Bank of England (1788 and later), a design which was actually built, was more uncompromising than anything achieved by the others. Stark and austere, it had a magnificent central domed rotunda in which decoration was almost completely eliminated and simplicity of form was everything. Gilly's great work, the Prussian National Theatre designed for Berlin, was never built; but it too shows an uncompromising attitude to geometric purity and surface simplicity. The simple rectangular stage tower set against the hemicyclical auditorium was a concept as suited to the architecture of the 20th century as to that of the 18th.

The group of architects to which Boullée and Ledoux belonged became known as 'the revolutionaries'. On the whole, this described an architectural rather than a social attitude. Ledoux at least was a royalist and an 'architecte du roi', and there is something oppressive as well as liberating in his designs and the attitudes that formed them. Nevertheless these *architectes révolutionnaires* were working at a time when the idea of social revolution was very much part of intellectual life. Rousseau, for example, in *Du Contrat Social*, strongly advocated popular sovereignty in order to attain the supremacy of the 'general will'. In 1775, the theories were put to a practical test as the American colonies, dissatisfied at being taxed without being represented at Westminster, came into open conflict with England. At first, there was no general revolutionary aim – Washington himself was a monarchist and sought only to bring Britain to its senses – but gradually the opportunity for independence was grasped. By 1783, a revolution had taken place.

Now the French bourgeoisie had another model of progress to set beside the example of England. They began firmly to believe that they deserved more power and status, and the main political change of the 18th century occurred as a result of

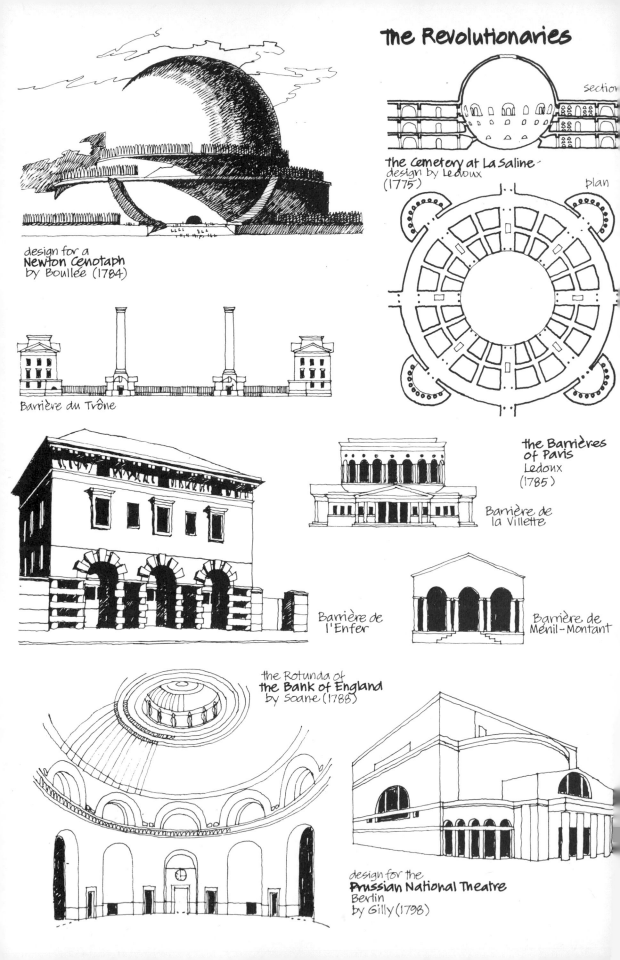

the Revolutionaries

design for a
Newton Cenotaph
by Boullée (1784)

section

the Cemetery at La Saline
design by Ledoux
(1775)

plan

Barrière du Trône

the **Barrières
of Paris**
Ledoux
(1785)

Barrière de
la Villette

Barrière de
l'Enfer

Barrière de
Ménil-Montant

the Rotunda of
the Bank of England
by Soane (1788)

design for the
Prussian National Theatre
Berlin
by Gilly (1798)

this belief. The ideas of Thomas Paine (1737–1809) crystallised the progressive attitude of the time. His book *Common Sense* and his 'Crisis' papers had already done much to strengthen and direct the efforts of the Americans towards independence. In 1789, revolution broke out in France with the aim of achieving a parliamentary democracy similar to England's, and Paine's *The Rights of Man* (1791) became a bible for democrats everywhere. As it was, of the many guises the revolution went through, none was democratic, and popular sovereignty was not achieved. What did happen, however, was that the royal family and the aristocracy were removed, leaving the way open, as it was already in England, for the middle classes to expand their role.

The age of iron

1815-1850

The intellectual turmoil of the age of revolution is typified by its great artists, who stood midway between the classical world of the 18th century and the modern one of the 19th. After Beethoven's 'Eroica' symphony (1804), music was never the same again. Goethe's varied talents and affinity with the classical world made him one of the last 'renaissance men', but *Faust* (1832) nevertheless introduced concepts – such as the eternal search for truth, the idea of creative toil, the creation of a new life and the attainment of spiritual freedom – which became intellectual hallmarks of the modern world.

The architecture of the time had no Goethe or Beethoven. There are several reasons why architects failed at first to make the leap forward into the 19th century, and why they responded to the new opportunities of the industrial revolution merely by retreating into traditional forms and methods. For one thing, the architects themselves had worked over the years to achieve status in society. As taste-makers in a world in which taste counted for a great deal, they had created a set of design rules accepted everywhere from Petersburg to Washington. The new techniques threatened their world and it was understandable that they preferred to close their minds to them.

In fact, though the underlying economic structure of society was changing, outwardly the old order appeared to continue: the conservatism of Metternich dominated the politics of Italy and the German states, the French revolution had ended in the dictatorship of Napoleon, and in England the flamboyant reign of George IV brought the monarchy into the public eye. The liberalism on which industrial capitalism depended, with its ideals of *liberté, égalité, fraternité,* posed a threat to the old order. There must have been considerable pressure from the ruling class, and from those of the bourgeoisie who aspired to it, to persist with the traditional architectural forms as symbols of continuity in a changing world.

Politically, there was a need for a civic architecture to impart grandeur and dignity to the various aspiring regimes – from Napoleon's nascent empire to the fast-developing Union of American states. Renaissance and baroque architects had used the elements of classical architecture as the starting-point in the development of an original style; but now architects were turning to the faithful reproduction of the forms of the classical world. The use of this neo-classical style allowed the politicians of Prussia and England, as well as those of America and France, to consider themselves by implication the rightful heirs of democratic Athens or imperial Rome. The new American capital of Washington was designed by the French architect Pierre Charles l'Enfant (1754–1825) with a grand baroque layout in the tradition of Versailles, made more magnificent by its riverside location. But the Capitol, the White House and a succession of other government buildings which adorned the site were built as, or remodelled into, severe and elegant Greek-revival monuments. Leading the neo-classical movement in America was Benjamin Latrobe (1764–1820). His early career was associated with President Thomas Jefferson

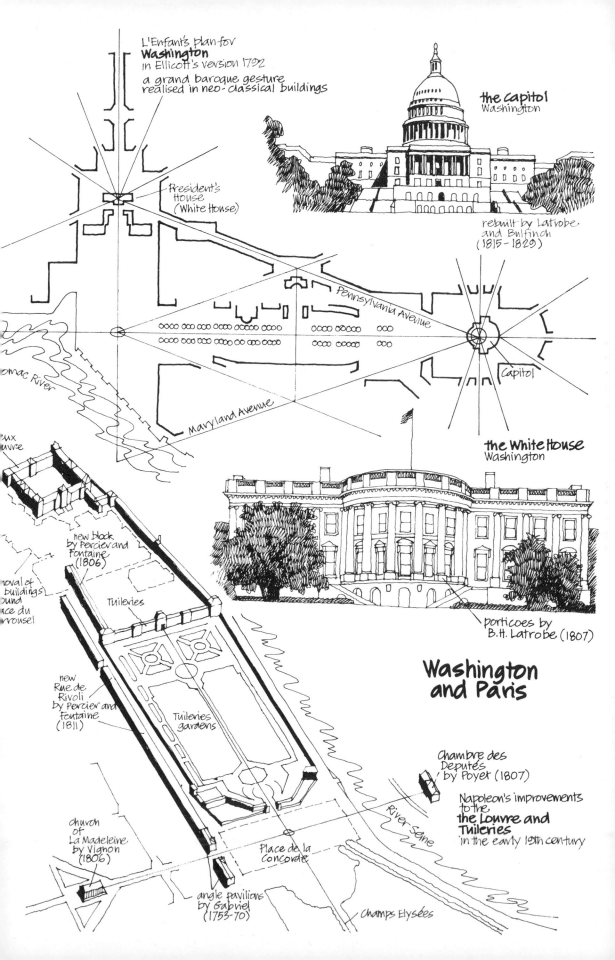

L'Enfant's plan for
Washington
in Ellicott's version 1792
a grand baroque gesture
realised in neo-classical buildings

the Capitol
Washington

rebuilt by Latrobe
and Bulfinch
(1815-1829)

President's
House
(White House)

Pennsylvania Avenue

Capitol

omac River

Maryland Avenue

ux
uvre

the White House
Washington

new block
by Percier and
Fontaine
(1806)

oval of
buildings
ound
ace du
rousel

Tuileries

porticoes by
B.H. Latrobe (1807)

new
Rue de
Rivoli
by Percier and
Fontaine
(1811)

Tuileries
gardens

**Washington
and Paris**

Chambre des
Deputés
by Poyet (1807)

Napoleon's improvements
to the
**the Louvre and
Tuileries**
in the early 19th century

River Seine

church
of
La Madeleine
by Vignon
(1806)

Place de la
Concorde

angle pavilions
by Gabriel
(1753-70)

Champs Elysées

Jefferson's house,
Monticello (1770)
at Charlottesville, Va

the State Capitol of
Richmond, Va (1789)
by Jefferson
with Latrobe's
assistance

another joint design — **the University of
Virginia** (1817) at Charlottesville near
Monticello

gardens

library

teaching
pavilions

students'
rooms

campus

servants' rooms

this 'academical village' set a pattern
for future campus planning

Latrobe's finest work was **the Roman
Catholic Cathedral at Baltimore**, Md (1805)

Latrobe's English training makes likely the
influence of Soane

(1734–1826), himself an accomplished architect, whose house Monticello, near Charlottesville, Va. (1770), was an imaginative essay in the Palladian style. Together they designed the State Capitol at Richmond, Va. (1789), a fine building in the form of a Greek Ionic temple which set a pattern for future public buildings. Latrobe's own remodelling of the White House (1807) is a good example, but his finest work is perhaps the Roman Catholic cathedral of Baltimore, Md. (1805), with its Latin-cross plan and spacious, domed crossing.

In Napoleon's France, civic architecture was moving towards a similar neo-classical monumentality, for which Roman grandeur rather than Greek democracy was the model. An early forerunner was Soufflot's church of Ste Geneviève in Paris (1755), later to become a national shrine known as the Panthéon. Its stark window-less walls, central dome and colonnaded portico recall the mood, if not the detail, of its great Roman predecessor. Vignon's church of La Madeleine (1806), however, was an almost literal reproduction of a Roman temple. The intended association between Napoleon and the Caesars is clear, and shows how architects were seeking inspiration from the past to produce buildings which would represent their patrons as upholders of eternal values.

This attitude is demonstrated particularly by Karl Friedrich von Schinkel (1781–1841) and his two great works in Berlin, the Schauspielhaus (1819) and the Altes Museum (1824). Though the bold, dramatic massing of these buildings has great integrity and is strongly expressive of the way they are planned, the persistent use of the Ionic order to dress the elevations represents a regression from the position of Gilly, whose pupil Schinkel was. Schinkel's philosophy appears to have been particularly influenced by the writings of J.-N.-L. Durand whose two books on architecture (1801–2) sponsored a mechanical approach to design which provided an acceptable formula for the numerous public buildings then being put up. The Rue de Rivoli in Paris, by Percier and Fontaine, was part of a sweeping improvement scheme for the city initiated by Napoleon in 1811. Continuous five-storey residential blocks line the street, with arcaded ground storeys containing shops, in a scheme designed, like Bath, to invest individual bourgeois houses with a collective palatial dignity.

This characteristic is seen at its best in the improvements to London of John Nash (1752–1835). A combination of royal patronage, middle-class support and his own entrepreneurial skill allowed Nash to place his stamp on the West End of London in a way Wren had never been able to do in the City. A system of new buildings and public spaces stretching from Buckingham Palace in the south to the terraces of Regent's Park in the north, demonstrated Nash's mastery over large-scale spatial effects. Unadventurous in style, slipshod in detail and cheap in construction, the elements of Nash's grand design which remain nevertheless impart to London a great theatrical panache. They include Carlton House Terrace (1827), the plan-form but not the buildings of Regent Street, and the terraces of Regent's Park, of which Cumberland Terrace (1827) is probably the best example. The cluster of detached houses in various styles, including classical and gothic, which form Park Village (1824) are among the earliest recognisable examples of English suburbia.

During the 18th century, attitudes to design had been moving in a general direction which continued well into the 19th. An individual genius like Gilly might dispense with style almost completely or, like Hawksmoor, might treat it eclectically, as something independent of the real architecture underneath. But to the Palladians,

169

'La Gloire' in France

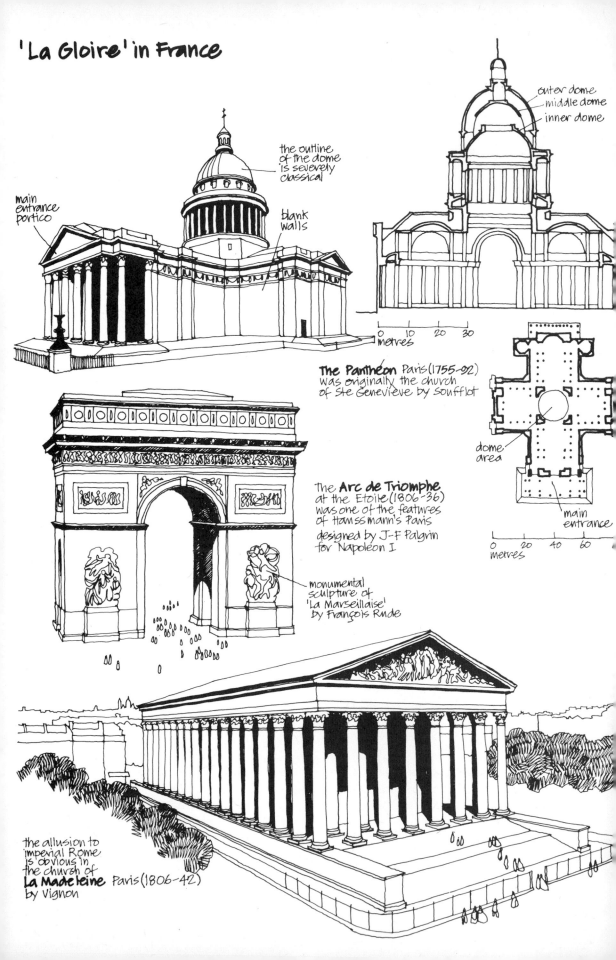

the outline of the dome is severely classical

main entrance portico

blank walls

outer dome
middle dome
inner dome

0 10 20 30
metres

The Panthéon Paris (1755-92) was originally the church of Ste Geneviève by Soufflot

dome area

main entrance

The **Arc de Triomphe** at the Etoile (1806-36) was one of the features of Haussmann's Paris designed by J-F Palgrin for Napoléon I

0 20 40 60
metres

monumental sculpture of 'La Marseillaise' by François Rude

the allusion to imperial Rome is obvious in the church of **La Madeleine** Paris (1806-42) by Vignon

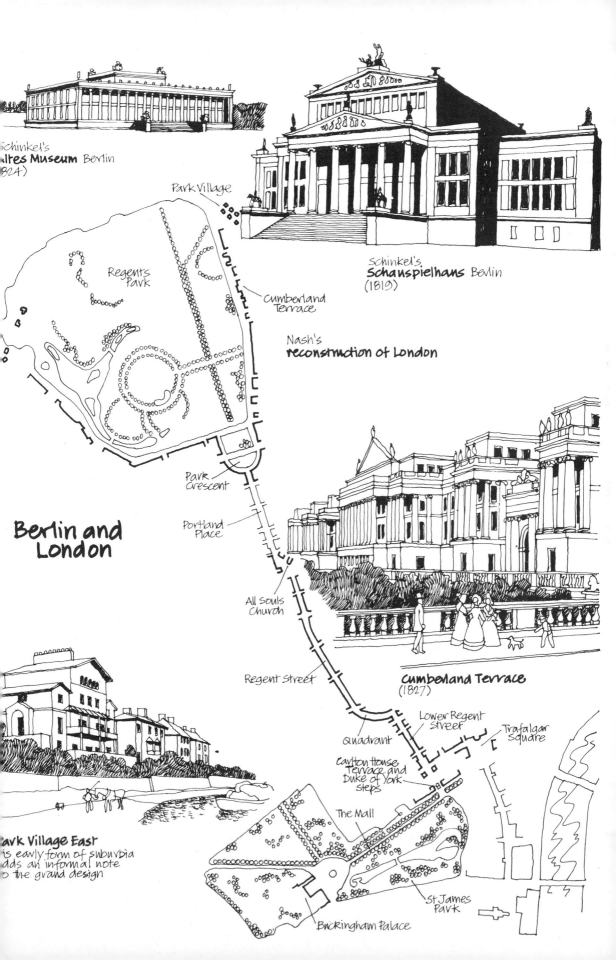

Schinkel's
Altes Museum Berlin
(1824)

Park Village

Schinkel's
Schauspielhaus Berlin
(1819)

Regents Park

Cumberland Terrace

Nash's
reconstruction of London

Park Crescent

Berlin and London

Portland Place

All Souls Church

Regent Street

Cumberland Terrace
(1827)

Lower Regent Street

Trafalgar Square

Quadrant

Carlton House Terrace and Duke of York steps

The Mall

Park Village East
is early form of suburbia
adds an informal note
to the grand design

St James Park

Buckingham Palace

style had been intrinsic, the very essence of architecture. This attitude prevailed into the 19th century; almost all architects were pre-occupied with style and its significance, which prevented them at first from appreciating the structural possibilities of the new materials of the industrial revolution. Feelings on the subject of style ran high, and Neo-Classical and Gothic in particular had firm and even fanatical adherents.

The Gothic revival, from tentative beginnings in the 18th century, became firmly established when in 1834 the old medieval palace of Westminster was destroyed by fire. It was decided that the gothic style was most suited to the memory of the old building and would harmonise best with Westminster Abbey and the old Westminster Hall, which still remained. The architect, Charles Barry (1785–1860), was a confirmed classicist and produced a formal, symmetrical plan with an octagonal central hall. The job of converting this into Gothic was entrusted to Augustus Pugin (1812–52), an eccentric and fervent catholic convert who advocated the gothic style as a matter of religious principle and considered the Italian renaissance style not only bad architecture but also immoral. Interestingly, his love for Gothic extended to an appreciation of its constructional integrity, and in his book *The True Principles of Pointed or Christian Architecture* (1841) he showed how the decorative aspects of Gothic grew out of its function. His single-minded realisation of the new Palace of Westminster with its romantic silhouette and intricate gothic decoration, coaxed from a specially selected team of Victorian craftsmen, remains one of the finest achievements of English architecture.

Support for the gothic style increased as the influential art critic John Ruskin (1819–1900) weighed in on its side. His book *The Seven Lamps of Architecture* (1849) put forward seven prerequisites for good architecture, among them truth to materials, the beauty of natural forms and the life given to anything which is hand-crafted rather than machine-made. Early Gothic he saw as fulfilling these requirements, and he enlarged on this theme in *The Stones of Venice* (1851) in which he analysed Venetian Gothic and, importantly, attributed its success as an architectural style to the sense of achievement felt by craftsmen in producing it. Despite Ruskin's traditionalism, for this recognition alone of the alienation of the industrial age he is still profoundly relevant.

But probably the most perceptive and brilliant theorist of the gothic style was the Frenchman Eugène-Emanuel Viollet-le-Duc (1814–79). His interest in Gothic was inspired by enthusiastic friends who included the writers Mérimée and Hugo, and he began as a scholarly restorer of medieval buildings, including the Sainte-Chapelle and Notre Dame. An active revolutionary, he recognised that the achievements of the High Gothic period were the result of laymen overcoming the restrictions placed on them by the church. He was the first to point out, in his *Dictionnaire raisonné de l'architecture française* (1845), that gothic architecture obeyed rational structural laws. Indeed, he went further and drew a parallel between the rib-vault and buttress system of the Middle Ages and the iron skeleton construction of his own day, which architects till then had largely ignored. In his book *Entretiens* he did much to awaken architects' interest in the engineering opportunities of the 19th century.

In fact, the development of these techniques had been proceeding for some decades, outside the confines of conventional architecture, for another class of designers had emerged, ready to fulfil the role demanded of them by industrial ambition. These were the engineers – among them the most agile minds of their

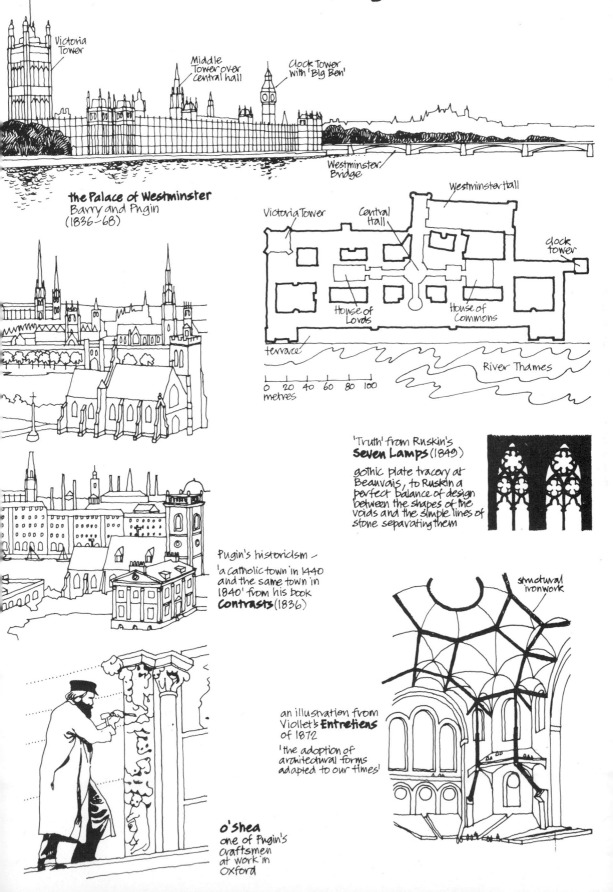

the gothic revival

Victoria Tower

Middle Tower over central hall

Clock Tower with 'Big Ben'

Westminster Bridge

the Palace of Westminster
Barry and Pugin
(1836–68)

Westminster Hall

Victoria Tower

Central Hall

clock tower

House of Lords

House of Commons

terrace

River Thames

0 20 40 60 80 100
metres

'Truth' from Ruskin's
Seven Lamps (1849)

gothic plate tracery at Beauvais, to Ruskin a perfect balance of design between the shapes of the voids and the simple lines of stone separating them

Pugin's historicism –
'a Catholic town in 1440 and the same town in 1840' from his book
Contrasts (1836)

structural ironwork

an illustration from Viollet's **Entretiens** of 1872
'the adoption of architectural forms adapted to our times'

o'shea
one of Pugin's craftsmen at work in Oxford

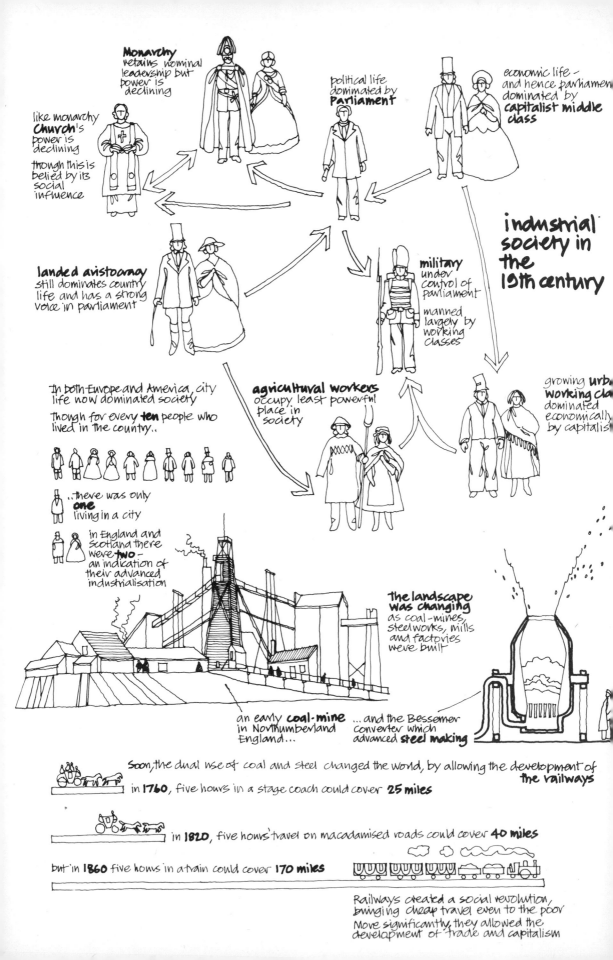

Monarchy retains nominal leadership but power is declining

like monarchy **Church**'s power is declining

though this is belied by its social influence

political life dominated by **Parliament**

economic life — and hence parliament dominated by **capitalist middle class**

landed aristocracy still dominates country life and has a strong voice in parliament

military under control of parliament

manned largely by working classes

industrial society in the 19th century

In both Europe and America, city life now dominated society

Though for every **ten** people who lived in the country..

..there was only **one** living in a city

in England and Scotland there were **two** — an indication of their advanced industrialisation

agricultural workers occupy least powerful place in society

growing urb working cla dominated economically by capitalis

the landscape was changing as coal-mines, steelworks, mills and factories were built

an early **coal-mine** in Northumberland England...

... and the Bessemer converter which advanced **steel making**

Soon, the dual use of coal and steel changed the world, by allowing the development of **the railways**

in **1760**, five hours in a stage coach could cover **25 miles**

in **1820**, five hours' travel on macadamised roads could cover **40 miles**

but in **1860** five hours in a train could cover **170 miles**

Railways created a social revolution, bringing cheap travel even to the poor More significantly, they allowed the development of trade and capitalism

generation – who alone had come to terms with the constructional opportunities offered by the industrial revolution. From ancient times till the 18th century, the technologies of manufacturing, building and travel had developed very little. But the early 19th century was a cultural watershed; from then on, the harnessing of energy, the scientific application of knowledge and the speed of communication allowed the western world to develop at an unprecedented rate. The revolution took place in England between about 1780 and 1850. It reached France, Germany, Belgium and Switzerland by the mid-19th century and northern Italy, Sweden and Russia by the 1900s. The origins went back to the population growth of the early Middle Ages, and to the urbanisation of the 11th and 12th centuries. But it did not reach fruition until the unique economic freedom enjoyed by the English bourgeoisie at the end of the 18th century and the Europeans during the 19th allowed the development of industrial capitalism.

London was the first world city to reach a population of one million. In the early 19th century, though ten per cent of Europe's people lived in towns, the figure for England and Scotland was twenty per cent, a reflection of their industrialisation. The basic activity was still agriculture, but now that the enclosures had put an end to the peasant economy, progressive land-owners could experiment with crops, animals and methods and the yields, supplemented by the increasing importation of food from abroad, had become high enough to support a large population.

Industry was moving into the towns and, conversely, towns were growing up around the industries, because new large-scale production required a large labour-force. Cotton imports grew rapidly as the cloth industry increased and the cotton-towns grew in size and wealth.

The main technical developments of the age were, of course, in the interdependent coal and iron industries. In a small way, coal had been used as a fuel for centuries, but the undreamed-of power it brought to the 19th century came from its use with iron machinery. The early steam-powered machines of Newcomen and Watt were developed for mining, to pump out shafts and raise loads. As metallurgy improved, the use of steam-driven machines was rapidly extended to factories, to the fast-growing railways and to the newly developing machine-tool industry.

In 1779, the iron-master Abraham Darby III built an arched bridge over the gorge of the River Severn at Coalbrookdale, then a major centre of the English iron and coal industries. This elegant structure still remains, a testimony to its maker's understanding of the material and the first important example in the world of the structural use of cast-iron. During the 18th century, the building of canals and turnpike roads stimulated bridge-building, with the developers all the time pushing their engineers to greater feats of daring. Techniques were learned by trial and error, though collapses and accidents were rare. The engineer Thomas Telford (1757–1834) built several cast-iron bridges. The arched form was found to be the most appropriate to the particular properties of cast-iron, whose high carbon content and granular structure made it strong in compression but weak in tension. When a large-span suspension bridge was needed to carry the Holyhead road over the Menai Strait (1819), Telford developed chains of wrought-iron, whose directional cell-structure, like the grain in wood, was capable of resisting higher tensile forces.

The coming of the railways began a frenzy of competition, with hastily formed speculative companies placing ever-greater demands on their engineers. The High Level Bridge over the Tyne at Newcastle, designed by Robert Stephenson and begun

early iron engineering 1

Abraham Darby's cast **iron bridge** over the Severn at Coalbrookdale (1779) was the first in the world

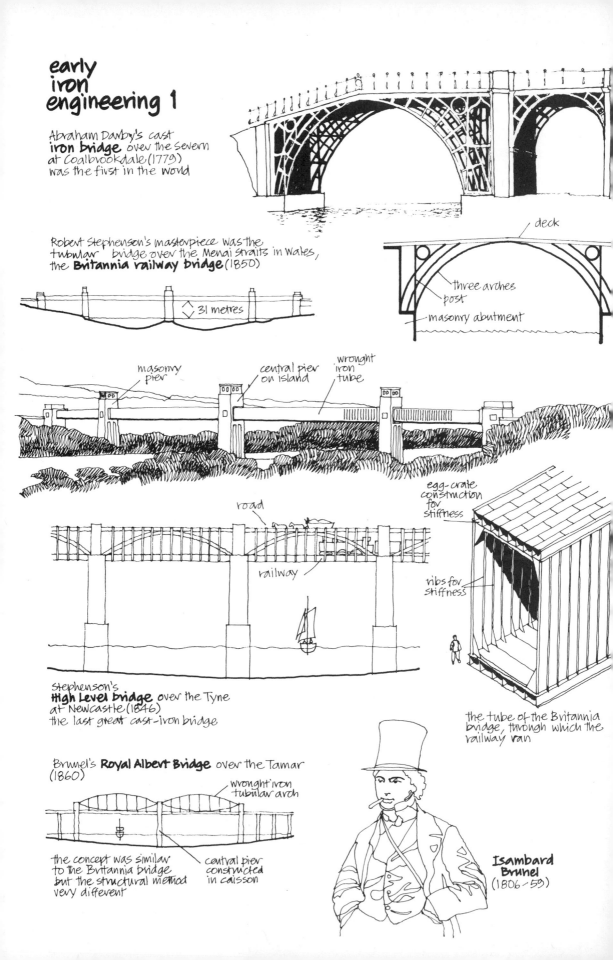

Robert Stephenson's masterpiece was the tubular bridge over the Menai Straits in Wales, the **Britannia railway bridge** (1850)

31 metres

deck

three arches

post

masonry abutment

masonry pier

central pier on island

wrought iron tube

road

railway

egg-crate construction for stiffness

ribs for stiffness

Stephenson's **High Level bridge** over the Tyne at Newcastle (1846) the last great cast-iron bridge

the tube of the Britannia bridge, through which the railway ran

Brunel's **Royal Albert Bridge** over the Tamar (1860)

wrought iron tubular arch

the concept was similar to the Britannia bridge but the structural method very different

central pier constructed in caisson

Isambard Brunel (1806-59)

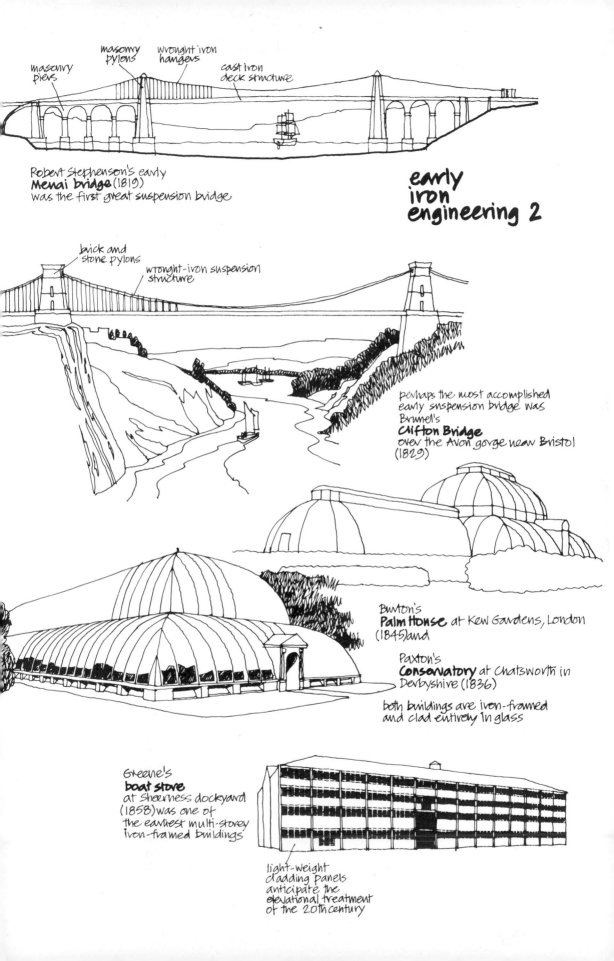

masonry
piers

masonry
pylons

wrought iron
hangers

cast iron
deck structure

Robert Stephenson's early
Menai bridge (1819)
was the first great suspension bridge

brick and
stone pylons

wrought-iron suspension
structure

perhaps the most accomplished
early suspension bridge was
Brunel's
Clifton Bridge
over the Avon gorge near Bristol
(1829)

Burton's
Palm House at Kew Gardens, London
(1845) and

Paxton's
Conservatory at Chatsworth in
Derbyshire (1836)

both buildings are iron-framed
and clad entirely in glass

Greene's
boat store
at Sheerness dockyard
(1858) was one of
the earliest multi-storey
iron-framed buildings

light-weight
cladding panels
anticipate the
elevational treatment
of the 20th century

in 1846, was probably the last great cast-iron bridge, a daring conception in which the bow-and-string principle of the main girders was evolved to lessen the tension in the cast-iron members. Stephenson's other great work was the Britannia railway bridge over the Menai Strait (1850). The total span of almost 300 metres seemed to preclude a suspension bridge like Telford's a mile farther north, despite a rock in mid-stream which would serve for a central pier. Further, an Admiralty requirement for uniform head-room on the underside precluded an arch. The solution was to provide two spans of box-girder construction, massive square tubes of wrought-iron through which the trains ran. This design, based on exhaustive tests and much calculation, was a major step forward in the science of structural mechanics.

Isambard Brunel (1806–59) was forced through the competitive nature of the 'railway mania' into rivalry with Stephenson. Like many engineers, he doubted the wisdom of competition. 'The whole world', he wrote, 'is railway mad. I am really sick of hearing proposals made ... The dreadful scramble in which I am obliged to get through my business is by no means a good sample of the way in which work ought to be done.' Projects were pushed ahead too fast, and more construction workers were killed on the railways in England in the first half of the 19th century than in all the battles of the same period – which included the Napoleonic Wars. The engineers themselves saw the professional wisdom of collaboration: a close friendship existed between Stephenson and Brunel and much technical exchange took place. Brunel's most famous work is perhaps the elegant wrought-iron suspension bridge over the Avon gorge at Clifton, Bristol, begun in 1829, but his greatest is probably the Royal Albert Bridge over the Tamar at Saltash, completed in 1860. Brunel knew Stephenson's Britannia bridge well and the problem he had to solve was similar. The overall span was comparable with Stephenson's, but the central rock did not exist and Brunel was obliged to build a central pier in mid-stream, inside a pressurised iron caisson which was an engineering feat in itself. As before, a flat underside was required: Brunel's solution was two spans of arched wrought-iron tubes carrying the bridge deck slung below.

Iron was coming into use for buildings as well as bridges, though seldom for conventional building-types and never, as yet, by conventional architects. The beautiful conservatory at Chatsworth, Derbyshire (1836), was designed by Joseph Paxton, a garden superintendent. Some 90 metres long, framed in curving bars of cast-iron and wood and clad entirely in glass, this building had numerous progeny including the equally elegant Palm House at Kew Gardens, designed by Decimus Burton – one time assistant to Paxton – and Richard Turner in 1845. The iron-framed boat-store at the navy dockyard, Sheerness, by G. T. Greene (1858) is a simple four-storey building which in terms of architectural expression was considerably ahead of its time, and Oriel Chambers in Liverpool (1864) by Peter Ellis is a fine five-storey office building, completely framed in cast-iron, which uses this new material in a rich and ornate yet appropriate way.

The railway stations of the period express perfectly the division which still existed between conventional architecture and the adventure of iron engineering. King's Cross (1850), one of the earliest of the great termini, was designed by an engineer, Lewis Cubitt. Apart from a small Italianate clock-tower stuck on for architectural effect, its plain brick entrance façade is unpretentious, and in keeping with the double-span arched train-shed behind. But at Paddington (1852) the front of Brunel's amazing train-shed, with its three wrought-iron framed spans intersected

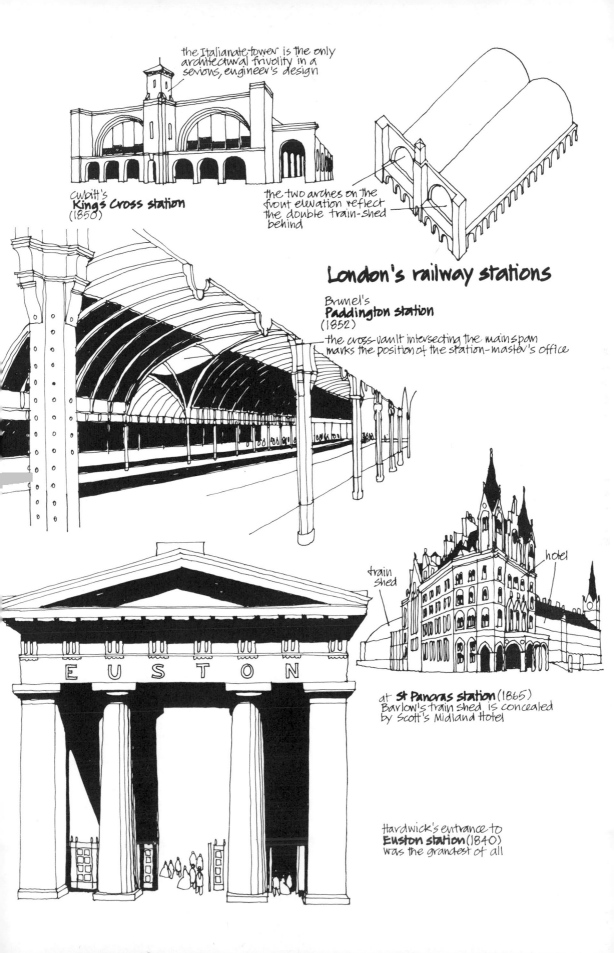

the Italianate tower is the only architectural frivolity in a serious, engineer's design

Cubitt's
Kings Cross station
(1850)

the two arches on the front elevation reflect the double train-shed behind

London's railway stations

Brunel's
Paddington station
(1852)

the cross-vault intersecting the main span marks the position of the station-master's office

E U S T O N

hotel

train shed

at **St Pancras station** (1865)
Barlow's train shed is concealed by Scott's Midland Hotel

Hardwick's entrance to
Euston station (1840)
was the grandest of all

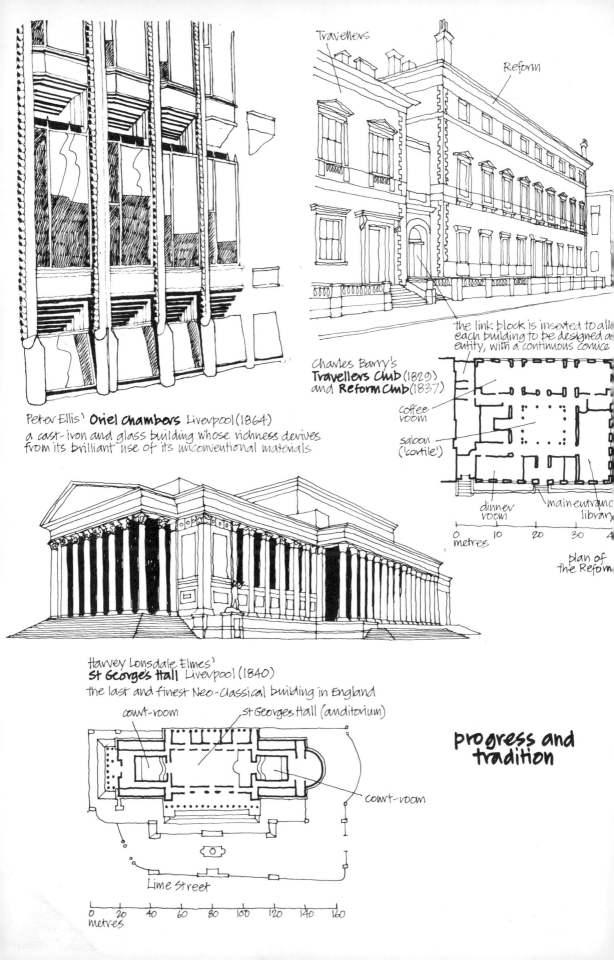

Peter Ellis' **Oriel Chambers** Liverpool (1864)
a cast-iron and glass building whose richness derives
from its brilliant use of its unconventional materials

Travellers

Reform

the link block is inserted to allow
each building to be designed as a
entity, with a continuous cornice

Charles Barry's
Travellers Club (1829)
and **Reform Club** (1837)

coffee
room

saloon
('cortile')

dinner
room

main entrance
library

0   10   20   30   4
metres

plan of
the Reform

Harvey Lonsdale Elmes'
St George's Hall Liverpool (1840)
the last and finest Neo-Classical building in England

court-room   St Georges Hall (auditorium)

court-room

Lime Street

0   20   40   60   80   100   120   140   160
metres

progress and
tradition

by cross-vaults, was disguised with a pretentious hotel building. At St Pancras Station (1865) the juxtaposition of engineering and architecture results in one of the century's most bizarre masterpieces. At the rear is the spectacular train shed by W. H. Barlow, a single curving span of 75 metres, 30 metres in height. At the front are the neo-gothic turrets and pinnacles of George Gilbert Scott's Midland Hotel. It is apparent that these pompous façades were designed with an ulterior purpose in mind: the Inigo Jones style of Bath Queen Square, the Tudor of Bristol Temple Meads, and the baroque of Newmarket Station were intended to make the railways respectable to a suspicious public. Approaching Euston through Hardwick's Doric propaeleum (1840) redolent with feelings of history and culture, the traveller might feel himself bound on some epic pilgrimage.

This unashamed use of architectural style for the associations it evoked became more explicit during the 19th century. Successful businessmen with a sense of tradition could see themselves as the successors of the Medici when they entered Charles Barry's Traveller's Club (1829) or his Reform Club (1837), both designed in the style of Florentine *palazzi* – with the central *cortile* translated into a roofed-in saloon to suit the London climate. As time went on, more and more styles from the past came into vogue, each with its own adherents and each with its own associational meanings to set beside the religiosity of Gothic and the aristocratic dignity of Neo-Classical.

Neo-Classical itself was in its final phase. Its last great manifestation in England was St George's Hall in Liverpool (1840–54) by Harvey Elmes. A massive and monumental building on an island site, combining the unlikely functions of concert hall and assize courts, with its clear articulation of the separate elements within the overall mass, it is firmly in the tradition of Gilly. Neo-Classical, with its overtones of Athenian democracy, was an accepted style for law-courts. It appears again in the Palais de Justice, Brussels (1866), by Joseph Poelaert, in a coarse and inflated design with none of the clarity of Liverpool. It appears too in the United States' Capitol in Washington, where the central feature, with its high rotunda and dome, were added in 1851 when the original Palladian building was remodelled by Thomas Walter.

In America, Neo-Classical gained greater acceptance than in England. Its use for country mansions, particularly in the south, was a natural progression from Palladianism, and the archetypal plantation house, with its hexastyle Doric portico, dates from this period. So also does a development in timber-framing which was to be a major American contribution to building techniques for smaller houses – the perfection of the 'balloon-frame' system, used for timber buildings in Europe since about the 16th century but now brought to a level of sophistication which allowed it to remain in common use until the present day. Instead of the independent structural frame of earlier centuries, a system was evolved which used the framing as an integral part of each wall, floor or roof element, turned into a diaphragm by timber sheathing. Considerable economy of timber brought the possibility of cheap, decently-built houses to all levels of the social scale.

In fact, 19th-century society, despite prosperity and despite revolution, was still desperately unequal; exploitation by the aristocracy had been exchanged for exploitation by the bourgeoisie, and the black slaves in America, the peasants in Europe and industrial workers everywhere formed a submerged majority whose rights were ignored. As industrial capitalism expanded, supported by the theories of the liberal economists Adam Smith and David Ricardo, the condition of the poor worsened

North American timber construction

the dignity of the timber Doric portico at the **Orton Plantation House** Wilmington N.C. (1734 and later)...

... the functionalism of **Kingsley Plantation House** Jacksonville Fla., (early 19th century)...

timber boarding

look-out position

basement in masonry construction containing slave prison-rooms

brick chimney stack

... and the simple timber framed construction of **Telfair House** Washington N.C., (1818)

masonry plinth with basement

corner brace

corner post

'girt'
cill

the strength of medieval European **braced framing** depended on the use of heavy hardwood members

separate studding for each storey

but North American framed construction used softwood in smaller sections, as in this **platform construction**..

continuous studs give great rigidity despite their small size

continuous studding required supply of softwood long enough and in sufficient quantity

... or in this **balloon framing**, the rapid building system on which the phenomenal growth of Chicago and San Francisco depended

balloon framing

head plate

upper floor joists

ribbon board carries floor joists

studs

sole plate or cill
masonry plinth

floor joists

50mm wide studs

fire stop

ribbo

studs

sole plate

timber cladding

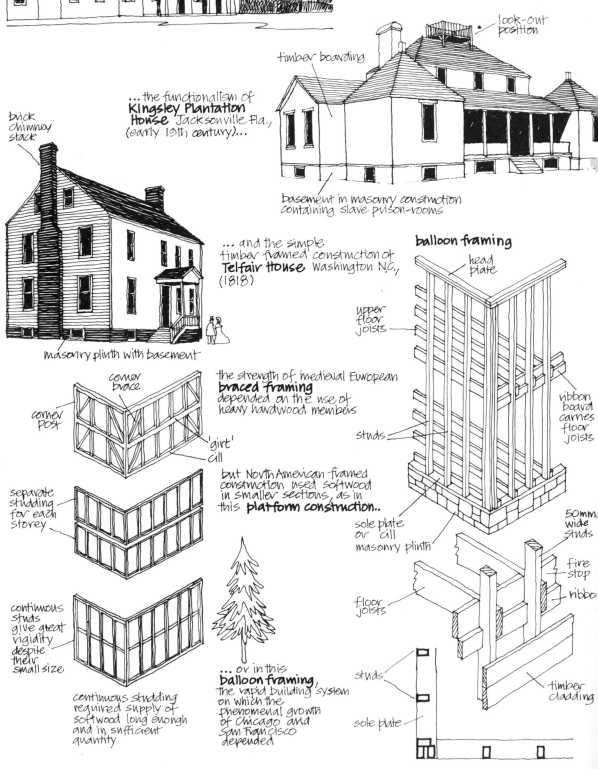

instead of improving, and the essays of Thomas Malthus fatalistically predicted that mass starvation was unavoidable. The old personal relationship between employer and employee had broken down and the rewards due to a worker now depended not on his ability but on the vagaries of an anonymous market. Entrepreneurs were growing rich at the expense of the workers, for whom long hours, poor conditions and low pay had become a way of life. Their old craft skills, from which they might have derived satisfaction, were required less and less, and their families suffered from the social uprooting which industrialisation had brought.

Progressive thinkers began to examine this situation more critically. John Stuart Mill recognised the value of individual liberty, the need for greater democracy and for social reform. The French philosopher Saint-Simon, a Christian and socialist, believed in the abolition of private property, while his compatriots Fourier and Proudhon, in the tradition of the *philosophes*, believed that the ideal future lay in the development of man's reason, from which would come a moral, healthy and truly anarchical society. In England, where industrialisation was most developed and its effects most acute, various Acts of Parliament in the early 19th century eliminated some of the exploitation of women and children. Commentators in Britain and Europe began to address themselves to the problem of poverty and its appalling effects on human life, and Robert Owen (1771–1858) devised practical schemes to relieve it.

Owen, a successful capitalist, with one fortune made in the textile industry and another through marrying a millionaire's daughter, took over a factory for 2000 people in 1799 at New Lanark near Glasgow, which he developed into a world-famous model community. In a scheme which today appears paternalistic and autocratic but which then must have been a considerable advance on the brutalities of the open market system, he built blocks of flats, a school, a shop selling goods to his workers at advantageous prices and community buildings which included an Institution for the Formation of Character. He later sank his entire fortune into a 20,000-acre farming community in Indiana, USA.

Owen's method was essentially to work within the system to alleviate the worst of its effects. He looked hopefully to an abstract millennium in which Unity and Justice would prevail. There were others, however, who saw that the situation was too desperate to wait for a gradual improvement. Thousands of workers and their families in the fast growing industrial cities lived in the most terrible conditions.

> Here one is in an almost undisguised working-men's quarter, for even the shops and beerhouses hardly take the trouble to exhibit a trifling degree of cleanliness. But all this is nothing in comparison with the courts and lanes which lie behind, to which access can be gained only through covered passages in which no two human beings can pass at the same time. Of the irregular cramming together of dwellings in ways which defy all rational plan ... it is impossible to convey an idea ... He who turns in thither gets into a filth and disgusting grime, the equal of which is not to be found. The only entrance to most of the houses is by means of narrow dirty stairs and over heaps of refuse and filth.

This description by Friedrich Engels (1820–95), writing in 1844 of *The Condition of the Working Class in England*, is of the Old Town in Manchester, the pre-industrial centre of the city hurriedly adapted with makeshift hovels and shacks to house the sudden influx of population. The nearby New Town, built by local builders to

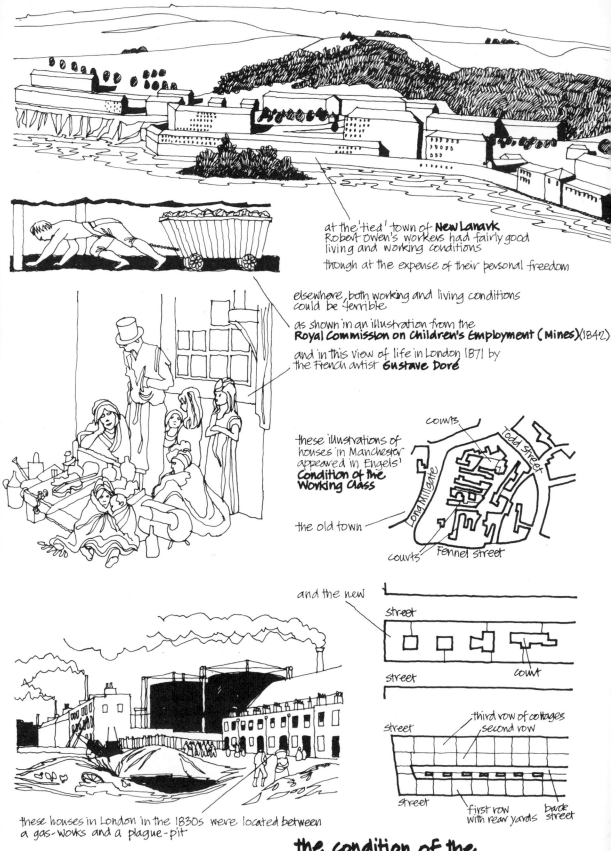

at the 'tied' town of **New Lanark**
Robert Owen's workers had fairly good
living and working conditions

though at the expense of their personal freedom

elsewhere, both working and living conditions
could be terrible

as shown in an illustration from the
Royal Commission on Children's Employment (Mines) (1842)

and in this view of life in London 1871 by
the French artist **Gustave Doré**

these illustrations of
houses in Manchester
appeared in Engels'
**Condition of the
Working Class**

courts

Todd street

Long millgate

the old town

courts

Fennel street

and the new

street

street

court

street

third row of cottages
second row

street

first row
with rear yards

back
street

these houses in London in the 1830s were located between
a gas-works and a plague-pit

the condition of the
working class

capitalise on the demand for living space, was scarcely better. Engels found a greater regularity of layout, but the houses were no more spacious, usually built back to back, lit and ventilated only from internal light-wells and with walls only half-a-brick – that is, $4\frac{1}{2}$ inches – in thickness. Homes, tanneries and gas-works were crowded together on the banks of stagnant canals which received factory waste and untreated sewage. Drainage and clean water supplies were non-existent, and disease was endemic.

Engels began to conclude that the desperate class-struggle which he saw around him was essentially the result of the economic structure of the modern world. In 1844 he established a life-long friendship with Karl Marx (1818–83) who, with Engels' close collaboration, became the first and greatest thinker to describe the multiple causes and effects of industrial society by means of a coherent methodology – which included an analysis of its past and a vision of the future.

Through his writings, culminating in *Capital* (1867 and later), Marx formulated an approach to the problems of the industrial age. Beginning with a utopian dream of what *could* be – of all men working in a creative collaboration with the world around – he showed how far the capitalist system fell short of this. Full of inherent tensions, capitalism would eventually be destroyed by worsening crises of its own making, but positive steps could be taken towards replacing it with a classless society by wresting power from the bourgeoisie, through a workers' revolution.

During the early 19th century, in fact, the working-class movement was gathering strength. In 1848, Europe was once more in a state of revolution – the first in which the workers as a class played a significant part. It began in France where it challenged not only the king but also bourgeois liberalism, then spread to Italy, where it was bound up with the struggle for independence from Austria, and to Germany, Switzerland, Holland, Belgium and Scandinavia. The struggle was short and violent and ended almost everywhere with the re-establishment of the old order.

But Europe had changed as a result. The ruling classes in general were less assured, more prepared to adapt and concede. The bourgeoisie, though now stronger economically than ever before, were less confident in the liberal idea of unlimited progress for its own sake: henceforward the development of capitalism was more pragmatic and realistic. And the workers, though defeated, had at least entered the political arena and gained greatly in strength and confidence.

At the time of the French Revolution in 1789, artists had supported the cause of freedom and liberty, the ideology of the liberal bourgeoisie. Now it was apparent what revolution had really achieved: not freedom for humanity as a whole but the fragmentation of society and the alienation of the individual. Critics of society were beginning to sympathise overtly with socialist aims: Byron with the oppressed Greeks, Stendhal with the Italians and Pushkin with the revolutionary Decembrists in Russia. The poetry of Baudelaire was a protest against bourgeois society and Courbet's painting showed his strong sympathy for the common people. Architects and engineers had no such freedom of expression. The nature of their profession and the way it had developed placed them firmly under the control of the ruling classes, whose principal means of communication they now were. The great architectural and engineering works which were to follow 1848 – uniquely impressive, popularly appealing – were an important means of giving a false air of unity to a divided society.

Tradition and progress

1850-1914

After the 1848 revolution Napoleon Bonaparte's nephew became president of France. Within four years he had proclaimed himself Napoleon III and France had entered its Second Empire. The emperor was a shrewd and cynical ruler, whose methods in some ways anticipated the dictators of the 20th century. He was careful to appease both the influential industrialists and the troublesome workers, by handing out attractive concessions. At the same time he was stern and repressive with minorities, the schools and universities, and the press. Under him, France prospered, and entered its real industrial revolution: banks were founded, factories and railways built and major public works begun, including an addition to the Louvre by Visconti and Lefuel (1852) in an ornate neo-renaissance style.

One of the greatest works of the Second Empire was the reconstruction by Baron Haussmann of the centre of Paris, which turned the old medieval city into a grand baroque gesture. In fact, aesthetic appeal was not Haussmann's only consideration: in the aftermath of the revolutionary street-fighting, security was a primary aim. Between 1853 and 1869, small buildings around the palaces and barracks which might offer cover to attackers were swept away and broad avenues, giving rapid access for troops, were ruthlessly cut in all directions. The opportunity was taken to destroy areas of potential opposition; the Boulevard St Michel cut a swathe through the university quarter, then as now a source of radical discontent. The radiating street-pattern, inspired by Versailles, was given a new meaning: from a single *rond-point* at the centre, a small detachment of artillery could control an entire district.

It was recognised now that the potential enemy was not outside the city but within. In 1858, the walls of Vienna were demolished at the command of the emperor Franz Josef and replaced with the *Ringstrasse*, a broad horseshoe-shaped avenue designed by Ludwig Förster, which gave the army access to all parts of the old city.

The new boulevards of Paris were lined with blocks of bourgeois apartments, similar in conception to those of the Place Royale and Rue de Rivoli, but rather more economical and less elegant. Typically they had four or five storeys of flats above a ground floor of shops and were two rooms deep, the outer and grander ones facing the street and the inner ones a narrow, claustrophobic light-well disdainfully known as a *cour anglaise*.

The Paris Opéra by Charles Garnier (1861) epitomises the bourgeois opulence of the Second Empire. Here the rich neo-renaissance style of the New Louvre was used to invest the frivolous world of the theatre with a ceremonial grandeur. The stage area is enormous, with a high tower suitable for flying the numerous scene changes required by *Les Huguenots* or *Guillaume Tell*. The auditorium is large and decorative, but comparable in size and even richer is the entrance hall, with painted ceilings, gilded statuary, ornate chandeliers and grand *escalier d'honneur*, a place for the fashionable opera-goer to see and be seen in a performance to rival that on the stage.

The Ecole des Beaux Arts in Paris, brought under state control in 1864 by

Haussmann's Paris

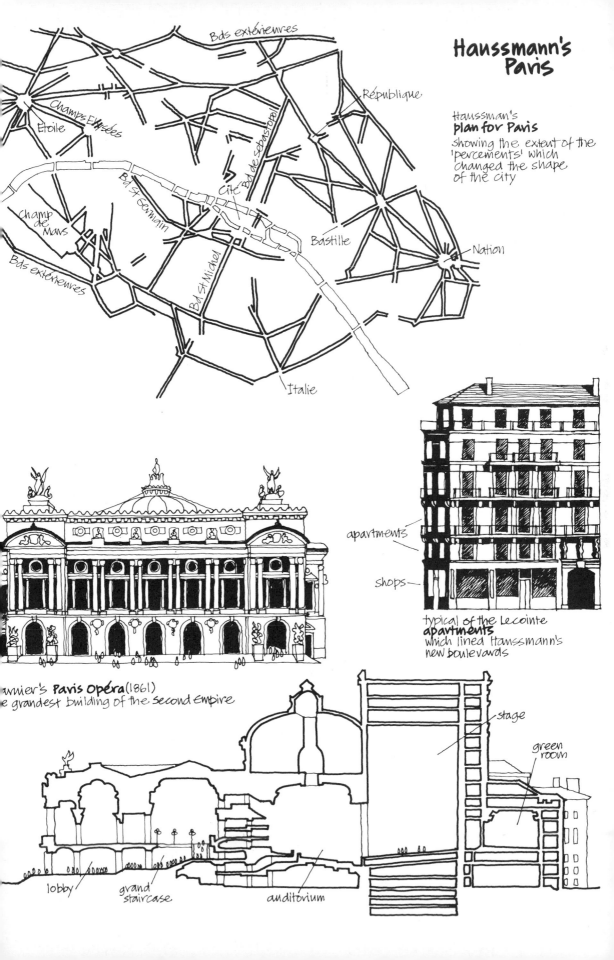

Bds extérieures

Champs Elysées
Etoile
République
Bd de sébastopol
Bd St Germain
Cité
Champ de Mars
Bd St Michel
Bds extérieures
Bastille
Nation
Italie

Haussman's
plan for Paris
showing the extent of the 'percements' which changed the shape of the city

apartments

shops

typical of the Lecointe
apartments
which lined Haussmann's
new boulevards

...rnier's **Paris Opéra** (1861)
...e grandest building of the **second Empire**

stage

green room

lobby

grand staircase

auditorium

Napoleon III, began to propagate a dry academic approach to design in which the styles of the French past played an important part. Through its students its influence spread over the world. Canada with its French traditions, and the USA with its much-travelled students, were particularly receptive. The French Gothic of the Ottawa Parliament buildings (1861) by Thomas Fuller and F. W. Stent, and the renaissance-style Vanderbilt Mansion in New York (1879) and Biltmore House at Ashville, NC (1890), both by R. M. Hunt, are good examples.

But the dominant style of the second half of the 19th century was still neo-gothic, which under the influence of Pugin, Ruskin and Viollet-le-Duc had become more eclectic and adventurous, drawing its inspiration from a greater variety of sources. The church of All Saints, Margaret Street, London (1849), was built by William Butterfield as a major centre of High Anglicanism. Its polychromatic brick and faience work were a re-creation of the richness of the medieval style in modern terms, and the ingenuity of its planning, on a congested urban site, is worthy of Wren. In the same tradition were the simple yet richly textured churches of G. E. Street, notably those of St Philip and St James, Oxford (1860) and of St James the Less, Westminster (1858). The Victorian Gothic high noon continued with the Albert Memorial in London (1863) by Scott and Manchester Town Hall (1868) by Waterhouse and ended in 1871 with Street's Law Courts in the Strand, London.

Gothic had also become accepted as an appropriate style for the country-houses of the wealthy, especially those of a romantic or eccentric disposition. The influence of the 'gothic' novels of Horace Walpole and Mary Shelley and the consuming interest of poets, painters and composers in a revival of the Arthurian legend were responsible for many neo-gothic sham castles. Cardiff castle and the nearby Castell Coch were real enough, but after their reconstruction (1868 and 1875) by William Burges for the Marquess of Bute they became fine examples of medieval scholarship combined with happy decorative invention. The gothic style was not particularly popular in the United States, where there was a strong classical tradition, but was frequently used to adorn the romantic hillsides and the forests of southern Germany and Austria. Archetypal is the mountainside *Schloss* of Neuschwanstein (1869) built by Georg von Dollman and Eduard Riedel for Wagner's friend and patron Ludwig II of Bavaria. Here, function counts for nothing: the whole building is a symbol, consonant with an image of Ludwig as a fairy-tale hero.

Romantic images were not confined to rich, eccentric princes. As city centres grew more foul, the middle classes, assisted by the expansion of suburban railways, moved out of town to newly-built, speculative suburbs. The aim, particularly in England, was to counteract the filth and noise of the city by re-creating some half-remembered image of the country mansion – or at the very least the country cottage. So, in emulation of Nash's Park Village, each house was if possible built 'detached', standing within its own plot, even when the plot was so narrow that the houses almost touched. Closer to the centre, the houses built for petty bourgeois shop-keepers and clerks might for economy be in continuous terraces, but even here the rural image was maintained by the provision of vestigial front gardens. The architectural style was almost everywhere a debased and highly eclectic Gothic, with high-pitched roofs, frequent dormers and gables, polychrome brickwork and stuccoed or artificial stone surrounds to windows and doors, adorned with factory-produced, neo-Ruskinian foliage.

But if most architects and builders were still concerned with creating an image of

NeoGothic

the Canadian
Parliament buildings
Ottawa (1861)
Fuller and Stent

grand
escalier

the Vanderbilt Mansion
New York (1879)
by Hunt
the style is that of the
early French chateaux

St Philip and St James
Oxford (1860)
by Street

a mixture of French
and English gothic

Butterfield's All Saints Margaret Street
London (1849)
the rich polychromatic decoration was
Butterfield's response to the Gothic idiom

court

hall

court

tower

0   20   40   60   80   100
metres

the plan of
Waterhouse's
Manchester
Town Hall
(1868)

Albert Memorial London 1863
Scott

Neuschwanstein in
Bavaria by Dollman and
Riedel (1869)

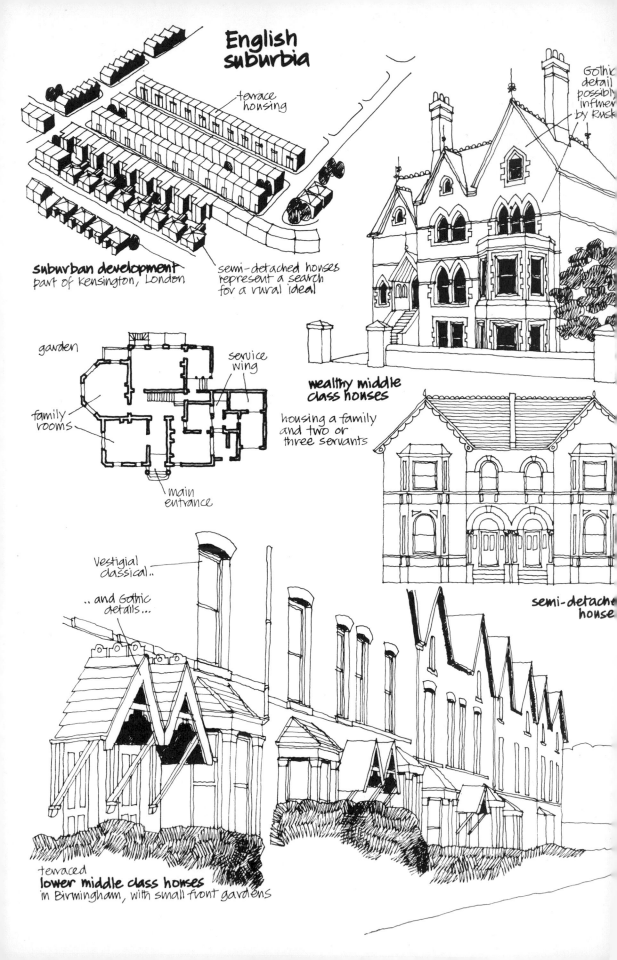

English suburbia

terrace housing

suburban development
part of Kensington, London

semi-detached houses represent a search for a rural ideal

Gothic detail possibly influenced by Ruskin

garden

service wing

family rooms

main entrance

wealthy middle class houses

housing a family and two or three servants

semi-detached house

Vestigial classical..

.. and Gothic details...

terraced
lower middle class houses
in Birmingham, with small front gardens

the past, there were now a few others, gradually increasing in number, with a more progressive attitude. The 'railway mania' of the thirties and forties had left a legacy of structural knowledge which, under the influence of Viollet-le-Duc, architects began to use. The Parisian churches of Ste Clotilde (1846) by F. C. Gau and St Eugène (1854) by F. C. Boileau made considerable use of ironwork, the former in the roof, the latter as a complete structural frame. The Halles Centrales in Paris (1853) by Victor Baltard, the city's main wholesale market till their demolition in 1971, were a vast complex of iron-framed pavilions separated by circulation routes and roofed almost completely in glass. Of the major Paris railway stations with iron roofs the Gare de l'Est (1847) by F. A. Duquesney and the Gare du Nord (1862) by J. I. Hitorff are the earliest and finest.

As industry expanded, it needed more and more outlets for its manufactured goods. During the 19th century, Europe's exports increased rapidly; England's, worth £100 million in 1854, had increased to £250 million by 1872. Domestic sales too, were strenuously promoted. Cities changed from being periodic outlets for market produce to permanent shopping centres selling manufactured goods. Regent Street and the Rue de Rivoli were elegantly colonnaded to protect their fashionable clients from the weather and pedestrian shopping streets, completely roofed over with iron-and-glass-vaulted arcades, became quite common in the larger cities. The earliest major example was the Galerie d'Orléans, Paris (1829), by P. F. L. Fontaine. The finest remaining ones are the Galleria Umberto I in Naples (1887), and the splendid Galleria Vittorio Emanuele II in Milan (1829 and later) by G. Mengoni which takes the form of a pair of pedestrian streets, intersecting at right angles, lined with dignified shopping façades and continuously roofed with iron-and-glass barrel-vaulting. The cruciform plan and the domed crossing make it superficially like a cathedral, but its mood is very different: humane, matter-of-fact and unmysterious in a way appropriate to a secular rather than religious meeting-place.

Capitalism needed to expand continuously to allow increased consumption to stimulate production. In the 19th century, importance was placed on international expositions, in which nations displayed their art and technology to the world. The first was the Great Exhibition, held in London in 1851, and many others followed: in Paris in 1855 and 1867, in Vienna in 1873, and in Paris again in 1878, 1889 and 1900. On the assumption that a confident display invokes the confidence of the customer, expenditure was lavish, and the architects and engineers responded with a vigour and assurance which resulted in some of the greatest building achievements of the century.

Joseph Paxton's Crystal Palace, built in Hyde Park, London, in 1851, was the culmination of cast-iron building technology. Designed in haste and erected in the remarkably short time of nine months, it showed a mastery of the iron techniques which Paxton had tried out at Chatsworth. It was famous not only for its elegance but also for its great size, 125×560 metres on plan and 22 metres high, tall enough to contain a living tree. Perhaps more significantly, it was pre-fabricated in sections off the site, a factor which obviously contributed to the short time it took to build but which demanded scrupulous pre-planning, remarkable for the period.

With the common use of wrought-iron, and then steel, exhibition structures became even more ambitious. Vienna 1873 saw the building of a gigantic iron cupola, over 100 metres in diameter, and Paris 1889 gave the world two engineering masterpieces. One was the Galérie des Machines, by Victor Contamin, a vast hall

Iron and glass

Les Halles centrales
Paris (1853)
by Victor Baltard

a completely iron-and-glass
structure, part of Haussmann's
reconstruction of the city

the main portico
of the,
Gare du Nord
Paris (1862)
by J. I. Hitorff
Ionic decoration
on an iron structure

NORD   NORD

Galleria Vittorio Emanuele II
Milan (1829)
by G. Mengoni

a religious form in a
new, secular context

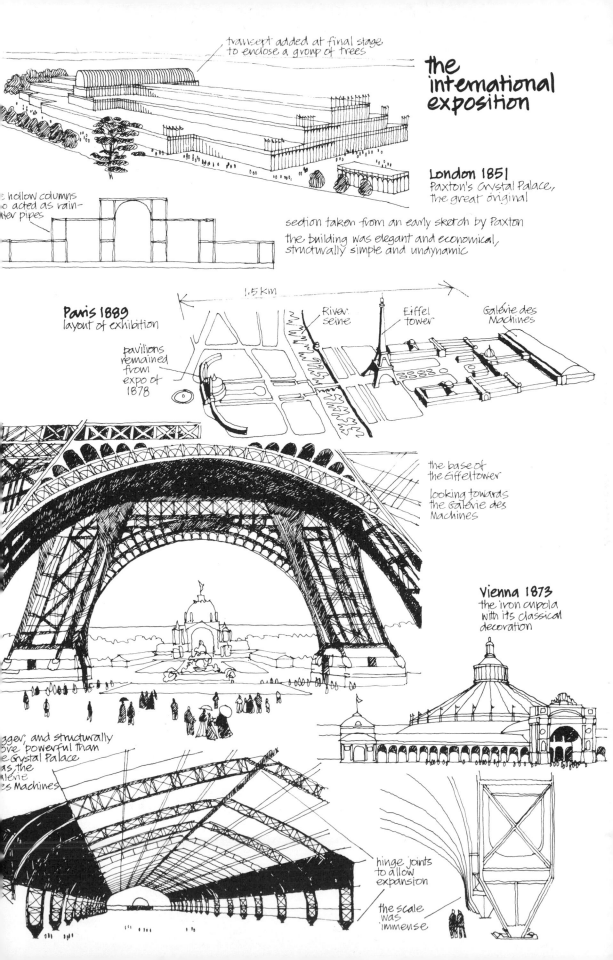

transcept added at final stage to enclose a group of trees

the international exposition

London 1851
Paxton's Crystal Palace, the great original

...e hollow columns ...o acted as rain-...ter pipes

section taken from an early sketch by Paxton

the building was elegant and economical, structurally simple and undynamic

Paris 1889
layout of exhibition

1.5 km

River Seine

Eiffel tower

Galérie des Machines

pavilions remained from expo of 1878

the base of the Eiffel tower

looking towards the Galérie des Machines

Vienna 1873
the iron cupola with its classical decoration

...gger, and structurally ...ve 'powerful' than ...e Crystal Palace ...as, the ...lérie ...es Machines

hinge joints to allow expansion

the scale was immense

430×120 metres, 45 metres high at the apex, clad entirely in glass. Its structure consisted of curving, trussed portal-frames, hinged at the apex and the base, and braced laterally by steel-framing, the widest span then built. The same exhibition also presented the world's highest structure, Gustave Eiffel's famous tower, an elegant lattice of steelwork curving parabolically from a wide, four-footed base to a height of some 300 metres. Both were conceived in terms of steel, higher in tensile strength than either cast- or wrought-iron; considering that steel-making was relatively new, it says much for Contamin and Eiffel that they mastered the material in such a confident way, in the face of criticism from rival engineers who predicted that the buildings would not stay up.

The architectural form of a great medieval church was only partly demanded by the need to enclose a large space. Much came from the way its designers saw the building in relation to society outside. Its relevance to the actual needs of society was probably less than is commonly supposed, but it did act as some kind of visual and social focus for the town, and also as a symbol, invoking certain concepts about God, the church and the world. In a great building like Durham or Vézelay, function and symbolism were combined in a perfect unity of form and content. But the structural masterpieces of the industrial age, though dazzling in terms of form alone, were almost empty of content. They performed no central social function – the Eiffel Tower had no real function at all – and were not symbols of any central philosophy of their time, except insofar as they were intended to evoke some generalised feeling of confidence in the achievements of the age. Their underlying purpose, like most major projects under capitalism, was the stimulation of capitalism itself and the promotion of economic growth. This is a basic architectural paradox of the modern world: the greatest resources and the highest technology are so often used on those projects of most questionable social value.

Perhaps the greatest and most prophetic critic of the effect of capitalism on architecture was the English poet, designer and revolutionary, William Morris (1834–96). Even in an age of giants, Morris stands out for the variety of his talents and the vigour of his approach to life. He learned architecture with Street, he painted with the Pre-Raphaelites, wrote novels and lyric poetry, and founded a design firm for the production of textiles, wallpapers, stained glass and illuminated books. All this he did within the context of a political philosophy which, by the 1870s, had independently reached a similar standpoint to that of Marx, and which made him more and more active in the socialist movement. For Morris, art and politics could not be separated. 'I do not want art for a few', he said in a famous passage from one of his many lectures, 'any more than education for a few, or freedom for a few.' He hated capitalism not only because it brought wage-slavery and alienation, but also because it created ugliness. The future, he was sure, would depend on the workers gaining freedom to expand their minds and skills and beginning once again to create the kind of beauty that the medieval cathedrals showed them capable of.

Morris's sympathy with the 13th century is often criticised as an unreal nostalgia and his preference for crafted goods over machine-made ones is interpreted as a dogmatic hatred of the machine which denies his own aim of 'art for the people' – the implication being that art can only be brought to the people by machine production. However, these views of Morris fail to incorporate his role as a socialist. Far from being a historicist – as Pugin and Ruskin both were – Morris had a positive, and frequently expressed, view of the future which was decidedly not a re-creation of

194

medieval England. In it, machinery had an important part to play as a background force to relieve man from toil and to free him to develop his talents. His art would not be just one more machine-made commodity imposed on him from outside, but something to which he himself would give expression. Clearly capitalism, with its invention of imaginary needs, its waste, pollution and inequality was not able to create this kind of society.

In the meantime capitalism was still expanding. Under Bismarck and Moltke, Prussia's military successes against Austria in 1866 and France in 1870 were the prelude to a spectacular economic expansion between 1870 and 1890. Italy, created by Garibaldi and Mazzini out of a number of separate states in 1860, also emerged as an industrial power. The United States was now colonising the west, building railways, expanding its industry, commerce and agriculture. Its freedom brought immigrants from Europe, escaping from political repression and poverty, who became a ready-made work-force for the industries of the eastern cities: New York, Boston, Chicago, Philadelphia and Pittsburgh expanded rapidly as industrial and commercial centres. Russia, on the other hand, excluded from western Europe since the Crimean War (1853–6), had relapsed into a repressive and reactionary autocracy which denied any real progress towards industrialisation.

The growth of capitalism had more apologists than critics; to many it seemed to represent all that was best in civilisation. To historians like Mommsen there were distinct similarities between 19th-century Germany and ancient Rome; to Burckhardt the industrial age fulfilled the promise of the Italian Renaissance. There were architectural apologists too, of course, who executed official commissions by drawing parallels between the present and its glorious heritage. The Reichstag in Berlin (1884) by P. Wallot was appropriately pompous and baroque, while the monument designed for the Capitol in Rome by G. Sacconi to commemorate Victor Emmanuel (1885) was an extraordinarily grandiose invocation of the imperial past.

In northern Europe there were fewer pretensions to imperial destiny, and public buildings were being designed within a more democratic and domestic tradition. The Rijksmuseum in Amsterdam (1877) by P. Cuijpers and the City Hall in Copenhagen (1893) by M. Nyrop are both unpretentious buildings of gothic character. Their picturesque outline, their use of local brick and their small-scale elevations make them much more humane than the pomposities of Berlin and Rome. The Stock Exchange (1898) and the Diamond Workers' Union (1899) in Amsterdam, both by H. P. Berlage, represent progress from traditionalism. The simple design of their brick exteriors and the straightforward structural expression of their interiors point the way to the functionalism of the 20th century.

In the United States, too, traditional forms were discarded as architects began to evolve an indigenous approach to design. The architecture of McKim, Meade and White during the eighties and nineties, like their brownstone houses in New York, still showed classical influences, with formal plans and strictly controlled elevations. In Stoughton House in Cambridge, Mass. (1882), on the other hand, Henry Hobson Richardson progressed to a looser and more informal plan arrangement which derived from the greater freedom offered by the use of a structural frame. This feature was taken up by Frank Lloyd Wright (1869–1959) in his early houses, which, whether of load-bearing or framed construction, demonstrate his early preoccupation with free-flowing, interpenetrating spaces.

national grandeur
and
civic pride

the Reichstag building
Berlin (1884)
by P. Wallot •

the Victor Emmanuel
monument
Rome (1885)
by G. Sacconi

the Palais de Justi
Brussels (186
by J. Poelae

copenhagen city Hall
(1893)
by M. Nyrop

the Rijksmuseum
Amsterdam (1877)
by P. Cuijpers

Wright, born in Wisconsin of Baptist parents, was something of a pioneer, who grew up with a love of the countryside and a distaste for city life. He learned his craft with the big-city architects Dankmar Adler (1844–1900) and Louis Sullivan (1856–1924) for whom he worked in Chicago till 1893. Sullivan, whom he revered for the rest of his life, was the only architect Wright would accept as having influenced him, though the influence came more from Sullivan's attitude than from his style: the concept of architectural honesty, embodied in Sullivan's famous dictum, 'form follows function'. This misunderstood phrase did not mean that beauty of form arose *inevitably* out of the expression of function, but that honesty of expression was an essential pre-condition in the creation of a beautiful building. In fact, Wright had little sympathy for the office-buildings which were Adler and Sullivan's stock-in-trade, and he began to concentrate on the firm's private houses. The Charnley House (1891) was entirely Wright's work, a simple geometric brick block of three storeys.

More commissions came Wright's way, and he set up on his own, developing a very personal style which began to express all he felt about the relationship between man and nature. His early houses in the Oak Park and Riverside suburbs of Chicago, now known as the Prairie houses, were clearly conceived with a more elemental landscape in mind. They demonstrate a pre-occupation with interlocking spaces, a blurring of the distinction between interior and exterior, terraces that link the house to the landscape around and horizontal pitched roofs that over-sail and dominate the whole composition. Conceived as true expressions of their simple materials, generally brick and timber, and with integral rather than applied decorative features, they represent Wright's search for a rugged American architecture owing nothing to the European past. The Winslow House at River Forest, Ill. (1893) and the famous Robie House in Chicago (1908) were his first mature works.

There were two other major works of these early years: the Unity Temple at Oak Park (1906) and the seven-storey Larkin Company administration building at Buffalo, NY (1904). The former was not a dramatic statement but two simple rooms linked together by an entrance lobby; heavy, simple concrete walls and a flat slab roof were part of a straightforward conception. The latter, till its destruction in 1950, remained unique among office buildings. It was built in brick, heavily modelled into plain, vertical slabs, like the pylons of an Egyptian or Mayan temple. Inside, a central five-storey-high hall was surrounded by tiers of galleries containing office space, and the whole was lit from a vast central rooflight. The Larkin building, simple, vertical and dramatic, and the Robie house, subtle, complex, calm and horizontal, soon became, internationally, Wright's two most admired buildings and had a strong influence on the ideas of the European avant-garde.

Tall office buildings were springing up all over America in its fast-growing city-centres, as a result of rising land-costs and a number of technical developments. The use of Elisha Otis's electric elevator from the 1860s onwards, combined with the great strength of structural steel, allowed the construction during the eighties and nineties of the world's first skyscrapers. They appeared in all the major cities, but above all in Chicago where they were conceived from the start by architects such as Richardson, Adler and Sullivan as a new architectural form. A simple, functional design approach was evolved, in which the structural supports – columns or piers – and the floor slabs became the main features of the elevations. Decoration was used sparingly, though Sullivan in particular was given to occasional outpourings of rich, decorative detail – a characteristic he bequeathed to Wright.

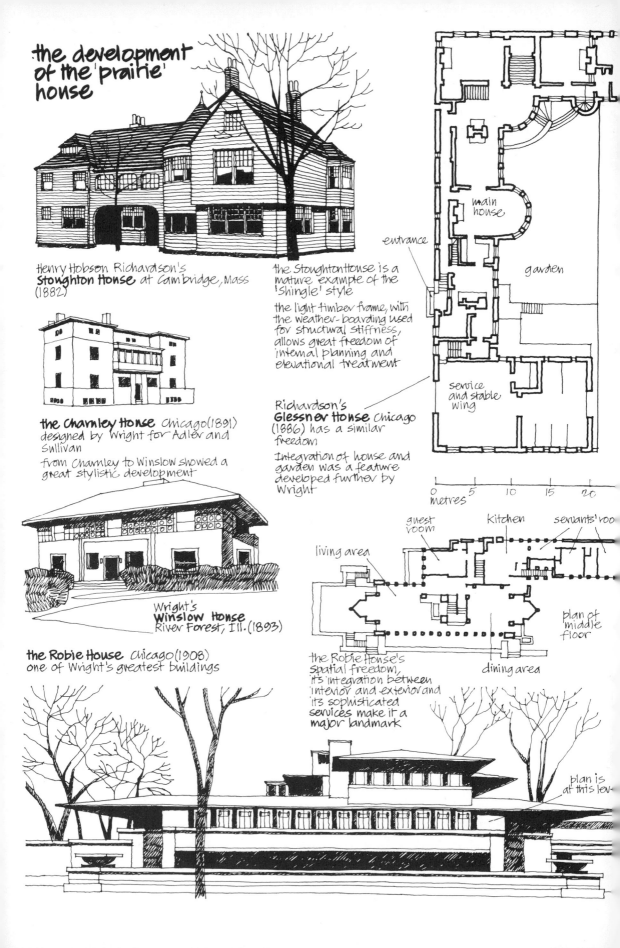

the development of the 'prairie' house

Henry Hobson Richardson's **Stoughton House** at Cambridge, Mass (1882)

the **Charnley House** Chicago (1891) designed by Wright for Adler and Sullivan

from Charnley to Winslow showed a great stylistic development

Wright's **Winslow House** River Forest, Ill. (1893)

the **Robie House** Chicago (1908) one of Wright's greatest buildings

the Stoughton House is a mature example of the 'shingle' style

the light timber frame, with the weather-boarding used for structural stiffness, allows great freedom of internal planning and elevational treatment

Richardson's **Glessner House** Chicago (1886) has a similar freedom

Integration of house and garden was a feature developed further by Wright

entrance

main house

garden

service and stable wing

0 5 10 15 20
metres

guest room

living area

Kitchen

servants' room

plan of middle floor

dining area

the Robie House's spatial freedom, its integration between interior and exterior and its sophisticated services make it a major landmark

plan is at this lev-

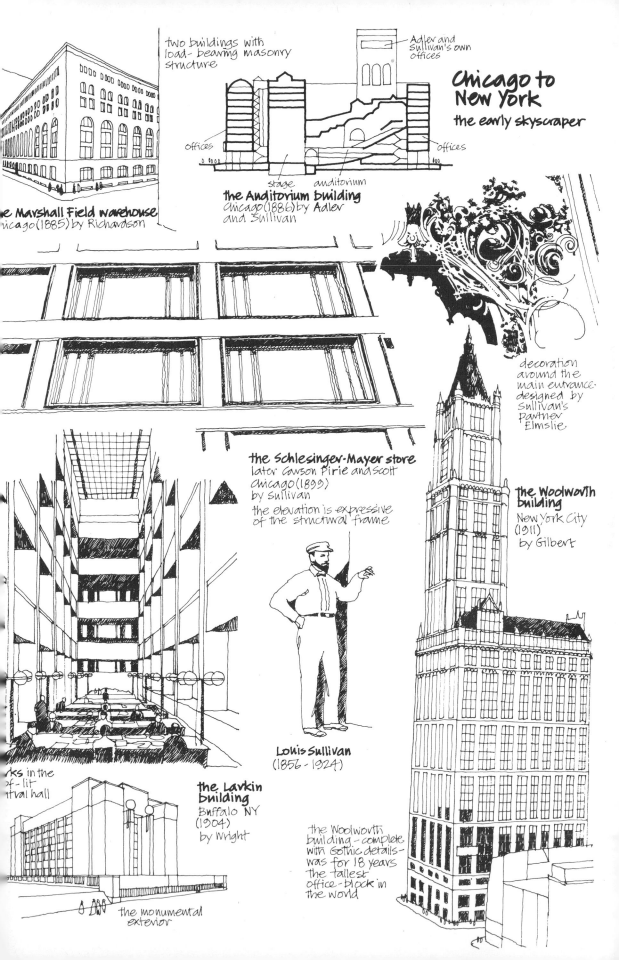

two buildings with load-bearing masonry structure

Adler and Sullivan's own offices

Offices

stage   auditorium

Offices

the Auditorium building
Chicago (1886) by Adler and Sullivan

the Marshall Field warehouse
Chicago (1885) by Richardson

decoration around the main entrance designed by Sullivan's partner Elmslie

the Schlesinger-Mayer store
later Cawson Pirie and Scott
Chicago (1899)
by Sullivan
the elevation is expressive of the structural frame

the Woolworth building
New York City (1911)
by Gilbert

Louis Sullivan
(1856 - 1924)

...rks in the
...of-lit
...tral hall

the Larkin building
Buffalo NY
(1904)
by Wright

the monumental exterior

the Woolworth building - complete with Gothic details - was for 18 years the tallest office-block in the world

At first, these buildings had load-bearing external walls as well as steel-framing, and considerable care was taken in designing the foundations to carry the enormous loads involved. Richardson's seven-storey Marshall Field Warehouse (1885) and the ten-storey Auditorium Building (1886) by Adler and Sullivan were examples. The first fully steel-framed block was built in 1883, and among its distinguished successors are the Gage Building (1898) and the Schlesinger-Mayer Store (1899), both by Sullivan. The latter has a simple elevation faced in white faience which follows the outline of the structure without obscuring it. Early skyscraper construction ends with the Woolworth Building in New York (1911) designed by Cass Gilbert. Though elevationally it was much less advanced than Sullivan's buildings, its height of 240 metres – fifty storeys – makes it a remarkable technical feat.

Steel was not ideal for structural frames. Though quick to erect, it was not fireproof, and de-formed drastically under intense heat. It was also expensive, and by the 1880s a cheaper alternative was developed. The long French tradition of civil engineering, fostered throughout the 19th century by the Ecole Centrale des Travaux Publiques, resulted in the development by Joseph Monier during the 1880s of reinforced concrete. This is a composite material, in which concrete, with its high compressive strength and high resistance to fire, is given tensile strength by the steel reinforcing rods embedded within it. An added advantage is its plasticity, its ability to assume the shape of the moulds in which it is cast. The engineers François Coignet and François Hennebique, in their pioneering work in the eighties and nineties, used this plasticity to advantage, finding it particularly appropriate for arched bridge construction.

The engineer-architect Auguste Perret (1874–1954) was among the first to exploit the properties of the new material in buildings. His early block of nine-storey apartments at 25bis Rue Franklin near the Trocadéro in Paris (1903) has an exposed concrete frame inset with decorative panels. Though predominantly rectilinear, the plan-form has a freedom which comes from a frame construction with bold projections and recessions on the front elevation. In his church of Notre Dame du Raincy, Seine-et-Oise (1922), the spatial freedom of Gothic is translated into modern materials. The thin-shell concrete vaulting supported on slim pillars, and the perforated concrete screens which serve as windows, give an air of lightness and elegance impossible to achieve with masonry.

The influence of the Ecole Centrale spread into Switzerland and Germany, resulting in the foundation of the Polytechnic at Zurich in 1854 and numerous *Technische Hochschulen* during the seventies and eighties. In 1895, the Ecole itself became the Ecole Polytechnique, an institution which has continued to dominate French public life. One of its pupils, the engineer Eugène Freyssinet, brought an analytical approach to design. His two airship hangars at Orly (1905) were simple, economical and conceived very much in terms of reinforced concrete: vast, folded slabs curved into the form of parabolic arches some 60 metres to the apex. Further advances were made by the Swiss engineer Robert Maillart (1872–1940), a student of Zurich, who is known particularly for his use, from 1908, of 'mushroom' construction in heavily loaded buildings, and for his curved-slab bridge designs, first used at Tavenasa in 1905 and reaching their greatest elegance at Salginatobel in 1929.

As a result of the industrial revolution, architecture had assumed many different forms, and the turn of the century presented a vivid contrast between extremes: on the one hand, Sullivan, Perret and the engineer-architects were moving towards an

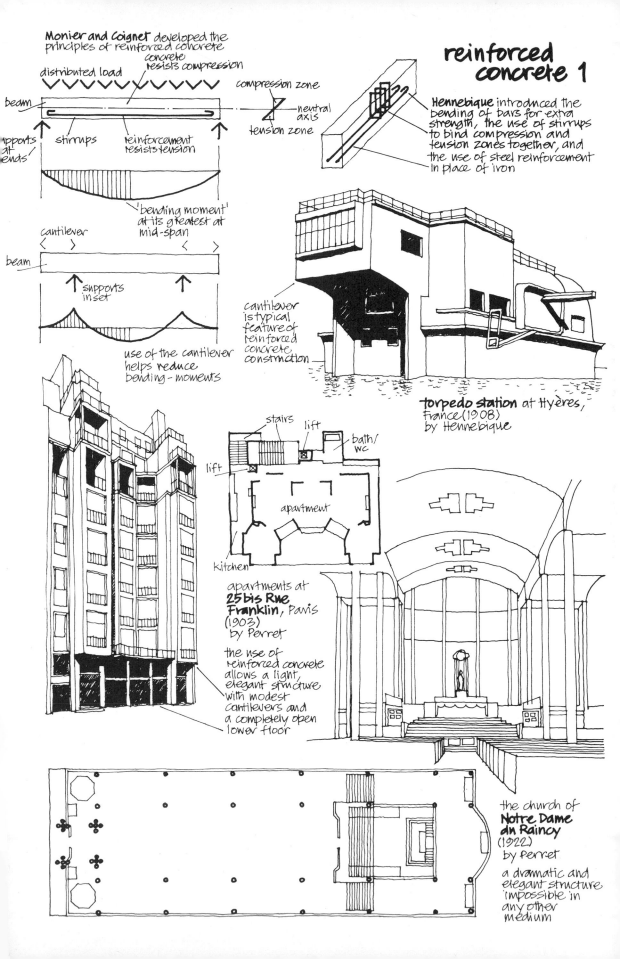

Monier and Coignet developed the principles of reinforced concrete

concrete resists compression

distributed load

beam

compression zone

neutral axis

tension zone

supports at ends

stirrups

reinforcement resists tension

'bending moment' at its greatest at mid-span

cantilever

beam

supports inset

use of the cantilever helps reduce bending-moments

Hennebique introduced the bending of bars for extra strength, the use of stirrups to bind compression and tension zones together, and the use of steel reinforcement in place of iron

cantilever is typical feature of reinforced concrete construction

torpedo station at Hyères, France (1908) by Hennebique

stairs

lift

lift

bath/wc

apartment

kitchen

apartments at 25 bis Rue Franklin, Paris (1903) by Perret

the use of reinforced concrete allows a light, elegant structure with modest cantilevers and a completely open lower floor

the church of Notre Dame du Raincy (1922) by Perret

a dramatic and elegant structure impossible in any other medium

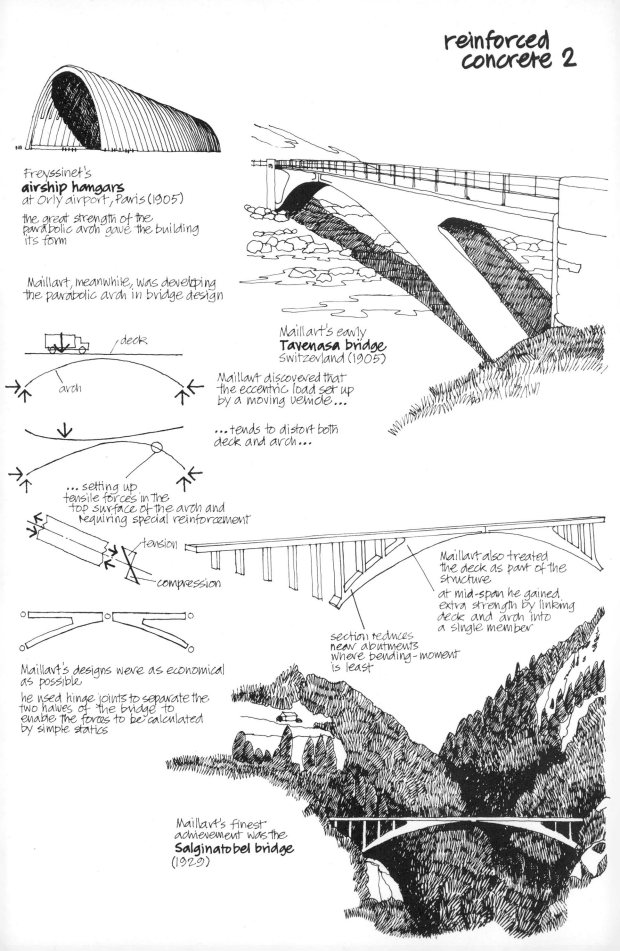

Freyssinet's
airship hangars
at Orly airport, Paris (1905)

the great strength of the
parabolic arch gave the building
its form

Maillart, meanwhile, was developing
the parabolic arch in bridge design

deck

arch

Maillart's early
Tavenasa bridge
Switzerland (1905)

Maillart discovered that
the eccentric load set up
by a moving vehicle...

...tends to distort both
deck and arch...

...setting up
tensile forces in the
top surface of the arch and
requiring special reinforcement

tension

compression

Maillart's designs were as economical
as possible

he used hinge joints to separate the
two halves of the bridge to
enable the forces to be calculated
by simple statics

Maillart also treated
the deck as part of the
structure

at mid-span he gained
extra strength by linking
deck and arch into
a single member

section reduces
near abutments
where bending-moment
is least

Maillart's finest
achievement was the
Salginatobel bridge
(1929)

aesthetic which derived from the structural method used; on the other, an attitude persisted that architecture was a matter of style. To the traditionalist, 'style' meant reproducing the styles of the past, but in the 1890s a feeling was growing among the more progressive stylists that the modern age should have its own style. For a brief decade, a design movement came and went, taking its name from a shop selling modern goods, opened in Paris in 1895: 'L'Art Nouveau'. Designers, artists and architects everywhere seemed concerned with the same new aesthetic, based on limp, flowing curves like the tendrils of growing plants and twisting wind-blown forms like flames, which contrasted strongly with the ordered geometry of Classicism and the stiffness of Neo-Gothic. The growth of the art nouveau style can be traced from such diverse antecedents as the paintings of Edvard Munch and Edward Burne-Jones or the decorative designs of Morris and Louis Sullivan, but it really came of age with the interior designs of the Belgian architects Victor Horta (1861–1947) and Henri van de Velde (1863–1957).

In Horta's masterpiece, the Hôtel Tassel at 6 Rue Paul-Emile Janson, Brussels (1892), the decorative iron main staircase is a forest of flowing curves. The curving iron façade of the Maison du Peuple (1896) and the department store 'L'Innovation' (1901), were further essays in the style. Van de Velde designed the interior of 'L'Art Nouveau' itself and went on to design buildings and interiors in Germany which furthered his reputation throughout Europe, especially in furniture design. In France Hector Guimard (1867–1943) designed the Castel Béranger in the Rue Fontaine at Passy (1894) with its sinuous wrought-iron entrance gate, and worked for the Paris Métro. The entrance to the Bastille station (1900) is a vegetable growth of iron-work and glass, an architectural statement which belongs very much to its time, owing little in its lines and form to any period of the past.

In one major respect Art Nouveau was, in fact, traditional: it was essentially decorative, even two-dimensional, and did not form part of any radical appraisal of the spatial possibilities of the new materials. Among architects, the two main exceptions to this rule stood somewhat on the edge of the movement. The first was the Spaniard, Antoni Gaudí (1852–1926), an enigmatic, ascetic figure whose buildings are among the most personal ever constructed. His style, while recognisably Art Nouveau, grew out of the Spanish past, both Christian and Arabic. His early Casa Vicens at Barcelona (1878), his park, the Parque Güell (1900), and his two blocks of apartments, the Casa Batlló (1905) and the Casa Milá (1905) show a mastery of form and space, rare in Art Nouveau and eccentric in the extreme. Much depends on his use of concrete to achieve flowing shapes, imbedded with shards of pottery and glass and clusters of decorative metalwork. His masterpiece, begun in 1883 and still unfinished now, was his extension to the neo-gothic church of La Sagrada Familia in Barcelona, a commission of great importance to the forces of right-wing catholicism to which he responded with architectural fervour. Gradually the existing neo-gothic design was transformed, first into Gaudí's own version of Gothic; then, with the addition of the four clustered transept spires and the strange, angular shapes of the internal arcades, the composition became a huge abstract sculpture, incomplete and hardly usable as a building but dramatically powerful as an image.

The other exception to the art nouveau norm was the Scot, Charles Rennie Mackintosh (1868–1928), who was studying at the Glasgow School of Art at the time when Art Nouveau caught the attention of young and progressive designers. Beginning as a freelance graphic designer and a salaried architect working for a local firm,

a wallpaper design by **William Morris** with the flowing lines and two-dimensional character later to be associated with Art Nouveau

6 Rue Paul-Émile Janson Brussels (1892) by Victor Horta

bedroom

anteroom

staircase

drawing room

Horta's plan is fairly conventional but the decoration is highly original

this is the staircase

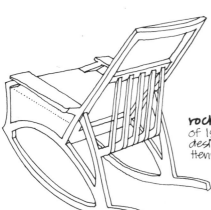

rocking chair of 1903 designed by Henri Van de Velde

Guimard's iron gateway to the **Castel Béranger** in Paris (1894)

the iron and glass facade of the **Maison du Peuple** Horta's building for the Parti Ouvrier Belge in Brussels (1897)

SORTIE ENTRÉE

one of Guimard's three standard designs for Métro entrances at the **Bastille** Paris (1900)

floor plan of the
Casa Batlló Barcelona
(1905)
by Gaudí

**Art nouveau
2**

Gaudí's
Casa Milá Barcelona
(1905)

begun in 1883 in Barcelona
Gaudí's church of the Holy Family
La Sagrada Familia

iron finial
above
entrance

Mackintosh's **Glasgow School of Art** (1896)

the
west facade

the entrance
elevation

he quickly came to public attention by winning a competition in 1896 for the design of a new School of Art. The building is as personal as those of Gaudí, but very different: disciplined and tensely organised, severe yet with touches of frivolity, designed to the last detail. Both inside and out, an art nouveau delicacy of detail contrasts with the tough, plain character of traditional Scottish stone. On the front elevation, large airy studio windows adorned with elegant wrought-iron brackets alternate with massive stone piers, and on the later west elevation the three tall oriel windows which light the library, framed up in light bronze-work, form a rich and dramatic contrast to the mass of stonework which surrounds them.

The rest of Mackintosh's work shows the same startling contrasts – from the rich, elegant and exciting interiors for Miss Cranston's chain of Glasgow tea-rooms, of which The Willow in Sauchiehall Street (1904) was the finest, to the simple yet original country houses Windyhill (1900) and Hill House (1902). Mackintosh's spare, cool interiors, often plain and white, did much to form a transition between the excesses of Art Nouveau and the more restrained approach shortly to emerge. His other major contribution to architecture was his ability to manipulate space: his interiors, enclosed here by solid walls, there by light screens, now low and constricted, now tall and free, anticipate the exciting spatial adventures of the 20th century.

Mackintosh's interest in simple, vernacular architecture as a reaction against the 19th century was also seen in the domestic work of Richard Norman Shaw (1831–1912), and even more strongly in the houses of C. F. A. Voysey (1857–1941) and of Edwin Lutyens (1869–1944). Shaw was largely influenced by the ideas of Morris and of his architect collaborator Philip Webb. Though beginning his career by indulging in Neo-Gothic, he graduated to a mature, restrained and elegant brick style, seen best in his own house in Hampstead (1875), his Swan House in Chelsea (1876) and his suburban housing estate Bedford Park to the west of London (1880). Lutyens, rich and successful, was given the task of expressing the imperial grandeur of his time, in great country houses, churches and official buildings, which culminated in his grandiose designs for the government buildings in New Delhi (1913). But he was also a sensitive designer, on a small scale, of houses and gardens, and places like The Orchards, Godalming (1899), and Folly Farm, Sulhampstead (1905), show an informal side of his architecture. Voysey too was a master at integrating an unpretentious house with its surrounding garden and landscape. Of the three, his architecture is the least formal, the least derivative while most consciously belonging to some long-standing tradition of local building; Annesley Lodge in Hampstead (1895), Broadleys and Moor Crag at Lake Windermere (1898) and The Orchard, Chorley Wood (1899) demonstrate his unsensational yet original style.

One aspect of 19th-century romanticism, its support for bourgeois liberalism in the days when liberalism had promised to make men free, had been revolutionary. Other aspects, such as the rejection of the modern world and the retreat to Nature or to Antiquity, were reactionary. The result had been a widening rift between artist and public: it became *de rigeur* for the artist to reject society and for society in return to scorn, misunderstand or merely ignore him. This situation naturally pertained more to poetry or painting than architecture, which required society's acquiescence if it was to be built. But even here, the principle of 'L'art pour l'art' was gaining acceptance, and architects entered the coterie of elitist intellectuals. The aesthetic movement, of which Art Nouveau was part, was a move in this direction. The various international exhibitions, held around the turn of the century by artists, architects and their patrons to promote new artistic ideas to the art-buying public, were held in a spirit of defiance and had a mixed reception. The Bavarian and Viennese 'Secessionists', whose name expressed their intransigent, break-away attitude, rejected not only traditional art but also each other. The Viennese exhibitions included work by Mackintosh and his Scottish contemporaries, by Otto Wagner (1841–1918), J. M. Olbrich (1876–1908), Peter Behrens (1868–1940), Josef Hoffman (1870–1956) and Adolf Loos (1870–1933).

Wagner, as a professor at the Vienna academy, had a great influence on numerous gifted students, including Olbrich, Hoffman and Loos. His best-known work is the Post Office Savings Bank building in Vienna (1904) with its barrel-vaulted glass interior, uncompromisingly modern in design even today. Olbrich was the designer of the light-hearted little Secession building in Vienna (1898) which acted as the headquarters of the movement – a small rectangular block covered with a metalwork dome, and also of the houses of the Mathildenhöhe at Darmstadt (1901), part of an artists' colony founded by the Grand Duke of Hesse and planned by Olbrich, with Behrens, as a group of cool, low buildings whose simple design had already moved away from the vegetable forms of Art Nouveau. The centrepiece of the composition was the 45-metre 'Wedding Tower' or 'Hochzeitsturm', an original design incorporating a crest of five rounded fin-like pinnacles.

The work of Hoffman also represented a step towards modernity. His Palais Stoclet in Brussels (1905) convincingly demonstrated that richness of effect did not depend only on decoration but could also be achieved through variety of form and by contrasting materials; his Convalescent Home at Purkersdorf, Vienna (1903) went even further and rejected varied textures in a plain, rectilinear design of almost banal simplicity. Behrens' part in the Darmstadt project was to design himself a whimsical house which gave little hint that he was to become one of the masters of early modern design. Influenced by the total design approach of Morris, he brought to his appointment as chief architect to AEG, the Berlin electricity company, a comprehensive design attitude which tackled everything from buildings to stationery. His AEG Turbine Factory (1909) has a strongly classical feeling which makes it unusually dignified for an industrial building, but it is a classicism of mood rather than of detail. It is a symmetrical, hall-like building, steel-framed with a barrel roof, great expanses of glazing set between the steel columns, and rusticated concrete piers on the end walls as bold as the work of Giulio Romano. In some of his later works, Behrens relapsed into an overt classicism; and so after 1910 did Loos, whose early works, such as the houses near Lake Geneva (1904) and the Steiner House in Vienna (1910), are plain and rectilinear, in keeping with his anti-ornament philosophy.

In 1907, the Deutscher Werkbund was formed in Germany, an association of architects, designers and artists concerned with the application of higher design standards to industrial products and of industrial techniques to building design. The need to come to terms with the industrialist evoked a more cautious architectural approach. The first Werkbund exhibition in 1914 displayed a kind of stripped-down classicism; the only significant exceptions were Bruno Taut's crystalline little Glass Pavilion, conceived wholly within the nature of its unconventional materials, and parts of the administrative building which, though it had a rigidly classical plan and symmetrical elevations, was relieved by the exciting circular staircases at the cor-

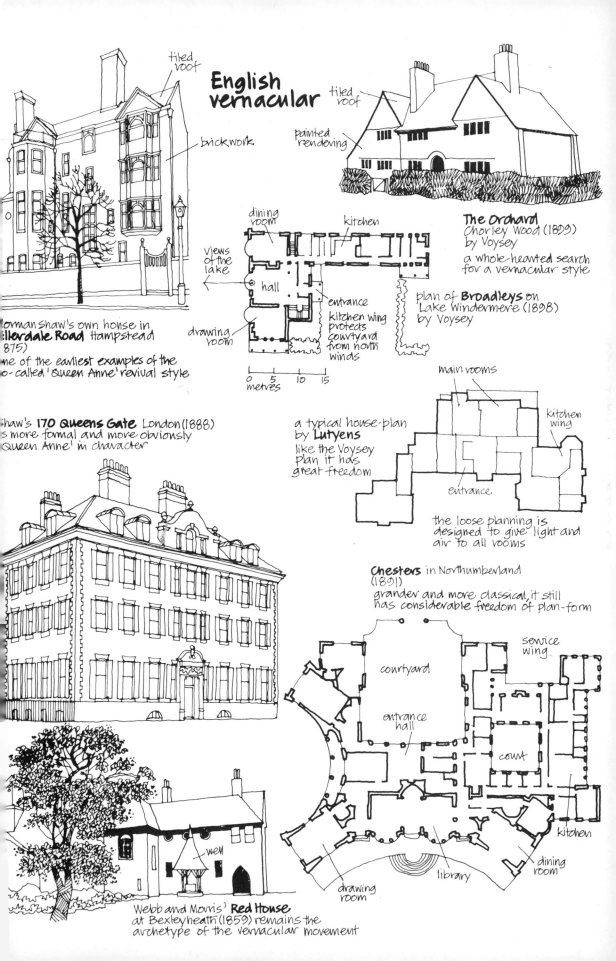

English vernacular

tiled roof

brickwork

tiled roof

painted rendering

The Orchard
Chorley Wood (1899)
by Voysey

a whole-hearted search
for a vernacular style

dining room

kitchen

views of the lake

hall

entrance

kitchen wing protects courtyard from north winds

drawing room

plan of **Broadleys** on
Lake Windermere (1898)
by Voysey

0 5 10 15
metres

main rooms

kitchen wing

a typical house-plan
by **Lutyens**
like the Voysey
plan it has
great freedom

entrance

the loose planning is
designed to give light and
air to all rooms

Norman Shaw's own house in
Ellerdale Road Hampstead
(1875)
one of the earliest examples of the
so-called 'Queen Anne' revival style

Shaw's **170 Queens Gate** London (1888)
is more formal and more obviously
'Queen Anne' in character

Chesters in Northumberland
(1891)
grander and more classical, it still
has considerable freedom of plan-form

courtyard

service wing

entrance hall

court

drawing room

library

kitchen

dining room

Webb and Morris' **Red House**
at Bexleyheath (1859) remains the
archetype of the vernacular movement

well

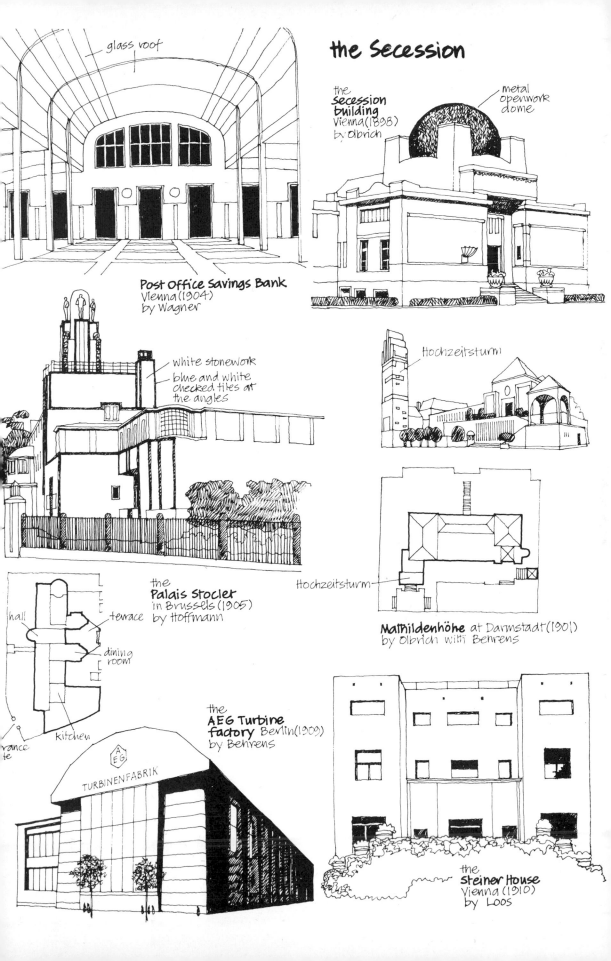

glass roof

Post Office Savings Bank
Vienna (1904)
by Wagner

the Secession

the
**secession
building**
Vienna (1898)
by Olbrich

metal
openwork
dome

white stonework
blue and white
checked tiles at
the angles

Hochzeitsturm

the
Palais Stoclet
in Brussels (1905)
by Hoffmann

hall

terrace

dining
room

entrance
gate

kitchen

Hochzeitsturm

Mathildenhöhe at Darmstadt (1901)
by Olbrich with Behrens

the
**AEG Turbine
factory** Berlin (1909)
by Behrens

A E G

TURBINENFABRIK

the
Steiner House
Vienna (1910)
by Loos

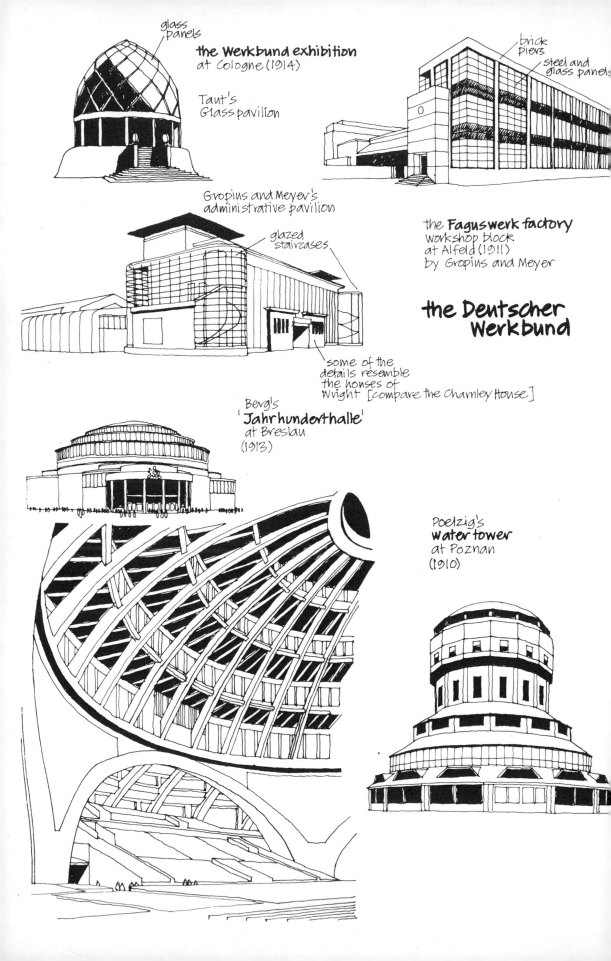

glass
panels

the Werkbund exhibition
at Cologne (1914)

Taut's
Glass pavilion

brick
piers

steel and
glass panels

Gropius and Meyer's
administrative pavilion

glazed
staircases

the Faguswerk factory
Workshop block
at Alfeld (1911)
by Gropius and Meyer

the Deutscher
Werkbund

some of the
details resemble
the houses of
Wright [compare the Charnley House]

Berg's
'Jahrhunderthalle'
at Breslau
(1913)

Poelzig's
water tower
at Poznan
(1910)

ners. The designer of the latter was Walter Gropius (1883–1969), an assistant in the office of Behrens who, with Adolf Meyer, had already designed a factory building at Alfeld for the Fagus company, makers of shoe-lasts and other metal goods. The Workshop block (1911) is one of the great works of modern architecture, a long, rectangular three-storey building with its clearly-seen framework of piers alternating with light infill panels of glass and steel. Even though the conception was still classical, the designers emphasised that this was no traditional structure by keeping the corners free of piers, which they set back some 3 metres, cantilevering the floor-slabs out in a way only possible in steel or reinforced concrete construction. The fully-glazed corners, which appeared here for the first time, became a hallmark of 20th-century design.

The main body of Werkbund architects, Behrens and Gropius included, kept firmly within the principles of classical composition. Others, however, were interested in devising totally new forms and concepts, among them the Werkbund 'expressionists' Max Berg (1870–1947) and Hans Poelzig (1869–1936). Berg designed what was possibly the most original building of the time, the Centennial Hall – 'Jahrhunderthalle' – in Breslau (1913). Externally this circular, domed building with its projecting portico is reminiscent of some enlarged Pantheon; but internally its vast circular space, 65 metres across and spanned by a huge ribbed, reinforced concrete dome, is a 20th-century conception far beyond any of Behrens. Poelzig's vast steel-and-brick circular water-tower at Poznan (1910) and his chemical factory at Luban (1911), an agglomeration of tall brick-built blocks whose semi-circular windows express the character of the material used, were also a reaction against staidness and Classicism.

Most vociferous of all in the fight against Classicism was the short-lived Futurist movement, founded by a group of Italian painters together with the writer Marinetti in about 1910. They evolved an attitude, proclaimed in successive Manifestos, before they invented a style which inevitably fell short of their theoretical aims. They set out to express the dynamism of the new machine age: for them, 'a roaring motor-car which runs like a machine-gun is more beautiful than the winged victory of Samothrace'. If Futurist painting was difficult to realise, Futurist architecture was even more so, and the designs of its greatest exponent, Antonio Sant' Elia (1888–1916), were never built. His brilliant pre-visions of the modern world, of glass towers and multi-level transport interchanges, have been fulfilled by proxy, through his deep and continuing influence on 20th-century architects.

Futurism was partly revolutionary in intent – at one stage during its decade of existence it was looking to 'an end to the architecture of big business' – and so it was perhaps not surprising that it failed to find commercial sponsors. Some Secession architects, however, and even more the Werkbund and its followers, had a growing conviction that architecture and design were commodities which the business community could be persuaded to want. Also growing was the architect's confidence in his own ability – a kind of intellectual arrogance, shared with the abstract painters, expressionist writers and atonal composers, which affirmed his belief that he knew what was best for the public. These revolutionary ideas in art and technology came at a time of general political reaction in which the architect and designer retreated from the position of Morris in two important ways: his respect for the capabilities of the machine was replaced by an obsession with its power, and capitalism was accepted without criticism as the best way forward.

design for an **electricity station** (1913)..

...and design for an **airship hangar** (1913) both by Sant'Elia

Constantin Brancusi's sculpture **bird in space** (1919)

sculpture **unique forms of continuity in space** (1913) by Umberto Boccioni

Sant'Elia's design for **La Città Nuova** (1914)

high-rise buildings, bridges, elevators, subways and access decks combined i a powerful and persistent image of the future

Futurism in Italy

design for an **apartment block** by Mario Chiattone an associate of Sant'Elia (1914) whose ideas were also influential

The development of trade unions in the 19th century put the workers in a stronger position, and continued criticism of the evils of industrialism achieved gradual improvements in factory and housing conditions, paradoxically making the likelihood of revolution more remote. The philanthropic movement of the 19th century, inspired by Christian charity and commercial expediency, was instrumental in making life better. Its early exponents were very much in the tradition of Owen; Saltaire, near Bradford, a town built for his workers by the industrialist Titus Salt in 1853, has much in common with New Lanark. The rural site on the river Aire was provided with 800 houses, a church and four chapels, public baths and wash-houses, hospital and school, all in a Venetian gothic style. The vast mill building was at one side, a constant reminder of the town's *raison d'etre*. Port Sunlight in Cheshire (1888), a tied town built by W. H. Lever the soap magnate, and Bournville near Birmingham (1895) by George Cadbury the chocolate and cocoa manufacturer, continued the tradition. The neatly packed terraces of Saltaire were rejected in favour of looser garden-city planning, with a large proportion of detached cottages with their own gardens. Street names such as Laburnum, Sycamore and Acacia reinforced the rural image.

For the workers who remained in the cities, numerous charitable trusts such as Peabody (1862) and Guinness (1889) began to provide improved housing. Estates were built, with tenement blocks in parallel rows far enough apart to allow sunlight and air to penetrate the windows. Typically five or six storeys with common staircases leading to self-contained flats, the estates were high-density, utilitarian and authoritarian, but in privacy and comfort they were infinitely better than the old back-to-backs. Then in 1899 the London County Council (LCC), formed ten years earlier, built the world's first local-authority flats, not radically different in form but significant in the fact that public money was being used to house the poor.

However much cities might be improved, it was evident that they had inherent disadvantages, among them the congestion, inefficiency and high costs which came from unplanned growth. A new type of planned city combining the liveliness and opportunity of the old city, the spaciousness of the countryside and the efficiency of a logical layout, was suggested in 1898 by Ebenezer Howard, a City of London clerk, in his book *Tomorrow*. Important features of Howard's city were its small size – 32,000 people was the optimum – and the sense of identity which came from its being self-contained rather than just another suburb of a metropolis. In this it differed from the rival theory of the Spanish transport engineer Soria y Mata who in 1882 had proposed his 'Ciudad Lineal', a continuous pattern of urban growth stretching through the countryside on either side of a rapid-transit 'spine' route, incorporating both old and new urban centres in a comprehensive whole.

In England, the mildly reformist utilitarian ideas of Howard proved appealing, and in 1905 the first of his 'garden cities' was begun at Letchworth in Hertfordshire, closely followed by another at Welwyn. Individual houses with gardens, in the tradition of Nash, of Bournville and of English suburbia in general, were interspersed liberally with open spaces and parks, which resulted in low densities and a prodigal consumption of land, offering plenty of light and air but little of the dynamism of the traditional city.

On the continent, low-density suburban living was less of a tradition, and most theories of town-planning were still based on the formal baroque approach of Haussmann and the Beaux Arts school. In 1889 the book *Der Städtebau* by the

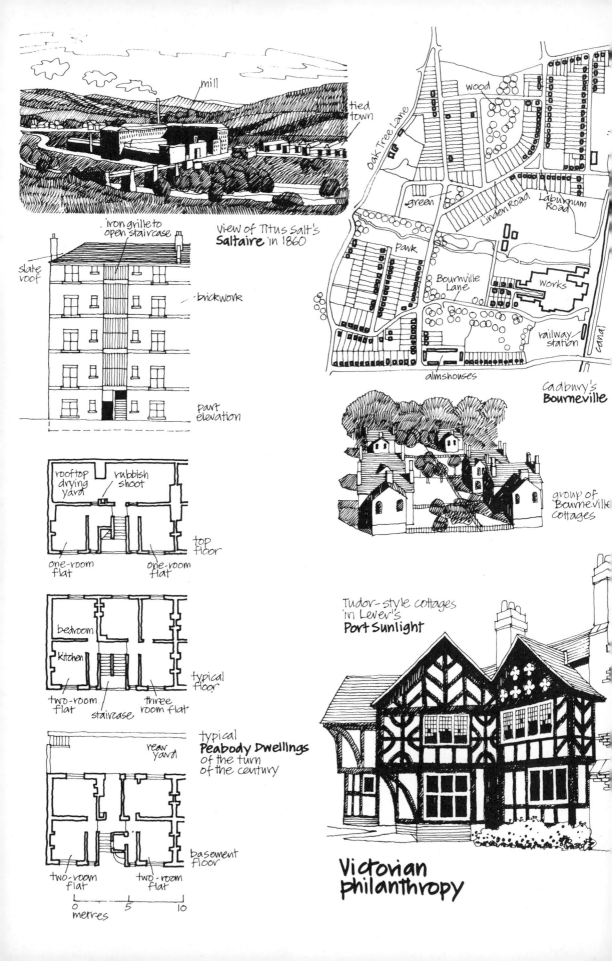

mill

tied town

View of Titus Salt's **Saltaire** in 1860

wood

Oak Tree Lane

green

Linden Road

Laburnum Road

park

Bournville Lane

Works

railway station

canal

almshouses

Cadbury's **Bourneville**

iron grille to open staircase

slate roof

brickwork

part elevation

group of Bourneville cottages

rooftop drying yard

rubbish shoot

top floor

one-room flat

one-room flat

bedroom

kitchen

two-room flat

staircase

three room flat

typical floor

Tudor-style cottages in Lever's **Port Sunlight**

typical **Peabody Dwellings** of the turn of the century

rear yard

basement floor

two-room flat

two-room flat

0   5   10
metres

Victorian philanthropy

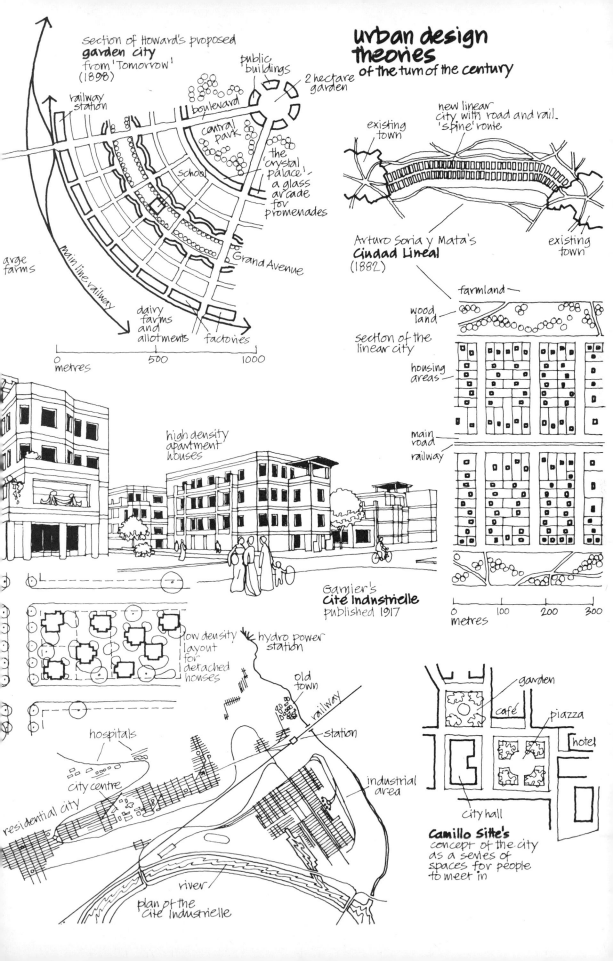

urban design theories
of the turn of the century

section of Howard's proposed **garden city** from 'Tomorrow' (1898)

railway station

public buildings

2 hectare garden

boulevard

central park

the 'crystal palace' a glass arcade for promenades

school

Grand Avenue

large farms

main line railway

dairy farms and allotments

factories

0 metres — 500 — 1000

new linear city with road and rail 'spine' route

existing town

existing town

Arturo Soria y Mata's **Ciudad Lineal** (1882)

farmland

woodland

section of the linear city

housing areas

main road railway

0 metres — 100 — 200 — 300

high density apartment houses

Garnier's **Cité Industrielle** published 1917

low density layout for detached houses

hydro power station

old town

railway

station

hospitals

city centre

residential city

industrial area

river

plan of the Cité Industrielle

garden

café

piazza

hotel

city hall

Camillo Sitte's concept of the city as a series of spaces for people to meet in

Austrian architect Camillo Sitte (1843–1903) put forward the idea of creating irregularities in a town design to obtain attractive, informal effects. It was, however, the French architect Tony Garnier (1869–1948) who overthrew the Beaux Arts approach with a scenario for the future so prophetic and complete that it still plays a major part in architectural thinking. Garnier built very little, but his reputation is assured by his design for an imaginary 'Cité Industrielle' prepared before 1904 and published in 1917. Like Howard's, it was for a city of about 30,000 people, but Garnier recognised the dynamic character of urban growth by planning his city in linear form, like that of Mata, to allow for expansion. For the exercise, he chose a real site near his home town of Lyon, and worked up the proposals in minute technical detail. As in Howard's plans, the industrial area was set apart to minimise pollution, and the focus of the town was a centre containing civic buildings, hospitals, libraries and entertainment. Garnier examined the design of the buildings in some detail, including the hydro-electric station, the municipal abattoir, factories and houses. The latter were to be provided in varying sizes and types to suit not incomes but different families' needs, including, in addition to detached houses, groups of four-storey apartment blocks giving higher densities towards the city centre. The main structural material was to be reinforced concrete, and the plain, simple style of the buildings is reminiscent partly of the French engineers, Hennebique and Perret, and partly of the classicism of the Werkbund. But perhaps the most significant aspect of the 'Cité Industrielle' was its socialism – inherited from Proudhon and Fourier – which distinguished it from the modified *laissez-faire* proposals of Howard. In many respects, Garnier presents us with an alternative prototype for the modern city to Howard's – not only physically, with its communal high-density housing schemes in reinforced concrete, but also in its administrative concepts of publicly owned services and buildings.

BUILDING DESIGN

Building Design is published from Morgan Grampian House, Calderwood Street, Woolwich, London SE18 6QH 01-855 7777.

Editor Martin Pawley
Managing editor Ian Rowden
News editor Hugh Pearman
Senior news reporter Ian Martin
Reporters Neal Morris
Janet Abrams
Features editor Lynda Relph-Knight
Chief sub editor Stuart Middleton

Publisher Stan Arnold
Advertisement Manager
Roger Murphy
Classified advertisement manager
Paul Nudds
Production manager
Angela Waterman

Editorial secretary
Sharon Filmer

Not just sharp edged geometrics

READERS Holyoak and Middleton have taken me to task for resurrecting yesterday's men as heroes of the 1980s (*Letters* pages 10 and 11). The time of modern architecture has passed, they claim, and the former wonders where I have been for the last 30 years that I have not noticed it. Well, it is true that I lack the cast iron alibi of Berthold Lubetkin and I have hardly space to elaborate on the folly of the romantics as Middleton wishes, but at least I can claim to have spent part of the time thinking, which is more than can be said for some.

The key to the whole question of the supposed death of the modern movement lies in the relationship of architecture to technology. Modern architecture, as its more enlightened exponents never cease to point out, was not and is not a style but a state of grace founded on the brilliant conception that buildings could become functional solutions to the problem of technology transfer. The crisis created by the need to assimilate new technology is in one sense ancient, but few would argue that it reached a new level of intensity during the industrial revolution. In the first half of the present century it emerged as a mainspring of architectural thought which did generate the international style, a plateau mistaken for a summit, as Reyner Banham brilliantly explained in *Theory and design*. The wiser heads among the moderns, like Frank Pick, always understood that the correct response was to "think out afresh all the problems of building in terms of current materials and current tools".

This is one sense in which Mies was a great architect. He spent a great part of his professional life developing one facet of modern technology, steel frame building, to such good effect that 13

The Editor's Comment

years after his death no better exponent of the art is to be found. To write about Mies van der Rohe being out of date is like calling Ferdinand Porsche out of date — it brings into question the writer's understanding of design in a technological age.

The presence or absence of technology transfer is the touchstone, which is why Clifton Nurseries is a modern building despite its columns and pediment.

The modern world

1914 to the present day - and beyond

By the early 20th century, the intellectual foundations had been laid for the development of modern architecture. Most of the west had become industrialised. Britain and France, no longer the economic leaders, had been overtaken by the rapid development of Germany and the USA. America's great resources of land, minerals and forests, and its small but dynamic population stimulated by the skills of refugees from European repression, encouraged an expansionism which contrasted with the conservatism and moribundity into which British capitalism had now drifted. The 'rugged individualist' of early British capitalism, vulnerable to those fluctuations of the market which Marx had predicted, was gradually replaced in America by the corporation, whose broad financial base enabled it to weather economic storms. Capitalism was adapting itself, and averting the collapse which its critics were expecting.

German capitalism was growing in another direction. The rigidity of the German class system, the prevailing philosophy of the power of the state, and above all, the Prussian army, brought German capitalism under close state supervision; the development of strategic rail-routes and of the armaments industry even gave it an overt military function. Physics and chemistry were put at the disposal of industrial technology. Coal and iron still remained paramount, but the electrical, chemical and petroleum industries also expanded. AEG, and those other great combines which employed the Werkbund architects and their circle, became part of a system of 'cartels', in which supplies and prices were controlled by agreement between competing companies, to the mutual benefit of them all. Compulsory military training helped support the whole structure; military intervention in economic life was so widespread that by 1917 most institutions were in effect controlled by the High Command.

The ideological battles between classes seen during France's revolution had, by 1870, been set aside. An era of pragmatic compromise was attained, both between nations and within each country. The west was now so interlinked, politically and economically, that any disturbance threatened the whole structure. This was the situation as Europe entered the cataclysmic First World War (1914–18), an event almost without specific causes but with the most specific of consequences. With the European balance of power destroyed and the German machine dismantled, leaving behind a memory of efficiency and power which in the future others would revive, Europe was open to influences from elsewhere. The first came from the United States which, having entered the war in 1917, now looked on Europe as a legitimate location for its neo-colonialism.

The second influence came from Russia, which between 1905 and 1922 underwent a great political turmoil and emerged transformed. The Tsar was besieged both by the bourgeoisie, who had missed out on their own liberal revolution, and by the workers, and it was the latter who under the guidance of Lenin (1870–1924) accomplished the world's first workers' revolution. The first years were character-

УРАН

Со ВТОРНКА
19
ЯНВАРЯ

1905
г

БРОНЕНОСЕЦ

ПОТЕМКИН

НАЧАЛО В БУДНИ 7 30 9 и 10 30 Ч 5 ПРАЗДНИКИ С 4 Ч

poster for S. M. Eisenstein's
film **Potemkin** 1925
which recalled the revolution
of 1905

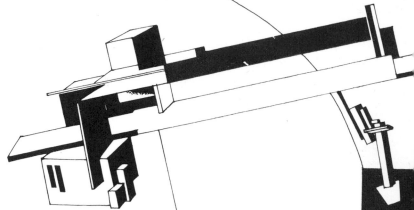

one of El Lissitzky's 'Prouns' 1919 which he
looked upon as a transition between
painting and building-design

this one is called **Bridge I**

soviet
constructivism

'**To whom + for
what purpose +
what = how**'
El Lissitzky 1931

the Vesnin brothers'
design for the **Pravda**
building Moscow 1924

a **Wolkenbügel** designed by El Lissitzky
and Mart Stam 1924, an office
building on legs, high above the
main roads of Moscow

the Tatlin **tower** designed to
celebrate the third International 1919
as a gigantic communications centre with
radio, film studios and meeting rooms

the radio masts
were a major
part of Soviet
architectural
thought

an important way
of educating people
in remote rural
areas

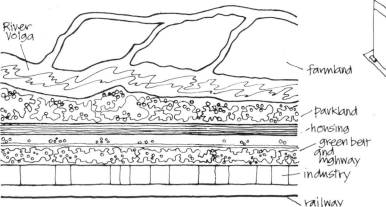

River
Volga

— farmland

— parkland

— housing

— green belt
  and
  highway

— industry

— railway

diagram of Miliutin's linear plan for
Magnitogorsk 1929

the Vesnins' design for a
Palace of the People
1922

ised by great intellectual ferment, as the new 'soviets' experimented with political and artistic ideas. Russia had gone from the past into the future, without being impeded by the capitalist present, and from 1917 to 1932 Russian artistic ideas were among the foremost in the world, as groups of artists and architects suddenly found both freedom of expression and a task to carry out. From this period came the early films of Eisenstein, including *Potemkin* (1925) and *Earth* (1930), and the early symphonies and operas of Shostakovitch. Art and architecture were examined for their social relevance and were taken into the streets in the form of festivals and concerts, symbolic constructions, murals, posters and slogans. The most famous example was Vladimir Tatlin's design (1919) for a great spiral tower to celebrate the Third International. Intended to exceed Eiffel's in height, it was built only in smaller-scale mock-ups, but it remained a potent image for those striving to find a design approach to revolutionary architecture.

Through the painter Kasimir Malevitch and notably through the architect-painter El Lissitzky (1890–1941), a relationship was established between architecture and abstract painting, initiating a search for an architecture of comparable simplicity and purity. Two distinct schools were forming. The first was that of the 'Rationalists', led by Nicolai Ladovsky (1881–1941) and dedicated to the honest expression of structure, the use of new materials and techniques and the analysis of spatial effects, for which it was hoped to set down design rules.

The second group was that of the 'Constructivists', led by the brilliant Vesnin brothers, Victor, Leonid and Alexander, who had a more abstract approach. For them, 'things created by modern artists must be pure constructions, devoid of the ballast of representation'. The Vesnins' designs for a Palace of the People in Moscow (1922) and their scheme for the *Pravda* building (1924) illustrate this attitude, the former with its untraditional, uncompromising forms, and the latter with its cool, rectangular elevations, like abstract paintings.

The need to increase factory production and to improve living conditions stimulated the planning of many new towns in Russia. Vladimir Semenov's proposals for the expansion of Moscow, Stalingrad and Astrakhan were in the tradition of Garnier. Semenov adopted the principles of zoning, to separate the housing areas from the noise and pollution of industry; he also perceived the town as a constantly changing phenomenon, which needed space to expand into. Foremost among the planning theorists of the time, however, was Nicolai Miliutin (1889–1942), who put forward proposals for the expansion of Magnitogorsk, Stalingrad and Gorki. He advocated a form developed from Mata's linear town. The zones were narrow, parallel strips of land running through the countryside, incorporating the old town centres where they occurred: a railway zone, a factory, workshop and technical college zone, a green belt with a main highway, a residential zone, a park and sports area, and a wide belt of farmland. Travel along the routes was rapid and efficient, and travel across them was made easy by the short distances involved. Miliutin envisaged a radically changed social system, which included the communal ownership of possessions, complete equality of the sexes, and the bringing-up of children in a communal way.

During his last years, Lenin thought increasingly about the implementation of Marx's main objective: how to achieve democracy and allow all citizens to participate creatively in their own future; but by 1930 power had been assumed by Stalin (1879–1953) who began to purge the country of intellectualism, stamping out

219

progressive ideas, controlling freedom of expression and assassinating or deporting those who resisted. Under the control of cultural commissars, art and architecture relapsed into representationalism, pseudo-naiveté or banal neo-classicism and many artists moved to the west.

Western Europe, like revolutionary Russia, was in intellectual ferment. The break-up of the old empires after the war – Austrian, German, Turkish and Russian – left a number of developing new states and a republican spirit in the air. The scientific theories of Darwin, Einstein and Freud had suddenly expanded man's consciousness of the universe and created both excitement and unease. Mass education was becoming universal, the spirit of experiment and inquiry spread widely and artistic life flourished.

The main political question was of German reparations for the war, on which France insisted. The payments imposed on Germany forced her to drive her industry strongly towards exporting, creating high employment but also high inflation. The victors, on the other hand, experienced lower inflation but high unemployment, and were burdened with the debt of war-loans from America. The promise to the soldiers had been 'homes fit for heroes' but they came back, shattered by the traumas of history's most devastating war, to countries whose economic problems were too great to allow the eradication of their squalid slum-housing.

European Marxists looked to Russia as an example – though without much hope of engineering a similar social revolution in the west. Nevertheless, there was a growing confidence among architects that better living conditions for all were almost within reach. The answer, it was thought, lay not so much in any structural change to society as in the proper harnessing of technology: new materials and techniques would bring new architectural forms to cities, ending overcrowding and squalor.

At the head of this movement was the Bauhaus, the industrial-design school founded at Weimar in 1919 by Walter Gropius. Following the Werkbund, Gropius placed his hopes on a closer relationship between 'the best artists and craftsmen on the one hand and trade and industry on the other'. However suspect the idea might be of forming close links with German industry in order to achieve progressive social aims, the Bauhaus was innovatory in two respects. The first was in its teaching method: in an atmosphere of almost monastic dedication, the student underwent a rigorous three-year course which began by clearing his attitude of pre-conceptions, continued by teaching him a craft in the workshop, and only then proceeded to the study of industrial design.

The second innovation was the design of the Bauhaus building itself, built by Gropius when the school moved to Dessau in 1925. It consists of three blocks, in an informal yet organised group. At the centre of gravity are the entrance and the all-important workshop block, which link eastwards by means of an assembly hall to a small tower of studio-flats for the students and northwards via a bridge over the access road to the classroom block. The fully-glazed workshops contrast with the more solid walls of the classrooms and the residential tower.

Gropius meant the building to be a manifesto, a demonstration of a rational design approach. So great was its influence, however, that it created an instant 'Bauhaus style', rather to the displeasure of Gropius, who rejected the very idea of style and demanded the working out of solutions from first principles. It is difficult, now that the formal vocabulary of this great building has passed into our architectural language and is used every day in the unthinking concoction of undistinguished

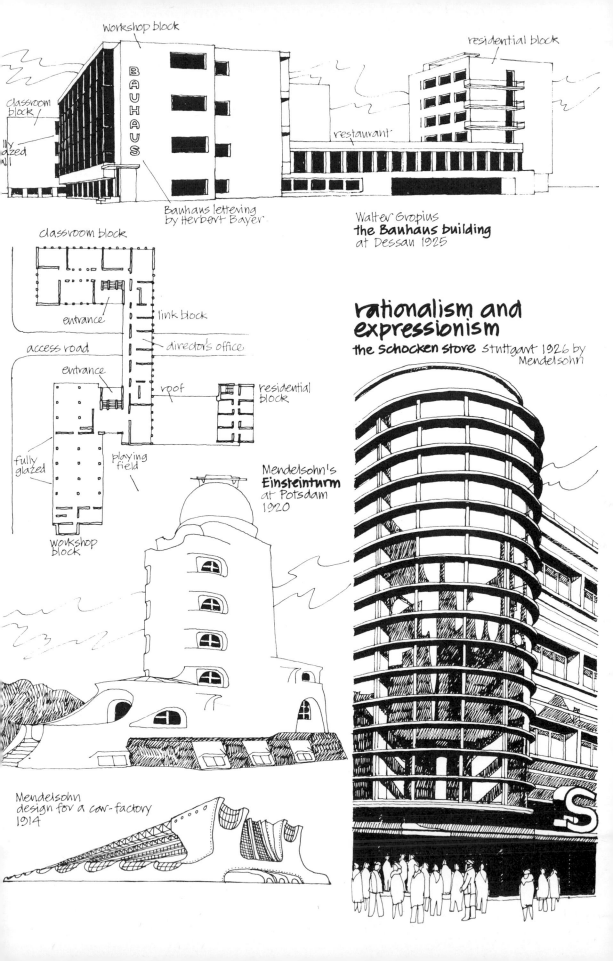

Workshop block

BAUHAUS

classroom block

lly glazed all

Bauhaus lettering by Herbert Bayer

residential block

restaurant

Walter Gropius
the Bauhaus building
at Dessau 1925

classroom block

entrance

access road

entrance

fully glazed

workshop block

link block

director's office

roof

playing field

residential block

Mendelsohn's
Einsteinturm
at Potsdam
1920

Mendelsohn
design for a car-factory
1914

rationalism and expressionism
the schocken store Stuttgart 1926 by Mendelsohn

S

buildings, to appreciate its originality. For just as Gothic began at St Denis, so was the Bauhaus the first major building in which all the features of today's architecture were brought together as a unified and convincing entity. It has an order which derives not from the imposition of any neo-classical rules of symmetry or proportion but from the logic of its structure, and a richness of effect which comes not from applied decoration but from its design detail. And its subtlety of form and spatial variety do not come from pre-conceived design formulae but are essentially the result of an ordered solution to the planning of the building.

At first, the Bauhaus courses placed little emphasis on architecture. In 1927 Gropius remedied this by appointing the Swiss architect Hannes Meyer to the staff. On Gropius's resignation the following year to devote more time to his own work, Meyer took over the school. To him, building was first and foremost a social activity, and he found the aesthetic preoccupations of the Bauhaus artists lacking in social purpose. His revision of the curriculum included not only the extension of the scientific and investigative side of the course, but also an increased emphasis on the architect's social responsibilities. Meyer's Marxist views, and his encouragement to the students to participate in political activity, brought a reaction from the conservative Dessau authorities; in 1930 he was asked to resign. Looking back on his two years as director, he was able to claim, 'I taught the students to relate building to the community; I weaned them from the formalistic, intuitive approach and taught them to undertake basic research; I showed them how to put the needs of the people first.'

Meyer's socialism and research-based design methods were not common among architects of his generation. Politically, the prevailing attitude was a kind of liberal humanism. In design, the methodology was intuitive rather than scientific, even in the Bauhaus, with its claims of rationality, and certainly so in the case of architects like Erich Mendelsohn (1887–1953). Mendelsohn's Einstein Tower at Potsdam (1920) was an individual, expressionist vision of the new age, a curious, solid, seven-storey laboratory surmounted by a domed observatory. A composition of sweeping, streamlined curves, it was designed to demonstrate the plasticity of reinforced concrete. The fact that it was built in plastered-over brickwork did not negate the conception: the intention was to symbolise modern technology rather than actually to use it. Mendelsohn's finest building was his store in Stuttgart for the Schocken company (1926) in which his predilection for sweeping curves was disciplined by a formal structural system; the result was one of the finest of early modern buildings, intellectual in approach and dynamic in effect.

Mendelsohn's strange genius sets him slightly apart from the architectural mainstream of the 1920s, which saw the development of what later became known as the 'international style'. The architectural features of the Bauhaus building became almost universal among the progressive architects: asymmetry, rectangularity of form, and the lightness which derived from the fact that frame construction had emancipated the external wall from its old load-bearing function. Colours were often natural and restrained and walls painted white to emphasise a departure from the heaviness and gloom of Neo-Classicism. The functional justification of the style was the use of steel and reinforced concrete, which enabled the achievement of unprecedented effects of lightness, space and precision – although where traditional materials could obtain the required mechanistic effect they were often used without compunction, the look of modernity being more important than the actuality.

Many architects were approaching modernism in the company of painters and sculptors, which sharpened their sense of form and space if not their scientific methodology. Notable among them were the Dutch architects known, from the title of the magazine they began in 1918, as 'De Stijl'. Their aim, couched in the resounding terms of the art manifestos of the time, was to reject the old which was 'based on the individual' and discover a harmony, through purity of form and colour, which was by contrast 'universal'. Their art and architecture, at its most pure, was purged of all forms except the most severely rectangular and of all colour except black, white and the three primary colours. Their chief theorist was Theo van Doesburg, also a lecturer at the Bauhaus, and their style is typified by that of the artist Piet Mondriaan (1872–1944) who carried cubism to a logical conclusion with his own pure and rectilinear painting.

De Stijl architecture began with Hendrikus Berlage, Rob van t'Hoff, Jan Wils and Jacobus Oud, whose early work dated from an exhibition in Holland in 1910 of the work of Wright, and showed distinct echoes of the Larkin Building and the Robie House. But the seminal works of the movement were two by the architect Gerrit Rietveld (1888–1965). The first was the design of the 'Red-Blue' chair of 1917, in which the functions of a chair were reduced to their bare essentials: a sheet of plywood for the seat and another for the back, both supported on a network of overlapping painted timber bars. Van Doesburg saw in it the 'silent eloquence of a machine'. The second was the Schroeder House (1924), a small two-storey building in a suburb of Utrecht. Its exterior is treated as the projection of a Mondriaan painting into three dimensions, a complex of flat planes – walls, floor-slabs, roofs, canopies, balconies – all overlapping, projecting and intersecting with each other to form an exciting architectural expression of De Stijl's stated desire 'for number and measure, for cleanliness and order'.

In 1922, Oud left De Stijl to pursue a more rational, less purely sculptural approach, and his blocks of workers' flats at Hoek van Holland (1924) are his attempt to apply the ideas of De Stijl to a realistic social aim. There were other rationalist Dutch architects, among them William Marinus Dudok whose rectilinear style owes something to De Stijl but is much calmer and less sculptural in effect and shows a stronger appreciation of the properties of materials, in particular of brickwork. His Vondelschool in Hilversum (1926) and the influential Hilversum Town Hall (1929) are among his best works – brick buildings in which horizontal masses are carefully balanced against verticals. Among the finest of Holland's rationalist buildings is the factory in Rotterdam (1928) designed for the Van Nelle tobacco company by Brinkman, van der Vlugt and the Bauhaus-trained designer Mart Stam. Like the Bauhaus workshop building, the main eight-storey block is in concrete construction – in this case with mushroom-headed columns – and clad externally in a curtain-wall of glass.

In 1923, a book called *Vers une Architecture* was published in Paris. It was a fighting manifesto advocating the adoption of a new attitude to architecture, and the implication of the title was that none of the styles of the past really deserved the name. 'A great epoch has begun. There exists a new spirit. There exists a mass of work conceived in the new spirit; it is to be met with particularly in industrial production. Architecture is stifled by custom. The "styles" are a lie.'

The writer was a thirty-six-year-old Swiss, Charles-Edouard Jeanneret (1887–1966), who was to become the greatest and most influential architect of the

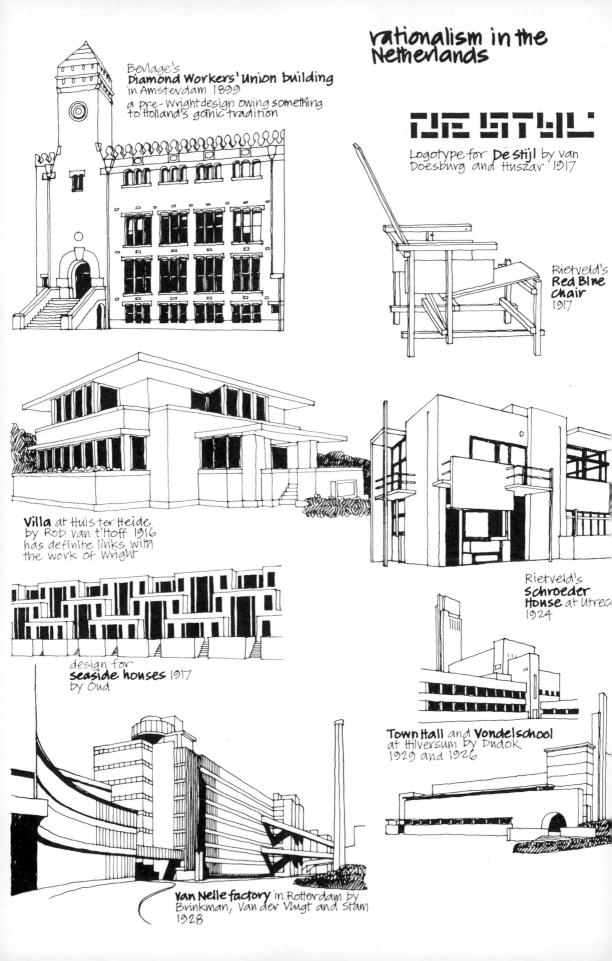

rationalism in the Netherlands

Berlage's
Diamond Workers' Union building
in Amsterdam 1899
a pre-Wright design owing something
to Holland's gothic tradition

DE STIJL

Logotype for **De Stijl** by van
Doesburg and Huszar 1917

Rietveld's
**Red Blue
chair**
1917

Villa at Huis ter Heide
by Rob van t'Hoff 1916
has definite links with
the work of Wright

design for
seaside houses 1917
by Oud

Rietveld's
**Schroeder
House** at Utrecht
1924

Town Hall and **Vondelschool**
at Hilversum by Dudok
1929 and 1926

Van Nelle factory in Rotterdam by
Brinkman, Van der Vlugt and Stam
1928

20th century. During his youth, he had displayed a certain indifference to architecture, but a succession of experiences acted as a catalyst to change his whole life: a tour of Europe in 1907, ending in Paris where he discovered Notre Dame, the Eiffel Tower and above all, Auguste Perret, for whom he worked for a time; a visit to Greece in 1911, where the Acropolis was a revelation; and a permanent return to Paris in 1917, where he met the post-cubist painter Amédée Ozenfant with whom in 1920 he founded a paper called *L'Esprit Nouveau*. This he used as a vehicle for his now rapidly forming ideas about painting, architecture and town design. He had become a new man, and it is significant that at this point he left his old identity behind, and became Le Corbusier.

His whole life was spent in pursuing new ideas, and the richness of his thought – comparable with that of Stravinsky and Picasso – kept him permanently ahead of critics and imitators. However, several continuous threads ran through his life, traceable to his formative years. His continued interest in simple, bold forms enhanced by carefully placed colour began with his own cubist paintings and gradually extended to his architecture. After his early contact with Perret he developed his interest in modern materials – steel, glass, reinforced concrete – and in their structural and spatial possibilities. With Ozenfant he shared a passionate belief in the new machine age and the achievements of its structural engineers, naval architects and car designers. Greece awoke in him an interest in proportion, and Italy encouraged the liberal humanistic philosophy which gave him his utopian vision of the future.

One of his greatest talents – and one which he shared with Garnier, whose work he knew well – was the ability to understand urban problems at every scale, to see the design of a living unit within its larger context, and conversely to design cities in the knowledge of how they were intended to work at the small scale; for him, the designing of small houses and of master plans for whole regions were part of the same problem. As early as 1914 he designed a prototype 'Dom-ino House', a framework of six columns, two floor-slabs and a roof, which offered flexibility in the location of internal partitions and external walls. In 1922 he published the first of his major contributions to town-planning theory, *Une Ville Contemporaine de 3,000,000 d'Habitants* in which the ideas of Garnier were transmuted into a dramatic vision of the future. Le Corbusier's own innovations were significant; they included a firm grasp of the concept of density and how it builds up in intensity towards a city centre – resulting in this case in sixty-storey office towers – and an appreciation of the implications of high-speed road and rail movement, which here for the first time became an integral part of town design. The residential areas of 'Une Ville Contemporaine' contained many of the ideas which he later published as the 'Citrohan House' (1924): housing-units with spacious, double-height living-rooms corresponding to two ordinary storeys; houses and flats with integral roof-gardens or balconies to provide private outdoor space; buildings raised off the ground on *pilotis* to allow the landscape to flow uninterrupted underneath.

In 1925, the Citrohan House was given concrete form, and became the 'Pavillon de L'Esprit Nouveau' at the Paris exposition of decorative arts. The international jury gave it a first prize, which was then successfully withdrawn by the French jury-member amid an atmosphere of shrill criticism of the building by the French architectural establishment.

Then came two early masterpieces, the elegant Maison Stein at Garches (1926)

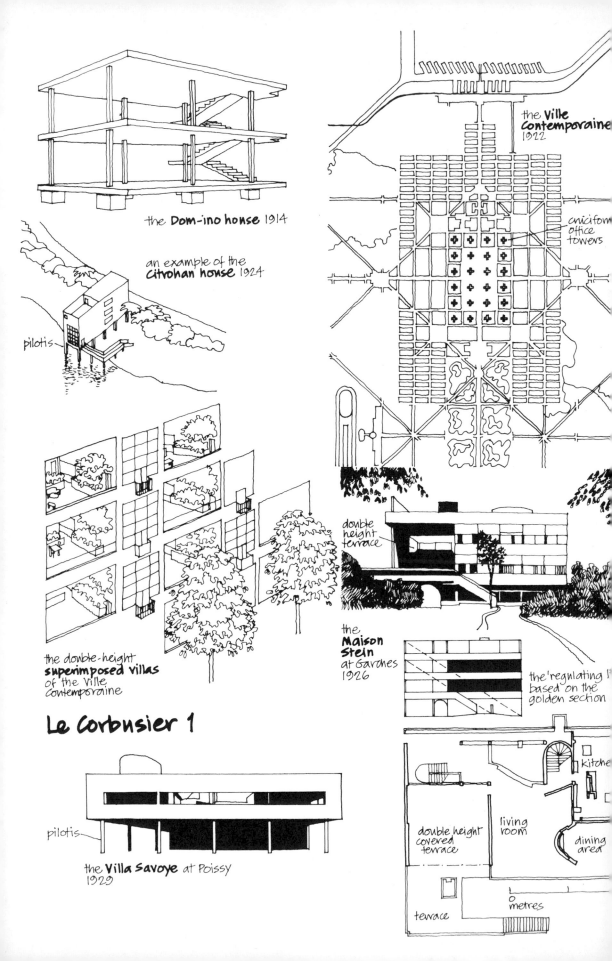

the **Dom-ino house** 1914

an example of the **Citrohan house** 1924

pilotis

the **Ville Contemporaine** 1922

cruciform office towers

the double-height **superimposed villas** of the Ville Contemporaine

double height terrace

the **Maison Stein** at Garches 1926

the 'regulating l' based on the golden section

Le Corbusier 1

pilotis

the **Villa Savoye** at Poissy 1929

kitchen

double height covered terrace

living room

dining area

terrace

metres

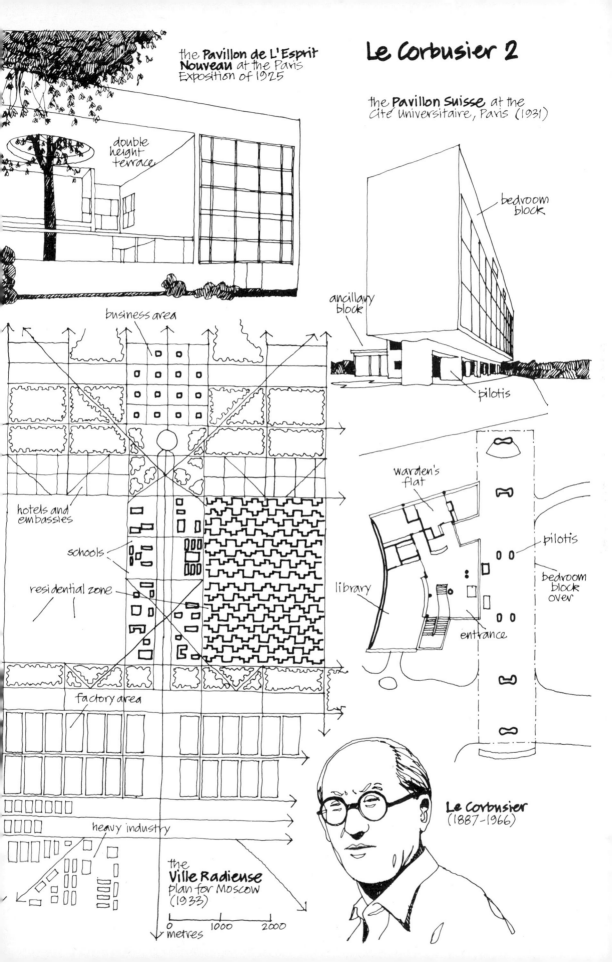

the **Pavillon de L'Esprit Nouveau** at the Paris Exposition of 1925

Le Corbusier 2

the **Pavillon Suisse** at the Cité Universitaire, Paris (1931)

double height terrace

bedroom block

ancillary block

pilotis

business area

hotels and embassies

schools

residential zone

factory area

warden's flat

pilotis

bedroom block over

library

entrance

heavy industry

the **Ville Radieuse** plan for Moscow (1933)

0   1000   2000
metres

Le Corbusier
(1887-1966)

and the beautiful Villa Savoye at Poissy (1928). The former is a simple three-storey block, derived from 'Esprit Nouveau' principles, with an integral roof-terrace and an inset, double-height garden area, the whole bound together by a system of harmonious proportions based on the golden section. The latter summarised all his ideas to date, and marked the beginning of Le Corbusier's architectural maturity. A two-storey house, it consists of a main upper storey designed as a simple, rectangular white box, with a single line of horizontal windows. This is raised on twelve concrete *pilotis* which form a loggia around the deeply recessed entrance floor, and give the impression of a building which floats above the landscape. From the main level, an internal ramp leads to the roof which contains a penthouse and terrace. Nothing could be a greater contrast to the Robie House of Wright, which deliberately hugs the ground. The Villa Savoye is an expression of pure, Voltairean rationalism, precise, geometric and man-made, whose relationship with nature is carefully controlled.

In 1926 the international style came to England when Behrens built a two-storey house, New Ways, for a Northampton industrialist. A house by the English architect Thomas Tait at Silver End (1928) and another by the New Zealander Amyas Connell, High and Over at Amersham (1929), gradually established a kind of Bauhaus-inspired cubism, which was to grow freer and more expressive during the 1930s when the ideas of Le Corbusier became better known.

Le Corbusier's most influential early building was perhaps the Pavillon Suisse, a hostel for Swiss university students at the Cité Universitaire in Paris. Built in 1931, it formed a prototype for many later buildings where the basic design problem was that of assembling a number of repetitive units together with a complex of ancillary accommodation. Le Corbusier's solution was to house the identical units, the students' bedrooms, in an elegant, regular slab-block which emphasised their repetitive nature. The communal accommodation – offices and common rooms – was in a single-storey rear block, as free in shape as the bedroom block was regular. Further emphasis was given to the distinction by lifting the slab off the ground on *pilotis*, the only link being a staircase tower.

During the late twenties and early thirties, architectural development was slowed down by the worsening economic situation. The liveliness of architectural and artistic ideas and the freneticism of the jazz and cinema age were in marked contrast to the grimness of the gradually deepening depression. Inflation and unemployment grew, the former at its worst in Weimar Germany and the latter in France and Britain, and everywhere there was less capital available for building. In 1929 the Wall Street crash seemed to threaten the very continuance of capitalism. Russia, on the other hand, under Stalin's direction, was entering its first five-year Plan (1928–33), the collective 'kolkhoz' was becoming a feature of life and, at the expense of drastic limits on personal freedom, economic progress was being made.

Le Corbusier was interested in Russia and in 1928 had prepared a design for the Centrosoyus in Moscow. As a result he had been denounced in the west as a communist, although in fact he saw Russia as no more than a likely vehicle for his architectural ideas. In 1933 he prepared a plan for Moscow which took his theories one step further: this was the famous 'Ville Radieuse', in which, possibly under the influence of Miliutin's linear city plan of 1929, the concept of planning for expansion entered his thinking.

In the west, some sort of economic adjustment appeared to be necessary to keep the system going, but a world conference on economic planning held in 1933 came to no conclusions: the United States was reluctant to share Europe's problems and Germany remained increasingly aloof. Each nation seemed prepared to go it alone. In England the approach was determined by the economist J. M. Keynes (1883–1946) whose *General Theory of Employment, Interest and Money* (1936) eventually had as much influence in the west as Marx in the east, in its proposals for easing unemployment and for setting up the controlled capitalist economy and the welfare state.

In Turkey, Portugal, Greece and particularly in Italy, Spain and Germany, other adjustments were being made, as politics moved sharply to the right. The aim of the emerging philosophy of fascism was to provide a single leader to act as a focus, and to subordinate the individual entirely to the state. Economic planning sought to free the country from dependence on others. Freedom of thought and action were controlled and Christian morality overturned. Minority groups were persecuted. Social improvements took place, production and employment ran high but at the expense of the worker's autonomy and freedom. The resemblance of this formula to Stalin's Russia has not escaped notice, but its two most important manifestations in the west were, of course, the Italy of Mussolini and Hitler's Germany.

The rise to power of Benito Mussolini (1883–1945) was in general tolerated by the Italians, who were ready to accept his brutalisation of political life for the sake of his welcome plans for increased employment, grand public works and national glory. Concessions given to the church won papal support, and from about 1922 onwards Italy appeared once again to have a purpose which awoke echoes of imperial Rome. The building of factories, power-stations, railways, airports and roads stimulated the economy, and at once presented architects with a dilemma: to reject the vicious regime or to accept it in order to obtain commissions. An uneasy, ambivalent attitude prevailed, with many architects, including some of genius like Giuseppe Terragni (1904–42), mentally glossing over fascism in order to put their architectural ideas into effect. Terragni, like Sant'Elia, was born in Como and was conscious of an architectural debt to his great predecessor. His works, mostly in Como, included a monument to Sant'Elia and the dead of the Great War, a structure distinctly Sant'Elian in style; the Casa Giuliana and the Novocomum, two blocks of flats in a rich modern style; and a little infants' school known as the Asilo Sant'Elia. His best-known work is the Casa del Fascio in Como (1932), now the Casa del Popolo, a plain, rectangular, beautifully-proportioned block of four-storey offices around a central courtyard.

Germany was the scene in the mid-1920s of the rise to power of Adolf Hitler (1889–1945). By 1932, the National Socialists were the biggest political party. The government's attempts to crush Hitler failed and he was eventually asked to form a government himself. A series of dramatic social reforms restored national pride and evoked memories of Prussian greatness: a public works programme, a national labour service, government support for the armaments industry, for manufacturers and farmers, and the introduction of conscription. Germany's rapid economic expansion blinded most eyes to the Nazis' repressive treatment of dissenters, communists and Jews. As in Italy, factories, power-stations, railways, airports and the system of *autobahnen* became the symbols of national regeneration. Even more symbolic were the stadiums: through international athletics and party rallies Hitler hoped to demonstrate Aryan supremacy to the world, and here the symbolism went

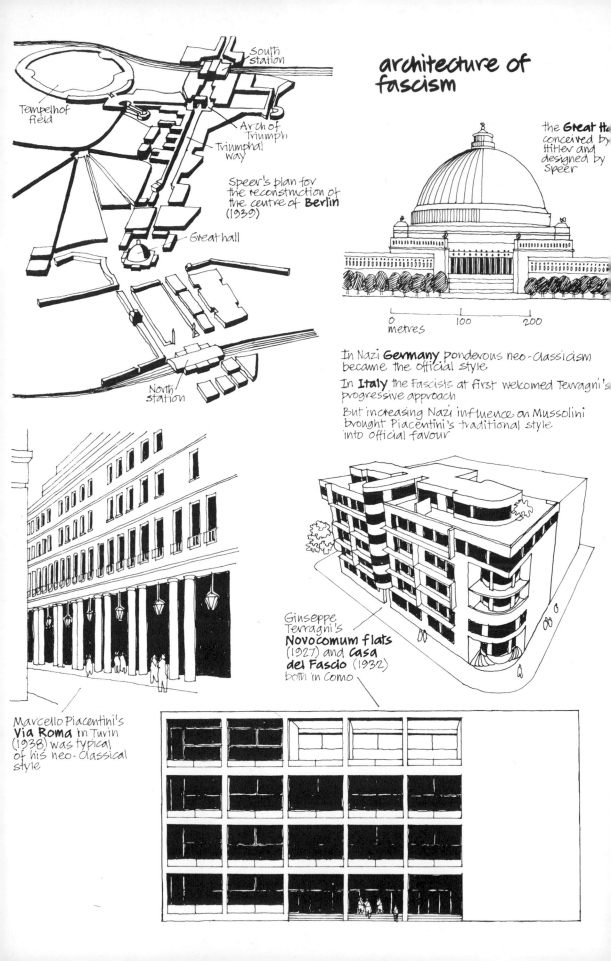

architecture of fascism

South station

Tempelhof field

Arch of Triumph

Triumphal Way

Speer's plan for the reconstruction of the centre of **Berlin** (1939)

Great hall

North station

the **Great Hall** conceived by Hitler and designed by Speer

0 metres   100   200

In Nazi **Germany** ponderous neo-classicism became the official style

In **Italy** the Fascists at first welcomed Terragni's progressive approach

But increasing Nazi influence on Mussolini brought Piacentini's traditional style into official favour

Giuseppe Terragni's **Novocomum flats** (1927) and **Casa del Fascio** (1932) both in Como

Marcello Piacentini's **Via Roma** in Turin (1938) was typical of his neo-classical style

beyond Prussia for inspiration, to ancient Greece and Rome. Hitler's own interest in architecture led him to befriend and give office in 1933 to a young German architect, Albert Speer (b. 1905), who was to create for the Reich 'buildings . . . such as have not been created for four thousand years'. A stadium was built in Berlin to house the 1936 Olympics, but a massive reconstruction planned for the centre of the city – to include a great domed hall, a processional way flanked by new public buildings, a triumphal arch and a new railway terminus – was overtaken by the war.

Speer's early training was within the Werkbund-Bauhaus orbit but his association with the Nazis put an end to any aspirations he might have had for modernism: a style was required which evoked the past, and a weighty neo-classicism was thought appropriate. Speer's most impressive architectural accomplishment was probably his stage-management of the 1934 Nuremburg Rally, for which most of Goering's stock of searchlights was brought to the Zeppelin Field:

> The hundred and thirty sharply defined beams, placed around the field at intervals of forty feet, were visible to a height of twenty to twenty-five thousand feet. . . . The feeling was of a vast room, with the beams serving as mighty pillars of infinitely high outer walls. Now and then a cloud moved through this wreath of lights, bringing an element of surrealistic surprise to the mirage . . . The effect . . . was like being in a cathedral of ice.

But theatricality and grandeur disguised a vicious regime. The repression of minority groups only hinted as yet at the horrors to come, but already an exodus of dissident intellectuals, liberals, communists and Jews was under way. The treatment by the Nazis of the Bauhaus was typical.

When the Dessau authorities forced Meyer's resignation in 1930, his place as director was taken by Ludwig Mies van der Rohe (1886–1969). Mies had long been connected with the Werkbund-Bauhaus tradition, having worked for Behrens between 1908 and 1911, and had made a brief excursion into expressionism with his richly-designed and exciting 'project for a glass skyscraper' in 1919. With the establishment of the rational Bauhaus style in the 1920s, however, Mies found his true metier, and his architecture gradually became more spare, calm and elegant. Housing projects in Berlin and Stuttgart, which included apartment houses at the Weissenhof Exhibition in 1927 – simple, well-proportioned four-storey blocks with roof terraces – established his name, and his move towards studied understatement continued. This reached a peak with his design for the German pavilion at the Barcelona exhibition of 1929.

Designed almost as a house – indeed the same principles were used at the Tugendhat House at Brno, Czechoslovakia, the following year – the pavilion was the epitome of Mies's careful yet confident attitude to design. The richest of materials were used – onyx, marble, tinted glass, chromed steel – and the most restrained of concepts: a small, asymmetrical, single-storey flat-roofed building, integrated spatially with a courtyard containing a pool. Divided by the simplest and most carefully-placed partition walls, the whole building was a sequence of elegant and varied spaces, given added lustre by the materials used. The pavilion contained no exhibits: the exhibit was the building itself.

When Mies took over the Bauhaus, he and Gropius tried to eradicate its Marxist past, apparently believing that architecture was apolitical and that, if this were made clear for all to see, it would be possible to co-exist with fascism. The Nazis disagreed;

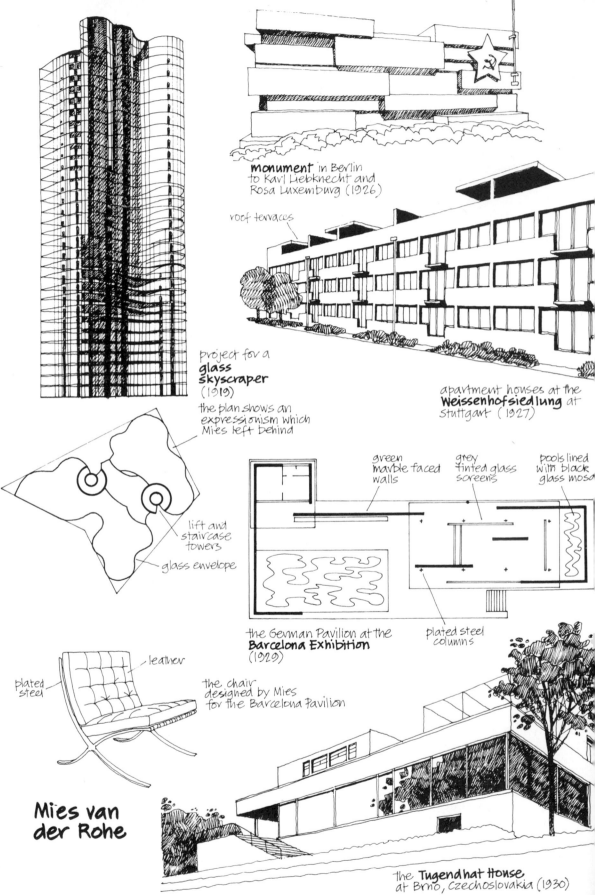

monument in Berlin
to Karl Liebknecht and
Rosa Luxemburg (1926)

roof terraces

project for a
**glass
skyscraper**
(1919)
the plan shows an
expressionism which
Mies left behind

apartment houses at the
Weissenhofsiedlung at
Stuttgart (1927)

lift and
staircase
towers

glass envelope

green
marble faced
walls

grey
tinted glass
screens

pools lined
with black
glass mosa

the German Pavilion at the
Barcelona Exhibition
(1929)

plated steel
columns

leather

plated
steel

the chair
designed by Mies
for the Barcelona Pavilion

Mies van
der Rohe

the **Tugendhat House**
at Brno, Czechoslovakia (1930)

by 1932 the Dessau district was governed by them and they forced the Bauhaus to move to Berlin. In 1933 Hitler himself came to power, and the school was once more under scrutiny. Seven years earlier, Mies had designed a monument in Berlin to the communist martyrs Rosa Luxemburg and Karl Liebknecht; the fact that he had fulfilled the commission for architectural and humanitarian rather than political reasons was lost on the suspicious Nazi 'cultural advisers'. For them, the Bauhaus was Bolshevist and un-German, and it was forced to close for ever. For four years Mies continued working in Germany, but at the invitation of the American architect Philip Johnson, he left in 1937 for the United States, where his appointment as head of Chicago's Armour Institute – now IIT – began a new chapter not only in his own life but also in that of American architecture.

During the thirties and forties, American and British cultural life was considerably enriched by intellectuals leaving Europe. Some of the architects settled in England, and others paused there briefly before crossing the Atlantic, leaving behind a handful of new buildings and a deep impression on the minds of their more progressive British colleagues. Gropius collaborated with Maxwell Fry on the design of a house in Chelsea (1936) and another at Sevenoaks (1937); Fry's Sun House in Hampstead (1936) was fully worthy of his eminent partner. Together they built the Impington Village College in Cambridgeshire (1936). Marcel Breuer collaborated with F. R. S. Yorke, on houses at Bristol (1936), at Eton (1938) and on a long, low, elegant brick-built house, raised on *pilotis*, at Angmering in Sussex (1937). The Russian Serge Chermayeff built a house at Rugby (1934) and one at Halland, Sussex (1939), and with the great Mendelsohn designed a house in Chelsea (1936) and the fine De La Warr Pavilion at the seaside resort of Bexhill (1935). The firm 'Tecton', set up by Bertold Lubetkin, built several houses, two enclosures at London Zoo, the Highpoint Flats at Highgate (1936–8) and the Finsbury Health Centre, London (1938–9). By 1937, both Gropius and Breuer had moved to Harvard, where they went into partnership and continued teaching, and in the early 1940s Mendelsohn and Chermayeff moved to California. They left behind a small group of British architects and planners whose confidence that a utopian future could be achieved through modern architecture was expressed by the increasing spatial and structural accomplishment of their buildings; the *Daily Express* offices in Fleet Street (1933) by Ellis and Clarke; the Peter Jones Store in Sloane Square, London (1935) by Crabtree, Slater and Moberly; and a number of fine houses by Amyas Connell, Basil Ward and Colin Lucas, which explored many of the design ideas currently preoccupying Le Corbusier. Making considerable use of concrete to achieve the rigidity of structure necessary for exciting spatial effects, they built a succession of houses at Ruislip (1935), Redhill and Henfield (1936), Wentworth and Moor Park (1937), culminating in the splendid 66 Frognal, Hampstead (1938).

These pioneer developments were still taking place against a background of public indifference or hostility. A gulf lay between this small group of architects, sure that they had the answer to society's problems, and a public which insisted on going elsewhere for its buildings. The most acceptable style for public buildings was heavy and neo-classical – even though modern structural methods were now common. The result was often a steel-framed, multi-storey building whose baroque stonework was not only out of character but also out of scale with the increased height that the steel frame made possible. In cinema and hotel design, modernism was more permissible, though it seldom took the form of anything more than fashionable applied decoration: the jagged forms of 'jazz modern' or the streamlined shapes of 'Art Deco'.

Cities were still growing at the rate of the industrial revolution, placing enormous demands on space as industry and housing, encouraged by the development of suburban railways and arterial roads, pushed their way out into the countryside. In the city centres, densities were drastically increased as land scarcity put building sites at a premium and the cheaper land at the outer edges of the city was used with prodigality.

Britain's building industry survived reasonably well during the 1920s and '30s, and the expansion of the suburbs continued, unaffected by the slump; 19th-century suburbs had represented the desire of the middle classes to escape the city, but now suburbs were being built for lower-middle class and working-class occupation too. The working-class suburb of Becontree in Essex, built between 1921 and 1934 by the LCC for a population of 90,000, was the largest single housing estate in the world. At the other end of the scale, unplanned and piecemeal development was taking place, as individual householders looked for plots on which to put their ideal houses.

Stylistically, the suburban house was often an unhappy mixture of mis-applied historical details derived from such varied sources as the houses of Voysey and those of Tudor England. There were many compensations however: two-storeyed, with front and rear gardens and space for a car, they were a great improvement on those left behind in the crowded city-centre. As a base for family life, they represented the aspirations of a large part of the population. But there were also disadvantages. At this time the local authorities' planning powers were weak: most of the existing controls were in the form of public health bye-laws, the creation of which had been an urgent task in the 19th century. Drainage, lighting, ventilation and space around buildings were thus controlled and ensured certain minimum standards for the house itself. But there was little machinery for making basic decisions about land-use. Estates were built without sufficient open space, because no-one was responsible for providing it; the provision of shops was haphazard; journeys to school might be long and difficult; estates as large as small towns had no focus for their social life.

There was often no architectural focus either: these houses, offering desirable features individually, were monotonous and stereotyped when repeated in their thousands. It was this feature above all which aroused the scorn of progressive architects and set them searching for other ways of designing mass housing to give it more architectural coherence.

One approach was represented by the ideas of Le Corbusier and Gropius; the former in *Vers Une Architecture* and the latter in his book *The New Architecture and the Bauhaus* (1935) were already beginning to show how houses could be piled on top of each other to form regular high-rise blocks and how the space saved could provide landscape for the benefit of all. What was lost, of course, was the autonomy of the individual plot, and the close relationship of the dwelling to the ground. Le Corbusier, with his experience of the long-standing French tradition of flat-dwelling in both cities and suburbs, was prepared to accept this. Less understandably, many of his English colleagues were, too: the desirability of replacing suburbia by high-rise buildings set in park-land became the conventional wisdom for architects, many of whom made their living designing detached houses for wealthy clients.

Another approach was represented by Howard's ordered, balanced garden-city idea which, perhaps because of its nearer approximation to the suburban ideal, continued to have some influence. The approach remained undeveloped in practice,

the discovery in 1923 of Tutankhamun's tomb created a vogue for Egyptian design as in this **table clock** by Meyrowitz

design on **elevator doors** in Wall Street office block of the early 1930s

the Art Deco style became popular after the Paris Exposition of 1925 where it was featured in all the pavilions except Le Corbusier's Purist 'Pavillon de L'Esprit Nouveau'

it was used in hotels, cinemas and commercial buildings to express an opulent kind of modernism..

..as in these gilt metal gates in the ballroom of **Claridge's**, London (1929)...

.. or the metalwork pinnacle of the **Chrysler building** New York by William van Alen (1929)

white-painted render

..dows with ..zontal ..cing bars

..dernistic styling was applied to small, speculative ..ses as in this example of the early 1930s ..ngland

brickwork

even the most traditionally designed speculative houses incorporated fashionable details, like the 'sun-burst' doors on these 1930s 'semi-detached English 'bungalows'

where designers clung to classical styles, the result was often inappropriate to the increased height of the buildings. This London office building is composed of two designs.

however. Letchworth and Welwyn were very slow to grow – at the end of the 1930s their combined population was less than 40,000 – and the only other major example was Dame Henrietta Barnett's Hampstead Garden Suburb, began in 1907. On the other hand, many theoretical ideas were being put forward in the United States, where a growing tradition of suburban living made the garden-city idea attractive.

In 1916, the American planner Clarence Perry coined the phrase 'neighbourhood unit'. This idea added a new dimension to garden-city theory by suggesting that each family needed to identify with its local area. This could be done, he suggested, by giving each neighbourhood distinct boundaries and certain specific facilities to act as social foci. Each area would contain about 5000 people – enough to support an elementary school – and would be about 1 kilometre across, so that the maximum walking-distance to the school and community facilities at the centre would be no more than 400 or 500 metres.

The high car-ownership in America meant that its planners had to come to terms earlier with how to integrate traffic movement into the design of housing. In the late 1920s a four-square-kilometre new town was begun at Radburn, NJ, by the City Housing Corporation. The intention was to build the first American garden city, housing 25,000 people in a number of neighbourhoods based on the Perry principle. The designers, Clarence Stein and Henry Wright, were able to try out their own ideas too, the most important being to separate pedestrian and vehicle movement. Each residential super-block, surrounded by distributor roads, had a central green-way, a completely pedestrian area onto which all the houses faced. Each greenway was linked to the next by an underpass below the surrounding roads and it was possible to walk through the town without even seeing a motor vehicle. Radburn was never completed, but the idea, with its emphasis on amenity and safety, remained a major feature of housing philosophy.

In the city centres, particularly those of New York, Chicago and Philadelphia, rising land values pushed office buildings higher and higher. The archetypal New York skyscraper appeared during the 1920s: Wall Street became a forest of tall buildings and even higher ones began to appear in the mid-town area. The City Zoning Ordinance required set-backs on successive floors as the buildings increased in height, which produced the characteristic tapering profile of the New York Life building, the Chrysler building and the Empire State building. At a height of 370 metres, the latter was for some time the tallest building in the world. The development of the Rockefeller Centre, dominated by the RCA building with its Radio City Music Hall, dates from 1930.

American investment in building was reduced drastically during the troubled 1930s, but these early years of the European presence in the United States saw the construction of a few fine buildings which represented the first real contact with the international style. At IIT, Mies began in 1939 to replan the campus, designing the buildings himself as simple, elegant glass boxes, bringing an unequivocal statement of the machine aesthetic to his adopted country. Even Wright, most American of architects, came as near during the 1930s as he ever did to the international style. His house Falling Water for Edgar Kaufman, at Bear Run, Pa. (1936), is built above a waterfall, and is as romantic a conception as any of his prairie houses. At the same time, its prominent, white reinforced-concrete cantilevers give it an air of undecorated simplicity, rare in Wright's work. A similar simplicity characterises his administration building for the Johnson Wax company at Racine, Wis. (1938).

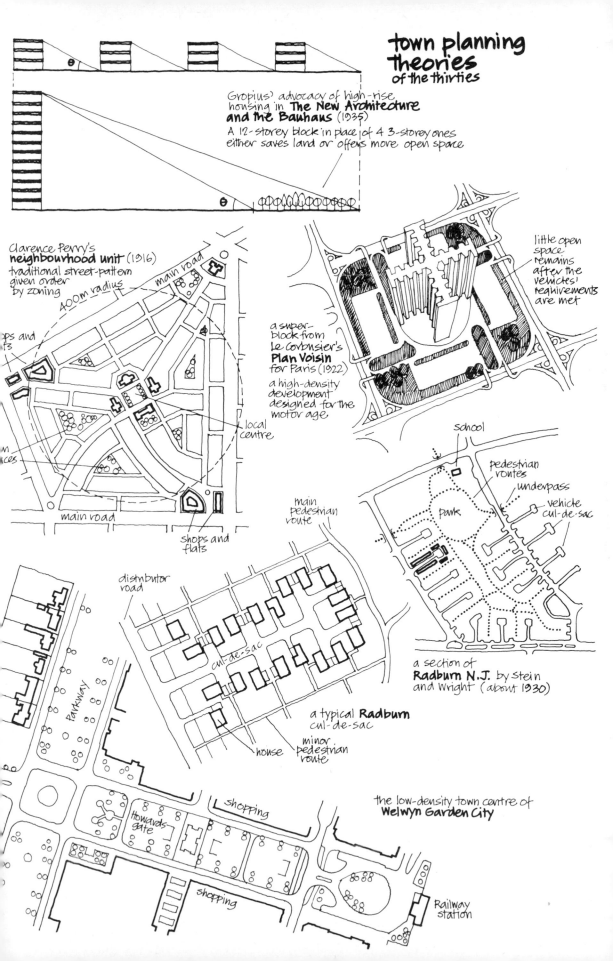

town planning theories
of the thirties

Gropius' advocacy of high-rise housing in **The New Architecture and the Bauhaus** (1935)

A 12-storey block in place of 4 3-storey ones either saves land or offers more open space

Clarence Perry's **neighbourhood unit** (1916) traditional street-pattern given order by zoning

400m radius

main road

ps and ts

main road

m ces

local centre

shops and flats

a super-block from Le Corbusier's **Plan Voisin** for Paris (1922)

a high-density development designed for the motor age

little open space remains after the vehicles' requirements are met

school

pedestrian routes

underpass

Park

vehicle cul-de-sac

a section of **Radburn N.J.** by Stein and Wright (about 1930)

distributor road

main pedestrian route

cul-de-sac

Parkway

a typical **Radburn** cul-de-sac

house

minor pedestrian route

the low-density town centre of **Welwyn Garden City**

shopping

Howards gate

shopping

Railway station

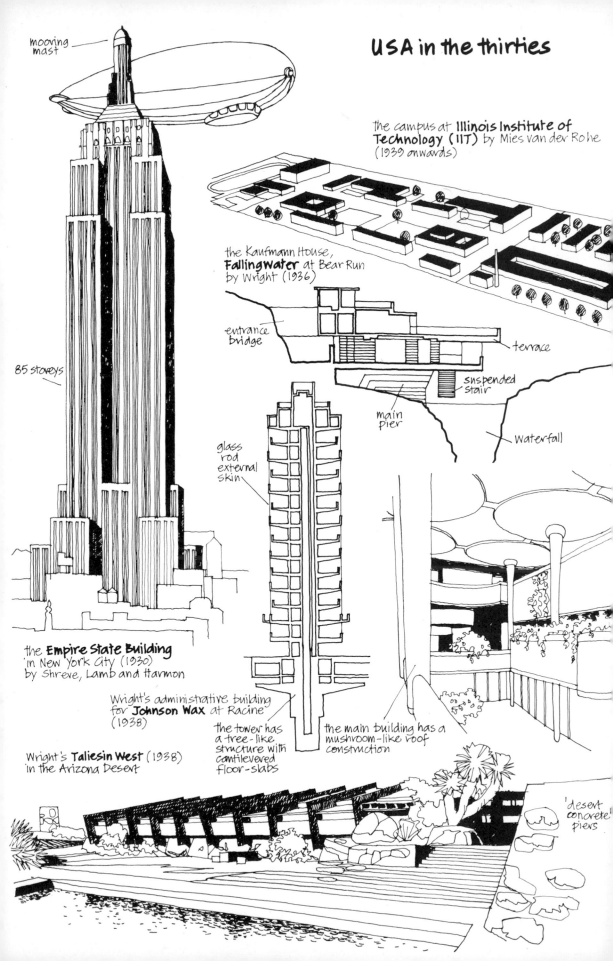

USA in the thirties

mooring mast

85 storeys

the **Empire State Building**
in New York City (1930)
by Shreve, Lamb and Harmon

the campus at **Illinois Institute of Technology (IIT)** by Mies van der Rohe (1939 onwards)

the Kaufmann House,
Fallingwater at Bear Run
by Wright (1936)

entrance bridge

terrace

suspended stair

main pier

Waterfall

glass rod external skin

Wright's administrative building
for **Johnson Wax** at Racine
(1938)

the tower has a tree-like structure with cantilevered floor-slabs

the main building has a mushroom-like roof construction

Wright's **Taliesin West** (1938)
in the Arizona Desert

'desert concrete piers

There is no decoration, and its brick and glass are used in a strong, original and honest manner. The great richness of the building comes mostly from its spatial and structural ingenuity. The same year, by contrast, Wright produced the most intuitive and most American of all his buildings. Taliesin West was built in 1938 as a studio-house where he and his students could develop their architectural ideas in monastic seclusion. The building is a romantic response to a spectacular desert site near Phoenix, Ariz. which for Wright was the epitome of the frontier. A long, low, tent-like structure, with a roof of canvas and cedar-wood held up on massive piers of 'desert concrete' – boulders held together with cement – it has ancient Mayan, and even Biblical, overtones.

In 1938 Taliesin could hardly have seemed more remote from the political situation in Europe. The growing tensions between the three rival political systems – Stalin's socialism, the fascism of Italy and Germany, and the struggling capitalism of the other countries – was given a new urgency by German rearmament. The First World War had begun almost accidentally; the Second, by contrast, was provoked almost unilaterally by the fascist countries' need to expand. Entire populations were affected: innocence and non-involvement were no longer a guarantee of safety. Yet socially, its effect was less devastating. The First War had marked a break between the old world and the new: the end of 19th-century Europe and its power structure. The Second was a temporary upheaval in a process which had already begun: the emergence of a weaker, less confident Europe, more dependent on mutual aid and on help from outside.

The war gave great impetus to technological development, particularly in aviation and in nuclear physics. The rapid post-war growth of air-travel and of electronic communication was comparable in some ways to the railway age of the 19th century, reducing the world to a 'global village'. Nuclear fission seemed to offer unlimited scope for the development of new sources of power and before, and during, the war, and immediately afterwards, there was confidence in the building of a better future.

A major influence on Europe was the example of Sweden which, due to its neutrality, had escaped much of the destruction of western Europe and was making steady social progress. A humane, social-democratic government had been in office since the early 1930s, and a high standard of living, publicly-provided social services, free education and good industrial relations seemed to be a pointer for the rest of Europe.

The Weissenhof exhibition in Stuttgart in 1927, at which Mies assembled the work of almost all the progressive European architects, was followed by a similar one in Stockholm in 1930. The co-ordinator, and designer of several of the buildings, was the Swede Sven Markelius. The mixed layout of public buildings, houses, flats and urban landscape, more organised than the Weissenhof, with its thirty-three scattered blocks of housing, created an exciting yet realistic image of the city of the future.

Among the ideas was that of the 'lamella' house, with a wide-fronted, shallow plan, giving good daylighting to all rooms, in contrast to the narrow-fronted poorly-lit houses of Swedish tradition. Lamella houses, in regular, continuous rows, were to make a considerable, if uninspiring, impact on many European townscapes. A typical scheme is the Hjorthagen area of Stockholm, with workers' houses designed by Hakon Ahlberg. The Swedish political system encouraged new ideas in housing. In 1937 the architect Eric Friberger evolved his 'element house', based on a pre-fabricated system flexible enough to be used for a variety of family sizes, and capable of being extended or reduced as the family size changed. Tower blocks of flats were also developed to provide an alternative type of accommodation to the lamella terrace, and began appearing in housing schemes even before the Second World War. Few Swedish housing schemes laid emphasis on private outdoor space. Sun-balconies might be provided in flat-blocks, but at ground level the land was usually communal, with public landscaped areas stretching right up to the walls of the houses. The provision of common facilities was a feature of Swedish planning and reached its conclusion in the building of 'collective' houses for families whose parents were at work, with communal restaurants, kitchens, laundries and day-nurseries, the first of which was designed by Markelius for Stockholm in 1935.

In Britain the 1944 Beveridge Report suggested how a comparable programme of social benefits might be achieved, and the labour government of 1945 began to put it into effect. The County of London Plan (1943) proposed the replanning of the London region, the rebuilding of devastated areas and the setting-up of a ring of new towns outside the city. To provide the machinery for this, the New Towns Act (1946) and the Town and Country Planning Act (1947) gave Britain the most powerful and advanced land-use planning laws in the world.

As yet, the British system was still only a system, and nothing concrete had been achieved. But an important example of what could be done was provided by the United States, whose housing policy during the war had been exemplary. Roosevelt's New Deal (1933–41), a result of the Depression, had introduced the country to the concept of state control of the economy and the carrying-out of major public works. Under acute wartime conditions, with production strained and one-third of the population still badly housed, state control was extended to the housing industry. A crash programme was set up to design and build factory-produced homes both temporary and permanent, communal and self-contained. Many architects, including Gropius and Breuer, were involved, and many ingenious designs were produced, economical and utilitarian but often the more elegant for it.

The lessons learned through wartime factory production seemed appropriate for meeting the challenge of post-war rebuilding. Not only had management become more efficient but new techniques had been evolved, often with the extra stimulus of material shortage. Among the most interesting and promising were those being investigated by Richard Buckminster Fuller (born 1895). As early as 1927 he had designed and built a prototype 'Dymaxion' house, consisting of two hexagonal metal decks suspended from a central mast which contained the services. The intention was to apply the efficiency and precision of car-building techniques to house con-struction. The Wichita House (1946) was a development produced on the assembly line of an aircraft company, to be packed in a crate and sent anywhere. Fuller's most successful work has been in the science of 'geodesics'. This technique involves the building-up of curved forms – in Fuller's case, domes – by linking together a number of pre-fabricated elements. The linkages are aligned along 'great circles', lines representing the shortest possible distance across the surface, and result in strong yet extremely light structures: a geodesic dome might easily weigh one-twentieth of an equivalent span in more conventional construction. Many thousands of Fuller domes have been manufactured in aluminium, plywood, plastic, corrugated iron, prestressed concrete or kraft paper and used for houses, factories, warehouses and exhibition buildings, both temporary and permanent. Fuller later progressed into

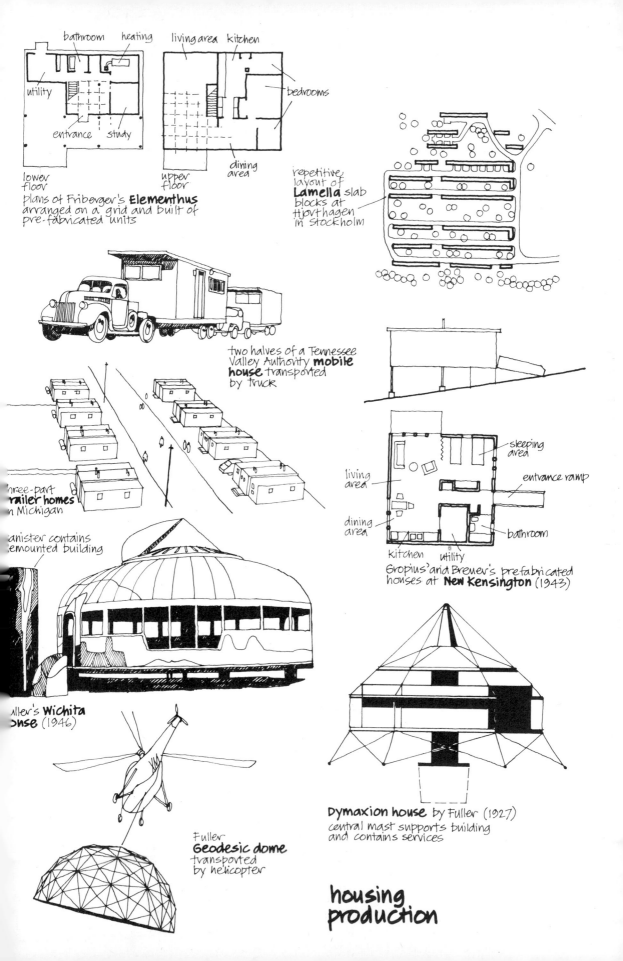

bathroom heating

living area kitchen

utility

bedrooms

entrance study

lower
floor

upper
floor

dining
area

plans of Friberger's **Elementhus**
arranged on a grid and built of
pre-fabricated units

repetitive
layout of
Lamella slab
blocks at
Hjorthagen
in Stockholm

two halves of a Tennessee
Valley Authority **mobile
house** transported
by truck

three-part
trailer homes
in Michigan

canister contains
remounted building

Fuller's **Wichita
House** (1946)

sleeping
area

living
area

entrance ramp

dining
area

bathroom

kitchen utility

Gropius' and Breuer's prefabricated
houses at **New Kensington** (1943)

Fuller
Geodesic dome
transported
by helicopter

Dymaxion house by Fuller (1927)
central mast supports building
and contains services

housing
production

the realm of 'tensegrity' structures, in which a distinction is made between members in compression and members in tension, allowing each member to be more efficiently and economically designed. The furniture designer and film-maker Charles Eames (1907–78) shared Fuller's interest in technology and his own house in Santa Monica, Ca. (1949), built from standard manufactured parts, did much to demonstrate the elegance that such an approach could obtain.

The strongly-held and fought-for ideas of the twenties and thirties were now common property and the technological imagery of the international style was being investigated and developed. The Royal Festival Hall in London (1951), designed by a team of LCC architects led by Robert Matthew, was perhaps one of the last great buildings of the international style, with all the formal purity and spatial richness of the great buildings of the thirties. Mies van der Rohe's two tower-blocks of luxury flats at 860 Lake Shore Drive, Chicago (1951) and his Farnsworth House at Plano, Ill. (1950) were a move towards even greater subtlety and refinement: the creation of almost negative architecture, containing pure, simple spaces which the inhabitants could use how they wished. Eero Saarinen's (1910–61) General Motors Technical Centre at Warren, Michigan (1951) consisted of luxurious, Miesian buildings in a large, open landscape, planned at the scale of the motor-car in a demonstration of conspicuous consumption. The Italian engineer Pier Luigi Nervi (born 1891) built two fine exhibition halls at Turin (1948–50) whose elegant reinforced-concrete roofs combined structural efficiency with a romantic delicacy of expression.

Meanwhile, some former champions of the international style, including Le Corbusier himself, seemed to be setting its principles aside in a search for a more personal mode of expression. His amazing pilgrimage chapel of Notre Dame du Haut at Ronchamp in France (1950) was an intriguing combination of functionalism and pure sculpture: its puzzled critics saw its bizarre, hybrid structure as a betrayal of the principles of modern architecture, perhaps without appreciating the rigorous functionalism of the building's planning.

One of the most dramatic examples of the appearance of a personal style was that of the Finnish architect Alvar Aalto (born 1898). Before the war he had been a practitioner in his own country of a fairly straightforward international style of design, demonstrated by the Viipuri library (1927), a factory with workers' housing at Sumila (1936) and his best-known early work, a large tuberculosis clinic at Paimio (1929), built in reinforced concrete. Because of their cost, modern materials like steel and concrete were alien to Finnish building experience, and Aalto became increasingly interested in the architectural character and the building techniques of local tradition: small-scale, low, modest buildings built in masonry and – in particular – timber. His experiments in the 1930s in the design of bent-wood furniture ran parallel with the development of the Finnish plywood and laminated timber business, which remains today the country's principal manufacturing industry. He was thus able to combine a feeling for Finnish tradition with a perception of the most up-to-date techniques it had to offer, and to synthesise the two into the most personal, most self-contained, least fashionable style of any of the great modern architects. His buildings have the spatial richness of Wright's, but without Wright's clutter of decoration; they have a Miesian precision without verging on over-simplification; and they have much of Le Corbusier's grandeur without his occasional grandiosity.

Aalto's post-war reputation rests mainly on two buildings. The first was his

242

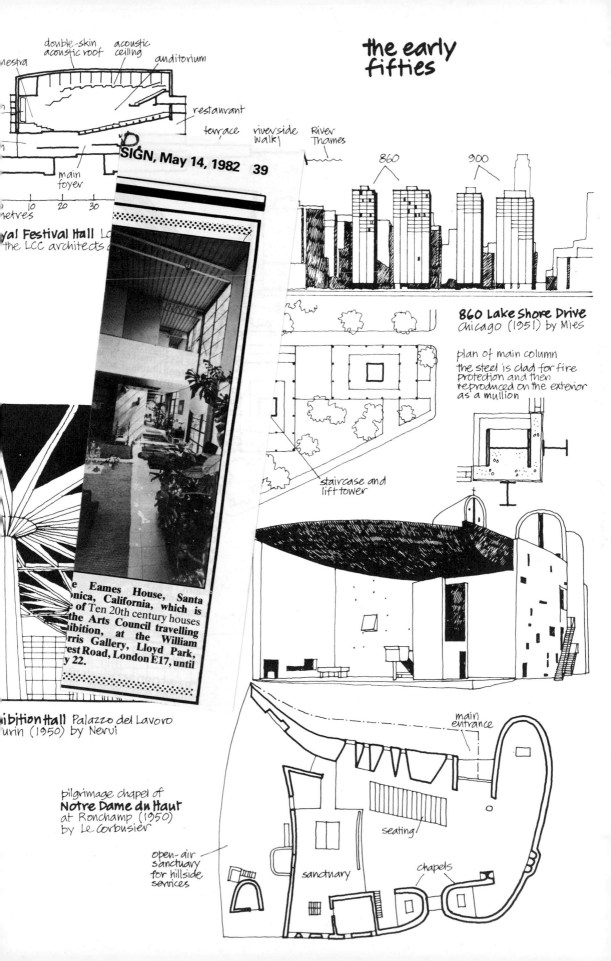

orchestra · double-skin acoustic roof · acoustic ceiling · auditorium

restaurant

terrace · riverside walk · River Thames

main foyer

metres 10 20 30

yal **Festival Hall** Lo
the LCC architects

860 · 900

860 Lake Shore Drive
Chicago (1951) by Mies

plan of main column
the steel is clad for fire
protection and then
reproduced on the exterior
as a mullion

staircase and lift tower

e Eames House, Santa
onica, California, which is
e of Ten 20th century houses
the Arts Council travelling
ibition, at the William
rris Gallery, Lloyd Park,
est Road, London E17, until
y 22.

ibition Hall Palazzo del Lavoro
urin (1950) by Nervi

pilgrimage chapel of
Notre Dame du Haut
at Ronchamp (1950)
by Le Corbusier

open-air sanctuary for hillside services

main entrance

seating

sanctuary

chapels

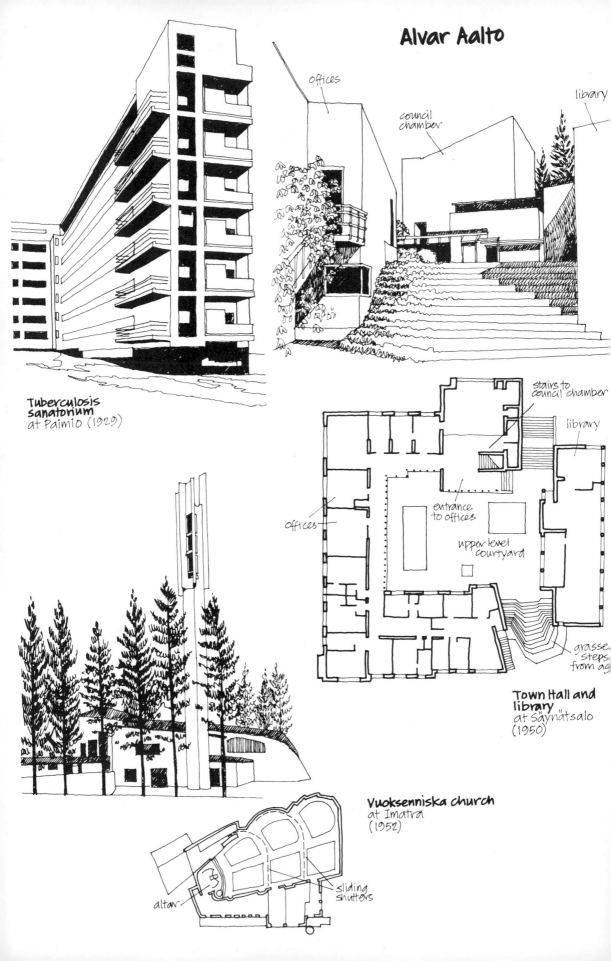

Alvar Aalto

Tuberculosis sanatorium at Paimio (1929)

offices

council chamber

library

stairs to council chamber

library

offices

entrance to offices

upper level courtyard

grasse steps from ag

Town Hall and library at Säynätsalo (1950)

Vuoksenniska church at Imatra (1952)

altar

sliding shutters

beautiful village hall for the tiny island of Säynatsälo. This is perhaps a more important commission than its small size and humble location would suggest: Finland's highly decentralised economy places great importance on local life and the design of a village hall inevitably says much about the relationship between people and authority. Säynatsälo was a new town for 3000 people, for which Aalto prepared the plan. At its centre was a loosely-planned 'market' area, a main meeting-place recalling the agora of ancient times. At one side were placed the village hall and library, regularly planned around a small courtyard, linked to the market-place by a set of steps. The characterful brickwork and pitched timber roofs of these small buildings give an air of informality and approachability absent from the design of most other civic buildings in Europe or America, either before or since.

His second great building was the Vuoksenniska church at Imatra (1952), contemporary with Ronchamp and an interesting contrast. Both buildings are highly sculptural and spatially and structurally free. But where Ronchamp is a bold composition of parabolic curves, Imatra is complex and intense. Ronchamp stands as a monument on an open hill-side, but Imatra lies low among pine-trees, with only its tall elegant tower to mark it from a distance. It consists of three interlinked compartments, separated or opened up at will by sliding screens, with a huddle of ancillary rooms round the edge. Three copper-clad hump-back roofs cover the three compartments, canted at one side to provide large areas of high-level glazing above the surrounding walls. The idea is simple, but the shapes themselves, and the detailing, are asymmetrical and complex.

Ronchamp was not Le Corbusier's only work of the period. In 1946 he began construction of a building in the suburbs of Marseille which became perhaps the single most influential architectural work of the post-war years. This was the 'Unité d'Habitation de grandeur conforme', completed in 1952, a massive housing project to rehouse the shipyard workers from the Vieux-Port quarter of the city destroyed in the war. Le Corbusier saw it as an opportunity to put into practice the theoretical ideas of his Ville Contemporaine and Ville Radieuse, and the Unité was only the first of a number of blocks proposed, with the intention of restructuring the whole social life of Marseille. The scale of the building is immense: an entire suburb of 1600 people was to be housed in a single rectangular block, 140 metres long and 24 deep, twenty storeys and more in height, containing not only living space but also shops and sports and play areas. The block is aligned north–south, with an east–west aspect, allowing all the units – mostly duplexes, ingeniously interlocking around a central access corridor – to receive both morning and evening sun. 'Soleil, espace, verdure', was Le Corbusier's approach, and the 'espace' comes partly from the double-height living-rooms, on the Citrohan principle, opening onto private open-air balconies, while the 'verdure' is the Provençal landscape, visible not only around the building but also below it, between its giant *pilotis*.

Le Corbusier's early interest in prefabrication is apparent in the construction. The main frame is an 'in situ' skeleton of reinforced-concrete columns and beams, within which the wall and floor panels of the flats are located, isolated from the main structure – for sound insulation – by pads of lead. Much of the repetitive cladding, including the sun-screens or 'brises-soleil', were precast and lifted into position. The dimensional control implicit in the use of precast elements was given extra point by the use of the 'Modulor', a system of harmonious proportion recently devised by Le Corbusier, based on the principles of the golden section.

At the time, one of the more startling things about the building was its surface texture. The idea of concrete as a smooth, precise material – an idea which had inspired much of the architecture of the 1920s, including Le Corbusier's own – was here set aside in recognition of its being a plastic material, dependent for its shape on the shutter-boards within which it is cast. It appeared in the Unité, heavily-textured, marked with the knots and grain of the formwork, totally in keeping with the elephantine scale of the building itself.

Le Corbusier followed the Unité with a pair of small houses for private clients, the Jaoul family, in the Parisian suburb of Neuilly (1954). Here the same roughness of detail is apparent: rustic brick walls and heavy concrete floorslabs, with low, barrel-vaulted roofs. The reversion from the machine aesthetic of the Villa Savoie to this earthiness could hardly have been more dramatic. The same aesthetic continued into his two final *chefs d'oeuvre*, the Parliamentary buildings at Chandigarh, new capital of the Punjab (1950–65), and the monastery of La Tourette (1960) near Lyon. The main feature of Chandigarh is the Capitol, a group of four buildings – Palace, Secretariat, Assembly and Supreme Court – enormous in scale and all but dwarfed by a vast, open landscape shaped by Le Corbusier's cosmic geometry. The combination of spatial complexity and textural roughness – intellectual yet technically primitive – seems highly appropriate to the function and the location. And the use of stark, exposed concrete could hardly be more appropriate than among the severe, disciplined Cistercians of La Tourette, in a simple, block-like building whose cunning roof-shapes make the plain interiors glow with light.

Le Corbusier's concrete work helped give birth to a new international style, and his term for it – *béton brut* – gave rise to the name 'brutalism'. Stirling and Gowan's low-rise Langham housing development at Ham Common, London (1958), has the roughness of the Maisons Jaoul. Churchill College, Cambridge (1960), by Richard Sheppard, though exposed brick and concrete, is rather neater and politer a building. The use of this tough and rugged style for institutional buildings was perhaps understandable but also of questionable humanity, and Aldo van Eyck's orphanage at Amsterdam (1958) and Vittoriano Viganò's Instituto Marchiondi (1959), an institute in Milan for deprived boys, seem to provide unnecessarily harsh environments. In the United States, brutalism was softened with touches of luxury, as in the elegantly-ribbed exposed concrete of Paul Rudolph's Art and Architecture building at Yale (1959). Japanese architects, possibly through the influence of Chandigarh, were particularly receptive, and the strong forms of *béton brut* were used in a way which resembled the over-lapping baulks of timber in traditional Japanese construction. Among the best examples are two early works by Kenzo Tange, his building for the Yamanshi Broadcasting company at Koufu (1967) and his magnificent City Hall at Kurashiki (1960). Perhaps the most fitting application of the properties of *béton brut* was in the small evangelical church of the Atonement built by Helmut Striffler in 1965 on the site of Dachau, a partly underground building approached by a broad set of steps and contained, with appropriate symbolism, inside a strong, jagged, ribbed-concrete retaining-wall.

Of all Le Corbusier's late buildings, the Unité had the widest influence. Among other things, it encouraged everywhere the building of high-rise flats for family living, a piece of conventional wisdom which was to persist for longer than it deserved. It should be said that the original concept of the Ville Radieuse, with its emphasis on spacious landscape, on community facilities within the block and on

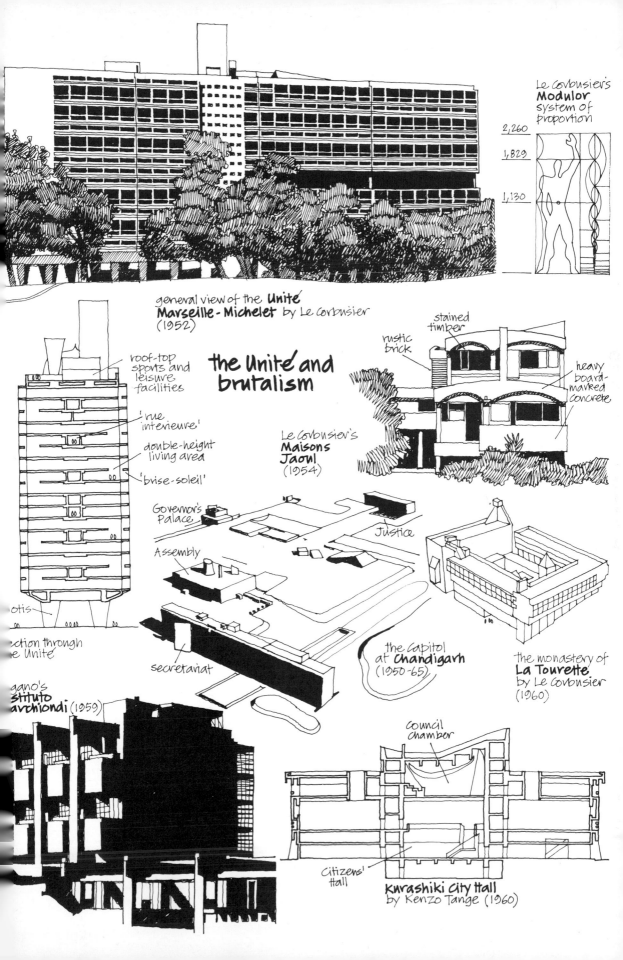

general view of the **Unité
Marseille - Michelet** by Le Corbusier
(1952)

Le Corbusier's
Modulor
system of
proportion

2,260

1,829

1,130

the Unité and brutalism

roof-top
sports and
leisure
facilities

'rue
interieure'

double-height
living area

'brise-soleil'

...otis

...ction through
...e Unité

Le Corbusier's
**Maisons
Jaoul**
(1954)

rustic
brick

stained
timber

heavy
board-
marked
concrete

Governor's
Palace

Justice

Assembly

secretariat

the Capitol
at **Chandigarh**
(1950-65)

the monastery of
La Tourette
by Le Corbusier
(1960)

...gano's
**...stituto
...avchiondi** (1959)

Council
chamber

Citizens'
Hall

Kurashiki City Hall
by Kenzo Tange (1960)

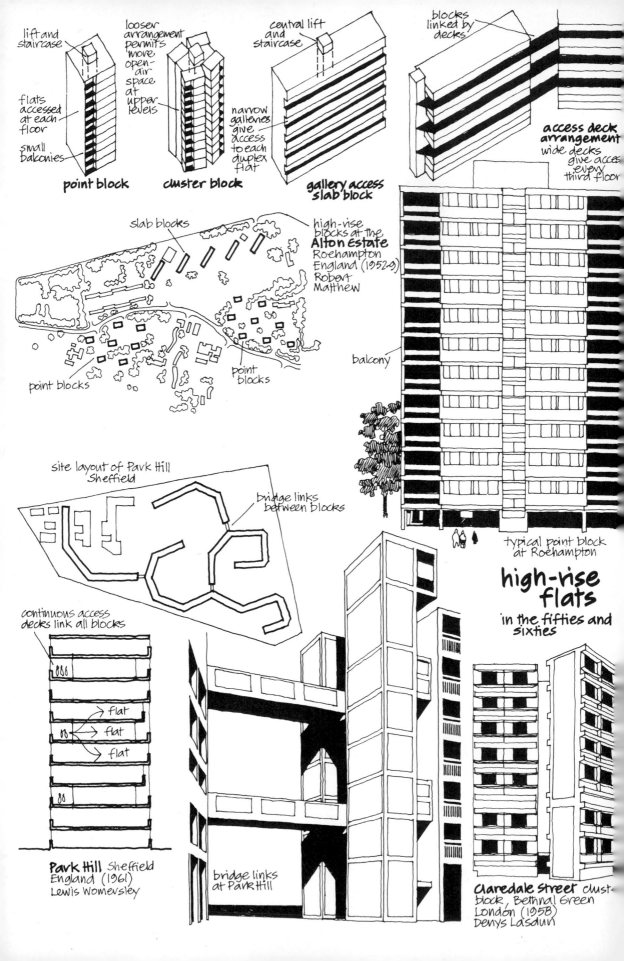

lift and staircase

flats accessed at each floor

small balconies

point block

looser arrangement permits 'more open-air space' at upper levels

cluster block

central lift and staircase

narrow galleries give access to each duplex flat

gallery access slab block

blocks linked by decks

access deck arrangement wide decks give access every third floor

slab blocks

point blocks

point blocks

high-rise blocks at the **Alton estate** Roehampton England (1952-9) Robert Matthew

balcony

typical point block at Roehampton

high-rise flats
in the fifties and sixties

site layout of Park Hill Sheffield

bridge links between blocks

continuous access decks link all blocks

flat

flat

flat

Park Hill Sheffield England (1961) Lewis Womersley

bridge links at Park Hill

Claredale street cluster block, Bethnal Green London (1958) Denys Lasdun

upper-level gardens for every flat, would have done much to counter the sense of isolation and the lack of outdoor space which have been major criticisms of high-rise living. The Unité itself fell somewhat short of the theory – certainly the small balconies were little substitute for high-level gardens – but the numerous subsequent imitations and mis-applications of Le Corbusier's ideas fell shorter still.

One of the best follow-ups was the Alton housing estate designed by the LCC architects, led by Robert Matthew, for the London suburb of Roehampton (1952–9). In this, the Ville Radieuse was translated from Provence to a romantic landscape of English parkland. It consists of five slab-blocks of duplex flats, a number of tower-blocks, and lower terraces of flats and houses, all set in a luxurious landscape of lawns and trees. The tall blocks are neater and politer versions of the Unité. One of the biggest differences is the absence of Le Corbusier's emphasis on community facilities. The Unité contains shops, cafés, a bar, a health clinic, crèche, nursery, club and play areas, but the blocks at Roehampton contain nothing but dwellings, inevitably increasing the sense of isolation.

The idea of community was, by contrast, uppermost in the minds of Lewis Womersley, Sheffield city architect, and the design team of the Park Hill flats (1961). This massive slum-clearance project, stretched out across a rocky hill-side in the city-centre, consists of a number of slab-blocks linked at various levels by continuous 'access-decks', from which open the doors of every flat. The idea of the deck, over 3 metres wide, is the backbone of the scheme. Used both by people and by lightweight delivery trucks, it is intended to work like a traditional street: not only a means of getting about, but also a place for people to meet and for children to play in. The concept is similar – though more thoroughgoing in its application – to the internal access corridor of the Unité.

The reason for simulating a traditional street, rather than actually building one, was a question of density. It was thought important to conserve as much land as possible, and Park Hill is in effect three streets of houses piled on top of one another; there was no other way of achieving the high densities required – for the scheme contains 500 people per hectare of land. Neither the Unité nor the Alton estate was built at a high density; the main reason for tall buildings had been the retention of as much as possible of the living landscape below. But inevitably, few sites were in areas of landscape. Inevitably too, higher densities meant less open space, fewer places for children to play and an increase in the psychological pressures that occur when privacy is at a premium. Denys Lasdun's sixteen-storey cluster of flats at Bethnal Green, London (1956), made the best use of a difficult site by providing outdoor spaces at the upper levels for sitting out and talking to neighbours. But other schemes were being built whose design and density were placing considerable strains on their inhabitants, producing isolation and loneliness where there should have been a sense of community, and exposure and insecurity where there should have been privacy.

In urban areas all over the world the design of high tower-blocks of flats continued to fall short of people's needs. There was little visual difference between the towers of Glasgow and the twenty-six-storey blocks of Co-Op City, New York (1968). The alienation and malaise of high-rise Birmingham had its counterpart in the *superbloques* of Caracas (1950–4), the petty crime and vandalism on the Southwark estates was exceeded at the vast Pruitt-Igoe redevelopment in St Louis (1952–5).

On the green-field sites of the new towns, there was the opportunity for a different approach. Here, low-rise housing provided a better home environment for a family,

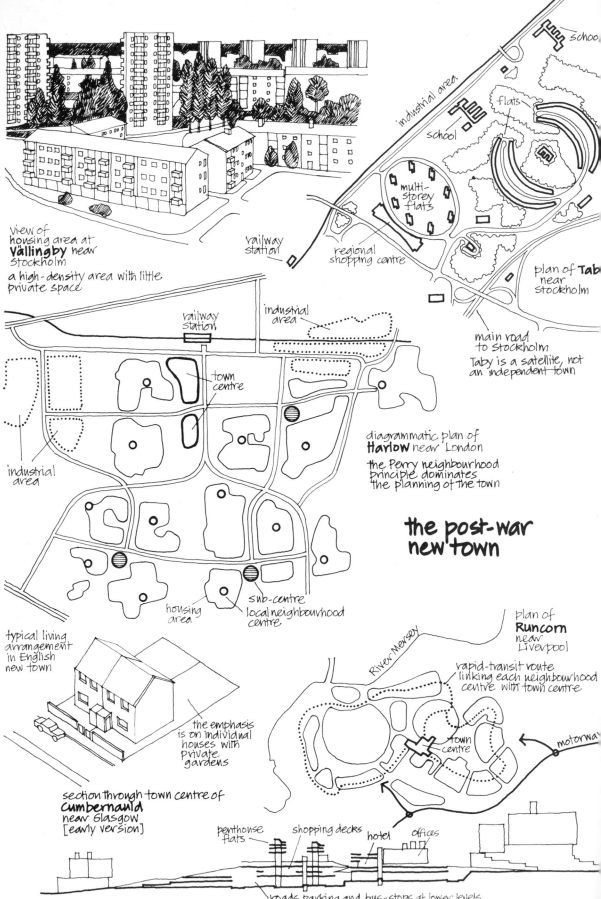

view of housing area at **Vällingby** near Stockholm

a high-density area with little private space

plan of **Taby** near Stockholm

industrial area

school

school

flats

multi-storey flats

regional shopping centre

railway station

main road to Stockholm

Taby is a satellite, not an independent town

railway station

industrial area

town centre

industrial area

diagrammatic plan of **Harlow** near London

the Perry neighbourhood principle dominates the planning of the town

the post-war new town

housing area

sub-centre

local neighbourhood centre

typical living arrangement in English new town

the emphasis is on individual houses with private gardens

plan of **Runcorn** near Liverpool

River Mersey

rapid-transit route linking each neighbourhood centre with town centre

town centre

motorway

section through town centre of **Cumbernauld** near Glasgow [early version]

penthouse flats

shopping decks

hotel

offices

roads, parking and bus-stops at lower levels

and the acres of green space made for healthier and cleaner surroundings. The early 1950s saw the development of new communities outside many major cities in Europe and America. In Scandinavia, they were mostly treated as satellites to their parent cities: Årsla, Vällingby, Farsta and Täby to Stockholm, Bellahøj to Copenhagen and Tapiola to Helsinki. Small in size, with their own community centres but depending largely for shopping and employment on the city, they were like well-planned suburbs. At their best, they were idyllic, as at Tapiola with its wide variety of buildings set in a spectacular landscape of forests and lakes.

In Britain, by the late 1960s, almost a million people had been housed in twenty-one new towns, eight of them near London. Larger in size and farther from the centre than their Swedish counterparts, they were as self-contained as possible. They were divided, according to the theories of Perry, into neighbourhoods of 5000 to 10,000 people, each area being planned to exclude through-traffic, often on the Radburn principle. The spacious, spread-out housing made for long travelling distances. Though some plans, such as Runcorn, provided efficient bus-services, in general it was necessary to rely on the motor-car. New towns demanded a certain affluence.

British and Swedish new towns were publicly financed. The relative lack of public enterprise in north America encouraged the private development of new towns. The best-known are perhaps Kitimat in Canada, a company town built by Alcan, and Reston, Va., near Washington, DC, financed by a variety of private interests. Reston, a series of neighbourhood 'villages' set in a landscape of boating lakes, golf-courses and riding-schools, is an unashamed demonstration of middle-class luxury. This feature is shared, to a lesser extent, by modern new towns: their expansive, successful economies attract the fairly young, resourceful and economically active, and the towns themselves, with their emphasis on self-contained living, on car-borne mobility, on the shopping centre as the focus of communal life and on the lavish provision of recreation, tend to emphasise the material welfare of this highly active group at the expense of others.

New-town house design tended to be unadventurous: it was important in attracting people from the cities to provide the same kind of safe, marketable product that they would have looked for in suburbia. It was instead the captive population remaining in the cities who provided the opportunity for architectural experiment. After the war, several European countries began to place considerable emphasis on solving their housing problems through 'industrialised building'. Complete buildings, manufactured in sections in the factory, could be assembled on site by a small, efficient work-force. In Russia, Denmark and Sweden, the long winters made it more sensible to transfer as much working-time as possible from the building site to the factory. For economic and practical reasons, the most favoured systems were those using heavyweight pre-cast concrete units in the form of wall and floor panels, bolted together at the junctions. France, with its tradition of reinforced-concrete engineering, was soon among the foremost in the field.

Deriving from economies of scale, industralised building encouraged the use of repetitive, identical wall units. Furthermore, as a load-bearing unit each wall panel had to be placed vertically below the one above, often resulting in flat elevations of extraordinary banality. The advantages of the system lay in its precision. Steel shuttering could be used to obtain a precise concrete finish, electrical conduit could be installed in the walls before erection, and complete 'heart' units – fully fitted bathrooms and kitchens – could be delivered to the site and merely lowered into place. The most spectacular example of heavyweight industrialised building in Britain was the Aylesbury Estate, built during the late 1960s in Southwark, London. This displays the advantages and disadvantages of the approach: the precision of its individual components and, with over 2000 dwellings, the soullessness of endless repetition. The planning of the blocks so that they can be erected from continuous 'crane-ways' makes the layout rectangular and the blocks themselves economically – but depressingly – long.

In 1968, a heavyweight panel system-built tower block in east London partly collapsed, like a pack of cards, as the result of a gas explosion which might have caused much less damage in a traditionally-built building. The stringent safety measures which immediately came in added a considerable cost to a form of development which many people already had misgivings about, and heavyweight panel building suffered a setback.

But there must be fewer doubts about the successful lightweight systems devised for school-building in England during the post-war years of material shortage. Using a specially devised system of standard components, the Hertfordshire Council, under C. H. Aslin, were able to build 100 schools during the nine years following 1946. In 1955, the CLASP system – Consortium of Local Authorities Special Programme – was begun by the Nottinghamshire Council under Donald Gibson. CLASP was a lightweight steel frame, suitable for one- and two-storey buildings, as flexible in its uses and as elegant in its application as the heavy concrete systems were inflexible and ponderous. CLASP had an enormous variety of components for different situations, and a great variety of external appearance was possible. More important, the project was well-researched in every detail, and resulted in buildings which were attractive and humane for those who used them; a good example of what system-building, used with compassion and understanding, could achieve.

Technology offered some hope for the future and, here and there, social progress was being made. Nevertheless, it would have been unrealistic to feel euphoric about the post-war world. The growth of fascism had been stopped, but a tension remained between capitalism and communism. The world war continued without a break into a political 'cold war', just as de-humanising in its effects. Nuclear war became a possibility and the aggressive neo-colonialism of the great powers and their satellites brought real and increasing violence to the underdeveloped third world, to Korea, the middle east, South America, black Africa, Cambodia and Vietnam.

To intellectuals in the 1930s and during the war, there had been hope of a new order. Orthodox communism had seemed, on the basis of the achievements of the twenties and thirties, to offer a solution to the world's problems, and the welfare state was an attempt to move capitalism a few steps nearer to a Marxist future. But after the war the despotic Russia of Stalin seemed less and less desirable as a model, and at the same time the adaptation and strengthening of capitalism in the west made a dramatic change in the system less likely.

Two features emerged. The first was economic co-operation at international level; the foundation of the International Monetary Fund in 1946 did a great deal to bring stability to capitalism, and created a world through which the fast-growing international corporations moved with ease. The second was the phenomenon, within each country, of the planned capitalist economy; it began to be clear that capitalism would survive longer if the conflicting demands of industry and labour could be balanced and controlled; bureaucratic intervention in all aspects of life, if not

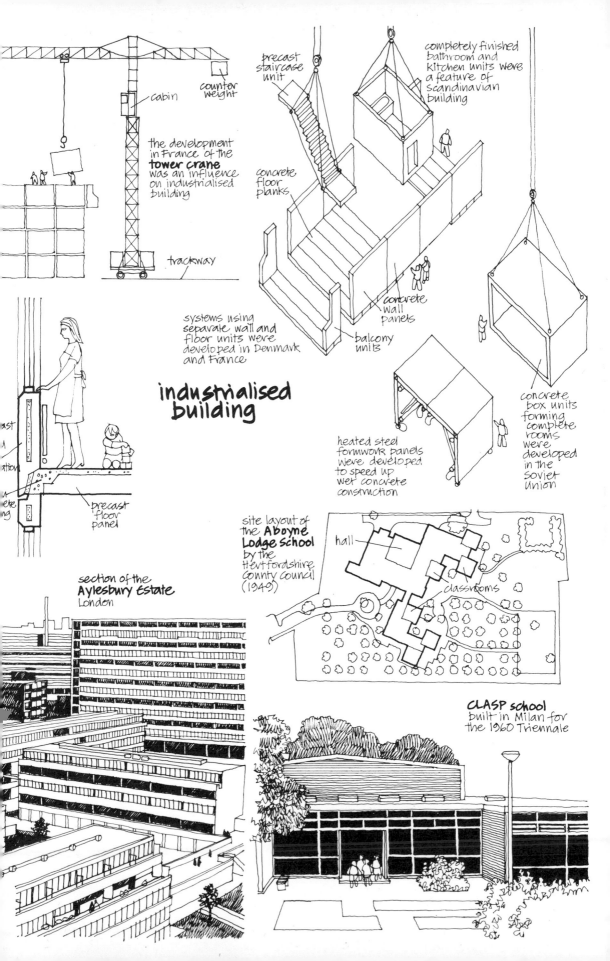

cabin

counter weight

the development in France of the **tower crane** was an influence on industrialised building

trackway

precast staircase unit

completely finished bathroom and kitchen units were a feature of scandinavian building

concrete floor planks

concrete wall panels

balcony units

systems using separate wall and floor units were developed in Denmark and France

concrete box units forming complete rooms were developed in the Soviet Union

heated steel formwork panels were developed to speed up wet concrete construction

precast floor panel

industrialised building

section of the **Aylesbury Estate** London

site layout of the **Aboyne Lodge School** by the Hertfordshire County Council (1949)

hall

classrooms

CLASP school built in Milan for the 1960 Triennale

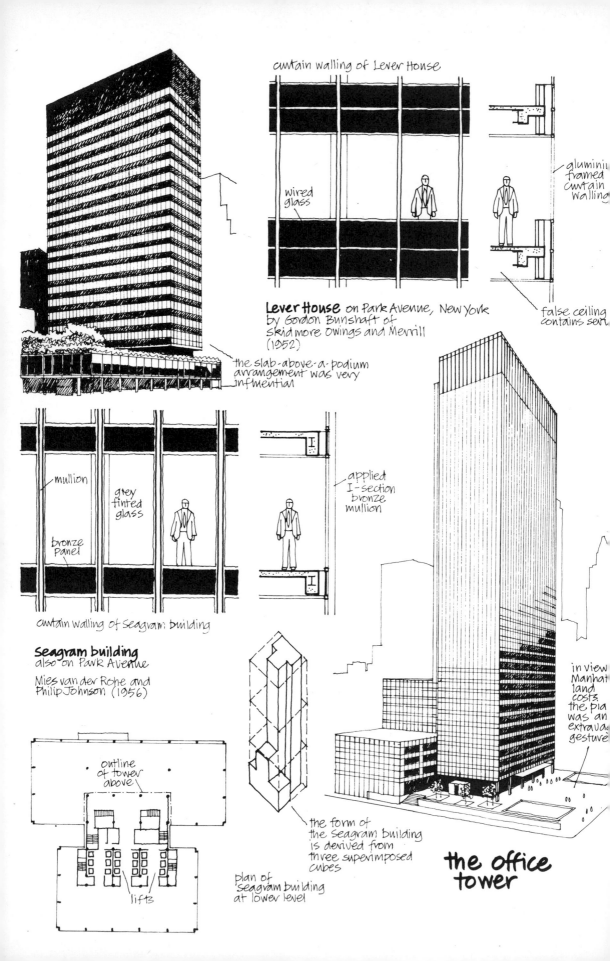

curtain walling of Lever House

wired glass

aluminium framed curtain walling

false ceiling contains ser...

Lever House on Park Avenue, New York
by Gordon Bunshaft of
Skidmore Owings and Merrill
(1952)

the slab-above-a-podium
arrangement was very
influential

mullion

grey tinted glass

bronze panel

applied I-section bronze mullion

curtain walling of Seagram building

Seagram building
also on Park Avenue

Mies van der Rohe and
Philip Johnson (1956)

in view Manhat... land costs the pia... was an extrava... gesture

outline of tower above

lifts

the form of
the Seagram building
is derived from
three superimposed
cubes

plan of
Seagram building
at lower level

the office tower

welcome, was accepted as necessary. There was a general drift towards pragmatic, consensus politics, with the right becoming more socially aware and the left dispensing with ideas of revolution. Extremism and idealism, both political and religious, tended to be subordinated to unadventurous materialism.

The public and private sectors began to merge and overlap. Most western countries were now controlled by vast corporate sub-cultures, in which central and local government and their agencies, together with the unions and semi-public institutions, shared power with the multi-national corporations: chemical and drug companies, insurance companies, motor manufacturers, the fuel and communications industries. Society was divided, not only between capital and labour but by the conflict between the power of bureaucracy and rights of the individual; 20th-century culture reflects the continuous struggle of the individual to be heard, from Kafka to Solzhenitsin, from existentialism to pop. This self-assertion, now common in literature, painting and music, had its counterpart in architecture: from the 1950s onwards, many architects turned their buildings into spectacular personal statements, in a brilliant variety of colours, textures and forms. Ironically, such statements could only be made through the patronage of the corporate world: the great modern buildings, each apparently a monument to its architect's individuality, are permanent reminders of his and our domination by the organisations which pay for them.

Lever House in New York (1952) was designed by Gordon Bunshaft of Skidmore, Owings and Merrill, and the nearby Seagram Building (1956) by Mies van der Rohe in association with Philip Johnson. Both are variations on a theme: simple, rectangular skyscrapers whose main difference is the treatment of the metal-framed glass curtain-walling. If the Seagram Building, with its applied I-section mullions, is more interesting, Lever House has probably been more influential, encouraging hundreds of imitators to whom the flat, graph-paper façade was the easiest and simplest way to clad an office block. The proliferation of the glass-clad office tower has tended to submerge the individuality of these two buildings. In their time, contrasting with the stone-clad skyscrapers of New York, their simple elegance and technical excellence helped to create a modern corporate identity for their clients: a whisky firm and a manufacturer of soap.

A similar job was done for the Pirelli rubber firm by Gio Ponti and Pier Luigi Nervi. The Pirelli tower in Milan (1957), an office-block of over thirty storeys, is elegant and visually satisfying. Nervi's structure is based on two full-width reinforced concrete diaphragm walls, which reduce in size towards the top. Around them, Ponti's façade is designed with classical completeness and symmetry, as distinct from the arbitrary repetitiveness of curtain walling, and emphasises the finiteness of the building. Nervi's present fame rests on this building and on his two halls for the Rome Olympics, brilliant *tours-de-force* in reinforced concrete.

The affluent and cultured elegance of Milanese and Roman society was expressed in the late 1950s by an outburst of luxurious and formalistic architecture, of which the Pirelli building was an immediate precursor. The promotion of the movement by the design magazine *Casabella* earned it wide recognition and its apparently perverse resemblance to the 'Liberty' style of Italian Art Nouveau earned it the epithet 'neo-Liberty'. Many office-blocks in Milan, the Rinascente department store in Rome by Franco Albini and Franca Helg (1961) and Ignazio Gardella's house on the Zattere, Venice, are all aspects of the same movement, away from the sterility of

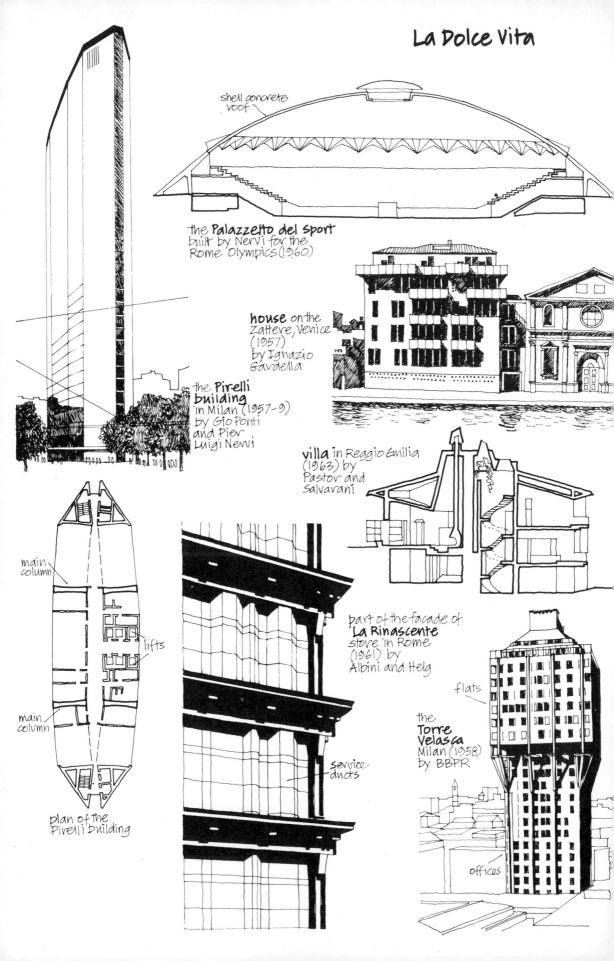

La Dolce Vita

shell concrete roof

the **Palazzetto del Sport**
built by Nervi for the
Rome Olympics (1960)

house on the
Zattere, Venice
(1957)
by Ignazio
Gardella

the **Pirelli
building**
in Milan (1957-9)
by Gio Ponti
and Pier
Luigi Nervi

villa in Reggio Emilia
(1963) by
Pastor and
Salvarani

main
column

lifts

main
column

plan of the
Pirelli building

part of the facade of
La Rinascente
store in Rome
(1961) by
Albini and Helg

service
ducts

flats

the
**Torre
Velasca**
Milan (1958)
by BBPR

offices

much of the current commercial and residential architecture towards something more interesting and humane. The archetypal building was the Torre Velasca skyscraper in Milan (1958) by Banfi, Belgiojoso, Peressuti and Rogers, a rectangular block whose top six storeys project out on brackets, giving a distinctly modern silhouette which yet refers obliquely to the towers of the Florentine renaissance. The 1950s and '60s also saw a great deal of public investment in major buildings by city councils, public trusts, airport authorities, universities and colleges. Louis Kahn's Richards Medical Centre laboratories in Philadelphia (1957) used the vocabulary of the modern movement but in a rich, expressive way which departed from the understatement of Gropius and Mies. The complexity of the duct-work serving the laboratories became the starting-point for a display of bold rectangular forms, projecting and recessing, and for a skyline of almost romantic irregularity. Even more romantic are the silhouettes of the Sydney Opera House by Jørn Utzon and Ove Arup (1957–73), with its cluster of sail-like roofs dominating the harbour area, and the TWA terminal at Kennedy Airport, New York (1962), by Eero Saarinen, whose sweeping bird-like roof is, consciously or not, a metaphor for flight.

Wright's last great work, the Guggenheim art museum in New York (1959), is a dramatic, spiral drum-like form placed above a cluster of ancillary accommodation. The concept is anything but self-effacing; instead of providing a building which takes second place to the exhibits, Wright imposes a highly personal design which dominates everything within it. The same could perhaps be said of Hans Scharoun's Berlin Philharmonic Hall (1963), specially built for Karajan's orchestra, unique among concert halls in its almost centrally placed platform. The auditorium is divided into small, self-contained sections as if to emphasise the intimate relationship between listener and musicians.

Among the major examples of public investment was the city of Brasilia, a new capital for Brazil, built largely during the 1960s by Lucio Costa and Oscar Niemeyer. The whole conception – of a new capital city built in the uninhabited bush, of a sweeping, formal town plan, of the grandiose buildings at the centre – is one of megalomania, reinforced by the panache of the buildings themselves, as in the vast, cool Presidential Palace and the dramatic, geometrical *grande geste* of the Parliament buildings.

Another big public undertaking, in Montreal in the late 1960s, included, within a few years, the building of a Métro, two major central area redevelopments at the Place Ville Marie and at the Place Bonaventure, a major international exposition (1967) and the Olympic Games (1968). The elegant, high-technology, German pavilion by Frei Otto, a steel, tent-like structure supported on posts, reappeared later in a developed form in the sports buildings for the Munich Olympics. Moshe Safdie's 'Habitat', designed for Expo '67 as a permanent feature, is a cluster of pre-cast concrete boxes put together to form a block of 158 flats.

In Britain James Stirling (b. 1926) with James Gowan (b. 1924) built the Leicester University engineering building (1963). He also designed the History Faculty Library in Cambridge (1965) and the Florey Building at Queen's College, Oxford (1968). A predilection for bold, brutal, solid forms in machine-made brick and concrete enclosing large areas of aluminium-framed glazing gives his buildings a highly individual and mechanistic character. The structure is clearly demonstrated, and the mechanical services are visibly arranged to be part of the architectural expression. Much is made of the way the components are put together: the concep-

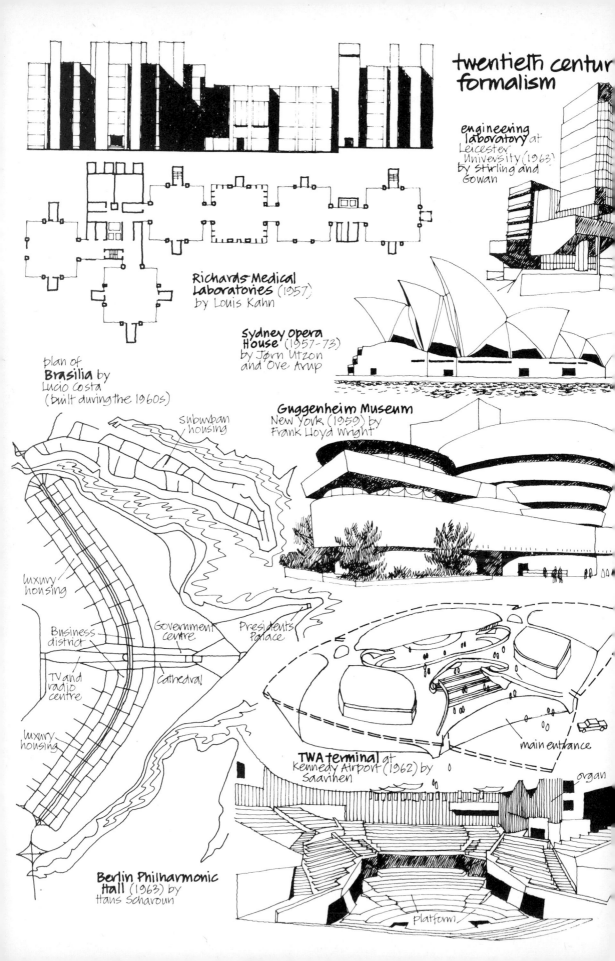

twentieth century formalism

engineering laboratory at Leicester University (1963) by Stirling and Gowan

Richards Medical Laboratories (1957) by Louis Kahn

Sydney Opera House (1957-73) by Jørn Utzon and Ove Arup

Guggenheim Museum New York (1959) by Frank Lloyd Wright

plan of Brasilia by Lucio Costa (built during the 1960s)

suburban housing

luxury housing

Business district

Government centre

President's Palace

TV and radio centre

Cathedral

luxury housing

main entrance

TWA terminal at Kennedy Airport (1962) by Saarinen

organ

Berlin Philharmonic Hall (1963) by Hans Scharoun

platform

tion is of the building as a machine, assembled out of parts. This characteristic is shared by the British architects Norman Foster, whose most successful buildings are the Willis Faber offices in Ipswich (1973) and the Sainsbury Gallery (1978) at East Anglia University, and Richard Rogers of Piano and Rogers, architects of the Centre Pompidou in Paris (1976).

In 1966, the year that the Lincoln Centre, an expensive monument to traditionalist culture, was built in New York, a cluster of hovels appeared in the Arizona landscape. This was Drop City, a young people's encampment, with geodesic-dome-like buildings constructed from old car bodies and other detritus of the consumer civilisation which had made the Lincoln Centre possible. Drop City was not unique: it took its cue from the growing squatter movement, a feature of western life since the war. Nor did it reflect an urgent social problem: these middle-class kids, trying to form a commune, were worlds apart from the building-workers in the French *bidonvilles* or the thousands of homeless in the *barriadas* of Peru. Nevertheless, it was unusual enough in America, and it excited some interest at a time when the values of western society were being questioned from within. Criticism centred on foreign policy in Vietnam, and in all sections of society the war, its brutality and its waste of lives and money, was seen by growing numbers as part of a cynical and continual exploitation by the major powers of the people of the underdeveloped countries.

Misgivings were felt about domestic affairs too, both in America and in other western countries: the linked problems of racialism and poverty in a supposedly humane and affluent society, which now appeared to be permanent; the problems of inner cities, starved of resources and drained of manpower by the suburbs and new towns; the continued existence of bad housing, despite slum-clearance programmes; the manifest inadequacies of much new housing, soulless, ugly, a prey to vandalism; the deteriorating environment of traffic-choked cities, and the increasing failure of their public services; and the mounting evidence of society's profligate use of the world's resources and its pollution of those that remained.

The protest movement reached a climax in 1968, in both America and Europe. It undoubtedly helped to end the war in Vietnam – though there were other, more compelling, reasons too, such as the enormous strain it placed on America's resources. At the same time, the politicians, under pressure, began to look more closely at urban problems, at the inner city, racism, pollution, the energy crisis, and at the growing demand for local autonomy. Inevitably, their first concern was to keep the structure intact and the majority satisfied: minority views did not count highly. Programmes were set up here and there, and a few concessions were made but did little to get to the roots of the problems. It was publicly admitted that environmental mistakes had been made in the past. Tower blocks, which in any case had been rather expensive to build, were now agreed to be socially undesirable. In recognition of their extreme unpopularity with tenants and the high incidence of vandalism, the decision was taken in 1972 to demolish some of the Pruitt-Igoe flats in St. Louis, built only seventeen years earlier.

Perhaps the most important result of the protest movement was to give young people a more important role to play, in architecture as in politics. During the 1950s and '60s the architectural avant-garde was perhaps typified by 'Archigram', a group of designers excited by the imagery of aerospace technology yet seemingly indifferent to social relevance in architecture. This has changed and, tentative

259

though many of the ideas may be, today's architectural fringe has a firmer social commitment.

Two main issues emerge. One is that of ecology. The report *Limits of Growth* by the Club of Rome (1972) did much to alert the world to the fact that its natural resources were finite. Supported by the economists Galbraith and Mishan, who argued against the concept of unrestrained economic growth, and by the writers Erlich and Schumacher who put forward the idea of a small-scale 'alternative' technology, the ecological movement grew. It was taken up officially by governments, not to the extent of discrediting economic growth but in the less contentious field of energy conservation. Only the young and unofficial, however, have turned this concept into a philosophy in which energy-conservation is seen in the wider context of food production, of the relationship between people and between man and nature. Many experimental houses have been tried out using solar heating, wind pumps for power, heat exchangers, waste re-cycling systems and high levels of heat insulation. The concept of re-using waste as building material is embodied in Martin Pawley's *Garbage Housing*, which casts doubts on the validity of a high-technology approach to architecture. This alternative attitude is given an image by the work of the 'Post-Modern' architects, such as Robert Venturi's Guild House apartments (1960) or Charles Moore's Sea Ranch housing (1963), which deliberately look to a low-key, 'vernacular' type of design as a reaction against the conspicuous consumption of the corporate world. A major problem remains: that of reconciling small-scale or inter-mediate technology with the sheer size of the world's problems of starvation and homelessness.

The second issue is the extent of people's control over environmental decisions, which can range from token gestures of 'participation' by the authorities on the one hand, to complete local autonomy on the other. The further one moves towards the latter, the more need there is to see the architect less as the imposer of solutions from outside and more as a collaborator with the building's intended users. The Byker 'Wall' in Newcastle, England, was designed by Ralph Erskine in collaboration with the people of Byker themselves. Erskine, an expatriate Englishman working in Sweden, is notable for the humanity of his approach; his residences for Clare Hall in Cambridge are by far the least pompous of the modern buildings in the city. The massive Byker housing scheme, though not radical in its general form – a continuous slab-block sheltering clusters of lower housing from traffic noise – is unusual in the extent to which it involved people in the design of their own housing. Its success seems proved by the unconventional, tailor-made appearance of the buildings, by the appreciation of the tenants and by the lack of vandalism. Another experiment has been Lucien Kroll's work at the Flemish University of Louvain, where the building of a 'social zone' and students' residence involved a lengthy design exercise in which both students and building-workers participated and the architect acted only as 'orchestrator' of other peoples' ideas. Both Byker and Louvain are organised build-ings, in the sense that they were co-ordinated by a single mind and made use of a deliberately limited palette of elements and materials. At the same time they are excitingly anarchic by comparison with most other modern buildings. The question must remain as to whether this anarchy is a true expression of the tenants' freedom or whether it is purely visual. There is more to freedom than living in an interesting building, even if you did help to design it.

Perhaps the biggest social task which faces us today is to find the means of

images of freedom

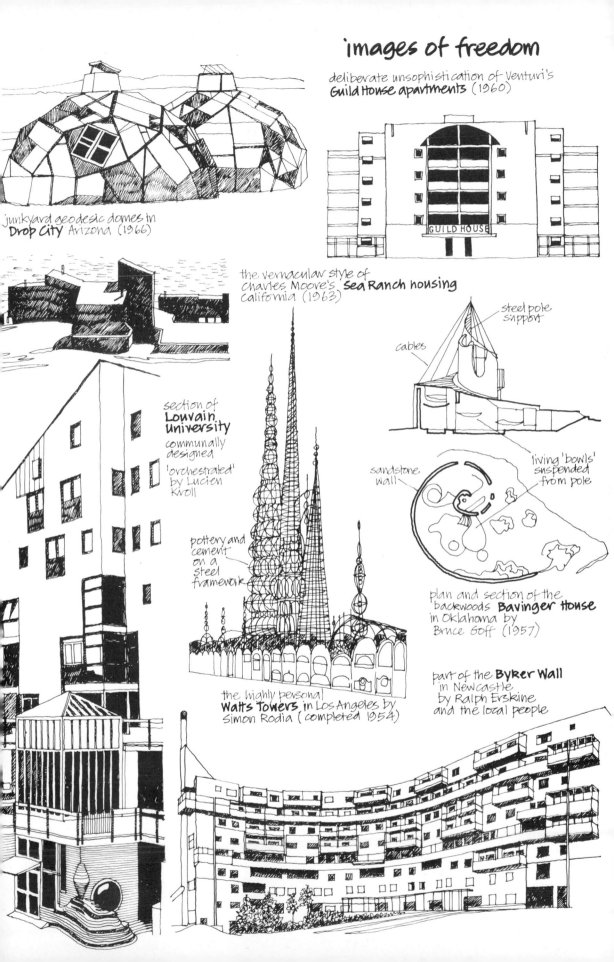

junkyard geodesic domes in
Drop City, Arizona (1966)

deliberate unsophistication of Venturi's
Guild House apartments (1960)

the vernacular style of
Charles Moore's **Sea Ranch housing**
California (1963)

steel pole
support

cables

section of
**Louvain
University**

communally
designed
'orchestrated'
by Lucien
Kroll

living 'bowls'
suspended
from pole

sandstone
wall

pottery and
cement
on a
steel
framework

plan and section of the
backwoods **Bavinger House**
in Oklahoma by
Bruce Goff (1957)

part of the **Byker Wall**
in Newcastle
by Ralph Erskine
and the local people

the highly personal
Watts Towers in Los Angeles by
Simon Rodia (completed 1954)

becoming a society of free, fulfilled individuals. The scale of the world's problems grows larger yet the manifestations of these problems at a personal level become more complex and acute. The solutions imposed by our massive corporate system generally fail on two counts, through their inadequacy on the one hand to match the size of the problem, and on the other their crudity of execution, whereby they ignore or even worsen the problems at a personal level. The Vietnam war as a solution to the political and economic problems of South-East Asia and the Aylesbury Estate as a solution to Southwark's housing problems are only two examples.

Science and technology, properly used, have the capacity to deal with many of our problems, but the constraints placed on science by the need for political dominance, for national prestige, or simply for crude financial gain, have diverted it from a better purpose. Our present system, based on exploitation and profligate consumption, will eventually fail, but before it does so we can expect more planning, stricter controls, firmer expressions of authority, directed towards saving the economy from collapse. The danger to personal freedom will become greater, and those individual needs which the crudity of the system leaves unfulfilled will bring greater discontent.

The way these two questions resolve themselves – who controls scientific progress, and how the need for personal autonomy expresses itself – will determine how we move into the post-industrial phase of history. The future, as in the 12th century, in 1789 and in 1917, lies with the progressive elements of society, and it may still be possible for an enlightened group to ensure a humane future. The hope lies not with the present power-structure, imposing its solutions from above, but perhaps in the growth of what Antonio Gramsci calls a 'new historic bloc' within society, allowing solutions to emerge from below. The collaboration of scientists and technologists, artists, professionals and workers is alone able to infuse society with a new creativity.

Within this context, architecture would become more relevant to human needs. Technology could be used seriously – not merely as a demonstration of political or economic power. Till now, modern technology has implied mechanistic and soulless buildings, but only because of the soullessness of the decision-makers themselves. The development of technology not only for construction but, more importantly, for analysing problems and discovering needs in a more sophisticated way, could result in architecture of greater humanity. The architect himself must change his role. He must be willing to share the design process with others; he must expand his awareness of his social role, and cease to be ambivalent about who he works for; he must expand his capabilities to embrace a more rigorous and scientific attitude; and he must see his work within a wider context: an awareness of the implications of small-scale decisions at the larger scale and of large-scale ones at the smaller. The architecture that results could be the most humane and most relevant in history to society's needs.

List of Illustrations

263

Bibliography

THE PROCESS OF HISTORY

Architecture is part of our social life and any view of architectural history should be part of an overall idea about the nature of history itself. The following encompass the approach attempted by this book:
Carr, E. H. *What is History?* Macmillan, London, 1961; Random House, New York, 1967
Fleischer, H. *Marxism and History* Allen Lane, London, 1973
Marx, K. and Engels, F. *The German Ideology* Lawrence & Wishart, London, 1974; Progress Pubns, Chicago, 1976

GENERAL HISTORY: A SUMMARY

These books provide a basic historical framework for the story of western architecture:
Bainton, R. *The Penguin History of Christianity* (2 vols) Penguin, London and New York, 1967
Kirchner, W. *Western Civilisation* Barnes & Noble, New York, 1958 (new edn 1975); distrib. UK, Methuen & Co., London
McEvedy, C. *The Penguin Atlas of Medieval History* Penguin, London and New York, 1961
McEvedy, C. *The Penguin Atlas of Modern History* Penguin, London and New York, 1972
McNeill, W. H. *The Rise of the West: A History of the Human Community* University of Chicago Press, 1963

GENERAL HISTORY: PERIODS

These books put the architecture of each period into an economic and social context. They are given in roughly chronological order:
Balsdon, J. P. (ed.) *Roman Civilisation* Penguin, London and New York, 1965
Quennell, M. and C. H. B. *Everyday Life in Roman Britain* Batsford, London, 1959
Kautsky, K. *Foundations of Christianity* International Publishers Co. Inc., 1925; Orbach & Chambers, London, 1973; Path Press, New York, 1972
Ross, A. *Everyday Life of the Pagan Celts* Batsford, London, 1970; Putnam, New York, 1970
Todd, M. *Everyday Life of the Barbarians* Batsford, London, 1972; Putnam, New York, 1973
Thomas, C. *Britain and Ireland in Early Christian Times* Thames & Hudson, London, 1971; McGraw-Hill, New York, 1971
Lasko, P. *The Kingdom of the Franks* Thames & Hudson, London, 1971; McGraw-Hill, New York, 1971
Trevor-Roper, H. *The Rise of Christian Europe* Thames & Hudson, London, 1965; Harcourt Brace, New York, 1966
Quennell, M. and C. H. B. *Everyday Life in Anglo-Saxon Times* Batsford, London, 1965
Quennell, M. and C. H. B. *Everyday Life in Roman Anglo-Saxon Times* Putnam, New York, 1974
Rowling, M. *Everyday Life in Medieval Times* Batsford, London, 1968; Putnam, New York, 1968
Hodgett, G. *A Social and Economic History of Medieval Europe* Methuen, London, 1972; Harper & Row, New York, 1974
Bauther, R.-H. *The Economic Development of Medieval Europe* Thames & Hudson, London, 1971; Harcourt Brace, New York, 1971
Pirenne, H. *Medieval Cities; their origins and the revival of trade* (trans. Halsey) Princeton University Press, 1952
Heer, F. *The Medieval World* Weidenfeld & Nicolson, London, 1962; New American Library, New York, 1964
Power, E. *Medieval People* Methuen, London, 1966; Barnes & Noble, New York, 1963
Burckhardt, J. *The Civilisation of the Renaissance in Italy* Phaidon, London, 1960; Harper & Row, New York, 1975
Hale, J. R. *Renaissance Europe* Fontana, London, 1971
Chamberlin, E. R. *Everyday Life in Renaissance Times* Batsford, London, 1965; Putnam, New York, 1967
Ogg, D. *Europe of the Ancien Régime* Fontana, London, 1965
Cipolla, C. M. *Before the Industrial Revolution* Methuen, London, 1976; Norton, New York, 1976
Asimov, I. *The Shaping of North America* Dobson, London, 1974; Houghton Mifflin, Boston, Mass., 1973
Rudé, G. *Revolutionary Europe* Fontana, London, 1964; Harper & Row, New York, 1966
Hobsbawm, E. *The Age of Revolution* Weidenfeld & Nicolson, London, 1962; New American Library, New York, 1962
Asimov, I. *The Birth of the United States* Dobson, London, 1974; Houghton Mifflin, Boston, Mass., 1974
Hobsbawm, E. *Industry and Empire* Weidenfeld & Nicolson, London, 1968; Pantheon, New York, 1968
Inglis, B. *Poverty and the Industrial Revolution* Hodder, London, 1971
Silberschmidt, M. *The United States and Europe* Thames & Hudson, London, 1972; Harcourt Brace, New York, 1972
Lichtheim, G. *Europe in the Twentieth Century* Weidenfeld & Nicolson, London, 1972
Coates, K. and Silburn, R. *Poverty: The Forgotten Englishmen* Penguin, London, 1970
Harrington, M. *The Other America* Macmillan, London, 1963; Macmillan, New York, 1970

HISTORY OF ARCHITECTURE AND TOWN DESIGN

A number of basic background works, some of them well-established classics.
Bacon, E. N. *The Design of Cities* Penguin, London and New York, 1976

Fletcher, Banister *A History of Architecture* (18th edn, ed. J. C. Palmes) Athlone Press, University of London, 1975; Scribner, New York, 1975

Furneaux Jordan, R. *A Concise History of Western Architecture* Thames & Hudson, London, 1969; Harcourt Brace, New York, 1970

Holt, E. G. (ed.) *A Documentary History of Art* Princeton University Press, 1957

Korn, A. *History Builds the Town* Lund Humphries, London, 1953

Levey, M. *A History of Western Art* Thames & Hudson, London, 1968; Oxford University Press, New York, 1977

Mumford, L. *The City in History* Secker & Warburg, London, 1961; Harcourt Brace, New York, 1968

Pevsner, N. *An Outline of European Architecture* (7th edn) Penguin, London, 1963; Allen Lane, London and New York, 1974

Pevsner, N. (with J. Fleming and H. Honour) *A Dictionary of Architecture* Penguin, London, 1966; Overlook Press, New York, 1976

Harvey, J. *The Medieval Architect* Wayland, London, 1972; St Martin's Press, New York, 1972

Henderson, G. *Gothic* Penguin, London, 1967

Macaulay, D. *Cathedral* Collins, London, 1964; Houghton Mifflin, Boston, Mass., 1973

Wittkower, R. *Architectural Principles in the Age of Humanism* Tiranti, London, 1952; Norton, New York, 1971

Summerson, J. *The Classical Language of Architecture* BBC, London, 1963; MIT Press, Cambridge, Mass., 1966

Murray, P. *Architecture of the Italian Renaissance* Thames & Hudson, London, 1969; Schocken, New York, 1966

Benevolo, L. *The Architecture of the Renaissance* (2 vols) Routledge, London, 1977; Westview Press, Boulder, Co, 1977

Tapié, V.-L. *The Age of Grandeur* Weidenfeld & Nicolson, London, 1960

Kaufman, E. *Architecture in the Age of Reason* Dover, New York, 1968 (UK distrib. Tiptree)

Rosenau, H. *Social Purpose in Architecture* Studio Vista, London, 1970

Clark, K. *The Gothic Revival* Murray, London, 1962; Harper & Row, New York, 1974

Pevsner, N. *Pioneers of Modern Design* Penguin, London, 1961

Furneaux Jordon, R. *Victorian Architecture* Penguin, London, 1966

Bell, C. and R. *City Fathers: Early History of Town Planning in Britain* Barrie, London, 1969; Humanities Press, Atlantic Highlands, NJ, 1974

HISTORICAL ARCHITECTURE: PERIODS

A roughly chronological list of books on periods, styles and ideas.

Wheeler, M. *Roman Art and Architecture* Thames & Hudson, London, 1964; Oxford University Press, New York, 1977

Krautheimer, R. *Early Christian and Byzantine Architecture* Penguin, London and New York, 1965

Conant, K. *Carolingian and Romanesque Architecture* Penguin, London and New York, 1974

Harvey, J. *The Master Builders: Architecture in the Middle Ages* Thames & Hudson, London, 1971; McGraw-Hill, New York, 1972

Giedion, S. *Space, Time and Architecture* Harvard University Press, 1941

Benevolo, L. *History of Modern Architecture* (2 vols) Routledge, London, 1971; MIT Press, Cambridge, Mass., 1972

Banham, R. *Guide to Modern Architecture* Architectural Press, London, 1962; Harper & Row, New York, 1975

Blake, P. *The Master Builders* Gollancz, London, 1960; Norton, New York, 1976

Tetlow, J. and Goss, A. *Homes, Towns and Traffic* Faber, London, 1965; Praeger, New York, 1965

Jencks, C. *Modern Movements in Architecture* Penguin, London, 1973; Doubleday, New York, 1975

Turner, J. *Housing by People* Marion Boyars, London, 1976; Pantheon, New York, 1977

Jacobs, J. *Death and Life of Great American Cities* Random House, New York, 1961

Goodman, R. *After the Planners* Penguin, London, 1972; Simon & Schuster, New York, 1972

Pawley, M. *Architecture versus Housing* Studio Vista, London, 1971; Praeger, New York, 1971

HISTORICAL ARCHITECTURE: PLACES

General surveys of national and local planning activity.

Braun, H. *English Abbeys* Faber, London, 1971; Transatlantic Arts, New York, 1973

Braun, H. *Parish Churches* Faber, London, 1970; Transatlantic Arts, New York, 1970

Briggs, M. *Architecture in Italy* Dent, London, 1961; Dutton, New York, 1961

Brown, R. A. *English Castles* Batsford, London, 1954; Norton, New York, 1962

Burchard, J. and Bush-Brown, A. *The Architecture of America* Gollancz, London, 1967; Atlantic Monthly, Boston, Mass., 1961

Cantacuzino, S. *European Domestic Architecture* Studio Vista, London, 1969; Dutton, New York, 1969

Condit, C. W. *American Building* University of Chicago Press, 1968

Cox, J. C. and Ford, C. B. *The Parish Churches of England* Batsford, London, 1935

Hamilton, G. H. *The Art and Architecture of Russia* Penguin, London, 1954; Viking, New York, 1976

Knox, B. *The Architecture of Prague and Bohemia* Faber, London, 1965

Lavedan, P. *French Architecture* Penguin, London, 1956

Lloyd, N. *A History of the English House* Architectural Press, London, 1974; Architectural Book Publishing Co., Inc., New York, 1974

McCallum, I. *Architecture USA* Architectural Press, London, 1959

Paulsson, T. *Scandinavian Architecture* Leonard Hill, London, 1958

Rolt, L. T. C. *Victorian Engineering* Allen Lane, London and New York, 1970

Scully, V. *The Shingle Style and the Stick Style* Yale University Press, New Haven, Conn. and London, 1971

Summerson, J. *Georgian London* Barrie, London, 1970

Woodforde, J. *The Truth about Cottages* Routledge, London, 1969; Kelley Publishers, Fairfield, NJ, 1970

Yarwood, D. *The Architecture of Britain* Batsford, London, 1976; Scribner, New York, 1976

Yarwood, D. *The Architecture of Italy* Chatto, London, 1970.

Index

267

268

271